BATTLE OF CULLODEN.

Painted by Capt.n W. McKenzie

An Historical Account Of The Settlements Of

Scotch Highlanders In America

Prior To The Peace Of 1783 Together With Notices Of Highland Regiments And Biographical Sketches

J. P. MacLean

HERITAGE BOOKS
2008

HERITAGE BOOKS
AN IMPRINT OF HERITAGE BOOKS, INC.

Books, CDs, and more—Worldwide

For our listing of thousands of titles see our website at
www.HeritageBooks.com

Published 2008 by
HERITAGE BOOKS, INC.
Publishing Division
100 Railroad Ave. #104
Westminster, Maryland 21157

Copyright © 1900 J. P. MacLean

Other books by the author:

A History of the Clan MacLean from its first settlement at Duard Castle, in the Isle of Mull, to the Present Period, including a Genealogical Account of Some of the Principal Families together with their heraldry, legends, superstitions, etc
CD: *An Historical Account of the Settlements of Scotch Highlanders In America*

All rights reserved. No part of this book may be reproduced or transmitted in any form or by any means, electronic or mechanical, including photocopying, recording or by any information storage and retrieval system without written permission from the author, except for the inclusion of brief quotations in a review.

International Standard Book Numbers
Paperbound: 978-0-7884-1742-9
Clothbound: 978-0-7884-7105-6

PREFACE.

An attempt is here made to present a field that has not been preoccupied. The student of American history has noticed allusions to certain Scotch Highland settlements prior to the Revolution, without any attempt at either an account or origin of the same. In a measure the publication of certain state papers and colonial records, as well as an occasional memoir by an historical society have revived what had been overlooked. These settlements form a very important and interesting place in the early history of our country. While they may not have occupied a very prominent or pronounced position, yet their exertions in subduing the wilderness, their activity in the Revolution, and the wide influence exercised by the descendants of these hardy pioneers, should, long since, have brought their history and achievements into notice.

The settlement in North Carolina, embracing a wide extent of territory, and the people numbered by the thousands, should, ere this, have found a competent exponent. But it exists more as a tradition than an actual colony. The Highlanders in Georgia more than acted their part against Spanish encroachments, yet survived all the vicissitudes of their exposed position. The stay of the Highlanders on the Mohawk was very brief, yet their flight into Canada and final settlement at Glengarry forms a very strange episode in the history of New York. The heartless treatment of the colony of Lachlan Campbell by the governor of the province of New York, and their long delayed recompense stands without a parallel, and is so strange and fanciful, that long since it should have excited the poet or novelist. The settlements in Nova Scotia and Prince Edwards Island, although scarcely commenced at the breaking out of the Revolution, are more important in later events than those chronicled in this volume.

The chapters on the Highlands, the Scotch-Irish, and the Darien scheme, have sufficient connection to warrant their insertion.

It is a noticeable fact that notwithstanding the valuable services rendered by the Highland regiments in the French and Indian war, but little account has been taken by writers, except in Scotland, although General David Stewart of Garth, as early as 1822, clearly paved the way. Unfortunately, his works, as well as those who have followed him, are comparatively unknown on this side the Atlantic.

I was led to the searching out of this phase of our history, not only by the occasional allusions, but specially from reading works devoted to other nationalities engaged in the Revolution. Their achievements were fully set forth and their praises sung. Why should not the oppressed Gael, who sought the forests of the New World, struggled in the wilderness, and battled against foes, also be placed in his true light? If properly known, the artist would have a subject for his pencil, the poet a picture for his praises, and the novelist a strong background for his romance.

Cleveland, O., October, 1898.

TABLE OF CONTENTS.

CHAPTER I.
THE HIGHLANDERS OF SCOTLAND.

Division of Scotland—People of the Highlands—Language—Clanship—Chiefs—Customs—Special Characteristics—Fiery-Cross—Slogan—Mode of Battle—Forays—Feasts—Position of Woman—Marriage—Religious Toleration—Superstitions—Poets—Pipers—Cave of Coir-nan-Uriskin—The Harp—Gaelic Music—Costume—Scotland's Wars—War with Romans—Battle of Largs—Bannockburn—Flodden—Pinkie—Wars of Montrose—Bonnie Dundee—Earl of Mar—Prince Charles Stuart—Atrocities in the Wake of Culloden—Uncertainty of Travelers' Observations—Kidnapping—Emigration 17

CHAPTER II.
THE SCOTCH-IRISH IN AMERICA.

Origin of the name of Scotland—Scoto-Irish—Ulster—Clandonald—Protestant Colonies in Ireland—Corruption of Names—Percentage of in Revolution—Characteristics—Persecuted—Emigration from Ulster—First Scotch-Irish Clergyman in America—Struggle for Religious Liberty—Settlement at Worcester—History of the Potato—Pelham—Warren and Blandford—Colerain—Londonderry—Settlements in Maine—New York—New Jersey—Pennsylvania—The Revolution—Maryland—Virginia—Patrick Henry—Daniel Morgan—George Rogers Clark—North Carolina—Battle of King's Mountain—South Carolina—Georgia—East Tennessee—Kentucky—Canada—Industrial Arts—Distinctive Characteristics............40

CHAPTER III.
CAUSES THAT LED TO EMIGRATION.

Results of Clanship—Opposed to Emigration—Emigration to Ulster—Expatriation of 7000—Changed Condition of Highlanders—Lands Rented—Dissatisfaction—Luxurious Landlords—Action of Chiefs in Skye—Deplorable State of Affairs—Sheep-Farming—Improvements—Buchanan's Description—Famine—Class of Emigrants—America—Hardships and Disappointments 60

CHAPTER IV.
DARIEN SCHEME.

First Highlanders in America—Disastrous Speculation—Ruinous Legislation—Massacre of Glencoe—Darien Scheme Projected—William Paterson—Fabulous Dreams—Company Chartered—Scotland Excited—Subscriptions—List of Subscribers—Spanish Sovereignty over Darien—English Jealousy and Opposition—Dutch East India Company—King William's Duplicity—English and Dutch Subscriptions Withdrawn—Great Preparations—Purchase of Ships—Sailing of First Expedition—Settlement of St. Andrews—Great Sufferings—St. Andrews Abandoned—The Caledonia and Unicorn Arrive at New York—Recriminations—The St. Andrews—The Dolphin—King Refuses Supplies—Relief Sent—Spaniards Aggressive—Second Expedition—Highlanders—Disappointed Expectations—Discordant Clergy—How News was Received in Scotland—Give Vent to Rage—King William's Indifference—Campbell of Fonab—Escape—Capitulation of Darien Colony—Ships Destroyed—Final End of Settlers.................. 75

CHAPTER V.

HIGHLANDERS IN NORTH CAROLINA.

On the Cape Fear—Town Established—Highlanders Patronized—Arrival of Neil McNeill—Action of Legislature—List of Grantees—Wave of Emigration—Represented in Legislature—Colony Prosperous—Stamp Act—Genius of Liberty—Letter to Highlanders—Emigrants from Jura—Lands Allotted—War of Regulators—Campbelton Charter—Public Road—Public Buildings at Campbelton—Petition for Pardon—Highland Costume—Clan Macdonald Emigration—Allan Macdonald of Kingsborough—American Revolution—Sale of Public Offices—Attitude of Patriots—Provincial Congress—Highlanders Objects of Consideration—Reverend John McLeod—Committee to Confer with Highlanders—British Confidence—Governor Martin—Provincial Congress of 1775—Farquhard Campbell—Arrival of the George—Other Arrivals—Oaths Administered—Distressed Condition—Petition to Virginia Convention—War Party in the Ascendant—American Views—Highlanders Fail to Understand Conditions—Reckless Indifference of Leaders—General Donald Macdonald—British Campaign—Governor Martin Manipulates a Revolt—Macdonald's Manifesto—Rutherford's Manifesto—Highlanders in Rebellion—Standard at Cross Creek—March for Wilmington—Country Alarmed—Correspondence—Battle of Moore's Creek Bridge—Overthrow of Highlanders—Prescribed Parole—Prisoners Address Congress—Action of Sir William Howe—Allan Macdonald's Letter—On Parole—Effects His Exchange—Letter to Members of Congress—Cornwallis to Clinton—Military at Cross Creek—Women Protected—Religious Status 102

CHAPTER VI.

HIGHLANDERS IN GEORGIA.

English Treatment of Poor—Imprisonment for Debt—Oglethorpe's Philanthropy—Asylum Projected—Oglethorpe Sails for Georgia—Selects the Site of Savannah—Fort Argyle—Colonists of Different Nationalities—Towns Established—Why Highlanders were Selected—Oglethorpe Returns to England—Highland Emigrants—Character of—John Macleod—Founding of New Inverness—Oglethorpe Sails for Georgia—Visits the Highlanders—Fort St. Andrews—Spaniards Aggressive—Messengers Imprisoned—Spanish Perfidy—Suffering and Discontent in 1737—Dissension Increases—Removal Agitated—African Slavery Prohibited—Petition and Counter Petition—Highlanders Oppose African Slavery—Insufficient Produce Raised

CONTENTS. xi

—Murder of Unarmed Highlanders—Florida Invaded—St. Augustine Blockaded—Massacre of Highlanders at Fort Moosa—Failure of Expedition—Conduct of William MacIntosh—Indians and Carolinians Desert—Agent Reprimanded by Parliament—Clansmen at Darien—John MacLeod Abandons His Charge—Georgia Invaded—Highlanders Defeat the Enemy—Battle of Bloody Marsh—Spaniards Retreat—Ensign Stewart—Oglethorpe Again Invades Florida—Growth of Georgia—Record in Revolution—Resolutions—Assault on British War Vessels—Capture of—County of Liberty—Settlement Remained Highland 146

CHAPTER VII.

CAPTAIN LACHLAN CAMPBELL'S NEW YORK COLONY.

Lachlan Campbell—Donald Campbell's Memorial—Motives Controlling Royal Governors—Governor Clarke to Duke of Newcastle—Same to Lords of Trade—Efforts of Captain Campbell—Memorial Rejected—Redress Obtained—Grand Scheme—List of Grantees—A Desperado—Township of Argyle—Records of—Change of Name of County—Highland Soldiers Occupy Lands—How Allotted—Selling Land Warrants—New Hampshire Grants—Ethan Allan—Revolution—An Incident—Indian Raid—Massacre of Jane McCrea—Religious Sentiment........................ 176

CHAPTER VIII.

HIGHLAND SETTLEMENT ON THE MOHAWK.

Sir William Johnson—Highlanders Preferred—Manner of Life—Changed State of Affairs—Sir John Johnson—Highlanders not Civic Officers—Sir John Johnson's Movements Inimical—Tryon County Committee to Provincial Congress—Action of Continental Congress—Sir John to Governor Tryon—Action of General Schuyler—Sir John's Parole—Highlanders Disarmed—Arms Retained—Highland Hostages—Instructions for Seizing Sir John—Sir John on Removal of Highlanders—Flight of Highlanders to Canada—Great Sufferings—Lady Johnson a Hostage—Highland Settlement a Nest of Treason—Exodus of Highland Women—Some Families Detained—Letter of Helen McDonell—Regiment Organized—Butler's Rangers—Cruel Warfare—Fort Schuyler Besieged—Battle of Oriskany—Heroism of Captain Gardenier—Parole of Angus McDonald—Massacre of Wyoming—Bloodthirsty Character of Alexander McDonald—Indian Country Laid Waste—Battle of Chemung—Sir John Ravages Johnstown—Visits Schoharie with Fire and Sword—Flight from Johnstown—Exploit of Donald McDonald—Shell's Defence—List of Officers of Sir John Johnson's Regiment—Settlement in Glengarry—Allotment of Lands—Story of Donald Grant—Religious Services Established................... 196

CHAPTER IX.

GLENALADALE HIGHLANDERS OF PRINCE EDWARD ISLAND.

Highlanders in Canada—John Macdonald—Educated in Germany—Religious Oppression—Religion of the Yellow-Stick—Glenaladale Becomes Protector—Emigration—Company Raised Against Americans—Capture of American Vessel—Estimate of Glenaladale—Offered Governorship of Prince Edward Island 231

CHAPTER X.

HIGHLAND SETTLEMENT IN PICTOU, NOVA SCOTIA.

, Emigration to Nova Scotia—Ship Hector—Sails from Lochbroom—Great Sufferings and Pestilence—Landing of Highlanders—Frightening of Indians—Bitter Disappointment—Danger of Starvation—False Reports—Action of Captain Archibald—Truro Migration—Hardships—Incidents of Suffering—Conditions of Grants of Land—Hector's Passengers—Interesting Facts Relative to Emigrants—Industries—Plague of Mice—American Revolution—Divided Sentiment—Persecution of American Sympathizers—Highlanders Loyal to Great Britain—Americans Capture a Vessel—Privateers—Wreck of the Malignant Man-of-War—Indian Alarm—Itinerant Preachers—Arrival of Reverend James McGregor.................... 235

CHAPTER XI.

FIRST HIGHLAND REGIMENTS IN AMERICA.

Cause of French and Indian War—Highlanders Sent to America—The Black Watch—Montgomery's Highlanders—Fraser's Highlanders—Uniform of—Black Watch at Albany—Lord Loudon at Halifax—Surrender of Fort William Henry—Success of the French—Defeat at Ticonderoga—Gallant Conduct of Highlanders—List of Casualties—Expedition Against Louisburg—Destruction French Fleet—Capture of Louisburg—Expedition Against Fort Du Quesne—Defeat of Major Grant—Washington—Name Fort Changed to Fort Pitt—Battalions of 42nd United—Amherst Possesses Ticonderoga—Army at Crown Point—Fall of Quebec—Journal of Malcolm Fraser—Movements of Fraser's Highlanders—Battle of Heights of Abraham—Galling Fire Sustained by Highlanders—Anecdote of General Murray—Retreat of French—Officers of the Black Watch—Highland Regiments Sail for Barbadoes—Return to New York—Black Watch Sent to Pittsburg—Battle of Bushy Run—Black Watch Sent Against Ohio Indians—Goes to Ireland—Impressions of in America—Table of Losses—Montgomery Highlanders Against the Cherokees—Battle with Indians—Allan Macpherson's Tragic Death—Retreat from Indian Country—Return to New York—Massacre at Fort Loudon—Surrender of St. Johns—Tables of Casualties—Acquisition of French Territory a Source of Danger....... 252

CHAPTER XII.

SCOTCH HOSTILITY TOWARDS AMERICA.

Causes of American Revolution—Massacre at Lexington—Insult to Franklin—England Precipitates War—Americans Ridiculed—Pitt's Noble Defence—Attitude of Eminent Men—Action of Cities—No Enthusiasm in Enlistments in England and Ireland—The Press-Gang—Enlistment of Criminals—Sentiment of People of Scotland—Lecky's Estimate—Addresses Upholding the King—Summary of Highland Addresses—Emigration Prohibited—Resentment Against Highlanders—Shown in Original Draft of Declaration of Independence—Petitions of Donald Macleod.. 292

CHAPTER XIII.

HIGHLAND REGIMENTS IN AMERICAN REVOLUTION.

Eulogy of Pitt—Organizing in America—Secret Instructions to Governor Tryon—Principal Agents—Royal Highland Emigrants—How Re-

CONTENTS. xiii

ceived—Colonel Maclean Saves Quebec—Siege of Quebec—First Battalion in Canada—Burgoyne's Doubts—Second Battalion—Sufferings of—Treatment of—Battle of Eutaw Springs—Royal Highland Emigrants Discharged—List of Officers—Grants of Land—John Bethune—42nd or Royal Highlanders—Embarks for America—Capture of Highlanders—Capture of Oxford Transport—Prisoners from the Crawford—British Fleet Arrives at Staten Island—Battle of Long Island—Ardor of Highlanders—Americans Evacuate New York—Patriotism of Mrs. Murray—Peril of Putnam—Gallant Conduct of Major Murray—Battle of Harlem—Capture of Fort Washington—Royal Highlanders in New Jersey—Attacked at Pisquatiqua—Sergeant McGregor—Battle of Brandywine—Wayne's Army Surprised—Expeditions During Winter of 1779—Skirmishing and Suffering—Infusion of Poor Soldiers—Capture of Charleston—Desertions—Regiment Reduced—Sails for Halifax—Table of Casualties—Fraser's Highlanders—Sails for America—Capture of Transports—Reports of Captain Seth Harding and Colonel Archibald Campbell—Confinement of Colonel Campbell—Interest in by Washington—Battle of Brooklin—Diversified Employment—Expedition Against Little Egg Harbor—Capture of Savannah—Retrograde Movement of General Prevost—Battle of Brier Creek—Invasion of South Carolina—Battle of Stono Ferry—Retreat to Savannah—Siege of—Capture of Stony Point—Surrender of Charleston—Battle of Camden—Defeat of General Sumter—Battle of King's Mountain—Battle of Blackstocks—Battle of the Cowpens—Battle of Guilford Court-House—March of British Army to Yorktown—Losses of Fraser's Highlanders—Surrender of Yorktown—Highlanders Prisoners—Regiment Discharged at Perth—Argyle Highlanders—How Constituted—Sails for Halifax—Two Companies at Charleston—At Penobscot—Besieged by Americans—Regiment Returns to England—Macdonald's Highlanders—Sails for New York—Embarks for Virginia—Bravery of the Soldiers—Highlanders on Horseback—Surrender of Yorktown—Cantoned at Winchester—Removed to Lancaster—Disbanded at Stirling Castle—Summary—Estimate of Washington—His Opinion of Highlanders—Not Guilty of Wanton Cruelty................308

CHAPTER XIV.

DISTINGUISHED HIGHLANDERS WHO SERVED IN AMERICA IN THE INTERESTS OF GREAT BRITAIN.

General Sir Alan Cameron—General Sir Archibald Campbell—General John Campbell—Lord William Campbell—General Simon Fraser of Balnain—General Simon Fraser of Lovat—General Simon Fraser—General James Grant of Ballindalloch—General Allan Maclean of Torloisk—Sir Allan Maclean—General Francis Maclean—General John Small—Flora Macdonald 377

CHAPTER XV.

DISTINGUISHED HIGHLANDERS IN AMERICAN INTERESTS.

General Alexander McDougall—General Lachlan McIntosh—General Arthur St. Clair—Serjeant Macdonald......... 398

xiv   CONTENTS.

APPENDIX.

Note A.—First Emigrants to America............................417
Note B.—Letter of Donald Macpherson..........................417
Note C.—Emigration during the Eighteenth Century..................419
Note D.—Appeal to the Highlanders lately arrived from Scotland.....422
Note E.—Ingratitude of the Highlanders...........................426
Note F.—Were the Highlanders Faithful to their Oath to the American.426
Note G.—Marvellous Escape of Captain McArthur....................430
Note H.—Highlanders in South Carolina...........................442
Note I.—Alexander McNaughton....................................443
Note J.—Allan McDonald's Complaint to the President of Congress....444
Note K.—The Glengarry Settlers..................................445
Note to Chapter VIII..448
Note L.—Moravian Indians 448
Note M.—Highlanders Refused Lands in America....................450
Note N.—Captain James Stewart commissioned to raise a company
    Highlanders 453

ILLUSTRATIONS.

Battle of Culloden	Frontispiece
Coire-nan-Uriskin	26
House of Henry McWhorter	52
View of Battle-Field of Alamance	55
Scottish India House	90
Barbacue Church, where Flora Macdonald Worshipped	144
Johnson Hall	204
View of the Valley of Wyoming	218
Highland Officer	256
Old Blockhouse Fort Duquesne	281
General Sir Archibald Campbell	397
Brigadier General Simon Fraser	382
General Simon Fraser of Loval	387
Sir Allan Maclean, Bart	391
Flora Macdonald	394
General Alexander McDougall	398
General Lachlan McIntosh	402
General Arthur St. Clair	405
Sergeant Macdonald and Colonel Gainey	413

PARTIAL LIST OF PRINCIPAL AUTHORITIES CONSULTED.

American Archives.
Answer of Cornwallis to Clinton, London, 1783.
Bancroft (George.) History of the United States, London, N. D.
Burt (Captain.) Letters from the North of Scotland, London, 1815.
Burton (J. H.) Darien Papers, Bannatyne Club, 1849.
Burton (J. H.) History of Scotland, Edinburgh, 1853.
Celtic Monthly, Inverness, 1876-1888.
Georgia Historical Society Collections.
Graham (James J.) Memoirs General Graham, Edinburgh, 1862.
Hotten (J. C.) List of Emigrants to America, New York, 1874.
Johnson (C.) History Washington County, New York, Philadelphia, 1878.
Keltie (J. S.). History of the Highland Clans, Edinburgh, 1882.
Lecky (W. E. H.) History of England, London, 1892.
Lossing (B. J.) Field-Book of the American Revolution, New York, 1855.
Macaulay (T. B.) History of England, Boston, N. D.
McDonald (H.) Letter-Book, New York Historical Society, 1892.
Macdonell (J. A.) Sketches of Glengarry, Montreal, 1893.
McLeod (D.) Brief Review of the Settlement of Upper Canada, Cleveland, 1841.
Martin (M.) Description Western Isles, Glasgow, 1884.
National Portrait Gallery of Distinguished Americans, Philadelphia, 1852.
New York Documentary and Colonial History.
North Carolina Colonial Record.
Paterson (J.) History Pictou County, Nova Scotia, Montreal, 1893.
Proceedings Scotch-Irish American Congress, 1889-1896.
Rogers (H.) Hadden's Journal and Orderly Book, Albany, 1884.
Scott (Sir W.) Lady of the Lake, New York, N. D.
Scott (Sir W.) Tales of a Grandfather, Boston, 1852.
Smith (William) History of New York, New York, 1814.
Smith (W. H.) St. Clair Papers, Cincinnati, 1882.
Sparks (Jared) Writings of Washington, Boston, 1837.
Stephens (W. B.) History of Georgia, New York, 1859.
St. Clair (Arthur.) Narrative, Philadelphia, 1812.
Stewart (David.) Sketches of the Highlanders, Edinburgh, 1822.
Stone (W. L.) Life of Joseph Brant, New York, 1838.
Stone (W. L.) Orderly Book of Sir John Johnson, Albany, 1882.
Tarleton (Lieut. Col.) Campaigns of, 1780-1781, London, 1787.
Washington and his Generals, Philadelphia, 1848.

CHAPTER I.

THE HIGHLANDERS OF SCOTLAND.

A range of mountains forming a lofty and somewhat shattered rampart, commencing in the county of Aberdeen, north of the river Don, and extending in a south-west course across the country, till it terminates beyond Ardmore, in the county of Dumbarton, divides Scotland into two 'distinct parts. The southern face of these mountains is bold, rocky, dark and precipitous. The land south of this line is called the Lowlands, and that to the north, including the range, the Highlands. The maritime outline of the Highlands is also bold and rocky, and in many places deeply indented by arms of the sea. The northern and western coasts are fringed with groups of islands. The general surface of the country is mountainous, yet capable of supporting innumerable cattle, sheep and deer. The scenery is nowhere excelled for various forms of beauty and sublimity. The lochs and bens have wrought upon the imaginations of historians, poets and novelists.

The inhabitants living within these boundaries were as unique as their bens and glens. From the middle of the thirteenth century they have been distinctly marked from those inhabiting the low countries, in consequence of which they exhibit a civilization peculiarly their own. By their Lowland neighbors they were imperfectly known, being generally regarded as a horde of savage thieves, and their country as an impenetrable wilderness. From this judgment they made no effort to free themselves, but rather inclined to confirm it. The language spoken by the two races greatly varied which had a tendency to establish a marked characteristic difference between them. For a period of seven centuries the entrances or passes into the Grampians constituted a boundary between both the people and their language. At the south the Saxon language was universally spoken, while beyond the range the Gaelic formed the mother tongue, accompanied by the plaid, the claymore and other specialties which accompanied Highland characteristics. Their language was one of the oldest and least mongrel types of the great Aryan family of speech.

The country in which the Gaelic was in common use among all classes of people may be defined by a line drawn from the western opening of the Pentland Frith, sweeping around St. Kilda, from thence embracing the entire cluster of islands to the east and south, as far as Arran; thence to the Mull of Kintyre, re-entering the mainland at Ardmore, in Dumbartonshire, following the southern face of the Grampians to Aberdeenshire, and ending on the north-east point of Caithness.

For a period of nearly two hundred years the Highlander has been an object of study by strangers. Travellers have written concerning them, but dwelt upon such points as struck their fancy. A people cannot be judged by the jottings of those who have not studied the question with candor and sufficient information. Fortunately the Highlands, during the present century, have produced men who have carefully set forth their history, manners and customs. These men have fully weighed the questions of isolation, mode of life, habits of thought, and wild surroundings, which developed in the Highlander firmness of decision, fertility in resource, ardor in friendship, love of country, and a generous enthusiasum, as well as a system of government.

The Highlanders were tall, robust, well formed and hardy. Early marriages were unknown among them, and it was rare for a female of puny stature and delicate constitution to be honored with a husband. They were not obliged by art in forming their bodies, for Nature acted her part bountifully to them, and among them there are but few bodily imperfections.

The division of the people into clans, tribes or families, under separate chiefs, constituted the most remarkable circumstance in their political condition, which ultimately resulted in many of their peculiar sentiments, customs and institutions. For the most part the monarchs of Scotland had left the people alone, and, therefore, had but little to do in the working out of their destiny.

Under little or no restraint from the State, the patriarchal form of government became universal. It is a singular fact that although English ships had navigated the known seas and transplanted colonies, yet the Highlanders were but little known in London, even as late as the beginning of the eighteenth century. To the people of England it would have been a matter of surprise to learn that in the north of Great Britain, and at a distance of less than five hundred miles from their metropolis, there were many miniature courts, in each of which there was a hereditary ruler, attended by guards, armor-bearers, musicians, an orator, a poet, and who kept a rude state, dispensed justice, exacted tribute, waged war, and contracted treaties.

The ruler of each clan was called a chief, who was really the chief man of his family. Each clan was divided into branches who had chieftains over them. The members of the clan claimed consanguinity to the chief. The idea never entered into the mind of a Highlander that the chief was anything more than the head of the clan. The relation he sustained was subordinate to the will of the people. Sometimes his sway was unlimited, but necessarily paternal. The tribesmen were strongly attached to the person of their chief. He stood in the light of a protector, who must defend them and right their wrongs. They rallied to his support, and in defense they had a contempt for danger. The sway of the chief was of such a nature as to cultivate an imperishable love of independence, which was probably strengthened by an exceptional hardiness of character.

The chief generally resided among his clansmen, and his castle was the court where rewards were distributed and distinctions conferred. All disputes were settled by his decision. They followed his standard in war, attended him in the chase, supplied his table and harvested the products of his fields. His nearest kinsmen became sub-chiefs, or chieftains, held their lands and properties from him, over which they exercised a subordinate jurisdiction. These became counsellors and assistants in all emergencies. One chief was distinguished from another by having a greater number of attendants, and by the exercise of general hospitality, kindness and condescension. At the castle everyone was made welcome, and treated according to his station, with a degree of courtesy and regard for his feelings. This courtesy not only raised the clansman in his own estimation, but drew the ties closer that bound him to his chief.

While the position of chief was hereditary, yet the heir was obliged in honor to give a specimen of his valor, before he was assumed or declared leader of his people. Usually he made an incursion upon some chief with whom his clan had a feud. He gathered around him a retinue of young men who were ambitious to signalize themselves. They were obliged to bring, by open force, the cattle they found in the land they attacked, or else die in the attempt. If successful the youthful chief was ever after reputed valiant and worthy of the government. This custom being reciprocally used among them, was not reputed robbery; for the damage which one tribe sustained would receive compensation at the inauguration of its chief.

Living in a climate, severe in winter, the people inured themselves to the frosts and snows, and cared not for the exposure to the severest storms or fiercest blasts. They were content to lie down, for a night's rest, among the heather on the hillside, in snow or rain, covered only by their plaid. It is related that the laird of Keppoch, chieftain of a branch of the MacDonalds, in a winter campaign against a neighboring clan, with whom he was at war, gave orders for a snow-ball to lay under his head in the night; whereupon, his followers objected, saying, "Now we despair of victory, since our leader has become so effeminate he can't sleep without a pillow."

The high sense of honor cultivated by the relationship sustained to the chief was reflected by the most obscure inhabitant. Instances of theft from the dwelling houses seldom ever occurred, and highway robbery was never known. In the interior all property was safe without the security of locks, bolts and bars. In summer time the common receptacle for clothes, cheese, and everything that required air, was an open barn or shed. On account of wars, and raids from the neighboring clans, it was found necessary to protect the gates of castles.

The Highlanders were a brave and high-spirited people, and living under a turbulent monarchy, and having neighbors, not the most peaceable, a warlike character was either developed or else sustained. Inured to poverty they acquired a hardihood which enabled them to sustain severe privations. In their school of life it was taught to consider courage an honorable virtue and cowardice the most disgraceful failing. Loving their native glen, they were ever ready to defend it to the last extremity. Their own good name and devotion to the clan emulated and held them to deeds of daring.

It was hazardous for a chief to engage in war without the consent of his people; nor could deception be practiced successfully. Lord Murray raised a thousand men on his father's and lord Lovat's estates, under the assurance that they were to serve king James, but in reality for the service of king William. This was discovered while Murray was in the act of reviewing them; immediately they broke ranks, ran to an adjoining brook, and, filling their bonnets with water, drank to king James' health, and then marched off with pipes playing to join Dundee.

The clan was raised within an incredibly short time. When a sudden or important emergency demanded the clansmen the chief slew a goat, and making a cross of light wood, seared its extremities with fire, and extinguished them in the blood of the animal. This was called the *Fiery Cross,* or Cross of Shame, because disobedience to what the symbol implied inferred infamy. It was delivered to a swift trusty runner, who with the utmost speed carried it to the first hamlet and delivered it to the principal person with the word of rendezvous. The one receiving it sent it with the utmost despatch to the next village; and thus with the utmost celerity it passed through all the district which owed allegiance to the chief, and if the danger was common, also among his neighbors and allies. Every man between the ages of sixteen and sixty, capable of bearing arms, must immediately repair to the place of rendezvous, in his best arms and accoutrements. In extreme cases childhood and old age obeyed it. He who failed to appear suffered the penalties of fire and sword, which were emblematically denounced to the disobedient by the bloody and burnt marks upon this warlike signal.

In the camp, on the march, or in battle, the clan was commanded by the chief. If the chief was absent, then some responsible chieftain of the clan took the lead. In both their slogan guided them, for every clan had its own war-cry. Before commencing an attack the warriors generally took off their jackets and shoes. It was long remembered in Lochabar, that at the battle of Killiecrankie, Sir Ewen Cameron, at the head of his clan, just before engaging in the conflict, took from his feet, what was probably the only pair of shoes, among his tribesmen. Thus freed from everything that might impede their movements, they advanced to the assault, on a double-quick, and when within a few yards of the enemy, would pour in a volley of musketry and then rush forward with claymore in hand, reserving the pistol and dirk for close action. When in close quarters the bayonets of the enemy were received on their targets; thrusting them aside, they resorted to the pistol and dirk to complete the confusion made by the musket and claymore. In a close engagement they could not be withstood by regular troops.

Another kind of warfare to which the Highlander was prone, is called *Creach,* or foray, but really the lifting of cattle. The *Creach* received the approbation of the clan, and was planned by some responsible individual. Their predatory raids were not made for the mere pleasure of plundering their neighbors. To them it was legitimate warfare, and generally in retaliation for recent injuries, or in revenge of former wrongs. They were strict in not offending those with whom they were in amity. They had high notions of the duty of observing faith to allies and hospitality to guests. They were warriors receiving the lawful prize of war, and when driving the herds of the Lowland farmers up the pass which led to their native glen considered it just as legitimate as did the Raleighs and Drakes when they divided the spoils of Spanish galleons. They were not always the aggressors. Every evidence proves that they submitted to grievances before resorting to arms. When retaliating it was with the knowledge that their own lands would be exposed to rapine. As an illustration of the view in which the *Creach* was held, the case of Donald Cameron may be taken, who was tried in 1752, for cattle stealing, and executed at Kinloch Rannoch. At his execution he dwelt with surprise and indignation on his fate. He had never committed murder, nor robbed man or house, nor taken anything but cattle, and only then when on the grass, from one with whom he was at feud; why then should he be punished for doing that which was a common prey to all?

After a successful expedition the chief gave a great entertainment, to which all the country around was invited. On such an occasion whole deer and beeves were roasted and laid on boards or hurdles of rods placed on the rough trunks of trees, so arranged as to form an extended table. During the feast spirituous liquors went round in plenteous libations. Meanwhile the pipers played, after which the women danced, and, when they retired, the harpers were introduced.

Great feasting accompanied a wedding, and also the burial of a great personage. At the burial of one of the Lords of the Isles, in Iona, nine hundred cows were consumed.

The true condition of a people may be known by the regard held for woman. The beauty of their women was extolled in song. Small eye-brows was considered as a mark of beauty, and names were bestowed upon the owners from this feature. No country in Europe held woman in so great esteem as in the Highlands of Scotland. An unfaithful, unkind, or even careless husband was looked upon as a monster. The parents gave dowers according to their means, consisting of cattle, provisions, farm stocking, etc. Where the parents were unable to provide sufficiently, then it was customary for a newly-married couple to collect from their neighbors enough to serve the first year.

The marriage vow was sacredly kept. Whoever violated it, whether male or female, which seldom ever occurred, was made to stand in a barrel of cold water at the church door, after which the delinquent, clad in a wet canvas shirt, was made to stand before the congregation, and at the close of service, the minister explained the nature of the offense. A separation of a married couple among the common people was almost unknown. However disagreeable the wife might be, the husband rarely contemplated putting her away. Being his wife, he bore with her failings; as the mother of his children he continued to support her; a separation would have entailed reproach upon his posterity.

Young married women never wore any close head-dress. The hair, with a slight ornament was tied with ribbons; but if she lost her virtue then she was obliged to wear a cap, and never appear again with her head uncovered.

Honesty and fidelity were sacredly inculcated, and held to be virtues which all should be careful to practice. Honesty and fair dealing were enforced by custom, which had a more powerful influence, in their mutual transactions, than the legal enactments of later periods. Insolvency was considered disgraceful, and *prima facie* a crime. Bankrupts surrendered their all, and then clad in a party colored clouted garment, with hose of different sets, had their hips dashed against a stone in presence of the people, by four men, each seizing an arm or a leg. Instances of faithfulness and attachment are innumerable. The one most frequently referred to occurred during the battle of Inverkeithing, between the Royalists and the troops of Cromwell, during which seven hundred and fifty of the Mac Leans, led by their chief, Sir Hector, fell upon the field. In the heat of the conflict, eight brothers of the clan sacrificed their lives in defense of their chief. Being hard pressed by the enemy, and stoutly refusing to change his position, he was supported and covered by these intrepid brothers. As each brother fell another rushed forward, covering his chief with his body, crying *Fear eil airson Eachainn* (Another for Hector). This phrase has continued ever since as a proverb or watch-word when a man encounters any sudden danger that requires instant succor.

The Highlands of Scotland is the only country of Europe that has never been distracted by religious controversy, or suffered from religious persecution. This possibly may have been due to their patriarchal form of government. The principles of the Christian religion were warmly accepted by the people, and cherished with a strong feeling. In their religious convictions they were peaceable and unobtrusive, never arming themselves with Scriptural texts in order to carry on offensive operations. Never being perplexed by doubt, they desired no one to corroborate their faith, and no inducement could persuade them to strut about in the garb of piety in order to attract respect. The reverence for the Creator was in the heart, rather than upon the lips. In that land papists and protestants lived together in charity and brotherhood, earnest and devoted in their churches, and in contact with the world, humane and charitable. The pulpit administrations were clear and simple, and blended with an impressive and captivating spirit. All ranks were influenced by the belief that cruelty, oppression, or other misconduct, descended to the children, even to the third and fourth generations.

To a certain extent the religion of the Highlander was blended with a belief in ghosts, dreams and visions. The superstitions of the Gael were distinctly marked, and entirely too important to be overlooked. These beliefs may have been largely due to an uncultivated imagination and the narrow sphere in which he moved. His tales were adorned with the miraculous and his poetry contained as many shadowy as substantial personages. Innumerable were the stories of fairies, kelpies, urisks, witches and prophets or seers. Over him watched the Daoine Shi', or men of peace. In the glens and corries were heard the eerie sounds during the watches of the night. Strange emotions were aroused in the hearts of those who heard the raging of the tempest, the roaring of the swollen rivers and dashing of the water-fall, the thunder peals echoing from crag to crag, and the lightning rending rocks and shivering to pieces the trees. When a reasonable cause could not be assigned for a calamity it was ascribed to the operations of evil spirits. The evil one had power to make compacts, but against these was the virtue of the charmed circle. One of the most dangerous and malignant of beings was the Water-kelpie, which allured women and children into its element, where they were drowned, and then became its prey. It could skim along the surface of the water, and browse by its side, or even suddenly swell a river or loch, which it inhabited, until an unwary traveller might be engulfed. The Urisks were half-men, half-spirits, who, by kind treatment, could be induced to do a good turn, even to the drudgeries of a farm. Although scattered over the whole Highlands, they assembled in the celebrated cave—*Coire-nan-Uriskin*—situated near the base of Ben Venue, in Aberfoyle.

COIRE-NAN-URISKIN.

"By many a bard, in Celtic tongue,
Has Coir-nan-Uriskin been sung:
A softer name the Saxons gave,
And call'd the grot the Goblin-cave,

*   *   *   *   *

Gray Superstition's whisper dread
Debarr'd the spot to vulgar tread;
For there, she said, did fays resort,
And satyrs hold their sylvan court."—
Lady of the Lake.

The Daoine Shi' were believed to be a peevish, repining race of beings, who, possessing but a scant portion of happiness, envied mankind their more complete and substantial enjoyments. They had a sort of a shadowy happiness, a tinsel grandeur, in their subterranean abodes. Many persons had been entertained in their secret retreats, where they were received into the most splendid apartments, and regaled with sumptuous banquets and delicious wines. Should a mortal, however, partake of their dainties, then he was forever doomed to the condition of shi'ick, or Man of

Peace. These banquets and all the paraphernalia of their homes were but deceptions. They dressed in green, and took offense at any mortal who ventured to assume their favorite color. Hence, in some parts of Scotland, green was held to be unlucky to certain tribes and counties. The men of Caithness alleged that their bands that wore this color were cut off at the battle of Flodden; and for this reason they avoided the crossing of the Ord on a Monday, that being the day of the week on which the ill-omened array set forth. This color was disliked by both those of the name of Ogilvy and Graham. The greatest precautions had to be taken against the Daoine Shi' in order to prevent them from spiriting away mothers and their newly-born children. Witches and prophets or seers, were frequently consulted, especially before going into battle. The warnings were not always received with attention. Indeed, as a rule, the chiefs were seldom deterred from their purpose by the warnings of the oracles they consulted.

It has been advocated that the superstitions of the Highlanders, on the whole, were elevating and ennobling, which plea cannot well be sustained. It is admitted that in some of these superstitions there were lessons taught which warned against dishonorable acts, and impressed what to them were attached disgrace both to themselves and also to their kindred; and that oppression, treachery, or any other wickedness would be punished alike in their own persons and in those of their descendants. Still, on the other hand, it must not be forgotten that the doctrines of rewards and punishments had for generations been taught them from the pulpit. How far these teachings had been interwoven with their superstitions would be an impossible problem to solve.

The Highlanders were poetical. Their poets, or bards, were legion, and possessed a marked influence over the imaginations of the people. They excited the Gael to deeds of valor. Their compositions were all set to music,—many of them composing the airs to which their verses were adapted. Every chief had his bard. The aged minstrel was in attendance on all important occasions: at birth, marriage and death; at succession, victory, and defeat. He stimulated the warriors in battle by chanting the glorious deeds of their ancestors; exhorted them to emulate those distinguished examples, and, if possible, shed a still greater lustre on the warlike reputation of the clan. These addresses were delivered with great vehemence of manner, and never failed to raise the feelings of the listeners to the highest pitch of enthusiasm. When the voice of the bard was lost in the din of battle then the piper raised the inspiring sound of the pibroch. When the conflict was over the bard and the piper were again called into service—the former to honor the memory of those who had fallen, to celebrate the actions of the survivors, and excite them to further deeds of valor. The piper played the mournful Coronach for the slain, and by his notes reminded the survivors how honorable was the conduct of the dead.

The bards were the *senachies* or historians of the clans, and were recognized as a very important factor in society. They represented the literature of their times. In the absence of books they constituted the library and learning of the tribe. They were the living chronicles of past events, and the depositories of popular poetry. Tales and old poems were known to special reciters. When collected around their evening fires, a favorite pastime was a recital of traditional tales and poetry. The most acceptable guest was the one who could rehearse the longest poem or most interesting tale. Living in the land of Ossian, it was natural to ask a stranger, "Can you speak of the days of Fingal?" If the answer was in the affirmative, then the neighbors were summoned, and poems and old tales would be the order until the hour of midnight. The reciter threw into the recitation all the powers of his soul and gave vent to the sentiment. Both sexes always participated in these meetings.

The poetry was not always of the same cast. It varied as greatly as were the moods of the composer. The sublimity of Ossian had its opposite in the biting sarcasm and trenchant ridicule of some of the minor poets.

Martin, who travelled in the Western Isles, about 1695, remarks: "They are a very sagacious people, quick of apprehension, and even the vulgar exceed all those of their rank and education I ever yet saw in any other country. They have a great genius for music and mechanics. I have observed several of their children that before they could speak were capable to distinguish and make choice of one tune before another upon a violin; for they appeared always uneasy until the tune which they fancied best was played, and then they expressed their satisfaction by the motions of their head and hands. There are several of them who invent tunes already taking in the South of Scotland and elsewhere. Some musicians have endeavored to pass for first inventors of them by changing their name, but this has been impracticable; for whatever language gives the modern name, the tune still continues to speak its true original. * * *. Some of both sexes have a quick vein of poetry, and in their language—which is very emphatic—they compose rhyme and verse, both which powerfully affect the fancy. And in my judgment (which is not singular in this matter) with as great force as that of any ancient or modern poet I ever read. They have generally very retentive memories; they see things at a great distance. The unhappiness of their education, and their want of converse with foreign nations, deprives them of the opportunity to cultivate and beautify their genius, which seems to have been formed by nature for great attainments." *

The piper was an important factor in Highland society. From the earliest period the Highlanders were fond of music and dancing, and the notes of the bagpipe moved them as no other instrument could. The piper performed his duty in peace as well as in war. At harvest homes, Hallowe'en christenings, weddings, and evenings spent in dancing, he was the hero for the occasion. The people took delight in the high-toned warlike notes to which they danced, and were charmed with the solemn and melancholy airs which filled up the pauses. Withal the piper was a humorous fellow and was full of stories.

The harp was a very ancient musical instrument, and was called *clarsach*. It had thirty strings, with the peculiarity that the front arm was not perpendicular to the sounding board, but turned considerably towards the left, to afford a greater opening for the voice of the performer, and this construction showed that the accompaniment of the voice was a chief province of the harper. Some harps had but four strings. Great pains were taken to decorate the instrument. One of the last harpers was Roderick Morrison, usually called Rory Dall. He served the chief of Mac Leod. He flourished about 1650.

Referring again to Gaelic music it may be stated that its air

---

* "Description of the Western Islands," pp. 199, 200.

can easily be detected. It is quaint and pathetic, moving one with intervals singular in their irregularity. When compared with the common airs among the English, the two are found to be quite distinct. The airs to which "Scots wha hae," "Auld Langsyne," "Roy's Wife," "O a' the Airts," and "Ye Banks and Braes" are written, are such that nothing similar can be found in England. They are Scottish. Airs of precisely the same character are, however, found among all Keltic races.

No portraiture of a Highlander would be complete without a description of his garb. His costume was as picturesque as his native hills. It was well adapted to his mode of life. By its lightness and freedom he was enabled to use his limbs and handle his arms with ease and dexterity. He moved with great swiftness. Every clan had a plaid of its own, differing in the combination of its colors from all others. Thus a Cameron, a Mac Donald, a Mac Kenzie, etc., was known by his plaid; and in like manner the Athole, Glenorchy, and other colors of different districts were easily discernible. Besides those of tribal designations, industrious housewives had patterns, distinguished by the set, superior quality, and fineness of the cloth, or brightness and variety of the colors. The removal of tenants rarely occurred, and consequently, it was easy to preserve and perpetuate any particular set, or pattern, even among the lower orders. The plaid was made of fine wool, with much ingenuity in sorting the colors. In order to give exact patterns the women had before them a piece of wood with every thread of the stripe upon it. Until quite recently it was believed that the plaid, philibeg and bonnet formed the ancient garb. The philibeg or kilt, as distinct from the plaid, in all probability, is comparatively modern. The truis, consisting of breeches and stockings, is one piece and made to fit closely to the limbs, was an old costume. The belted plaid was a piece of tartan two yards in breadth, and four in length. It surrounded the waist in great folds, being firmly bound round the loins with a leathern belt, and in such manner that the lower side fell down to the middle of the knee joint. The upper part was fastened to the left shoulder with a large brooch or pin, leaving the right arm uncovered and at full liberty. In wet weather the plaid was thrown loose, covering both shoulders and body. When the use of both arms was required, it was fastened across the breast by a large bodkin or circular brooch. The sporan, a large purse of goat or badger's skin, usually ornamented, was hung before. The bonnet completed the garb. The garters were broad and of rich colors, forming a close texture which was not liable to wrinkle. The kilted-plaid was generally double, and when let down enveloped the whole person, thus forming a shelter from the storm. Shoes and stockings are of comparatively recent times. In lieu of the shoe untanned leather was tied with thongs around the feet. Burt, writing about the year 1727, when some innovations had been made, says: "The Highland dress consists of a bonnet made of thrum without a brim, a short coat, a waistcoat longer by five or six inches, short stockings, and brogues or pumps without heels * * * Few besides gentlemen wear the truis, that is, the breeches and stockings all of one piece and drawn on together; over this habit they wear a plaid, which is usually three yards long and two breadths wide, and the whole garb is made of checkered tartan or plaiding; this with the sword and pistol, is called a *full dress,* and to a well proportioned man with any tolerable air, it makes an agreeable figure."* The plaid was the undress of the ladies, and to a woman who adjusted it with an important air, it proved to be a becoming veil. It was made of silk or fine worsted, checkered with various lively colors, two breadths wide and three yards in length. It was brought over the head and made to hide or discover the face, according to the occasion, or the wearer's fancy; it reached to the waist behind; one corner dropped as low as the ankle on one side, and the other part, in folds, hung down from the opposite arm. The sleeves were of scarlet cloth, closed at the ends as man's vests, with gold lace round them, having plate buttons set with fine stones. The head-dress was a fine kerchief of linen, straight about the head. The plaid was tied before on the breast, with a buckle of silver or brass, according to the quality of the person. The plaid was tied round the waist with a belt of leather.

The Highlanders bore their part in all of Scotland's wars. An appeal, or order, to them never was made in vain. Only a

---

* "Letters from the North," Vol. II., p. 167.

brief notice must here suffice. Almost at the very dawn of Scotland's history we find the inhabitants beyond the Grampians taking a bold stand in behalf of their liberties. The Romans early triumphed over England and the southern limits of Scotland. In the year 78 A. D., Agricola, an able and vigorous commander, was appointed over the forces in Britain. During the years 80, 81, and 82, he subdued that part of Scotland south of the friths of Forth and Clyde. Learning that a confederacy had been formed to resist him at the north, during the summer of 83, he opened the campaign beyond the friths. His movements did not escape the keen eyes of the mountaineers, for in the night time they suddenly fell upon the Ninth Legion at Loch Ore, and were only repulsed after a desperate resistance. The Roman army receiving auxiliaries from the south, Agricola, in the summer of 84, took up his line of march towards the Grampians. The northern tribes, in the meantime, had united under a powerful leader whom the Romans called Galgacus. They fully realized that their liberties were in danger. They sent their wives and children into places of safety, and, thirty thousand strong, waited the advance of the enemy. The two armies came together at *Mons Grampius.* The field presented a dreadful spectacle of carnage and destruction; for ten thousand of the tribesmen fell in the engagement. The Roman army elated by its success passed the night in exultation. The victory was barren of results, for, after three years of persevering warfare, the Romans were forced to relinquish the object of the expedition. In the year 183 the Highlanders broke through the northern Roman wall. In 207 the irrepressible people again broke over their limits, which brought the emperor Severus, although old and in bad health, into the field. Exasperated by their resistance the emperor sought to extirpate them because they had prevented his nation from becoming the conquerors of Europe. Collecting a large body of troops he directed them into the mountains, and marched from the wall of Antoninus even to the very extremity of the island; but this year, 208, was also barren of fruits. Fifty thousand Romans fell a prey to fatigue, the climate, and the desultory assaults of the natives. Soon after the entire country north of the

Antonine wall, was given up, for it was found that while it was necessary for one legion to keep the southern parts in subjection two were required to repel the incursions of the Gael. Incursions from the north again broke out during the year 306, when the restless tribes were repelled by Constantius Chlorus. In the year 345 they were again repelled by Constans. During all these years the Highlanders were learning the art of war by their contact with the Romans. They no longer feared the invaders, for about the year 360, they advanced into the Roman territories and committed many depredations. There was another outbreak about the year 398. Finally, about the year 446, the Romans abandoned Britain, and advised the inhabitants, who had suffered from the northern tribes, to protect themselves by retiring behind and keeping in repair the wall of Severus.

The people were gradually forming for themselves distinct characteristics, as well as a separate kingdom confined within the Grampian boundaries. This has been known as the kingdom of the Scots; but to the Highlander as that of the Gael, or Albanich. The epithets, Scots and English, are totally unknown in Gaelic. They call the English Sassanachs, the Lowlanders are Gauls, and their own country Gaeldach.

Passing over several centuries and paying no attention to the rapines of the Danes and the Norse, we find that the power of the Norwegians, under king Haco, was broken at the battle of the Largs, fought October 2d, 1263 . King Alexander III. summoned the Highlanders, who rallied to the defence of their country and rendered such assistance as was required. The right wing of the Scottish army was composed of the men of Argyle, Lennox, Athole, and Galloway, while the left wing was constituted by those from Fife, Stirling, Berwick, and Lothian. The center, commanded by the king in person, was composed of the men of Ross, Perth, Angus, Mar, Mearns, Moray, Inverness, and Caithness.

The conquest of Scotland, undertaken by the English Edwards, culminated in the battle of Bannockburn, fought Monday, June 24, 1314, when the invaders met with a crushing defeat, leaving thirty thousand of their number dead upon the field, or two-thirds as many as there were Scots on the field. In this battle the reserve, composed of the men of Argyle, Carrick, Kintyre, and the Isles, formed the fourth line, was commanded by Bruce in person. The following clans, commanded in person by their respective chiefs, had the distinguished honor of fighting nobly: Stewart, Macdonald, Mackay, Mackintosh, Macpherson, Cameron, Sinclair, Drummond, Campbell, Menzies, Maclean, Sutherland, Robertson, Grant, Fraser, Macfarlane, Ross, Macgregor, Munro, Mackenzie, and Macquarrie, or twenty-one in all.

In the year 1513, James IV. determined on an invasion of England, and summoned the whole array of his kingdom to meet him on the common moor of Edinburgh. One hundred thousand men assembled in obedience to the command. This great host met the English on the field of Flodden, September 9th. The right divisions of James' army were chiefly composed of Highlanders. The shock of the mountaineers, as they poured upon the English pikemen, was terrible; but the force of the onslaught once sustained became spent with its own violence. The consequence was a total rout of the right wing accompanied by great slaughter. Of this host there perished on the field fifteen lords and chiefs of clans.

During the year 1547, the English, under the duke of Somerset, invaded Scotland. The hostile armies came together at Pinkie, September 18th. The right and left wings of the Scottish army were composed of Highlanders. During the conflict the Highlanders could not resist the temptation to plunder, and, while thus engaged, saw the division of Angus falling back, though in good order; mistaking this retrograde movement for a flight, they were suddenly seized with a panic and ran off in all directions. Their terror was communicated to other troops, who immediately threw away their arms and followed the Highlanders. Everything was now lost; the ground over which the fight lay was as thickly strewed with pikes as a floor with rushes; helmets, bucklers, swords, daggers, and steel caps lay scattered on every side; and the chase beginning at one o'clock, continued till six in the evening with extraordinary slaughter.

During the reign of Charles I. civil commotions broke out

which shook the kingdom with great violence. The Scots were courted by king and parliament alike. The Highlanders were devoted to the royal government. In the year 1644 Montrose made a diversion in the Highlands. With dazzling rapacity, at first only supported by a handful of followers, but gathering numbers with success, he erected the royal standard at Dumfries. The clans obeyed his summons, and on September 1st, at Tippermuir, he defeated the Covenanters, and again on the 12th at the Bridge of Dee. On February 2nd, 1645, at Inverlochy, he crushed the Argyle Campbells, who had taken up the sword on behalf of Cromwell. In rapid succession other victories were won at Auldearn, Alford and Kilsyth. All Scotland now appeared to be recovered for Charles, but the fruit of all these victories was lost by the defeat at Philiphaugh, September 13th, 1645.

Within the brief space of three years, James II., of England, succeeded in fanning the revolutionary elements both in England and Scotland into a flame which he was powerless to quench. The Highlanders chiefly adhered to the party of James which received the name of Jacobites. Dundee hastened to the Highlands and around him gathered the Highland chiefs at Lochabar. The army of William, under Hugh Mackay, met the forces of Dundee at Killiecrankie, July 29th, 1689, where, under the spirited leadership of the latter, and the irresistible torrent of the Highland charge, the forces of the former were almost annihilated; but at the moment of victory Bonnie Dundee was killed by a bullet. No one was left who was equal to the occasion, or who could hold the clans together, and hence the victory was in reality a defeat.

The exiled Stuarts looked with a longing eye to that crown which their stupid folly had forfeited. They seemed fated to bring countless woes upon the loyal hearted, brave, self-sacrificing Highlanders, and were ever eager to take advantage of any circumstance that might lead to their restoration. The accession of George I, in 1714, was an unhappy event for Great Britain. Discontent soon pervaded the kingdom. All he appeared to care about was to secure for himself and his family a high position, which he scarcely knew how to occupy; to fill the pockets of his

German attendants and his German mistresses; to get away as often as possible from his uncongenial islanders whose language he did not understand, and to use the strength of Great Britain to obtain petty advantages for his German principality. At once the new king exhibited violent prejudices against some of the chief men of the nation, and irritated without a cause a large part of his subjects. Some believed it was a favorable opportunity to reinstate the Stuart dynasty. John Erskine, eleventh earl of Mar, stung by studied and unprovoked insults, on the part of the king, proceeded to the Highlands and placed himself at the head of the forces of the house of Stuart, or Jacobites, as they were called. On September 6, 1715, Mar assembled at Aboyne the noblemen, chiefs of clans, gentlemen, and others, with such followers as could be brought together, and proclaimed James, king of Great Britain. The insurrection, both in England and Scotland, began to grow in popularity, and would have been a success had there been at the head of affairs a strong military man. Nearly all the principal chiefs of the clans were drawn into the movement. At Sheriffmuir, the contending forces met, Sunday, November 13, 1715. The victory was with the Highlanders, but Mar's military talents were not equal to the occasion. The army was finally disbanded at Aberdeen, in February, 1716.

The rebellion of 1745, headed by prince Charles Stuart, was the grandest exhibition of chivalry, on the part of the Highlanders, that the world has ever seen. They were actuated by an exalted sense of devotion to that family, which for generations, they had been taught should reign over them. At first victory crowned their efforts, but all was lost on the disastrous field of Culloden, fought April 16, 1746.

Were it possible it would be an unspeakable pleasure to drop a veil over the scene, at the close of the battle of Culloden. Language fails to depict the horrors that ensued. It is scarcely within the bounds of belief that human beings could perpetrate such atrocities upon the helpless, the feeble, and the innocent, without regard to sex or age, as followed in the wake of the victors. Highland historians have made the facts known. It must suffice here to give a moderate statement from an English writer:

"Quarter was seldom given to the stragglers and fugitives, except to a few considerately reserved for public execution. No care or compassion was shown to their wounded; nay more, on the following day most of these were put to death in cold blood, with a cruelty such as never perhaps before or since has disgraced a British army. Some were dragged from the thickets or cabins where they had sought refuge, drawn out in line and shot, while others were dispatched by the soldiers with the stocks of their muskets. One farm-building, into which some twenty disabled Highlanders had crawled, was deliberately set on fire the next day, and burnt with them to the ground. The native prisoners were scarcely better treated; and even sufficient water was not vouchsafed to their thirst. * * * * Every kind of havoc and outrage was not only permitted, but, I fear, we must add, encouraged. Military license usurped the place of law, and a fierce and exasperated soldiery were at once judge—jury—executioner. * * * * The rebels' country was laid waste, the houses plundered, the cabins burnt, the cattle driven away. The men had fled to the mountains, but such as could be found were frequently shot; nor was mercy always granted even to their helpless families. In many cases the women and children, expelled from their homes and seeking shelter in the clefts of the rocks, miserably perished of cold and hunger; others were reduced to follow the track of the marauders, humbly imploring for the blood and offal of their own cattle which had been slaughtered for the soldiers' food! Such is the avowal which historical justice demands. But let me turn from further details of these painful and irritating scenes, or of the ribald frolics and revelry with which they were intermingled—races of naked women on horseback for the amusement of the camp at Fort Augustus." *

The author and abettor of these atrocities was the son of the reigning monarch.

Not satisfied with the destruction which was carried into the very homes of this gallant, brave and generous race of people, the British parliament, with a refined cruelty, passed an act that, on and after August 1, 1747, any person, man, or boy, in Scotland, who should on any pretense whatever wear any part of the Highland garb, should be imprisoned not less than six months; and on conviction of second offense, transportation abroad for seven years. The soldiers had instructions to shoot upon the

---

* Lord Mahon's "History of England," Vol. III, pp. 308-311.

spot any one seen wearing the Highland garb, and this as late as September, 1750. This law and other laws made at the same time were unnecessarily severe.

However impartial or fair a traveller may be his statements are not to be accepted without due caution. He narrates that which most forcibly attracts his attention, being ever careful to search out that which he desires. Yet, to a certain extent, dependence must be placed in his observations. From certain travellers are gleaned fearful pictures of the Highlanders during the eighteenth century, written without a due consideration of the underlying causes. The power of the chiefs had been weakened, while the law was still impotent, many of them were in exile and their estates forfeited, and landlords, in not a few instances, placed over the clansmen, who were inimical to their best interests. As has been noticed, in 1746 the country was ravaged and pitiless oppression followed. Destruction and misery everywhere abounded. To judge a former condition of a people by their present extremity affords a distorted view of the picture.

Fire and sword, war and rapine, desolation and atrocity, perpetrated upon a high-spirited and generous people, cannot conduce to the best moral condtion. Left in poverty and galled by outrage, wrongs will be resorted to which otherwise would be foreign to a natural disposition. If the influences of a more refined age had not penetrated the remote glens, then a rougher reprisal must be expected. The coarseness, vice, rapacity, and inhumanity of the oppressor must of necessity have a corresponding influence on their better natures. If to this it be added that some of the chiefs were naturally fierce, the origin of the sad features could readily be determined. Whatever vices practiced or wrongs perpetrated, the example was set before them by their more powerful and better conditioned neighbors. Among the crimes enumerated is that some of the chiefs increased their scanty incomes by kidnapping boys or men, whom they sold as slaves to the American planters. If this be true, and in all probability it was, there must have been confederates engaged in maritime pursuits. But they did not have far to go for this lesson, for this nefarious trade was taught them, at their very doors, by the merchants of Aberdeen, who were "noted for a scandalous system of decoying young boys from the country and selling them as slaves to the planters in Virginia. It was a trade which in the early part of the eighteenth century, was carried on to a considerable extent through the Highlands; and a case which took place about 1742 attracted much notice a few years later, when one of the victims having escaped from servitude, returned to Aberdeen, and published a narrative of his sufferings, seriously implicating some of the magistracy of the town. He was prosecuted and condemned for libel by the local authorities, but the case was afterwards carried to Edinburgh. The imquitous system of kidnapping was fully exposed, and the judges of the supreme court unanimously reversed the verdict of the Aberdeen authorities and imposed a heavy fine upon the provost, the four bailies, and the dean of guild. * * * An atrocious case of this kind, which shows clearly the state of the Highlands, occurred in 1739. Nearly one hundred men, women and children were seized in the dead of night on the islands of Skye and Harris, pinioned, horribly beaten, and stowed away in a ship bound for America, in order to be sold to the planters. Fortunately the ship touched at Donaghadee in Ireland, and the prisoners, after undergoing the most frightful sufferings, succeeded in escaping."*

Under existing circumstances it was but natural that the more enterprising, and especially that intelligent portion who had lost their heritable jurisdiction, should turn with longing eyes to another country. America offered the most inviting asylum. Although there was some emigration to America during the first half of the eighteenth century, yet it did not fairly set in until about 1760. Between the years 1763 and 1775 over twenty thousand Highlanders left their homes to seek a better retreat in the forests of America.

---

* Lecky's "History of England," Vol. II, p. 274.

CHAPTER II.

THE SCOTCH-IRISH IN AMERICA.

The name Scotland was never applied to that country, now so designated, before the tenth century, but was called Alban, Albania, Albion. At an early period Ireland was called Scotia, which name was exclusively so applied before the tenth century. Scotia was then a territorial or geographical term, while Scotus was a race name or generic term, implying people as well as country. "The generic term of *Scoti* embraced the people of that race whether inhabiting Ireland or Britain. As this term of Scotia was a geographical term derived from the generic name of a people, it was to some extent a fluctuating name, and though applied at first to Ireland, which possessed the more distinctive name of Hibernia, as the principal seat of the race from whom the name was derived, it is obvious that, if the people from whom the name was taken inhabited other countries, the name itself would have a tendency to pass from the one to the other, according to the prominence which the different settlements of the race assumed in the history of the world; and as the race of the Scots in Britain became more extended, and their power more formidable, the territorial name would have a tendency to fix itself where the race had become most conspicuous. * * * The name in its Latin form of Scotia, was transferred from Ireland to Scotland in the reign of Malcolm the Second, who reigned from 1004 to 1034. The 'Pictish Chronicle,' compiled before 997, knows nothing of the name of Scotia as applied to North Britain; but Marianus Scotus, who lived from 1028 to 1081, calls Malcolm the Second 'rex *Scotiae*,' and Brian, king of Ireland, 'rex *Hiberniae*.' The author of the 'Life of St. Cadroe,' in the eleventh century, likewise applies the name of *Scotia* to North Britain." *

A strong immigration early set in from the north of Ireland to the western parts of Scotland. It was under no leadership, but more in the nature of an overflow, or else partaking of the spirit

---

*Skene's " Chronicles of the Picts and Scots," p. 77.

of adventure. This was accelerated in the year 503, when a new colony of Dalriadic Scots, under the leadership of Fergus, son of Erc, left Ireland and settled on the western coast of Argyle and the adjacent isles. From Fergus was derived the line of Scoto-Irish kings, who finally, in 843, ascended the Pictish throne.

The inhabitants of Ireland and the Highlands of Scotland were but branches of the same Keltic stock, and their language was substantially the same. There was not only more or less migrations between the two countries, but also, to a greater or less extent, an impinging between the people.

Ulster, the northern province of Ireland, is composed of the counties of Antrim, Armagh, Cavan, Donegal, Down, Fermanagh, Londonderry, Monaghan and Tyrone. Formerly it was the seat of the O'Neills, as well as the lesser septs of O'Donnell, O'Cahan, O'Doherty, Maguire, MacMahon, etc. The settlements made by the earlier migrations of the Highlanders were chiefly on the coast of Antrim. These settlements were connected with and dependent on the Clandonald of Islay and Kintyre. The founder of this branch of that powerful family was John Mor, second son of "the good John of Islay," who, about the year 1400, married Majory Bisset, heiress of the Glens, in Antrim, and thus acquired a permanent footing. The family was not only strengthened by settling cadets of its own house as tenants in the territory of the Glens, but also by intermarriages with the families of O'-Neill, O'Donnell, and others. In extending its Irish possessions the Clandonald was brought into frequent conflicts and feuds with the Irish of Ulster. In 1558 the Hebrideans had become so strong in Ulster that the archbishop of Armagh urged on the government the advisability of their expulsion by procuring their Irish neighbors, O'Donnell, O'Neill, O'Cahan, and others, to unite against them. In 1565 the MacDonalds suffered a severe defeat at the hands of Shane O'Neill, earl of Tyrone. The Scottish islanders still continued to exercise considerable power. Sorley Buy MacDonald, a man of great courage, soon extended his influence over the adjacent territories, in so much so that in 1575-1585, the English were forced to turn their attention to the progress of the Scots. The latter having been defeated, an agreement was made in which Sorley Buy was granted four districts. His eldest son, Sir James MacSorley Buy, or MacDonell of Dunluce, became a strenuous supporter of the government of James on his accession to the British throne.

In the meantime other forces were at work. Seeds of discontent had been sown by both Henry VIII, and his daughter Elizabeth, who tried to force the people of Ireland to accept the ritual of the Reformed Church. Both reaped abundant fruit of trouble from this ill-advised policy. Being inured to war it did not require much fire to be fanned into a flame of commotion and discord. Soon after his accession to the English throne, James I caused certain estates of Irish nobles, who had engaged in treasonable practices, to be escheated to the crown. By this confiscation James had at his disposal nearly six counties in Ulster, embracing half a million of acres. These lands were allotted to private individuals in sections of one thousand, fifteen hundred, and two thousand acres, each being required to support an adequate number of English or Scottish tenantry. Protestant colonies were transplanted from England and Scotland, but chiefly from the latter, with the intent that the principles of the Reformation should subdue the turbulent natives. The proclamation inviting settlers for Ulster was dated at Edinburgh, March 28, 1609. Great care was taken in selecting the emigrants, to which the king gave his personal attention. Measures were taken that the settlers should be "from the inward parts of Scotland," and that they should be so located that "they may not mix nor inter-marry" with "the mere Irish." For the most part the people were received from the shires of Dumbarton, Renfrew, Ayre, Galloway, and Dumfries. On account of religious persecutions, in 1665, a large additional accession was received from Galloway and Ayre. The chief seat of the colonization scheme was in the county of Londonderry. The new settlers did not mix with the native population to any appreciable extent, especially prior to 1741, but mingled freely with the English Puritans and the refugee Huguenots. The native race was forced sullenly to retire before the colonists. Although the king had expressly forbidden any more of the inhabitants of the Western Isles to be taken to Ulster, yet the blood of the Highlander, to a great degree, permeated that of the Ulsterman, and had its due weight in forming the character of the Scotch-Irish. The commotions in the Highlands, during the civil wars, swelled the number to greater proportions. The rebellions of 1715 and 1745 added a large percentage to the increasing population. The names of the people are interesting, both as illustrating their origin, and as showing the extraordinary corruptions which some have undergone. As an illustration, the proscribed clan MacGregor, may be cited, which migrated in great numbers, descendants of whom are still to be found under the names of Grier, Greer, Gregor, etc., the *Mac* in general being dropped; MacKinnon becomes McKenna, McKean, McCannon; Mac Nish is McNeice, Menees, Munnis, Monies, etc.

The Scotch settlers retained the characteristic traits of their native stock and continued to call themselves Scotch, although molded somewhat by surrounding influences. They demanded and exercised the privilege of choosing their own spiritual advisers, in opposition to all efforts of the hierarchy of England to make the choice and support the clergy as a state concern.

From the descendants of these people came the Scotch-Irish emigrants to America, who were destined to perform an important part on the theatre of action by organizing a successful revolt and establishing a new government. Among the early emigrants to the New World, although termed Scotch-Irish, and belonging to them we have such names as Campbell, Ferguson, Graham, McFarland, McDonald, McGregor, McIntyre, McKenzie, McLean, McPherson, Morrison, Robertson, Stewart, etc.; all of which are distinctly Highlander and suggestive of the clans.

On the outbreak of the American Revolution the thirteen colonies numbered among their inhabitants about eight hundred thousand Scotch and Scotch-Irish, or a little more than one-fourth of the entire population. They were among the first to become actively engaged in that struggle, and so continued until the peace, furnishing fourteen major-generals, and thirty brigadier generals, among whom may be mentioned St. Clair, McDougall, Mercer, McIntosh, Wayne, Knox, Montgomery, Sullivan, Stark, Morgan, Davidson, and others. More than any other one element, unless the New England Puritans be excepted, they formed a sentiment for independence, and recruited the continental army. To their valor, enthusiasm and dogged persistence the victory for liberty was largely due. Washington pronounced on them a proud encomium when he declared, during the darkest period of the Revolution, that if his efforts should fail, then he would erect his standard on the Blue Ridge of Virginia. Besides warring against the drilled armies of Britain on the sea coast they formed a protective wall between the settlements and the savages on the west.

Among the fifty-six signers of the Declaration of Independence, nine were of this lineage, one of whom, McKean, served continuously in Congress from its opening in 1774 till its close in 1783, during a part of which time he was its president, and also serving as chief justice of Pennsylvania. The chairman of the committee that drafted the constitution of the United States, Rutledge, was, by ancestry, Scotch-Irish. When the same instrument was submitted, the three states first to adopt it were the middle states, or Delaware, Pennsylvania and New Jersey, so largely settled by the same class of people.

Turning again specifically to the Scotch-Irish emigrants it may be remarked that they had received in the old country a splendid physique, having large bones and sound teeth, besides being trained to habits of industry. The mass of them were men of intelligence, resolution, energy, religious and moral in character. They were a God-fearing, liberty-loving, tyrant-hating, Sabbath-keeping, covenant-adhering race, and schooled by a discipline made fresh and impressive by the heroic efforts at Derry and Enniskillin. Their women were fine specimens of the sex, about the medium height, strongly built, with fair complexion, light blue or grey eyes, ruddy cheeks, and faces indicating a warm heart, intelligence and courage; and possessing those virtues which constitute the redeeming qualities of the human race.

These people were martyrs for conscience sake. In 1711 a measure was carried through the British parliament that provided that all persons in places of profit or trust, and all common councilmen in corporations, who, while holding office, were proved to have attended any Nonconformist place of worship, should forfeit the place, and should continue incapable of public employment till they should depose that for a whole year they had not attended a conventicle. A fine of £40 was added to be paid to the informer. There were other causes which assisted to help depopulate Ulster, among which was the destruction of the woolen trade about 1700, when twenty thousand left that province. Many more were driven away by the Test Act in 1704, and in 1732. On the failure to repeal that act the protestant emigration recommenced which robbed Ireland of the bravest defenders of English interests and peopled America with fresh blood of Puritanism.

The second great wave of emigration from Ulster occurred between 1771 and 1773, growing out of the Antrim evictions. In 1771 the leases on the estate of the marquis of Donegal, in Antrim, expired. The rents were placed at such an exhorbitant figure that the demands could not be met. A spirit of resentment to the oppressions of the landed proprietors at once arose, and extensive emigration to America was the result. In the two years that followed the Antrim evictions of 1772, thirty thousand protestants left Ulster for a land where legal robbery could not be permitted, and where those who sowed the seed could reap the harvest. From the ports of the North of Ireland one hundred vessels sailed for the New World, loaded with human beings. It has been computed that in 1773 and during the five preceding years, Ulster, by emigration to the American settlements, was drained of one-quarter of the trading cash, and a like proportion of its manufacturing population. This oppressed people, leaving Ireland in such a temper became a powerful adjunct in the prosecution of the Revolution which followed so closely on the wrongs which they had so cruelly suffered.

The advent of the first Scotch-Irish clergyman in America, so far as is now known, was in 1682, signalled by the arrival of Francis Makemie, the father of American Presbyterianism. Almost promptly he was landed in jail in New York, charged with the offense of preaching the gospel in a private house. Assisted by a Scottish lawyer from Philadelphia (who was silenced for his courage), he defended the cause of religious liberty with heroic courage and legal ability, and was ultimately acquitted by a fearless New York jury. Thus was begun the great struggle for religious liberty in America. Among those who afterwards followed were George McNish, from Ulster, in 1705, and John Henry, in 1709.

Early in the spring of 1718, Rev. William Boyd arrived in Boston as an agent of some hundreds of people who had expressed a desire to come to New England should suitable encouragement be offered them. With him he brought a brief memorial to which was attached three hundred and ninteen names, all but thirteen of which were in a fair and vigorous hand. Governor Shute gave such general encouragement and promise of welcome, that on August 4, 1718, five small ships came to anchor at the wharf in Boston, having on board one hundred and twenty Scotch-Irish families, numbering in all about seven hundred and fifty individuals. In years they embraced those from the babe in arms to John Young, who had seen the frosts of ninety-five winters. Among the clergy who arrived were James McGregor, Cornwell, and Holmes.

In a measure these people were under the charge of Governor Shute. He must find homes for them. He dispatched about fifty of these families to Worcester. That year marked the fifth of its permanent settlement, and was composed of fifty log-houses, inhabited by two hundred souls. The new comers appear to have been of the poorer and more illiterate class of the five ship loads. At first they were welcomed, because needed for both civic and military reasons. In September of 1722 a township organization was effected, and at the first annual town meeting, names of the strangers appear on the list of officers. With these emigrants was brought the Irish potato, and first planted in the spring of 1719. When their English neighbors visited them, on their departure they presented them with a few of the tubers for planting, and the recipients, unwilling to show any discourtesy, accepted the same, but suspecting a poisonous quality, carried them to the first swamp and threw them into the water. The same spring a few potatoes were given to a Mr. Walker, of Andover, by a family who had wintered with him. He planted them in the ground, and in due time the family gathered the "*balls*" which they supposed was the fruit. These were cooked in various ways, but could not be made palatable. The next spring when plowing the garden, potatoes of great size were turned up, when the mistake was discovered. This introduction into New England is the reason why the now indispensable succulent is called "Irish potato." This vegetable was first brought from Virginia to Ireland in 1565 by slave-trader Hawkins, and from there it found its way to New England in 1718, through the Scotch-Irish.

The Worcester Scotch-Irish petitioned to be released from paying taxes to support the prevalent form of worship, as they desired to support their own method. Their prayer was contemptuously rejected. Two years later, or in 1738, owing to their church treatment, a company consisting of thirty-eight families, settled the new town of Pelham, thirty miles west of Worcester. The scandalous destruction of their property in Worcester, in 1740, caused a further exodus which resulted in the establishing the towns of Warren and Blandford, both being incorporated in 1741. The Scotch-Irish town of Colerain, located fifty miles northwest of Worcester was settled in 1739.

Londonderry, New Hampshire, was settled in April, 1719, forming the second settlement, from the five ships. Most of these pioneers were men in middle life, robust and persevering. Their first dwellings were of logs, covered with bark. It must not be thought that these people, strict in their religious conceptions, were not touched with the common feelings of ordinary humanity. It is related that when John Morrison was building his house his wife came to him and in a persuasive manner said, "Aweel, aweel, dear Joan, an' it maun be a log-house, do make it a log heegher nor the lave;" (than the rest). The first frame house built was for their pastor, James McGregor. The first season they felt it necessary to build two strong stone garrison-houses in order to resist any attack of the Indians. It is remarkable that in neither Lowell's war, when Londonderry was strictly a frontier town, nor in either of the two subsequent French and Indian wars, did any hostile force from the northward ever approach that town. During the twenty-five years preceding the revolution, ten distinct towns of influence, in New Hampshire, were settled by emigrants from Londonderry, besides two in Vermont and two in Nova Scotia; while families, sometimes singly and also in groups, went off in all directions, especially along the Connecticut river and over the ridge of the Green Mountains. To these brave people, neither the crown nor the colonies appealed in vain. Every route to Crown Point and Ticonderago had been tramped by them time and again. With Colonel Williams they were at the head of Lake George in 1755, and in the battle with Dieskau that followed; they were with Stark and lord Howe, under Abercrombie, in the terrible defeat at Ticonderago in 1758; others toiled with Wolfe on the Heights of Abraham; and in 1777, fought under Stark at Bennington, and against Burgoyne at Saratoga.

A part of the emigrants intended for New Hampshire settled in Maine, in what is now Portland, Topsham, Bath and other places. Unfortunately soon after these settlements were established some of them were broken up by Indian troubles, and some of the colonists sought refuge with their countrymen at Londonderry, but the greater part removed to Pennsylvania,—from 1730 to 1733 about one hundred and fifty families, principally of Scotch descent. In 1735, Warren, Maine, was settled by twenty-seven families, some of whom were of recent emigration and others from the first arrival in Boston in 1718. In 1753 the town received an addition of sixty adults and many children brought from Scotland.

The Scotch-Irish settlement at Salem in Washington county, New York, came from Monaghan and Ballibay, Ireland. Under the leadership of their minister, Rev. Thomas Clark, three hundred sailed from Newry, May 10, 1764, and landed in New York in July following. On September 30, 1765, Mr. Clark obtained twelve thousand acres of the "Turner Grant," and upon this land he moved his parishioners, save a few families that had been induced to go to South Carolina, and some others that remained in Stillwater, New York. The great body of these settlers took possession of their lands, which had been previously surveyed into tracts of eighty-eight acres each, in the year 1767. The previous year had been devoted to clearing the lands, building houses, etc. Among the early buildings was a log church, the first religious place of worship erected between Albany and Canada. March 2, 1774, the legislature erected the settlement into a township named New Perth. This name remained until March 7, 1788, when it was changed to Salem.

The Scotch-Irish first settled in Somerset county, New Jersey, early in the last century, but not at one time but from time to time.

These early settlers repudiated the name of Irish, and took it as an offense to be so called. They claimed, and truly, to be Scotch. The term "Scotch-Irish" is quite recent, but has come into general use.

From the three centers, Worcester, Londonderry and Wiscasset, the Scotch-Irish penetrated and permeated all New England; Maine the most of all, next New Hampshire, then Massachusetts, and in lessening order, Vermont, Connecticut and Rhode Island. They were one sort of people, belonging to the same grade and sphere of life. In worldly goods they were poor, but the majority could read and write, and if possessed with but one book that was the Bible, yet greatly esteeming Fox's "Book of Martyrs" and Bunyon's "Pilgrim's Progress." Whatever their views, they were held in common.

The three doors that opened to the Scotch-Irish emigrant, in the New World, were the ports of Boston, Charleston and New Castle, in Delaware, the great bulk of whom being received at the last named city, where they did not even stop to rest, but pushed their way to their future homes in Pennsylvania. No other state received so many of them for permanent settlers. Those who landed in New York found the denizens there too submissive to foreign dictation, and so preferred Pennsylvania and Maryland, where the proprietary governors and the people were in immediate contact. Francis Machemie had organized the first Presbyterian church in America along the eastern shore of Maryland and in the adjoining counties of Virginia.

The wave of Quaker settlements spent its force on the line of the Conestoga creek, in Lancaster county. The Scotch and Scotch-Irish arriving in great numbers were permitted to locate beyond that line, and thus they not only became the pioneers, but long that race so continued to be. In 1725, so great had been the wave of emigration into Pennsylvania, that James Logan, a native of Armagh, Ireland, but not fond of his own countrymen who were not Quakers, declared, "It looks as if Ireland were to send all her inhabitants hither; if they continue to come they will make themselves proprietors of the province;" and he further condemned the bad taste of the people who were forcing themselves where they were not wanted. The rate of this invasion may be estimated from the rise in population from twenty thousand, in 1701, to two hundred and fifty thousand in 1745, which embraced the entire population of that colony. Between the years 1729 and 1750, there was an annual arrival of twelve thousand, mostly from Ulster. Among the vessels that helped to inaugurate this great tide was the good ship "George and Ann," which set sail from Ireland on May 9th, 1729, and brought over the McDowells, the Irvines, the Campbells, the O'Neills, the McElroys, the Mitchells, and their compatriots.

Soon after the emigrants landed at New Castle they found their way along the branches of various rivers to the several settlements on the western frontier. The only ones known to have come through New York was the "Irish settlement" in Allen township, Northampton county, composed principally of families from Londonderry, New Hampshire, where, owing to the rigid climate, they could not be induced to remain. It grew but slowly, and after 1750 most of the descendants passed on towards the Susquehanna and down the Cumberland.

As early as 1720 a colony was formed on the Neshaminy, in Bucks County, which finally became one of the greatest landmarks of that race. The settlements that commenced as early as 1710, at Fagg Manor, at Octorara, at New London, and at Brandywine Manor, in Chester County, formed the nucleus for subsequent emigration for a period of forty years, when they also declined by removals to other sections of the State, and to the colonies of the South. Prior to 1730 there were large settlements in the townships of Colerain, Pequea, and Leacock, in Lancaster County. Just when the pioneers arrived in that region has not been accurately ascertained, but some of them earlier than 1720. Within a radius of thirty-five miles of Harrisburgh are the settlements of Donegal, Paxtang, Derry, and Hanover, founded between 1715 and 1724; from whence poured another stream on through the Cumberland Valley, across the Potomac, down through Virginia and into the Carolinas and Georgia. The valley of the Juniata was occupied in 1749. The settlements in the lower part of York County date from 1726. From 1760 to 1770 settlements rapidly sprung up in various places throughout Western Pennsylvania. Soon after 1767 emigrants settled on the Youghiogheny, the Monongahela and its tributaries, and in the years 1770 and 1771, Washington County was colonized. Soon after the wave of population extended to the Ohio River. From this time forward Western Pennsylvania was characteristically Scotch-Irish.

These hardy sons were foremost in the French and Indian Wars. The Revolutionary struggle caused them to turn their attention to statesmanship and combat,—every one of whom was loyal to the cause of indepndence. The patriot army had its full share of Scotch-Irish representation. That thunderbolt of war, Anthony Wayne,* hailed from the County of Chester, The ardent manner in which the cause of the patriots was espoused is illustrated, in a notice of a marriage that took place in 1778, in Lancaster County, the contracting parties being of the Ulster race. The couple is denominated "very sincere Whigs."

It "was truly a Whig wedding, as there were present many young gentlemen and ladies, and not one of the gentlemen but had been out when called on in the service of his country; and it was well known that the groom, in particular, had proved his heroism, as well as Whigism, in several battles and skirmishes. After the marriage was ended, a motion was made, and heartily agreed to by all present, that the young unmarried ladies should form themselves into an association by the name of the 'Whig Association of Unmarried Young Ladies of America,' in which they should pledge their honor that they would never give their

---

*Stille, Life of Wayne, p. 5, says he was not Scotch-Irish.

hand in marriage to any gentleman until he had first proved himself a patriot, in readily turning out when called to defend his country from slavery, by a spirited and brave conduct, as they would not wish to be the mothers of a race of slaves and cowards.'" *

Pennsylvania was the gateway and first resting place, and the source of Scotch-Irish adventure and enterprise as they moved west and south. The wave of emigration striking the eastern border of Pennsylvania, in a measure was deflected southward through Maryland, Virginia, the Carolinas, reaching and crossing the Savannah river, though met at various points

BUILT BY HENRY McWHORTER, IN 1787, AT JANE LEW, WEST VIRGINIA.
PHOTOGRAPHED IN 1893.

by counter streams of the same race, which had entered the continent through Charleston and other southern ports. Leaving Pennsylvania and turning southward, the first colony into which the stream poured, was Maryland, the settlements being principally in the narrow strip which constitutes the western portion, although they never scattered all over the colony.

Proceeding southward traces of that race are found in Virginia east of the Blue Ridge, in the latter part of the seventeenth and early in the eighteenth century. They were in Albe-

---

*Dunlap's " Pennsylvania Packet," June 17, 1778.

marle, Nelson, Campbell, Prince Edward, Charlotte and Orange counties, and even along the great valley west of the Blue Ridge. It was not, however, until the year 1738 that they entered the valley in great numbers, and almost completely possessed it from the Pennsylvania to the North Carolina line. During the French and Indian wars the soldiers of Virginia were mainly drawn from this section, and suffered defeat with Washington at the Great Meadows, and with Braddock at Fort Duquesne, but by their firmness saved the remnant of that rash general's army. In 1774 they won the signal victory at Point Pleasant which struck terror into the Indian tribes across the Ohio.

The American Revolution was foreshadowed in 1765, when England began her oppressive measures regardless of the inalienable and chartered rights of the colonists of America. It was then the youthful Scotch-Irishman, Patrick Henry, introduced into the Virginia House of Burgesses, the resolutions denying the validity of the Act of the British parliament, and by Scotch-Irish votes he secured their adoption against the combined efforts of the old leaders. . At the first call for troops by congress to defend Boston, Daniel Morgan at once raised a company from among his own people, in the lower Virginia valley, and by a forced march of six hundred miles reached the beleagured city in three weeks. With his men he trudged through the wilderness of Maine and appeared before Quebec; and later, on the heights of Saratoga, with his riflemen, he poured like a torrent upon the ranks of Burgogne. Through the foresight of Henry, a commission was given to George Rogers Clark, in 1778, to lead a secret expedition against the northwestern forts. The soldiers were recruited from among the Scotch-Irish settlements west of the Blue Ridge. The untold hardships, sufferings and final success of this expedition, at the Treaty of Peace, in 1783, gave the great west to the United States.

The greater number of the colonists of North Carolina was Scotch and Scotch-Irish, in so much so as to have given direction to its history. There were several reasons why they should be so attracted, the most potent being a mild climate, fertile lands, and freedom of religious worship. The greatest accession at any one time was that in 1736, when Henry McCulloch secured sixty-four thousand acres in Duplin county, and settled upon these lands four thousand of his Ulster countrymen. About the same time the Scotch began to occupy the lower Cape Fear. Prior to 1750 they were located in the counties of Granville, Orange, Rowan and Mecklenburg, although it is uncertain when they settled between the Dan and the Catawba. Braddock's defeat, in 1755, rendered border life dangerous, many of the newcomers turning south into North Carolina, where they met the other stream of their countrymen moving upward from Charleston along the banks of the Santee, Wateree, Broad, Pacolet, Ennoree and Saluda, and this continued till checked by the Revolution. These people generally were industrious, sober and intelligent, and with their advent begins the educational history of the state. Near Greensborough, in 1767, was established a classical school, and in 1770, in the town of Charlotte, Mecklenburg county, was chartered Queen's College, but its charter was repealed by George III. However, it continued to flourish, and was incorporated as "Liberty Hall," in 1777. The Revolution closed its doors; Cornwallis quartered his troops within it, and afterwards burned the buildings.

Under wrongs the Scotch-Irish of North Carolina were the most restless of all the colonists. They were zealous advocates for freedom of conscience and security against taxation unless imposed by themselves. During the administration of acting Governor Miller, they imprisoned the president and six members of the council, convened the legislature, established courts of justice, and for two years exercised all the functions of government; they derided the authority of Governor Eastchurch; they imprisoned, impeached, and sent into exile Governor Sothel, for his extortions, and successfully resisted the effort of lord Granville to establish the Church of England in that colony. In 1731, Governor Burrington wrote: "The people of North Carolina are neither to be cajoled or outwitted; * * * always behaved insolently to their Governors. Some they imprisoned, others they have drove out of the country, and at other times set up a govern-

THE SCOTCH-IRISH IN AMERICA.

ment of their own choice." In 1765, when a vessel laden with stamp paper arrived, the people over-awed the captain, who soon sailed away. The officers then adopted a regular system of oppression and extortion, and plundered the people at every turn of life. The people formed themselves into an association "for regulating public grievances and abuse of powers." The royal governor, Tryon (the same who later originated the infamous plot

VIEW OF BATTLE FIELD OF ALAMANCE.

to poison Washington), raised an army of eleven hundred men, and marched to inflict summary punishment on the defiant sons of liberty. On May 16, 1771, the two forces met on the banks of the Great Alamance. After an engagement of two hours the patriots failed. These men were sturdy, patriotic members of three Presbyterian churches. On the field of battle were their pastors, graduates of Princeton. Tryon used his victory so savagely as to drive an increasing stream of settlers over the mountains into Tennessee, where they made their homes in the valley of the Watauga, and there nurtured their wrongs; but the day of their vengeance was rapidly approaching.

The stirring times of 1775 found the North Carolinians ready for revolt. They knew from tradition and experience the monstrous wrongs of tyrants. When the people of Mecklenburg county learned in May, 1775, that parliament had declared the colonies in a state of revolt, they did not wait for the action of congress nor for that of their own provincial legislature, but adopted resolutions, which in effect formed a declaration of independence.

The power, valor and uncompromisng conduct of these men is illustrated in their conduct at the battle of King's Mountain, fought October 7, 1780. It was totally unlike any other in American history, being the voluntary uprising of the people, rushing to arms to aid their distant kinsmen, when their own homes were menaced by savages. They served without pay and without the hope of reward. The defeat of Gates at Camden laid the whole of North Carolina at the feet of the British. Flushed with success, Colonel Furguson, of the 71st Regiment, at the head of eleven hundred men marched into North Carolina and took up his position at Gilbert Town, in order to intercept those retreating in that direction from Camden, and to crush out the spirit of the patriots in that region. Without any concert of action volunteers assembled simultaneously, and placed themselves under tried leaders. They were admirably fitted by their daily pursuits for the privations they were called upon to endure. They had no tents, baggage, bread or salt, but subsisted on potatoes, pumpkins and roasted corn, and such venison as their own rifles could procure. Their army consisted of four hundred men, under Colonel William Campbell, from Washington county, Virginia, two hundred and forty were under Colonel Isaac Shelby, from Sullivan county, North Carolina, and two hundred and forty men, from Washington county, same state, under John Sevier, which assembled at Watauga, September 25, where they were joined by

Colonel Charles McDowell, with one hundred and sixty men, from the counties of Burke and Rutherford, who had fled before the enemy to the western waters. While McDowell, Shelby and Sevier were in consultation, two paroled prisoners arrived from Furguson with the message that if they did not "take protection under his standard, he would march his army over the mountains, hang their leaders, and lay waste their country with fire and sword." On their march to meet the army of Furguson they were for twenty-four hours in the saddle. They took that officer by surprise, killed him and one hundred and eighty of his men, after an engagement of one hour and five minutes, the greater part of which time a heavy and incessant fire was kept up on both sides, with a loss to themselves of only twenty killed and a few wounded. The remaining force of the enemy surrendered at discretion, giving up their camp equipage and fifteen hundred stand of arms. On the morning after the battle several of the Royalist (Tory) prisoners were found guilty of murder and other high crimes, and hanged. This was the closing scene of the battle of King's Mountain, an event which completely crushed the spirit of the Royalists, and weakened beyond recovery the power of the British in the Carolinas. The intelligence of Furguson's defeat destroyed all Cornwallis's hopes of aid from those who still remained loyal to Britain's interests. The men oppressed by British laws and Tryon's cruelty were not yet avenged, for they were with Morgan at the Cowpens and with Greene at Guildford Court House, and until the close of the war.

In the settling of South Carolina, every ship that sailed from Ireland for the port of Charleston, was crowded with men, women and children, which was especially true after the peace of 1763. About the same date, within one year, a thousand families came into the state in that wave that originated in Pennsylvania, bringing with them their cattle, horses and hogs. Lands were aloted to them in the western woods, which soon became the most popular part of the province, the up-country population being overwhelmingly Scotch-Irish. They brought with them and retained, in an emiment degree, the virtues of industry and economy, so peculiarly necessary in a new country. To them the state is indebted for much of its early literature. The settlers in the western part of the colony, long without the aid of laws, were forced to band themselves together for mutual protection. The royal governor, Montague, in 1764, sent an army against them, and with great difficulty a civil war was averted. The division thus created reappeared in 1775, on the breaking out of the Revolution. The state suffered greatly from the ravages of Cornwallis, who rode roughly over it, although her sons toiled heroically in defence of their firesides. The little bands in the east gathered around the standard of Marion, and in the north and west around those of Sumter and Pickens. They kept alive the flame of liberty in the swamps, and when the country appeared to be subdued, it burst forth in electric flashes striking and withering the hand of the oppressor. Through the veins of most of the patriots flowed Scotch-Irish blood; and to the hands of one of this class, John Rutledge, the destinies of the state were committed.

Georgia was sparsely settled at the time of the Revolution. In 1753 its population was less than twenty-four hundred. Emigration from the Carolinas set in towards North Georgia, bringing many Scotch-Irish families. The movement towards the mountain and Piedmont regions of the southeast began about 1773. In that year, Governor Wright purchased from the Indians that portion of middle Georgia lying between the Oconee and the Savannah. The inducements he then offered proved very attractive to the enterprising sons of Virginia and the Carolinas, who lived in the highlands of those states. These people who settled in Georgia have thus been described by Governor Gilmer: "The pretty girls were dressed in striped and checked cotton cloth, spun and woven with their own hands, and their sweethearts in sumach and walnut-dyed stuff, made by their mothers. Courting was done when riding to meeting on Sunday, and walking to the spring when there. Newly married couples went to see the old folks on Saturday, and carried home on Sunday evening what they could spare. There was no *ennui* among the women for something to do. If there had been leisure to read, there were but few books for the indulgence. Hollow trees supplied cradles for babies."

A majority of the first settlers of East Tennessee were of

Scotch-Irish blood, having sought homes there after the battle of Alamance, and hence that state became the daughter of North Carolina. The first written constitution born of a convention of people on this continent, was that at Watauga, in 1772. A settlement of less than a dozen families was formed in 1778, near Bledsoe, isolated in the heart of the Chickasaw nation, with no other protection than a small stockade enclosure and their own indomitable courage. In the early spring of 1779, a little colony of gallant adventurers, from the parent line of Watauga, crossed the Cumberland mountain, and established themselves near the French Lick, and planted a field of corn where the city of Nashville now stands. The settlement on the Cumberland was made in 1780, after great privations and sufferings on the journey. The settlers at the various stations were so harrassed by the Indians, incited thereto by British and Spanish agents, that all were abandoned except Elatons and the Bluffs (Nashville). These people were compelled to go in armed squads to the springs, and plowed while guarded by armed sentinels. The Indians, by a well planned stratagem, attempted to enter the Bluffs, on April 22d, 1781. The men in the fort were drawn into an ambush by a decoy party. When they dismounted to give battle, their horses dashed off toward the fort, and they were pursued by some Indians, which left a gap in their lines, through which some whites were escaping to the fort; but these were intercepted by a large body of the enemy from another ambush. The heroic women in the fort, headed by Mrs. James Robertson, seized the axes and idle guns, and planted themselves in the gate, determined to die rather than give up the fort. Just in time she ordered the sentry to turn loose a pack of dogs which had been selected for their size and courage to encounter bears and panthers. Frantic to join the fray, they dashed off, outyelling the savages, who recoiled before the fury of their onset, thus giving the men time to escape to the fort. So overjoyed was Mrs. Robertson that she patted every dog as he came into the fort.

So thoroughly was Kentucky settled by the Scotch-Irish, from the older colonies, that it might be designated as of that race, the first emigrants being from Virginia and North Carolina.

It was first explored by Thomas Walker in 1747; followed by John Finley, of North Carolina, 1767; and in 1769, by Daniel Boone, John Stewart, and three others, who penetrated to the Kentucky river. By the year 1773, lands were taken up and afterwards there was a steady stream, almost entirely from the valley and southwest Virginia. No border annals teem with more thrilling incidents or heroic exploits than those of the Kentucky hunters, whose very name finally struck terror into the heart of the strongest savage. The prediction of the Cherokee chief to Boone at the treaty at Watauga, ceding the territory to Henderson and his associates, was fully verified: "Brother," said he, "we have given you a fine land, but I believe you will have much trouble in settling it."

The history of the Scotch-Irish race in Canada, prior to the peace of 1783, is largely that of individuals. It has already been noted that two settlements had been made in Nova Scotia by the emigrants that landed from the five ships in Boston harbor. It is recorded that Truro, Nova Scotia, was settled in 1762, and in 1756 three brothers from Ireland settled in Colchester, same province. If the questions were thoroughly investigated it doubtless would lead to interesting results.

It must not be lost sight of that one of the important industrial arts brought to America was of untold benefit. Not only did every colony bring with them agricultural implements needful for the culture of flax, but also the small wheels and the loom for spinning and weaving the fibre. Nothing so much excited the interest of Puritan Boston, in 1718, as the small wheels worked by women and propelled by the foot, for turning the straight flax fibre into thread. Public exhibitions of skill in 1719 took place on Boston common, by Scotch-Irish women, at which prizes were offered. The advent of the machine produced a sensation, and societies and schools were formed to teach the art of making linen thread.

The distinctive characteristics which the Scotch-Irish transplanted to the new world may be designated as follows: They were Presbyterians in their religion and church government; they were loyal to the conceded authority to the king, but considered him bound as well as themselves to "the Solemn League and Covenant," entered into in 1643, which pledged the support of the Reformation and of the liberties of the kingdom; the right to choose their own ministers, untrammeled by the civil powers; they practiced strict discipline in morals, and gave instruction to their youth in schools and academies, and in teaching the Bible as illustrated by the Westminster Assembly's catechism. To all this they combined in a remarkable degree, acuteness of intellect, firmness of purpose, and conscientious devotion to duty.

CHAPTER III.

THE CAUSES THAT LED TO EMIGRATION.

The social system of the Highlanders that bound the members of the clan together was conducive to the pride of ancestry and the love of home. This pride was so directed as to lead to the most beneficial results on their character and conduct: forming strong attachments, leading to the performance of laudable and heroic actions, and enabling the poorest to endure the severest hardships without a murmur, and never complaining of what they received to eat, or where they lodged, or of any other privation. Instead of complaining of the difference in station or fortune, or considering a ready obedience to the call of the chief as a slavish oppression, they felt convinced that they were supporting their own honor in showing their gratitude and duty to the generous head of the family. In them it was a singular and characteristic feature to contemplate with early familiarity the prospect of death, which was considered as merely a passage from this to another state of existence, enlivened by the assured hope that they should meet their friends and kindred in a fairer and brighter world than this. This statement may be perceived in the anxious care with which they provided the necessary articles for a proper and becoming funeral. Even the poorest and most destitute endeavored to save something for this last solemnity. It was considered to be a sad calamity to be consigned to the grave among strangers, without the attendance and sympathy of friends, and at a distance from the family. If a relative died away from home, the greatest exertions were made to carry the body back for interment among the ashes of the forefathers. A people so nurtured could only contemplate with despair the idea of being forced from the land of their nativity, or emigrating from that beloved country, hallowed by the remains of their kindred.

THE CAUSES THAT LED TO EMIGRATION.

The Highlander, by nature, was opposed to emigration. All his instincts, as well as training, led him to view with delight the permanency of home and the constant companionship of those to whom he was related by ties of consanguinity. Neither was he a creature of conquest, and looked not with a covetous eye upon the lands of other nations. He would do battle in a foreign land, but the Highlands of Scotland was his abiding place. If he left his native glen in order to become a resident elsewhere, there must have been a special or overpowering reason. He never emigrated through choice. Unfortunately the simplicity of his nature, his confiding trust, and love of chief and country, were doomed to receive such a jolt as would shake the very fibres of his being, and that from those to whom he looked for support and protection. Reference here is not made to evictions awful crimes that commenced in 1784, but to the change, desolation and misery growing out of the calamity at Culloden.

Notwithstanding the peculiar characteristics of the Highlander, there would of necessity arise certain circumstances which would lead some, and even many, to change their habitation. From the days of the Crusader downwards he was more or less active in foreign wars; and coming in contact with different nationalities his mind would broaden and his sentiment change, so that other lands and other people would be viewed in a more favorable light. While this would not become general, yet it would follow in many instances. Intercourse with another people, racially and linguistically related, would have a tendency to invite a closer affiliation. Hence, the inhabitants of the Western Isles had almost constant communication, sometimes at war, it is true, but generally in terms of amity, with the natives of North Ireland. It is not surprising then that as early as 1584, Sorley Buy MacDonald should lead a thousand Highlanders, called Redshanks, of the clans or families of the MacDonalds, Campbells, and Magalanes, into Ulster, and in time intermarry with the Irish, and finally become the most formidable enemies of England in her designs of settling that country. Some of the leading men were forced to flee on account of being attainted for treason, having fought under Dundee in 1689, or under Mar in

1715, and after Culloden in 1745 quite a hegira took place, many of whom found service in the army of France. Individuals, seeking employment, found their way into England before 1724. Although there was a strong movement for England from the Lowlands, yet many were from the Highlands, to whom was partly due the old proverb, "There never came a fool from Scotland." These emigrants, from the Highlands, were principally those having trades, who sought to better their condition.

Seven hundred prisoners taken at Preston were sold as slaves to some West Indian merchants, which was a cruel proceeding, when it is considered that the greater part of these men were Highlanders, who had joined the army in obedience to the commands of their chiefs. Wholly unfitted for such labor as would be required in the West Indies and unacclimated, their fate may be readily assumed. But this was no more heartless than the execution in Lancashire of twenty-two of their companions.

The specifications above enumerated have no bearing on the emigration which took place on a large scale, the consequences of which, at the time, arrested the attention of the nation. The causes now to be enumerated grew out of the change of policy following the battle of Culloden. The atrocities following that battle were both for vengeance and to break the military spirit of the Highlanders. The legislative enactments broke the nobler spirit of the people. The rights and welfare of the people at large were totally ignored, and no provisions made for their future welfare. The country was left in a state of commotion and confusion resulting from the changes consequent to the overthrow of the old system, the breaking up of old relationship, and the gradual encroachment of Lowland civilization, and methods of agriculture. While these changes at first were neither great nor extensive, yet they were sufficient to keep the country in a ferment or uproar. The change was largely in the manner of an experiment in order to find out the most profitable way of adaptation to the new regime. These experiments resulted in the unsettling of old manners, customs, and ideas,, which caused discontent and misery among the people. The actual change was slow; the innovations, as a rule, began in those districts bordering on the Lowlands, and thence proceeded in a northwesterly direction.

THE CAUSES THAT LED TO EMIGRATION.

In all probability the first shock felt by the clansmen, under the new order of things, was the abolishing the ancient clan system, and the reduction of the chiefs to the condition of landlords. For awhile the people failed to realize this new order of affairs, for the gentlemen and common people still continued to regard their chief in the same light as formerly, not questioning but their obedience to the head of their clan was independent of legislative enactment. They were still ready to make any sacrifice for his sake, and felt it to be their duty to do what they could for his support. They still believed that the chief's duty to his people remained unaltered, and he was bound to see that they did not want, and to succor them in distress.

The first effects in the change in tribal relations were felt on those estates that had been forfeited on account of the chiefs and gentlemen having been compelled to leave the country in order to save their lives. These estates were entrusted to the management of commissioners who rudely applied their powers under the new arrangement of affairs. When the chiefs, now reduced to the position of lairds, began to realize their condition, and the advantage of making their lands yield them as large an income as possible, followed the example of demanding a rent. A rental value had never been exacted before, for it was the universal belief that the land belonged to the clan in common. Some of the older chiefs, then living, held to the same opinion, and among such, a change was not perceptible until a new landlord came into possession. The gentlemen of the clan and the tacksmen, or large farmers, firmly believed that they had as much right to a share of the lands as the chief himself. In the beginning the rent was not high nor more than the lands would bear; but it was resented by the tacksmen, deeming it a wanton injury inflicted in the house of their dearest friend. They were hurt at the idea that the chief,—the father of his people—should be controlled by such a mercenary idea, and to exercise that power which gave him the authority to lease the lands to the highest bidder. This policy, which they deemed selfish and unjust, naturally cut them to the quick. They and their ancestors had occupied their farms for many generations; their birth was as good and their genealogy as old as that of the chief himself, to whom they were all blood relations, and whose loyalty was unshaken. True, they had no written document, no "paltry sheep-skin," as they called it, to prove the right to their farms, but such had never been the custom, and these parchments quite a modern innovation, and, in former times, before a chief would have tried to wrest from them that which had been given by a former chief to their fathers, would have bitten out his tongue before he would have asked a bond. There can be no doubt that originally when a chief bestowed a share of his property upon his son or other near relation, he intended that the latter should keep it for himself and his descendants. To these tacksmen it was injury enough that an alien government should interfere in their domestic relations, but for the chief to turn against them was a wound which no balm could heal. Before they would submit to these exactions, they would first give up their holdings; which many of them did and emigrated to America, taking with them servants and sub-tenants, and enticing still others to follow them by the glowing accounts which they sent home of their good fortune in the favored country far to the west. In some cases the farms thus vacated were let to other tacksmen, but in most instances the new system was introduced by letting the land directly to what was formerly sub-tenants, or those who had held the land immediately from the ousted tacksmen.

There was a class of lairds who had tasted the sweets of southern luxuries and who vied with the more opulent, increased the rate of rent to such an extent as to deprive the tacksmen of their holdings. This caused an influx of lowland farmers, who with their improved methods could compete successfully against their less favored northern neighbors. The danger of southern luxuries had been foreseen and an attempt had been made to provide against it. As far back as the year 1744, in order to discourage such things, at a meeting of the chiefs of the Isle of Skye, Sir Alexander MacDonald of MacDonald, Norman MacLeod of MacLeod, John MacKinnon of MacKinnon, and Malcolm MacLeod of Raasay, held in Portree, it was agreed to discontinue and discountenance the use of brandy, tobacco and tea.

THE CAUSES THAT LED TO EMIGRATION.

The placing of the land in the hands of aliens was deplored in its results as may be seen from the following portrayal given by Buchanan in his "Travels in the Hebrides," referring to about 1780:—"At present they are obliged to be much more submissive to their tacksmen than ever they were in former times to their lairds or lords. There is a great difference between that mild treatment which is shown to sub-tenants and even scallags, by the old lessees, descended of ancient and honorable families, and the outrageous rapacity of those necessitous strangers who have obtained leases from absent proprietors, who treat the natives as if they were a conquered and inferior race of mortals. In short, they treat them like beasts of burden; and in all respects like slaves attached to the soil, as they cannot obtain new habitations, on account of the combinations already mentioned, and are entirely at the mercy of the laird or tacksman . Formerly, the personal service of the tenant did not usually exceed eight or ten days in the year. There lives at present at Scalpa, in the isle of Harris, a tacksman of a large district, who instead of six days' work paid by the sub-tenants to his predecessor in the lease, has raised the predial service, called in that and in other parts of Scotland, *manerial bondage,* to fifty-two days in the year at once; besides many other services to be performed at different though regular and stated times; as tanning leather for brogans, making heather ropes for thatch, digging and drying peats for fuel; one pannier of peat charcoal to be carried to the smith; so many days for gathering and shearing sheep and lambs; for ferrying cattle from island to island, and other distant places, and several days for going on distant errands; so many pounds of wool to be spun into yarn. And over and above all this, they must lend their aid upon any unforseen occurrence whenever they are called on. The constant service of two months at once is performed at the proper season in making kelp. On the whole, this gentleman's sub-tenants may be computed to devote to his service full three days in the week. But this is not all: they have to pay besides yearly a certain number of cocks, hen, butter, and cheese, called CAORIGH-FERRIN, the Wife's Portion. This, it must be owned, is one of the most severe and rigorous tacksmen descended from the old inhabitants, in all the Western Hebrides; but the situation of his sub-tenants exhibits but too faithful a picture of the sub-tenants of those places in general, and the exact counterpart of such enormous oppression is to be found at Luskintire."*

---

*Keltie's "History of the Highland Clans," Vol. II, p. 35.

The dismissal of retainers kept by the chiefs during feudal times added to the discontent. For the protection of the clan it had been necessary to keep a retinue of trained warriors. These were no longer necessary, and under the changed state of affairs, an expense that could be illy afforded. This class found themselves without a vocation, and they would sow the seeds of discontent, if they remained in the country. They must either enter the army or else go to another country in search of a vocation.

Unquestionably the most potent of all causes for emigration was the introduction of sheep-farming. That the country was well adapted for sheep goes without disputation. Sheep had always been kept in the Highlands with the black cattle, but not in large numbers. The lowland lessees introduced sheep on a large scale, involving the junction of many small farms into one, each of which had been hitherto occupied by a number of tenants. This engrossing of farms and consequent depopulation was also a fruitful source of discontent and misery to those who had to vacate their homes and native glens. Many of those displaced by sheep and one or two Lowland shepherds, emigrated like the discontented tacksmen to America, and those who remained looked with an ill-will and an evil eye on the intruders. Some of the more humane landlords invited the oppressed to remove to their estates, while others tried to prevent the ousted tenants from leaving the country by setting apart some particular spot along the sea-shore, or else on waste land that had never been touched by the plow, on which they might build houses and have an acre or two for support. Those removed to the coast were encouraged to prosecute the fishing along with their agricultural labors. It was mainly by a number of such ousted Highlanders that the great and arduous undertaking was accomplished of bringing into a state of cultivation Kincardine Moss, in Perthshire. At that time, 1767, the task to be undertaken was one of stupendous magnitude; but was so successfully carried out that two thousand acres were reclaimed which for centuries had rested under seven feet of heath and vegetable matter. Similarly many other spots were brought into a state of cultivation. But this, and other pursuits then engaged in, did not occupy the time of all who had been despoiled of their homes.

THE CAUSES THAT LED TO EMIGRATION.

The breaking up of old habits and customs and the forcible importation of those that are foreign must not only engender hate but also cause misery. It is the uniform testimony of all travellers, who visited the Highlands during the latter half of the eighteenth century, especially Pennant, Boswell, Johnson, Newte, and Buchanan, that the condition of the country was deplorable. Without quoting from all, let the following lengthy extract suffice, which is from Buchanan:

"Upon the whole, the situation of these people, inhabitants of Britain! is such as no language can describe, nor fancy conceive. If, with great labor and fatigue, the farmer raises a slender crop of oats and barley, the autumnal rains often baffle his utmost efforts, and frustrate all his expectations; and instead of being able to pay an exorbitant rent, he sees his family in danger of perishing during the ensuing winter, when he is precluded from any possibility of assistance elsewhere. Nor are his cattle in a better situation; in summer they pick up a scanty support amongst the morasses or heathy mountains; but in winter, when the grounds are covered with snow, and when the naked wilds afford neither shelter nor subsistence, the few cows, small, lean, and ready to drop down through want of pasture, are brought into the hut where the family resides, and frequently share with them the small stock of meal which had been purchased, or raised, for the family only; while the cattle thus sustained, are bled occasionally, to afford nourishment for the children after it hath been boiled or made into cakes. The sheep being left upon the open heaths, seek to shelter themselves from the inclemency of the weather amongst the hollows upon the lee-side of the mountains, and here they are frequently buried under the snow for several weeks together, and in severe seasons during two months and upwards. They eat their own and each other's wool, and hold out wonderfully under cold and hunger; but even in moderate winters, a considerable number are generally found dead after the snow hath disappeared, and in rigorous seasons few or none are left alive. Meanwhile the steward, hard pressed by letters from Almack's or Newmarket, demands the rent in a tone which makes no great allowance for unpropitious seasons, the death of cattle, and other accidental misfortunes; disguising the feelings of his own breast —his Honor's wants must at any rate be supplied, the bills must be duly negotiated. Such is the state of farming, if it may be so called, throughout the interior parts of the Highlands; but as that country has an extensive coast, and many islands, it may be supposed that the inhabitants of those shores enjoy all the benefits of their maritime situation. This, however, is not the case; those gifts of nature, which in any other commercial kingdom would have been rendered subservient to the most valuable purposes, are in Scotland lost, or nearly so, to the poor natives and the public. The only difference, therefore, between the inhabitants of the interior parts and those of the more distant coasts, consists in this, that the latter, with the labors of the field, have to encounter alternately the dangers of the ocean and all the fatigues of navigation. To the distressing circumstances at home, as stated above, new difficulties and toils await the devoted farmer when abroad. He leaves his family in October, accompanied by his sons, brothers, and frequently an aged parent, and embarks on board a small open boat, in quest of the herring fishery, with no other provisions than oatmeal, potatoes, and fresh water; no other bedding than heath, twigs, or straw, the covering, if any, an old sail. Thus provided, he searches from bay to bay, through turbulent seas, frequently for several weeks together, before the shoals of herring are discovered. The glad tidings serve to vary, but not to diminish his fatigues. Unremitting nightly labor (the time when the herrings are taken), pinching cold winds, heavy seas, uninhabited shores covered with snow, or deluged with rain, contribute towards filling up the measure of his distresses; while to men of such exquisite feelings as the Highlanders generally possess, the scene which awaits him at home does it most effectually. Having disposed of his capture to the Busses, he returns in January through a long navigation, frequently amidst unceasing hurricanes, not to a comfortable home and a cheerful family, but to a hut composed of turf, without windows, doors, or chimney, environed with snow, and almost hid from the eye by its astonishing depth. Upon entering this solitary mansion, he generally finds a part of his family, sometimes the whole, lying upon heath or straw, languishing through want or epidemical disease; while the few surviving cows, which possess the other end of the cottage, instead of furnishing further supplies of milk or blood, demand his immediate attention to keep them in existence. The season now approaches when he is again to delve and labor the ground, on the same slender prospect of a plentiful crop or a dry harvest. The cattle which have survived the famine of the winter, are turned out to the mountains; and, having put his domestic affairs into the best situation which a train of accumulated misfortunes admits of, he resumes the oar, either in quest of herring or the white fishery. If successful in the latter, he sets out in his open boat upon a voyage (taking the Hebrides and the opposite coast at a medium distance) of two hundred miles, to vend his cargo of dried cod, ling, etc., at Greenock or Glasgow. The product, which seldom exceeds twelve or fifteen pounds, is laid out, in conjunction with his companions, upon meal and fishing tackle; and he returns through the same tedious navigation. The autumn calls his attention again to the field; the usual round of disappointment, fatigue, and distress awaits him; thus dragging through a wretched existence in the hope of soon arriving in that country where the weary shall be at rest." *

The writer most pitiably laments that twenty thousand of these wretched people had to leave their homes and famine-struck condition, and the oppression of their lairds, for lands and houses of their own in a fairer and more fertile land, where independence and affluence were at their command. Nothing but misery and degradation at home; happiness, riches and advancement beyond the ocean. Under such a system it would be no special foresight to predict a famine, which came to pass in 1770 and again in 1782-3. Whatever may be the evils under the clan system, and there certainly were such, none caused the oppression and misery which that devoted people have suffered since its abolishment. So far as contentment, happiness, and a wise regard for interest, it would have been better for the masses had the old system continued. As a matter of fact, however, those who emigrated found a greater latitude and brighter prospects for their descendants.

From what has been stated it will be noticed that it was a matter of necessity and not a spirit of adventure that drove the mass of Highlanders to America; but those who came, nevertheless, were enterprising and anxious to carve out their own fortunes. Before starting on the long and perilous journey across the Atlantic they were first forced to break the mystic spell that bound them to their native hills and glens, that had a charm and an association bound by a sacred tie. A venerable divine of a Highland parish who had repeatedly witnessed the fond affection of his parishioners in taking their departure, narrated how they approached the sacred edifice, ever dear to them, by the most hallowed associations, and with tears in their eyes kissed its

---

*Keltie's "History of the Highland Clans," Vol. II, p. 42.

very walls, how they made an emphatic pause in losing sight of the romantic scenes of their childhood, with its kirks and cots, and thousand memories, and as if taking a formal and lasting adieu, uncovered their heads and waived their bonnets three times towards the scene, and then with heavy steps and aching hearts resumed their pilgrimage towards new scenes in distant climes. *

"Farewell to the land of the mountain and wood,
    Farewell to the home of the brave and the good,
My bark is afloat on the blue-rolling main,
    And I ne'er shall behold thee, dear Scotland again!

Adieu to the scenes of my life's early morn,
    From the place of my birth I am cruelly torn;
The tyrant oppresses the land of the free;
    And leaves but the name of my sires unto me.

Oh! home of my fathers, I bid thee adieu,
    For soon will thy hill-tops retreat from my view,
With sad drooping heart I depart from thy shore,
    To behold thy fair valleys and mountains no more.

'Twas there that I woo'd thee, young Flora, my wife,
    When my bosom was warm in the morning of life.
I courted thy love 'mong the heather so brown,
    And heaven did I bless when it made thee my own.

The friends of my early years, where are they now?
    Each kind honest heart, and each brave manly brow;
Some sleep in the churchyard from tyranny free,
    And others are crossing the ocean with me.

Lo! now on the boundless Atlantic I stray,
    To a strange foreign realm I am wafted away,
Before me as far as my vision can glance,
    I see but the wave rolling wat'ry expanse.

So farewell my country and all that is dear,
    The hour is arrived and the bark is asteer,
I go and forever, oh! Scotland adieu!
    The land of my fathers no more I shall view."
                                             —*Peter Crerar.*

---

*"Celtic Magazine," Vol. I, p. 143.

THE CAUSES THAT LED TO EMIGRATION. 73

America was the one great inviting field that opened wide her doors to the oppressed of all nations. The Highlanders hastened thither; first in small companies, or singly, and afterwards in sufficient numbers to form distinctive settlements. These belonged to the better class, bringing with them a certain amount of property, intelligent, persevering, religious, and in many instances closely related to the chief. Who was the first Highlander, and in what year he settled in America, has not been determined. It is impossible to judge by the name, because it would not specially signify, for as has been noted, Highlanders had gone to the north of Ireland, and in the very first migrations of the Scotch-Irish, their descendants landed at Boston and Philadelphia. It is, however, positively known that individual members of the clans, born in the Highlands, and brought up under the jurisdiction of the chiefs, settled permanently in America before 1724. * The number of these must have been very small, for a greater migration would have attracted attention. In 1729, there arrived at the port of Philadelphia, five thousand six hundred and fifty-five Irish emigrants, and only two hundred and sixty-seven English, forty-three Scotch, and three hundred and forty-three Germans. Of the forty-three Scotch it would be impossible to ascertain how many of them were from the Highlands, because all people from Scotland were designated under the one word. But if the whole number were of the Gaelic race, and the ratio kept up it would be almost insignificant, if scattered from one end of the Colonies to the other. After the wave of emigration had finally set in then the numbers of small companies would rapidly increase and the ratio would be largely augmented. †

It is not to be presumed that the emigrants found the New World to be all their fancies had pictured. If they had left misery and oppression behind them, they were destined to encounter hardships and disappointments. A new country, however great may be its attractions, necessarily has its disadvantages. It takes time, patience, industry, perseverence and ingenuity to convert a wilderness into an abode of civilization. Innumerable obstacles

---

*See Appendix, Note A. †See Appendix, Note B.

must be overcome, which eventually give way before the indomitable will of man. Years of hard service must be rendered ere the comforts of home are obtained, the farm properly stocked, and the ways for traffic opened. After the first impressions of the emigrant are over, a longing desire for the old home engrosses his heart, and a self-censure for the step he has taken. Time ameliorates these difficulties, and the wisdom of the undertaking becomes more apparent, while contentment and prosperity rival all other claims. The Highlander in the land of the stranger, no longer an alien, grows stronger in his love for his new surroundings, and gradually becomes just as patriotic for the new as he was for the old country. All its civilization, endearments, and progress, become a part of his being. His memory, however, lingers over the scenes of his early youth, and in his dreams he once more abides in his native glens, and receives the blessings of his kind, tender, loving mother. Were it even thus to all who set forth to seek their fortunes it would be well; but to hundreds who left their homes in fond anticipation, not a single ray of light shone athwart their progress, for all was dark and forbidding. Misrepresentation, treachery, and betrayal were too frequently practiced, and in misery, heart-broken and despondent many dropped to rise no more, welcoming death as a deliverer.

CHAPTER IV.

THE DARIEN SCHEME.

The first body of Highlanders to arrive in the New World was as much military as civil. Their lines were cast in evil waters, and disaster awaited them. They formed a very essential part of a colony that engaged in what has been termed the Darien Scheme, which originated in 1695, and so mismanaged as to involve thousands in ruin, many of whom had enjoyed comparative opulence. Although this project did not materially affect the Highlands of Scotland, yet as Highland money entered the enterprise, and as quite a body of Highlanders perished in the attempted colonization of the isthmus of Panama, more than a passing notice is here demanded.

Scottish people have ever been noted for their caution, frugality, and prudence, and not prone to engage in any speculation unless based on the soundest business principles. Although thus characterized, yet this people engaged in the most disastrous speculation on record; established by act of the Scottish parliament, and begun by unprecedented excitement. The leading cause which impelled the people headlong into this catastrophe was the ruination of the foreign trade of Scotland by the English Navigation Act of 1660, which provided that all trade with the English colonies should be conducted in English ships alone. Any scheme plausibly presented was likely to catch those anxious to regain their commercial interests, as well as those who would be actuated to increase their own interests. The Massacre of Glencoe had no little share in the matter. This massacre, which occurred February 13, 1692, is the foulest blot in the annals of crime. It was deliberately planned by Sir John Dalrymple and others, ordered by king William, and executed by Captain Robert Campbell of Glenlyon, in the most treacherous, brutal, atrocious, and bloodthirsty manner imaginable, and perpetrated without the shadow of a reasonable excuse—infancy and old age, male and female alike perished. The bare recital of it is awful; and the barbarity of the American savage pales before it. In every quarter, even at court, the account of the massacre was received with horror and indignation. The odium of the nation rose to a great pitch, and demanded that an inquiry be made into this atrocious affair. The appointment of a commission was not wrung from the unwilling king until April 29, 1695. The commission, as a whole, acted with great fairness, although they put the best possible construction on the king's order, and threw the whole blame on Secretary Dalrymple. The king was too intimately connected with the crime to make an example of any one, although through public sentiment he was forced to dismiss Secretary Dalrymple. Not one of those actually engaged in the perpetration of the crime were dismissed from the army, or punished for the butchery, otherwise than by the general hatred of the age in which they lived, and the universal execration of posterity. The tide of feeling set in against king William, and before it had time to ebb the Darien Scheme was projected. The friends of William seized the opportunity to persuade him that some freedom and facilities of trade should be grantd the Scotch, and that would divert public attention from the Glencoe massacre. Secretary Dalrymple also was not slow to give it the support of his eloquence and interest, in hopes to regain thereby a part of his lost popularity.

The originator of the Darien Scheme was William Paterson, founder of the Bank of England, a man of comprehensive views and great sagacity, born in Scotland, a missionary in the Indies, and a buccaneer among the West India islands. During his roving course of life he had visited the isthmus of Panama—then called Darien—and brought away only pleasant recollections of that narrow strip of land that unites North and South America. On his return to Europe his first plan was the national establishment of the Bank of England. For a brief period he was admitted as a director in that institution, but it befell to Paterson that others possessed of wealth and influence, interposed and took advantage of his ideas, and then excluded him from the concern.

Paterson next turned his thoughts to the plan of settling a colony in America, and handling the trade of the Indies and the South Seas. The trade of Europe with the remote parts of Asia had been carried on by rounding the Cape of Good Hope. Paterson believed that the shorter, cheaper, and more expeditious route was by the isthmus of Panama, and, as he believed, that section of the country had not been occupied by any of the nations of Europe; and as it was specially adapted for his enterprise it should be colonized. He averred that the havens were capacious and secure; the sea swarmed with turtle; the country so mountainous, that though within nine degrees of the equator, the climate was temperate; and yet roads could be easily constructed along which a string of mules, or a wheeled carriage might in the course of a single day pass from sea to sea. Fruits and a profusion of valuable herbs grew spontaneously, on account of the rich black soil, which had a depth of seven feet; and the exuberant fertility of the soil had not tainted the purity of the atmosphere. As a place of residence alone, the isthmus was a paradise; and a colony there could not fail to prosper even if its wealth depended entirely on agriculture. This, however, would be only a secondary matter, for within a few years the entire trade between India and Europe would be drawn to that spot. The merchant was no longer to expose his goods to the capricious gales of the Antarctic Seas, for the easier, safer, cheaper route must be navigated, which was shortly destined to double the amount of trade. Whoever possessed that door which opened both to the Atlantic and Pacific, as the shortest and least expensive route would give law to both hemispheres, and by peaceful arts would establish an empire as splendid as that of Cyrus or Alexander. If Scotland would occupy Darien she would become the one great free port, the one great warehouse for the wealth that the soil of Darien would produce, and the greater wealth which would be poured through Darien, India, China, Siam, Ceylon, and the Moluccas; besides taking her place in the front rank among nations. On all the vast riches that would be poured into Scotland a toll should be paid which would add to her capital; and a fabulous prosperity would be shared by every Scotchman from the peer to the cadie. Along the desolate shores of the Forth Clyde villas and pleasure grounds would spring up; and Edinburgh would vie with London and Paris. These glowing prospects at first were only partially disclosed to the public, and the name of Darien was unpronounced save only to a few of Paterson's most confidential friends. A mystery pervaded the enterprise, and only enough was given out to excite boundless hopes and desires. He succeeded admirably in working up a sentiment and desire on the part of the people to become stockholders in the organization. The hour for action had arrived; so on June 26, 1695, the Scottish parliament granted a statute from the Crown, for creating a corporate body or stock company, by name of the Company of Scotland trading to Africa and the Indies, with power to plant colonies and build forts in places not possessed by other European nations, the consent of the inhabitants of the places they settled being obtained. The amount of capital was not fixed by charter, but it was stipulated that at least one-half the stock must be held by Scotchmen resident in Scotland, and that no stock originally so held should ever be transferred to any but Scotchmen resident in Scotland. An entire monopoly of the trade with Asia, Africa, and America was granted for a term of thirty-one years, and all goods imported by the company during twenty-one years, should be admitted duty free, except sugar and tobacco, unless grown on the company's plantations. Every member and servant of the company were privileged against arrest and imprisonment, and if placed in durance, the company was authorized to invoke both the civil and military power. The Great Seal was affixed to the Act; the books were opened; the shares were fixed at £100 sterling each; and every man from the Pentland Firth to the Galway Firth who could command the amount was impatient to put down his name. The whole kingdom apparently had gone mad. The number of shareholders were about fourteen hundred. The books were opened February 26, 1696, and the very first subscriber was Anne, dutchess of Hamilton. On that day there was subscribed £50,400. By the end of March the greater part of the amount had been subscribed. On March 5th, a separate book was opened in Glasgow and on it was entered £56,325. The books were closed

THE DARIEN SCHEME. 79

August 3rd of the same year, and on the last day of subscriptions there was entered £14,125, reaching the total of £400,000, the amount apportioned to Scotland. The cities of Edinburgh and Glasgow, in their corporate capacity, each took £3,000 and Perth £2,000. Of the subscriptions there were eight of £3,000 each; eight of £2,000 each; two of £1,500, and one each of £1,200 and £1,125; ninety-seven of £1,000 each; but the great majority consisted of £100 or £200 each. The whole amount actually paid up was £220,000. This may not seem to be a large amount for such a country as Scotland, but as already noted, the country had been ruined by the English Act of 1660. There were five or six shires which did not altogether contain as many guineas and crowns as were tossed about every day by the shovels of a single goldsmith in Lombard street. Even the nobles had but very little money, for a large part of their rents was taken in kind; and the pecuniary remuneration of the clergy was such as to move the pity of the most needy, of the present; yet some of these had invested their all in hopes that their children might be benefited when the golden harvest should come. Deputies in England received subscriptions to the amount of £300,000; and the Dutch and Hamburgers subscribed £200,000.

Those Highland chiefs who had been considered as turbulent, and are so conspicuous in the history of the day have no place in this record of a species of enterprise quite distinct from theirs. The houses of Argyle, Athol, and Montrose appear in the list, as families who, besides their Highland chiefships, had other stakes and interests in the country; but almost the only person with a Highland patronymic was John MacPharlane of that ilk, a retired scholar who followed antiquarian pursuits in the libraries beneath the Parliament House. The Keltic prefix of "Mac" is most frequently attached to merchants in Inverness, who subscribed their hundred.

It is probable that a list of Highlanders who subscribed stock may be of interest in this connection. Only such names as are purely Highland are here sub-joined with amounts given, and also in the order as they appear on the books:

26 February, 1696:
John Drummond of Newtoun.........................£	600
Adam Gordon of Dalphollie............................	500
Master James Campbell, brother-german to the Earle of Argyle	500
John McPharlane of that ilk............................	200
Sir Robert Gordon of Gordonstown....................	400
Sir Colin Campbell of Ardkinlass......................	500
Mr. Gilbert Campbell, son to Colin Campbell of Soutar houses	400

27 February, 1696:
John Robertson, merchant in Edinburgh...............	300
Matthew St. Clair, Doctor of Medicine.................	500
Daniel Mackay, Writer in Edinburgh....................	200
Mr. Francis Grant of Cullen, Advocate.................	100
Duncan Forbes of Culloden...........................	200
Arthur Forbes, younger of Echt.......................	200
George Southerland, merchant in Edinburgh............	200
Kenneth McKenzie of Cromartie......................	500
Major John Forbes	200

28 February, 1696:
William Robertsone of Gladney........................	1 000
Mungo Graeme of Gorthie............................	500
Duncan Campbell of Monzie..........................	500
James Mackenzie, son to the Viscount of Tarbat.........	1 000

2 March, 1696:
Jerome Robertson, periwig maker, burgess of Edinburgh..	100

3 March 1696:
David Robertsone, Vintner in Edinburgh...............	200
William Drummond, brother to Thomas Drummond of Logie Almond	500

4 March, 1696:
Sir Humphrey Colquhoun of Luss.....................	400

5 March, 1696:
James Robertson, tylor in Canonget....................	100
Sir Thomas Murray of Glendoick......................	1 000

6 March, 1696:
Alexander Murray, son to John Murray of Touchadam, and deputed by him.............................	300

7 March 1696:
John Gordon, Captain in Lord Stranraer's Regiment.....	100
Samuell McLelland, merchant in Edinburgh............	500

11 March 1696:

THE DARIEN SCHEME.

Aeneas McLeod, Town-Clerk of Edinburgh, in name and behalfe of George Viscount of Tarbat, and as having commission from him	£1 000
17 March, 1696:	
John Menzies, Advocate	200
William Menzies, merchant in Edinburgh	1 000
19 March, 1696:	
James Drummond, Writer in Edinburgh, deputed by Mr. John Graham of Aberuthven	100
Gilbert Campbell, merchant in Edinburgh, son to Colline Campbell of Soutar Houses	200
Gilbert Campbell, merchant in Edinburgh, son to Colline Campbell of Soutar Houses	100
Daniel McKay, Writer in Edinburgh, deputed by Captain Hugh McKay, younger of Borley	300
Patrick Campbell, Writer in Edinburgh, deputed by Captain Leonard Robertsone of Straloch	100
20 March, 1696:	
Alexander Murray, son to George Murray of Touchadam, deputed by him	200
Sir Colin Campbell of Aberuchill, one of the Senators of the Colledge of Justice	500
Andrew Robertson, chyrurgeon in Edinburgh, deputed by George Robertstone, younger, merchant in Glasgow	100
Andrew Robertson, chyrurgeon in Edinburgh	100
James Gregorie, student	100
George Earle of Southerland	1 000
21 March, 1696:	
John McFarlane, Writer to the Signet	200
23 March, 1696:	
John Forbes, brother-german to Samuell Forbes of Fovrain, deputed by the said Samuell Forbes	1 000
John Forbes, brother-german to Samuell Forbes of Fovrain,	500
James Gregory, Professor of Mathematiques in the Colledge of Edinburgh	200
24 March 1696:	
Patrick Murray of Livingstoun	600
Ronald Campbell, Writer to his Majesty's Signet, as having deputation from Alexander Gordoune, son to Alexander Gordoun, minister at Inverary	100
William Graham, merchant in Edinburgh	200
David Drummond, Advocate, deputed by Thomas Graeme of Balgowan	600

David Drummond, Advocate, deputed by John Drummond of Culqupalzie............................ £	600
25 March, 1696:	
John Murray of Deuchar.............................	800
Sir Robert Sinclair of Stevenstoun...................	400
John Sinclair of Stevenstoun........................	400
26 March, 1696:	
Helen Drummond, spouse to Colonel James Ferguson as commissionate by him............................	200
James Murray of Sundhope.........................	100
John Drummond of Newtoun........................	400
John Drummond of Newtoun, for John Stewart of Dalguis, conform to deputation.....................	100
March 27:	
Alexander Johnstoune of Elshieshells..................	400
John Forbes, brother-german to Samuell Forbes of Fovrain, conform to ane deputation by Captain James Stewart, in Sir John Hill's regiment, Governor of Fort William	100
Thomas Forbes of Watertoun.........................	200
William Ross, merchant in Edinburgh................	100
Rachell Johnstoun, relict of Mr. Robert Baylie of Jerviswood	200
March 28:	
John Fraser, servitor to Alexander Innes, merchant......	100
Mr. John Murray, Senior Advocate...................	100
John Stewart, Writer in Clerk Gibsone's chamber........	100
Mr. Gilbert Campbell, merchant in Edinburgh, son to Colline Campbell of Soutar Houses..................	200
Mr. Gilbert Campbell, merchant in Edinburgh, son to Colline Campbell of Soutar Houses, (more),............	100
James Gordon, Senior, merchant in Aberdeen...........	250
Thomas Gordon, skipper in Leith.....................	100
Adam Gordon of Dulpholly.........................	500
Colin Campbell of Lochlan..........................	200
Thomas Græme of Balgowane, by virtue of a deputation from David Græme of Kilor......................	200
Patrick Coutts, merchant in Edinburgh, being deputed by Alexander Robertsone, merchant in Dundie.........	200
David Drummond, of Cultimalindie...................	600
John Drummond, brother of David Drummond of Cultimalindie	200
30 March, 1696:	
James Marquess of Montrose........................	1 000

THE DARIEN SCHEME. 83

John Murray, doctor of medicine, for Mr. James Murray, Chirurgeon in Perth, conform to a deputation.........£	200
William Stewart, doctor of medicine at Perth............	100
Patrick Campbell, Writer in Edinburgh, being depute by Helen Steuart, relict of Doctor Murray.............	100
James Drummond, one of the Clerks to the Bills, being deputed by James Meinzies of Shian................	100
Robert Stewart, Junior, Advocate......................	300
Master Donald Robertsone, minister of the Gospel.......	100
Duncan Campbell of Monzie, by deputation from John Drummond of Culquhalzie.......................	100
John Marquesse of Athole..............................	500
John Haldane of Gleneagles, deputed by James Murray at Orchart Milne................................	100
Thomas Johnstone, merchant in Edinburgh...............	100
William Meinzies, merchant in Edinburgh...............	1 000
Alexander Forbes of Tolquhon.........................	500
Robert Murray, merchant in Edinburgh................	200
Walter Murray, merchant in Edinburgh................	100
Master Arthur Forbes, son of the Laird of Cragivar......	100
Robert Fraser, Advocate.............................	100
Barbara Fraser, relict of George Stirling, Chirurgeon apothecary in Edinburgh........................	200
Alexander Johnston, merchant in Edinburgh............	100
Sir Robert Sinclair of Stevenstoun, for Charles Sinclair, Advocate, his son...............................	100
The said Thomas Scott, deputed by Patrick Ogilvie of Balfour	400
The said Thomas Scott, deputed by Thomas Robertson, merchant there (i e Dundee)......................	125
The said Thomas Scott, deputed by David Drummond, merchant in Dundee.............................	100
Mrs. Anne Stewart, daughter to the deceased John Stewart of Kettlestoun..............................	100
31 March, 1696:	
Sir Archibald Murray of Blackbarrony................	500
William Stewart, clerk to his Majesty's Customs at Leith	100
Christian Grierson, daughter to the deceast John Grierson.	100
Jesper Johnstoune of Waristoun.......................	500
Alexander Forbes, goldsmith in Edinburgh.............	200
Master John Campbell, Writer to the Signet............	200
Thomas Campbell, flesher in Edinburgh................	200
Archibald Earle of Argyll..........................	1 500
James Campbell, brother-german to the Earle of Argyll....	200

William Johnston, postmaster of Hadingtoun............ £	100
Sir James Murray of Philiphaugh....................	500
Andrew Murray, brother to Sundhope................	100
William McLean, master of the Revelles..............	100
John Cameron, son to the deceast Donald Cameron, merchant in Edinburgh.............................	100
David Forbes, Advocate............................	200
Captain John Forbes of Forbestoune..................	200
Afternoon:	
Sir Alexander Monro of Bearcrofts....................	200
James Gregorie, student of medicine....................	100
Mungo Campbell of Burnbank......................	400
John Murray, junior, merchant in Edinburgh............	400
Robert Murray, burges in Edinburgh..................	150
Dougall Campbell of Sadell..........................	100
Ronald Campbell, Writer to his Majesty's Signet.........	200
Alexander Finlayson, Writer in Edinburgh..............	100
John Steuart, Writer in Edinburgh....................	100
William Robertson, one of the sub-clerks of the Session...	100
Lady Neil Campbell..................................	200
Mary Murray, Lady Enterkin, elder...................	200
Sir George Campbell of Cesnock.....................	1 000
7 April:	
Thomas Robertson of Lochbank.....................	400
Robert Fraser, Advocate, for Hugh Robertson, Provost of Inverness, conform to deputation.................	100
Robert Fraser, Advocate, for James McLean, baillie of Invernes, conform to deputation..................	100
Robert Fraser, Advocate, for John McIntosh, baillie of Invernes, conform to deputation.......................	100
Robert Fraser, Advocate, for Alexander McLeane, merchant of Invernes, conform to deputation...........	150
Robert Fraser, Advocate, for Robert Rose, late ballie of Invernes, conform to deputation....................	140
Robert Fraser, Advocate, for Alexander Stewart, skipper at Invernes, conform to deputation................	150
Robert Fraser, Advocate, for William Robertson of Inshes, conform to deputation.........................	100
9 April, 1696:	
James Drummond, one of the Clerks of the Bills, for Robert Menzies, in Aberfadie, conform to deputation....	100
John Drummond of Newtoun, depute by John Menzies of Camock, Advocate.............................	200
Archibald Sinclair, Advocate........................	100

THE DARIEN SCHEME. 85

Patrick Campbell, Writer in Edinburgh.............£	100
John Murray, doctor of medicine, for William Murray of Arbony, by virtue of his deputation................	200
Colen Campbell of Bogholt............................	100
William Gordone, Writer in Edinburgh...............	100
14 Apryle:	
The said Thomas Halliday, Conform to deputation from William Ogilvie in Todshawhill..................	100
16 Aprill:	
Patrick Murray, lawful son to Patrick Murray of Killor..	100
Walter Murray, servitor to George Clerk, junior, merchant in Edinburgh, deputed by Robert Murray of Levelands	150
John Campbell, Writer to the Signet, for Alexander Campbell, younger of Calder, conform to deputation......	500
Captain James Drummond of Comrie..................	200
April 21:	
James Cuming, merchant in Edinburgh.................	100
James Campbell of Kinpout..........................	100
James Drummond, Under-Clerk to the Bills, depute by Archibald Meinzies of Myln of Kiltney..............	100
Robert Blackwood, deputed by John Gordon of Collistoun, doctor of medicine............................	100
Robert Blackwood, merchant in Edinburgh, deputed by Charles Ogilvy, merchant and late baillie of Montrose.	200
James Ramsay, writer in Edinburg, commission at by Duncan Campbell of Duneaves.......................	100
Captain Patrick Murray, of Lord Murray's regiment of foot	100
May 5, 1696.	
John Haldane of Gleneagles, conform to deputation from Thomas Grahame in Auchterarder................	100
John Drummond of Newtoun, depute by David Græme of Jordanstoun	100
Samuel McLellan, merchant in Dundee, conform to deputation from William Stewart of Castle Stewart........	100
May 14, 1696.	
Andrew Robertsone, chirurgeon in Edinburgh, conform to deputation by George Robertsone, Writer in Dunblane	100
May 21, 1696.	
John Drummond of Newtoun, for Lodovick Drummond, chamberland to my Lord Drummond..............	100

May 26, 1696.
Thomas Drummond of Logie Almond.................. £ 500
June 2, 1696.
Robert Fraser, Advocate, by virtue of a deputation from
  Robert Cuming of Relugas, merchant of Inverness..   100
Robert Fraser, Advocate, in name of William Duff of
  Dyple, merchant of Inverness......................   100
Robert Fraser, Advocate, in name of Alexander Duffe of
  Drumuire, merchant of Inverness...................   100
June 4, 1696.
John Haldane of Gleneagles, depute by John Graham, son
  to John Graham, clerk to the chancellary...........   100
Adam Drummond of Meginch.........................   200
18.
Agnes Campbell, relict of Andrew Anderson, his Majesty's
  printer   100
July 10.
John Drummond of Newtoun, for Dame Margaret Gra-
  ham, Lady Kinloch................................   200
John Drummond of Newtoun.........................   200
James Menzies of Schian..............................   100
Mungo Græme of Garthie............................   200
21.
Sir Alexander Cumyng of Culter......................   200
31.
Mr. George Murray, doctor of physick.................   200
Patrick Campbell, brother to Monzie..................   100
August 1.
James Lord Drummond............................... 1 000
Friday, 6 March, 1696.
John Drummond of Newtoune........................ 1 125
Saturday, 7 March, 1696.
John Graham, younger of............................ 1 000
Daniel Campbell, merchant in Glasgow................ 1 000
George Robinsoune, belt-maker in Glasgow.............   100
John Robinsoune, hammerman in Glasgow.............   100
John Robertson, junior, merchant in Glasgow...........   500
Munday, 9 March, 1696.
Mattheu Cuming, junior, merchant in Glasgow.......... 1 000
William Buchanan, merchant in Glasgow..............   100
Marion Davidson, relict of Mr. John Glen, Minister of the
  Gospel   100
James Johnstoun, merchant in Glasgow................   200
Thomas Johnstoun, merchant in Glasgow..............   200

THE DARIEN SCHEME.

George Johnston, merchant in Glasgow	£ 200
John Buchanan, merchant in Glasgow	100
John Grahame, younger of Dougaldstoun	1,000

Tuesday, 10 March, 1696.

Neill McVicar, tanner in Glasgow	100
George Buchanan, Maltman in Glasgow	100

Saturday, 21 March, 1696.

Archibald Cambell, merchant in Glasgow	100

Tuesday, 24 March, 1696.

John Robertsone, younger, merchant in Glasgow, for Robert Robertsone, second lawfull sone to Umqll James Robertsone, merchant in Glasgow	100

Tuesday, March 31, 1696.

Mungo Campbell of Nether Place	100
Hugh Campbell, merchant, son to deceast Sir Hugh Campbell of Cesnock	100
Matthew Campbell of Waterhaugh	100

Thursday, Agr the 2d of Aprile.

Mungo Campbell, merchant in Ayr	100
David Fergursone, merchant in Ayr	100

Wednesday the 15th day, 1696.

Captain Charles Forbes, of Sir John Hill's regiment	200
Captain James Menzies, of Sir John Hill's regiment	100
Captain Francis Ferquhar, of Sir John Hill's regiment	100

Thursday, 16 Aprile, 1696.

Captain Charles Forbes, of Sir John Hill's regiment	200

Fryday, 17 Aprile.

Lieutenant Charles Ross, of Sir John Hill's regiment	100*

It is more than probable that some names should not be inserted above, as the name Græme, for it may belong to the clan Graham of the Highlands, or else to the debateable land, near Carlisle, which is more likely. We know that where they had made themselves adverse to both sides, they were forced to emigrate in large numbers. Some of them settled near Bangor, in the county of Down, Ireland. How large a per cent. of the subscribers who lived in the lowlands, and born out of the Highlands, would be impossible to determine. Then names of parties, born in the Highlands and of Gaelic blood have undoubtedly been omitted owing to change of name. By the change in spelling of the name, it would indicate that some had left Ulster where their forefathers had settled, and taken up their residence in Scotland.

---
* The Darien Papers, pp. 371-417.

It will also be noticed that the clans bordering the Grampians were most affected by the excitement while others seemingly did not even feel the breeze.

The Darien Scheme at best was but suppositious, for no experiment had been tried in order to forecast a realization of what was expected. There was, it is true, a glitter about it, but there were materials within the reach of all from which correct data might have been obtained. It seems incredible that men of sound judgment should have risked everything, when they only had a vague or general idea of Paterson's plans. It was also a notorious fact that Spain claimed sovereignty over the Isthmus of Panama, and, even if she had not, it was unlikely that she would tolerate such a colony, as was proposed, in the very heart of her transatlantic dominions. Spain owned the Isthmus both by the right of discovery and possession; and the very country which Paterson had described in such radiant colors had been found by the Castilian settlers to be a land of misery and of death; and on account of the poisonous air they had been compelled to remove to the neighboring haven of Panama. All these facts, besides others, might easily have been ascertained by members of the Company.

As has already been intimated, the Scots alone were not drawn into this vortex of wild excitement, and are no more to be held responsible for the delusion than some of other nationalities. The English people were seized with the dread of Scottish prosperity resulting from the enterprise, and England's jealousy of trade at once interfered to crush an adventure which seemed so promising. The English East India Company instigated a cry, echoed by the city of London, and taken up by the nation, which induced their parliament, when it met for the first time, after the elections of 1695, to give its unequivocal condemnation to the scheme. One peer declared, "If these Scots are to have their way I shall go and settle in Scotland, and not stay here to be made a beggar." The two Houses of Parliament went up together to Kensington and represented to the king the injustice of requiring England to exert her power in support of an enterprise which, if successful, must be fatal to her commerce and to her finances. William replied in plain terms that he had been illy-treated in Scotland, but that he would try to find a remedy for the evil which

THE DARIEN SCHEME.

had been brought to his attention. At once he dismissed Lord High Commissioner Tweeddale and Secretary Johnston; but the Act which had been passed under their management still continued to be law in Scotland.

The Darien Company might have surmounted the opposition of the English parliament and the East India Company, had not the Dutch East India Company—a body remarkable for its monopolizing character—also joined in the outcry against the Scottish enterprise; incited thereto by the king through Sir Paul Rycaut, the British resident at Hamburg, directing him to transmit to the senate of that commercial city a remonstrance on the part of king William, accusing them of having encouraged the commissioners of the Darien Company; requesting them to desist from doing so; intimating that the plan had not the king's support; and a refusal to withdraw their countenance from the scheme would threaten an interruption to his friendship with the good city of Hamburg. The result of this interference was the almost total withdrawal of the Dutch and English subscriptions, which was accelerated by the threatened impeachment, by the English parliament, of such persons who had subscribed to the Company; and, furthermore, were compelled to renounce their connection with the Company, besides misusing some native-born Scotchmen who had offended the House by subscribing their own money to a company formed in their own country, and according to their own laws.

The managers of the scheme, supported by the general public of Scotland, entered a strong protest against the king's hostile interference of his Hamburg envoy. In his answer the king evaded what he was resolved not to grant, and yet could not in equity refuse. By the double dealing of the monarch the Company lost the active support of the subscribers in Hamburg and Holland.

In spite of the desertion of her English and foreign subscribers the Scots, encouraged in their stubborn resolution, and flattered by hopes that captivated their imaginations, decided to enter the project alone. A stately house in Milne Square, then the most modern and fashionable part of Edinburgh, was purchased and fitted up for an office and warehouse. It was called the Scottish India House. Money poured faster than ever into the coffers of the Company. Operations were actively commenced during the month of May, 1696. Contracts were rapidly let and orders filled—smith and cutlery work at Falkirk; woollen stockings at Aberdeen; gloves and other leather goods at Perth; various metallic works, hats, shoes, tobacco-pipes, serges, linen cloth, bob-wigs and periwigs, at Edinburgh; and for home-spun and home-woven woollen checks or tartan, to various parts of the Highlands.

SCOTTISH INDIA HOUSE.

As the means for building ships in Scotland did not then exist, recourse was had to the dockyards of Amsterdam and Hamburg. At an expense of £50,000 a few inferior ships were purchased, and fitted out as ships of war; for their constitution authorized them to make war both by land and sea. The vessels were finally fitted out at Leith, consisting of the Caledonia, the St. Andrew, the Unicorn, and the Dolphin, each armed with fifty guns and two tenders, the Endeavor and Pink, afterwards sunk at Darien; and among the commodities stored away were axes, iron wedges, knives, smiths', carpenters' and coopers' tools, barrels, guns, pistols, combs, shoes, hats, paper, tobacco-pipes, and, as was supposed, provisions enough to last eight months. The value of the cargo of the St. Andrew was estimated at £4,006. The crew and colonists consisted of twelve hundred picked men, the greater part of whom were veterans who had served in king William's wars, and the remainder of Highlanders and others who had opposed the revolution, and three hundred gentlemen of family, desirous of trying their fortunes.

It was on July 26, 1698, that the vessels weighed anchor and put out to sea. A wild insanity seized the entire population of Edinburgh as they came to witness the embarkation. Guards were kept busy holding back the eager crowd who pressed forward, and, stretching out their arms to their departing countrymen, clamored to be taken on board. Stowaways, when ordered on shore, madly clung to rope and mast, pleading in vain to be allowed to serve without pay on board the ships. Women sobbed and gasped for breath; men stood uncovered, and with downcast head and choked utterance invoked the blessing of the Beneficent Being. The banner of St. Andrew was hoisted at the admiral's mast; and as a light wind caught the sails, the roar of the vast multitude was heard far down the waters of the frith.

The actual destination of the fleet was still a profound secret, save to a few. The supreme direction of the expedition was entrusted to a council of seven, to whom was entrusted all power, both civil and military. The voyage was long and the adventurers suffered much; the rations proved to be scanty, and of poor quality; and the fleet, after passing the Orkneys and Ireland, touched at Madeira, where those who had fine clothes were glad to exchange them for provisions and wines. Having crossed the Atlantic, they first landed on an uninhabited islet lying between Porto Rico and St. Thomas, which they took possession of in the name of their country, and hoisted the white cross of St. Andrew. Being warned off for trespassing on the territory of the king of Denmark, and having procured the services of an old buccaneer, under whose pilotage they departed, on November 1st they anchored close to the Isthmus of Panama, having lost fifteen of their number during the voyage. On the 4th they landed at Acla; founded there a settlement to which they gave the name of New St. Andrews; marked out the site for another town and called it New Edinburgh. The weather was genial and climate pleasant at the time of their arrival; the vegetation was luxuriant and promising; the natives were kind; and everything presaged a bright future for the fortune-seekers. They cut a canal through the neck of land that divided one side of the harbor from the ocean, and there constructed a fort, whereon they mounted fifty cannon. On a mountain, at the opposite side of the harbor, they built a watchhouse, where the extensive view prevented all danger of a surprise. Lands were purchased from the Indians, and messages of friendship were sent to the governors of the several Spanish provinces. As the amount of funds appropriated for the sustenance of the colony had been largely embezzled by those having the matter in charge, the people were soon out of provisions. Fishing and the chase were now the only sources, and as these were precarious, the colonists were soon on the verge of starvation. As the summer drew near the atmosphere became stifling, and the exhalations from the steaming soil, added to other causes, wrought death among the settlers. The mortality rose gradually to ten a day. Both the clergymen who accompanied the expedition were dead; one of them, Rev. Thomas James, died at sea before the colonists landed, and soon after the arrival Rev. Adam Scot succumbed. Paterson buried his wife in that soil, which, as he had assured his too credulous countrymen, exhaled health and vigor. Men passed to the hospital, and from thence to the grave, and the survivors were only kept alive through the friendly offices of the Indians. Affairs continued daily to grow worse. The Spaniards on the isthmus looked with complacency on the distress of the Scotchmen. No relief, and no tidings coming from Scotland, the survivors on June 22, 1699, less than eight months after their arrival, resolved to abandon the settlement. They re-embarked in three vessels, a weak and hopeless company, to sail whithersoever Providence might direct. Paterson, the first to embark at Leith, was the last to re-embark at Darien. He begged hard to be left behind with twenty or more companions to keep up a show of possession, and to await the next arrival from Scotland. His importunities were disregarded, and, utterly helpless, he was carried on board the St. Andrew, and soon after the vessels stood out to sea. The voyage was horrible. It might be compared to the horrors of a slave ship.

The ocean kept secret the sufferings on board these pestilential ships until August 8th, when the Caledonia, commanded by Captain Robert Drummond, drifted into Sandy Hook, New York, having lost one hundred and three men since leaving Darien, and twelve more within four days after arrival, leaving but sixty-five men on board fit for handling ropes. The three ships, on leaving Darien, had three hundred each, including officers, crew and colonists. On August 13th, the Unicorn, commanded by Captain John Anderson, came into New York in a distressed condition, having lost her foremast, fore topmast, and mizzen mast. She lost one hundred and fifty men on the way. It appears that Captain Robert Pennicuik of the St. Andrew knew of the helpless condition of the Unicorn, and accorded no assistance.* As might be expected, passion was engendered amidst this scene of misery. The squalid survivors, in the depths of their misery, raged fiercely against one another. Charges of incapacity, cruelty, brutal insolence, were hurled backward and forward. The rigid Presbyterians attributed the calamities to the wickedness of Jacobites, Prelatists, Sabbath-breakers and Atheists, as they denominated some of their fellow-sufferers. The accused parties, on the other hand, complained bitterly of the impertinence of meddling fanatics and hypocrites. Paterson was cruelly reviled, and was unable to defend himself. He sunk into a stupor, and became temporarily insane.

The arrival of the two ships in New York awakened different emotions. There certainly was no danger of these miserable people doing any harm, and yet their appearance awakened apprehension, on account of orders received from the king. After the proclamations which had been issued against these miserable fugitives, it became a question of difficulty, since the governor of New

---

*" Darien Papers," pp 195, 275.

York was absent in Boston, whether it was safe to provide the dying men with harborage and necessary food. Natural feelings overcame the difficulty; the more selfish and timid would have stood aloof and let fate take its course: there being a sufficient number of them to make the more generous feel that their efforts to save life were not made without risks. Even putting the most favorable construction on the act of the earl of Bellomont, governor of Rhode Island, who was appealed to for advice, by the lieutenant governor of New York, the colonists were provoked by the actions of those in authority. Bellomont, in his report to the Lords of Trade, under date of October 20, 1699, states that the sufferers drew up a memorial to the lieutenant governor for permission to buy provisions; would not act until Bellomont gave his instructions; latter thinks the colonists became insolent after being refreshed; and "your Lordships will see that I have been cautious enough in my orders to the lieutenant governor of New York, not to suffer the Scotch to buy more provisions than would serve to carry them home to Scotland."* On October 12th the Caledonia set sail from Sandy Hook, made the west coast of Ireland, November 11th, and on the 20th of same month anchored in the Sound of Islay, Scotland.

The story of the Unicorn is soon told. "John Anderson, a Scotch Presbyterian, who commanded a ship to Darien in the Scottish expedition thither and on his return in at Amboy, N. Jersey, & let his ship rot & plundered her & with ye plunder bought land." †

The St. Andrew parted company with the Caledonia the second day after leaving the settlement, and two nights later saw the Unicorn almost wholly dismasted, and on the following day was pursued by the Baslavento fleet. They put into Jamaica, but were denied assistance, in obedience to king William's orders; and a British admiral, Bembo, refused to give them some men to assist in bringing the ship to the isle of Port Royal. During the voyage to Port Royal, they lost the commander, Captain Pennicuik,

---

*" Documentary and Colonial History of New York," Vol. IV, p. 591.
†*Ibid*, Vol. V, p. 335.

most of the officers and one hundred and thirty of the men, before landing, on August 9, 1699.*

The Dolphin, Captain Robert Pincarton, commander, used as a supply and trading ship, of fourteen guns, on February 5, 1699, struck a rock and ran ashore at Carthagena, the crew seized by the Spaniards, and in irons were put in dungeons as pirates. The Spaniards congratulated themselves on having captured a few of "the ruffians" who had been the terror and curse of their settlements for a century. They were formally condemned to death, but British interference succeeded in preventing the sentence on the crew from being executed.

On the week following the departure of the expedition from Leith, the Scottish parliament met and unanimously adopted an address to the king, asking his support and countenance to the Darien colony. Notwithstanding this memorial the British monarch ordered the governors of Jamaica, Barbadoes and New York to refuse all supplies to the settlers. Up to this time the king had partly concealed his policy. No time was lost by the East India Companies in bringing every measure to bear in order to ruin the colony. To such length did rancor go that the Scotch commanders who should presume to enter English ports, even for repairs after a storm, were threatened with arrest. In obedience to the king's orders the governors issued proclamations, which they attempted strictly to enforce; and every species of relief, not only that which countrymen can claim of their fellow-subjects, and Christians of their fellow-Christians, and such as the veriest criminal has a right to demand, was denied the colonists of Darien.

On May 12, 1699, there sailed from Leith the Olive Branch, Captain William Johnson, commander, and the Hopeful, under Captain Alexander Stark, with ample stores of provisions, and three hundred recruits, but did not arrive at Darien until eight weeks after the departure of the colonists. Findnig that the settlement had been abandoned, and leaving six of their number, who preferred to remain, but were afterwards brought away, the Hopeful sailed for Jamaica, where she was seized and condemned as a prize. "The Olive Branch was unfortunately blown up at Caledonia" (Darien).†

---

*"Darien Papers," p. 150. †"Darien Papers," p. 160.

The Spaniards had not only become aggressive by seizing the Dolphin and incarcerating the officers and crew, but their government made no remonstrance against the invasion of its territory until May 3, 1699, when a memorial was presented to William by the Spanish ambassador stating that his sovereign looked on the proceedings as a rupture of the alliance between the two countries, and as a hostile invasion, and would take such measures as he thought best against the intruders. It is possible that at this time Spain would not have taken any action whatever, if William had pursued a different course; and seeing that the colonists had been abandoned and disowned by their own king, as if they had been vagabonds or outlaws, the Spaniards, in a manner, felt themselves invited to precipitate a crisis, which they accomplished.

In the meantime the directors of the Darien Company were actively organizing another expedition and hastily sent out four more vessels—the Rising Sun, Captain James Gibson; the Hope, Captain James Miller; the Hope of Barrowstouness, Captain Richard Daling; and the Duke of Hamilton, Captain Walter Duncan; with thirteen hundred "good men well appointed," besides materials of war. This fleet left Greenock August 18, 1699, but having been delayed by contrary winds, did not leave the Bay of Rothsay, Isle of Bute, until Sunday, Septemebr 24th. On Thursday, November 30, the fleet reached its destination, after considerable suffering and some deaths on board. These vessels contained engineers, fire-workers, bombardiers, battery guns of twenty-four pounds, mortars and bombs. The number of men mentioned included over three hundred Highlanders, chiefly from the estate of Captain Alexander Campbell of Fonab, most of whom had served under him, in Flanders, in Lorn's regiment. During the voyage the Hope was cast away. Captain Miller loaded the long boat very deep with provisions, goods and arms, and proceeded towards Havana. He arrived safely at Darien.

A large proportion of the second expedition belonged to the military, and were organized. Among the Highland officers are noticed the following names: Captains Colin Campbell, Thomas McIntosh, James Urquhart, Alexander Stewart, —— Ferquhar,

THE DARIEN SCHEME.

and —— Grant; Lieutenants Charles Stewart, Samuel Johnston, John Campbell and Walter Graham; Ensigns Hugh Campbell and Robert Colquhon, and Sergeant Campbell.

The members of this expedition were greatly disappointed on their arrival. They fully expected to find a secure fortification, a flourishing town, cultivated fields, and a warm reception. Instead they found a wilderness; the castle in ruins; the huts burned, and grass growing over the ruins. Their hearts sank within them; for this fleet had not been fitted out to found a colony, but to recruit and protect one already in a flourishing condition. They were worse provided with the necessaries of life than their predecessors had been. They made feeble attempts to restore the ruins. They constructed a fort on the old grounds; and within the ramparts built a hamlet consisting of about eighty-five cabins, generally of twelve feet by ten. The work went slowly on, without hope or encouragement. Despondency and discontent pervaded all ranks. The provisions became scanty, and unfair dealing resorted to. There were plots and factions formed, and one malcontent hanged. Nor was the ecclesiastical part happily arranged. The provision made by the General Assembly was as defective as the provision for the temporal wants had been made by the directors of the company. Of the four divines, one of them, Alexander Dalgleish, died at sea, on board of Captain Duncan's vessel. They were all of the established church of Scotland, who had the strongest sympathy with the Cameronians. They were at war with almost all the colonists. The antagonisms between priest and people were extravagant and fatal. They described their flocks as the most profligate of mankind, and declared it was most impossible to constitute a presbytery, for it was impossible to find persons fit to be ruling elders of a Christian church. This part of the trouble can easily be accounted for. One-third of the people were Highlanders, who did not understand a word of English, and not one of the pastors knew a word of Gaelic; and only through interpreters could they converse with this large body of men. It is also more than probable that many of these men, trained to war, had more or less of a tendency to fling off every corrective band. Both Rev. John Borland and Rev.

Alexander Shiels, author of the "Hynd let Loose," were stern fanatics who would tolerate nothing diverging a shade from their own code of principles. They treated the people as persons under their spiritual authority, and required of them fastings, humiliations, and long attendance on sermons and exhorations. Such pastors were treated with contempt and ignominy by men scarcely inclined to bear ecclesiastical authority, even in its lightest form. They mistook their mission, which was to give Christian counsel, and to lead gently and with dignity from error into rectitude. Instead of this they fell upon the flock like irritated schoolmasters who find their pupils in mutiny. They became angry and dominative; and the more they thus exhibited themselves, the more scorn and contumely they encountered. Meanwhile two trading sloops arrived in the harbor with a small stock of provisions; but the supply was inadequate; so five hundred of the party were ordered to embark for Scotland.

The news of the abandonment of the settlement by the first expedition was first rumored in London during the middle of September, 1699. Letters giving such accounts had been received from Jamaica. The report reached Edinburgh on the 19th, but was received with scornful incredulity. It was declared to be an impudent lie devised by some Englishmen who could not endure the sight of Scotland waxing great and opulent. On October 4th the whole truth was known, for letters had been received from New York announcing that a few miserable men, the remains of the colony, had arrived in the Hudson. Grief, dismay, and rage seized the nation. The directors in their rage called the colonists white-livered deserters. Accurate accounts brought the realization of the truth that hundreds of families, once in comparative opulence, were now reduced almost to beggary, and the flower of the nation had either succumbed to hardships, or else were languishing in prisons in the Spanish settlements, or else starving in English colonies. The bitterness of disappointment was succeded by an implacable hostility to the king, who was denounced in pamphlets of the most violent and inflammatory character, calling him a hypocrite, and a deceiver of those who had shed their best blood in his cause, and the author of the misfortunes of Scotland. Indemnification, redress, and revenge were demanded by every mouth, and each hand was ready to vouch for the claim. Never had just such a feeling existed in Scotland. It became a useless possession to the king, for he could not wring one penny from that kingdom for the public service, and, what was more important to him, he could not induce one recruit for his continental wars. William continued to remain indifferent to all complaints of hardships and petitions of redress, unless when he showed himself irritated by the importunity of the suppliants, and hurt at being obliged to evade what it was impossible for him, with the least semblance of justice to refuse. The feeling against William long continued in Scotland. As late as November 5, 1788, when it was proposed that a monument should be erected in Edinburgh to his memory, there appeared in one of the papers an anonymous communication ironically applauding the undertaking, and proposing as two subjects of the entabulature, for the base of the projected column, the massacre of Glencoe and the distresses of the Scottish colonists in Darien. On the appearance of this article the project was very properly and righteously abandoned. The result of the Darien Scheme and the cold-blooded policy of William made the Scottish nation ripe for rebellion. Had there been even one member of the exiled house of Stuart equal to the occasion, that family could then have returned to Scotland amid the joys and acclamations of the nation.

Amidst the disasters of the first expedition the directors of the company were not unmindful of the fate of those who had sailed in the last fleet. These people must be promptly succored. The company hired the ship Margaret, commanded by Captain Leonard Robertson, which sailed from Dundee, March 9, 1700; but what was of greater importance was the commission given to Captain Alexander Campbell of Fonab, under date of October 10, 1699, making him a councillor of the company and investing him with "the chief and supreme command, both by sea and by land, of all ships, men, forts, settlements, lands, possessions, and others whatsoever belonging to the said company in any part or parts of America,"* with instructions to lose no time in taking passage

---

*" Darien Papers," p. 176.

for Jamaica, or the Leeward Islands and there secure a vessel, with three or four months' provisions for the colony. Arriving at the Barbadoes, he then purchased a vessel with a cargo of provisions, and on January 24, 1700, sailed for Darien, which he reached February 5th, and just in time to be of active service; for intelligence had reached the colony that fifteen hundred Spaniards lay encamped on the Rio Santa Maria, waiting the arrival of an armament of eleven ships, with troops on board, destined to attack Ft. St. Andrew. Captain Campbell of Fonab, who had gained for himself great reputation in Flanders as an approved warrior, resolved to anticipate the enemy, and at once mustering two hundred of his veteran troops, accompanied by sixty Indians, marched over the mountains, and fell on the Spanish camp by night, and dispersed them with great slaughter, with a loss to the colony of nine killed and fourteen wounded, among the latter being their gallant commander. The Spaniards could not withstand the tumultuous rush of the Highlanders, and in precipitate flight left a large number of their dead upon the field. The little band, among the spoils, brought back the Spanish commander's decoration of the "Golden Fleece." When they recrossed the mountains it was to find their poor countrymen blockaded by five Spanish men-of-war. Campbell, and others, believing that no inequalities justified submission to such an enemy, determined on resistance, but soon discovered that resistance was in vain, when they could only depend on diseased, starving and broken-hearted men. As the Spaniards would not include Captain Campbell in the terms of capitulation, he managed, with several companions, dexterously to escape in a small vessel, sailed for New York, and from thence to Scotland. The defence of the colony under Fonab's genius had been heroic. When ammunition had given out, their pewter dishes were fashioned into cannon balls. On March 18, 1700, the colonists capitulated on honorable terms. It was a received popular opinion in Scotland that none of those who were concerned in the surrender ever returned to their native country. So weak were the survivors, and so few in numbers, that they were unable to weigh the anchor of their largest ship

THE DARIEN SCHEME.   101

until the Spaniards came to their assistance. What became of them? Their melancholy tale is soon told.

The Earl of Bellomont, writing to the Lords of the Admiralty, under date, New York, October 15, 1700, says:*

"Some Scotchmen are newly come hither from Carolina that belonged to the ship Rising Sun (the biggest ship they set out for their Caledonia expedition) who tell me that on the third of last month a hurricane happened on that coast, as that ship lay at anchor, within less than three leagues of Charles Town in Carolina with another Scotch ship called the Duke of Hamilton, and three or four others; that the ships were all shattered in pieces and all the people lost, and not a man saved. The Rising Sun had 112 men on board. The Scotch men that are come hither say that 15 of 'em went on shore before the storm to buy fresh provisions at Charles Town by which means they were saved. Two other of their ships they suppose were lost in the Gulph of Florida in the same storm. They came all from Jamaica and were bound hither to take in provisions on their way to Scotland. The Rising Sun had 60 guns mounted and could have carryed many more, as they tell me."

The colonists found a watery grave. No friendly hand nor sympathizing tear soothed their dying moments; no clergyman eulogized their heroism, self-sacrifice and virtues; no orator has pronounced a panegyric; no poet has embalmed their memory in song, and no novelist has taken their record for a fanciful story. Since their mission was a failure their memory is doomed to rest without marble monument or graven image. To the merciful and the just they will be honored as heroes and pioneers.

---

*" Documents Relating to Colonial History of New York," Vol. IV, p. 711.

CHAPTER V.

THE HIGHLANDERS IN NORTH CAROLINA.

The earliest, largest and most important settlement of Highlanders in America, prior to the Peace of 1783, was in North Carolina, along Cape Fear River, about one hundred miles from its mouth, and in what was then Bladen, but now Cumberland County. The time when the Highlanders began to occupy this territory is not definitely known; but some were located there in 1729, at the time of the separation of the province into North and South Carolina. It is not known what motive caused the first settlers to select that region. There was no leading clan in this movement, for various ones were well represented. At the headwaters of navigation these pioneers literally pitched their tent in the wilderness, for there were but few human abodes to offer them shelter. The chief occupants of the soil were the wild deer, turkeys, wolves, raccoons, opossums, with huge rattlesnakes to contest the intrusion. Fortunately for the homeless immigrant the climate was genial, and the stately tree would afford him shelter while he constructed a house out of logs proffered by the forest. Soon they began to fell the primeval forest, grub, drain, and clear the rich alluvial lands bordering on the river, and plant such vegetables as were to give them subsistence.

In course of time a town was formed, called Campbellton, then Cross Creek, and after the Revolution, in honor of the great Frenchman, who was so truly loyal to Washington, it was permanently changed to Fayetteville.

The immigration to North Carolina was accelerated, not only by the accounts sent back to the Highlanders of Scotland by the first settlers, but particularly under the patronage of Gabriel Johnston, governor of the province from 1734 until his death in 1752. He was born in Scotland, educated at the University of St.

Andrews, where he became professor of Oriental languages, and still later a political writer in London. He bears the reputation of having done more to promote the prosperity of North Carolina than all its other colonial governors combined. However, he was often arbitrary and unwise with his power, besides having the usual misfortune of colonial governors of being at variance with the legislature. He was very partial to the people of his native country, and sought to better their condition by inducing them to emigrate to North Carolina. Among the charges brought against him, in 1748, was his inordinate fondness for Scotchmen, and even Scotch rebels. So great, it was alleged, was his partiality for the latter that he showed no joy over the king's "glorious victory of Culloden;" and "that he had appointed one William McGregor, who had been in the Rebellion in the year 1715, a Justice of the Peace during the late Rebellion (1745) and was not himself without suspicion of disaffection to His Majesty's Government."*

The "Colonial Records of North Carolina" contain many distinctively Highland names, most of which refer to persons whose nativity was in the Scottish Highlands; but these furnish no certain criterion, for doubtless some of the parties, though of Highland parents, were born in the older provinces, while in later colonial history others belong to the Scotch-Irish, who came in that great wave of migration from Ulster, and found a lodgment upon the headwaters of the Cape Fear, Pee Dee and Neuse. Many of the early Highland emigrants were very prominent in the annals of the colony, among whom none were more so than Colonel James Innes, who was born about the year 1700 at Cannisbay, a town on the extreme northern point of the coast of Scotland. He was a personal friend of Governor Dinwiddie of Virginia, who in 1754 appointed him commander-in-chief of all the forces in the expedition to the Ohio,—George Washington being the colonel commanding the Virginia regiment. He had previously seen some service as a captain in the unsuccessful expedition against Carthagenia.

The real impetus of the Highland emigration to North Caro-

---

*North Carolina Colonial Records, Vol. IV, p. 931.

lina was the arrival, in 1739, of a "shipload," under the guidance of Neil McNeill, of Kintyre, Scotland, who settled also on the Cape Fear, amongst those who had preceded him. Here he found Hector McNeill, called "Bluff Hector," from his residence near the bluffs above Cross Creek.

Neil McNeill, with his countrymen, landed on the Cape Fear during the month of September. They numbered three hundred and fifty souls, principally from Argyleshire. At the ensuing session of the legislature they made application for substantial encouragement, that they might thereby be able to induce the rest of their friends and acquaintances to settle in the country. While this petition was pending, in order to encourage them and others and also to show his good will, the governor appointed, by the council of the province, a certain number of them justices of the peace, the commissions bearing date of February 28, 1740. The proceedings show that it was "ordered that a new commission of peace for Bladen directed to the following persons: Mathew Rowan, Wm. Forbes, Hugh Blaning, John Clayton, Robert Hamilton, Griffeth Jones, James Lyon, Duncan Campbel, Dugold McNeil, Dan McNeil, Wm. Bartram and Samuel Baker hereby constituting and appointing them Justices of the Peace for the said county."*

These were the first so appointed. The petition was first heard in the upper house of the legislature, at Newbern, and on January 26, 1740, the following action was taken:

"Resolved, that the Persons mentioned in said Petition, shall be free from payment of any Publick or County tax for Ten years next ensuing their Arrival.

"Resolved, that towards their subsistence the sum of one thousand pounds be paid out of the Publick money, by His Excellency's warrant to be lodged with Duncan Campbell, Dugald McNeal, Daniel McNeal, Coll. McAlister and Neal McNeal Esqrs., to be by them distributed among the several families in the said Petition mentioned.

"Resolved, that as an encouragement for Protestants to remove from Europe into this Province, to settle themselves in bodys or Townships, That all such as shall so remove into this

---

*Ibid, p. 447.

Province, Provided they exceed forty persons in one body or Company, they shall be exempted from payment of any Publick or County tax for the space of Ten years, next ensuing their Arrival.

"Resolved, that an address be presented to his Excellency the Governor to desire him to use his Interest, in such manner, as he shall think most proper to obtain an Instruction for giveing encouragement to Protestants from foreign parts, to settle in Townships within this Province, to be set apart for that purpose after the manner, and with such priviledges and advantages, as is practised in South Carolina."*

The petition was concurred in by the lower house on February 21st, and on the 26th, after reciting the action of the upper house in relation to the petition, passed the following:

"Resolved, That this House concurs with the several Resolves of the Upper House in the abovesd Message Except that relateing to the thousand pounds which this House refers till next Session of Assembly for Consideration."†

At a meeting of the council held at Wilmington, June 4, 1740, there were presented petitions for patents of lands, by the following persons, giving acres and location, as granted:

Name.	Acres.	County.
Thos Clarks	320	N. Hanover
James McLachlan	160	Bladen
Hector McNeil	300	"
Duncan Campbell	150	"
James McAlister	640	"
James McDugald	640	"
Duncan Campbell	75	"
Hugh McCraine	500	"
Duncan Campbell	320	"
Gilbert Pattison	640	"
Rich Lovett	855	Tyrrel
Rd Earl	108	N. Hanover
Jno McFerson	320	Bladen
Duncan Campbell	300	"
Neil McNeil	150	"
Duncan Campbell	140	"
Jno Clark	320	"
Malcolm McNeil	320	"
Neil McNeil	400	"
Arch Bug	320	"

---

*Ibid, p. 490. †Ibid, p. 583.

Name.	Acres.			County.
Duncan Campbel	640			Bladen
Jas McLachlen	320			"
Murdock McBraine	320			"
Jas Campbel	640			"
Patric Stewart	320			"
Arch Campley	320			"
Dan McNeil	105	(400)	400	"
Neil McNeil	400			"
Duncan Campbel	320			"
Jno Martileer	160			"
Daniel McNeil	320			"
Wm Stevens	300			"
Dan McNeil	400			"
Jas McLachlen	320			"
Wm Speir	160			Edgecombe
Jno Clayton	100			Bladen
Sam Portevint	640			N. Hanover
Charles Harrison	320			"
Robt Walker	640			"
Jas Smalwood	640			"
Wm Faris	400	640	640	"
Richd Carlton	180			Craven
Duncan Campbel	150			Bladen
Neil McNeil	321			"
Alex McKey	320			"
Henry Skibley	320			"
Jno Owen	200			"
Duncan Campbel	400			"
Dougal Stewart	640			
Arch Douglass	200			N. Hanover
James Murray	320			"
Robt Clark	200			
Duncan Campbel	148			Bladen
James McLachlen	320			"
Arch McGill	500			"
Jno Speir	100			Edgecombe
James Fergus	640			"
Rufus Marsden	640			
Hugh Blaning	320	(surplus land)		Bladen
Robt Hardy	400			Beaufort
Wm Jones	354	350		*

*Ibid, p. 453.

THE HIGHLANDERS IN NORTH CAROLINA. 107

All the above names, by no means are Highland; but as they occur in the same list, in all probability, came on the same ship, and were probably connected by kindred ties with the Gaels.

The colony was destined soon to receive a great influx from the Highlands of Scotland, due to the frightful oppression and persecution which immediately followed the battle of Culloden. Not satisfied with the merciless harrying of the Highlands, the English army on its return into England carried with it a large number of prisoners, and after a hasty military trial many were publicly executed. Twenty-two suffered death in Yorkshire; seventeen were put to death in Cumberland; and seventeen at Kennington Common, near London. When the king's vengeance had been fully glutted, he pardoned a large number, on condition of their leaving the British Isles and emigrating to the plantations, after having first taken the oath of allegiance.

The collapsing of the romantic scheme to re-establish the Stuart dynasty, in which so many brave and generous mountaineers were enlisted, also brought an indiscriminate national punishment upon the Scottish Gaels, for a blow was struck not only at those "who were out" with prince Charles, but also those who fought for the reigning dynasty. Left without chief, or protector, clanship broken up, homes destroyed and kindred murdered, dispirited, outlawed, insulted and without hope of palliation or redress, the only ray of light pointed across the Atlantic where peace and rest were to be found in the unbroken forests of North Carolina. Hence, during the years 1746 and 1747, great numbers of Highlanders, with their families and the families of their friends, removed to North Carolina and settled along the Cape Fear river, covering a great space of country, of which Cross Creek, or Campbelton, now Fayetteville, was the common center. This region received shipload after shipload of the harrassed, down-trodden and maligned people. The emigration, forced by royal persecution and authority, was carried on by those who desired to improve their condition, by owning the land they tilled. In a few years large companies of Highlanders joined their countrymen in Bladen County, which has since been subdivided into the counties of Anson, Bladen, Cumberland, Moore, Richmond,

Robeson and Sampson, but the greater portion established themselves within the present limits of Cumberland, with Fayetteville the seat of justice. There was in fact a Carolina mania which was not broken until the beginning of the Revolution.* The flame of enthusiasm passed like wildfire through the Highland glens and Western Isles. It pervaded all classes, from the poorest crofter to the well-to-do farmer, and even men of easy competence, who were according to the appropriate song of the day,

"Dol a dh'iarruidh an fhortain do North Carolina."

Large ocean crafts, from several of the Western Lochs, laden with hundreds of passengers sailed direct for the far west. In that day this was a great undertaking, fraught with perils of the sea, and a long, comfortless voyage. Yet all this was preferable than the homes they loved so well; but no longer homes to them! They carried with them their language, their religion, their manners, their customs and costumes. In short, it was a Highland community transplanted to more hospitable shores.

The numbers of Highlanders at any given period can only relatively be known. In 1753 it was estimated that in Cumberland County there were one thousand Highlanders capable of bearing arms, which would make the whole number between four and five thousand,—to say nothing of those in the adjoining districts, besides those scattered in the other counties of the province.

The people at once settled quietly and devoted their energies to improving their lands. The country rapidly developed and wealth began to drop into the lap of the industrious. The social claims were not forgotten, and the political demands were attended to. It is recorded that in 1758 Hector McNeil was sheriff of Cumberland County, and as his salary was but £10, it indicates his services were not in demand, and there was a healthy condition of affairs.

Hector McNeil and Alexander McCollister represented Cumberland County in the legislature that assembled at Wilmington April 13, 1762. In 1764 the members were Farquhar Campbell

---

*See Appendix, Note C.

and Walter Gibson,—the former being also a member in 1769, 1770, 1771, and 1775, and during this period one of the leading men, not only of the county, but also of the legislature. Had he, during the Revolution, taken a consistent position in harmony with his former acts, he would have been one of the foremost patriots of his adopted state; but owing to his vacillating character, his course of conduct inured to his discomfiture and reputation.

The legislative body was clothed with sufficient powers to ameliorate individual distress, and was frequently appealed to for relief. In quite a list of names, seeking relief from "Public duties and Taxes," April 16, 1762, is that of Hugh McClean, of Cumberland county. The relief was granted. This would indicate that there was more or less of a struggle in attaining an independent home, which the legislative body desired to assist in as much as possible, in justice to the commonwealth.

The Peace of 1763 not only saw the American Colonies prosperous, but they so continued, making great strides in development and growth. England began to look towards them as a source for additional revenue towards filling her depleted exchequer; and, in order to realize this, in March, 1765, her parliament passed, by great majorities, the celebrated act for imposing stamp duties in America. All America was soon in a foment. The people of North Carolina had always asserted their liberties on the subject of taxation. As early as 1716, when the province, all told, contained only eight thousand inhabitants, they entered upon the journal of their assembly the formal declaration "that the impressing of the inhabitants or their property under pretence of its being for the public service without authority of the Assembly, was unwarrantable and a great infringement upon the liberty of the subject." In 1760 the Assembly declared its indubitable right to frame and model every bill whereby an aid was granted to the king. In 1764 it entered upon its journal a peremptory order that the treasurer should not pay out any money by order of the governor and council without the concurrence of the assembly.

William Tryon assumed the duties of governor March 28, 1765, and immediately after he took charge of affairs the assembly was called, but within two weeks he prorogued it; said to have been done in consequence of an interview with the speaker of the assembly, Mr. Ashe, who, in answer to a question by the governor on the Stamp Act, replied, "We will fight it to the death." The North Carolina records show it was fought even to "the death."

The prevalent excitement seized the Highlanders along the Cape Fear. A letter appeared in "The North Carolina Gazette," dated at Cross Creek, January 30, 1766, in which the writer urges the people by every consideration, in the name of "dear Liberty" to rise in their might and put a stop to the seizures then in progress. He asks the people if they have "lost their senses and their souls, and are they determined tamely to submit to slavery." Nor did the matter end here; for, the people of Cross Creek gave vent to their resentment by burning lord Bute in effigy.

Just how far statistics represent the wealth of a people may not be wholly determined. At this period of the history, referring to a return of the counties, in 1767, it is stated that Anson county, called also parish of St. George, had six hundred and ninety-six white taxables, that the people were in general poor and unable to support a minister. Bladen county, or St. Martin's parish, had seven hundred and ninety-one taxable whites, and the inhabitants in middling circumstances. Cumberland, or St. David's parish, had eight hundred and ninety-nine taxable whites, "mostly Scotch —Support a Presbyterian Minister."

The Colonial Records of North Carolina do not exhibit a list of the emigrants, and seldom refer to the ship by name. Occasionally, however, a list has been preserved in the minutes of the official proceedings. Hence it may be read that on November 4, 1767, there landed at Brunswick, from the Isle of Jura, Argyleshire, Scotland, the following names of families and persons, to whom were allotted vacant lands, clear of all fees, to be taken up in Cumberland or Mecklenburgh counties, at their option:

Names of Families			Children		Total	Acres to Each Family
			Male	Female		
Alexander McDougald	and	wife		1	3	300
Malcolm McDougald	"	"		1	3	300
Neill McLean	"	"	1		3	300
Duncan McLean	"	"			2	200
Duncan Buea	"	"	1		3	300
Angus McDougald	"	"			2	200
Dougald McDougald	"	"	3	1	6	640
Dougald McDougald	"	"	2		4	400
John Campbell	"	"	1		3	300
Archibald Buea	"	"	1		3	300
Neill Buea					1	100
Neill Clark					1	100
John McLean					1	100
Angus McDougald					1	100
John McDougald					1	100
Donald McDougald					1	100
Donald McDougald					1	100
Alexander McDougald					1	100
John McLean					1	100
Peter McLean					1	100
Malcolm Buea					1	100
Duncan Buea					1	100
Mary Buea					1	100
Nancy McLean					1	100
Peggy Sinclair					1	100
Peggy McDougald					1	100
Jenny Darach					1	100
Donald McLean					1	100

These names show they were from Argyleshire, and probably from the Isle of Mull, and the immediate vicinity of the present city of Oban.

The year 1771 witnessed civil strife in North Carolina. The War of the Regulators was caused by oppression in disproportionate taxation; no method for payment of taxes in produce, as in other counties; unfairness in transactions of business by officials; the privilege exercised by lawyers to commence suits in any court they pleased, and unlawful fees extorted. The assembly was petitioned in vain on these points, and on account of these wrongs the people of the western districts attempted to gain by force what was denied them by peaceable means.

One of the most surprising things about this war is that it was ruthlessly stamped out by the very people of the eastern part of the province who themselves had been foremost in rebellion against the Stamp Act. And, furthermore, to be leaders against Great Britain in less than five years from the battle of the Alamance. Nor did they appear in the least to be willing to concede justice to their western brethren, until the formation of the state constitution, in 1776, when thirteen, out of the forty-seven sections, of that instrument embodied the reforms sought for by the Regulators.

On March 10, 1771, Governor Tryon apportioned the number of troops for each county which were to march against the insurgents. In this allotment fifty each fell to Cumberland, Bladen, and Anson counties. Farquhar Campbell was given a captain's commission, and two commissions in blank for lieutenant and ensign, besides a draft for £150, to be used as bounty money to the enlisted men, and other expenses. As soon as his company was raised, he was ordered to join, as he thought expedient, either the westward or eastward detachment. The date of his orders is April 18, 1771. Captain Campbell had expressed himself as being able to raise the complement.* The records do not show whether or not Captain Campbell and his company took an active part.

It cannot be affirmed that the expedition against the Regulators was a popular one. When the militia was called out, there arose trouble in Craven, Dobbs, Johnston, Pitt and Edgecombe counties, with no troops from the Albemarle section. In Bute county where there was a regiment eight hundred strong, when called upon for fifty volunteers, all broke rank, without orders, declaring that they were in sympathy with the Regulators.

The freeholders living near Campbelton on March 13, 1772, petitioned Governor Martin for a change in the charter of their town, alleging that as Campbelton was a trading town persons

---

Ibid, Vol. VIII. p. 708.

temporarily residing there voted, and thus the power of election was thrown into their hands, because the property owners were fewer in numbers. They desired "a new Charter impowering all persons, being Freeholders within two miles of the Courthouse of Campbelton or seized of an Estate for their own, or the life of any other person in any dwelling-house (such house having a stone or brick Chimney thereunto belonging and appendent) to elect a Member to represent them in General Assembly. Whereby we humbly conceive that the right of election will be lodged with those who only have right to Claim it and the purposes for which the Charter was granted to encourage Merchants of property to settle there fully answered."*

Among the names signed to this petition are those of Neill MacArther, Alexr. MacArther, James McDonald, Benja. McNatt, Ferqd. Campbell, and A. Maclaine. The charter was granted.

The people of Cumberland county had a care for their own interests, and fully appreciated the value of public buildings. Partly by their efforts, the upper legislative house, on February 24, 1773, passed a bill for laying out a public road from the Dan through the counties of Guilford, Chatham and Cumberland to Campbelton. On the 26th same month, the same house passed a bill for regulating the borough of Campbelton, and erecting public buildings therein, consisting of court house, gaol, pillory and stocks, naming the following persons to be commissioners: Alexander McAlister, Farquhard Campbell, Richard Lyon, Robert Nelson, and Robert Cochran.† The same year Cumberland county paid in quit-rents, fines and forfeitures the sum of £206.

In September, 1773, a boy named Reynold McDugal was condemned for murder. His youthful appearance, looking to be but thirteen, though really eighteen years of age, enlisted the sympathy of a great many, who petitioned for clemency, which was granted. To this petition were attached such Highland names as, Angus Camel, Alexr. McKlarty, James McKlarty, Malcolm McBride, Neil McCoulskey, Donald McKeithen, Duncan McKeithen, Gilbert McKeithen, Archibald McKeithen, Daniel McFarther, John McFarther, Daniel Graham, Malcolm Graham, Malcolm McFarland, Murdock Graham, Michael Graham, John

---

Ibid, Vol. IX. p. 79. †*Ibid*, p. 544.

McKown, Robert McKown, William McKown, Daniel Campbell, John Campbell, Iver McKay, John McLeod, Alexr. Graham, Evin McMullan, John McDuffie, William McNeil, Andw. McCleland, John McCleland, Wm. McRei, Archd. McCoulsky, James McCoulsky, Chas. McNaughton, Jno. McLason.

The Highland clans were fairly represented, with a preponderance in favor of the McNeils. They still wore their distinctive costume, the plaid, the kilt, and the sporan,—and mingled together, as though they constituted but one family. A change now began to take place and rapidly took on mammoth proportions. The MacDonalds of Raasay and Skye became impatient under coersion and set out in great numbers for North Carolina. Among them was Allan MacDonald of Kingsborough, and his famous wife, the heroine Flora, who arrived in 1774. Allan MacDonald succeeded to the estate of Kingsburgh in 1772, on the death of his father, but finding it incumbered with debt, and embarrassed in his affairs, he resolved in 1773 to go to North Carolina, and there hoped to mend his fortunes. He settled in Anson county. Although somewhat aged, he had the graceful mein and manly looks of a gallant Highlander. He had jet black hair tied behind, and was a large, stately man, with a steady, sensible countenance. He wore his tartan thrown about him, a large blue bonnet with a knot of black ribbon like a cockade, a brown short coat, a tartan waist-coat with gold buttons and gold button holes, a bluish philabeg, and tartan hose. At once he took precedence among his countrymen, becoming their leader and adviser. The Macdonalds, by 1775, were so numerous in Cumberland county as to be called the "Clan Donald," and the insurrection of February, 1776, is still known as the "Insurrection of the Clan MacDonald."

Little did the late comers know or realize the gathering storm. The people of the West Highlands, so remote from the outside world, could not apprehend the spirit of liberty that was being awakened in the Thirteen Colonies. Or, if they heard of it, the report found no special lodgement. In short, there were but few capable of realizing what the outcome would be. Up to the very breaking out of hostilities the clans poured forth emigrants into North Carolina.

THE HIGHLANDERS IN NORTH CAROLINA. 115

Matters long brewing now began to culminate and evil days grew apace. The ruling powers of England refused to understand the rights of America, and their king rushed headlong into war. The colonists had suffered long and patiently, but when the overt act came they appealed to arms. Long they bore misrule. An English king, of his own whim, or the favoritism of a minister, or the caprice of a woman good or bad, or for money in hand paid, selected the governor, chief justice, secretary, receiver-general, and attorney-general for the province. The governor selected the members of the council, the associate judges, the magistrates, and the sheriffs. The clerks of the county courts and the register of deeds were selected by the clerk of pleas, who having bought his office in England came to North Carolina and peddled out "county rights" at prices ranging from £4 to £40 annual rent per county. Scandalous abuses accumulated, especially under such governors as were usually chosen. The people were still loyal to England, even after the first clash of arms, but the open rupture rapidly prepared them for independence. The open revolt needed only the match. When that was applied, a continent was soon ablaze, controlled by a lofty patriotism.

The steps taken by the leaders of public sentiment in America were prudent and statesmanlike. Continental and Provincial Congresses were created. The first in North Carolina convened at Newbern, August 25, 1774. Cumberland county was represented by Farquhard Campbell and Thomas Rutherford. The Second Congress convened at the same place April 30, 1775. Again the same parties represented Cumberland county, with an additional one for Campbelton in the person of Robert Rowan. At this time the Highlanders were in sympathy with the people of their adopted country. But not all, for on July 3rd, Allan MacDonald of Kingsborough went to Fort Johnson, and concerted with Governor Martin the raising of a battalion of "the good and faithful Highlanders." He fully calculated on the recently settled MacDonalds and MacLeods. All who took part in the Second Congress were not prepared to take or realize the logic of their position, and what would be the final result.

The Highlanders soon became an object of consideration to

the leaders on both sides of the controversy. They were numerically strong, increasing in numbers, and their military qualities beyond question. Active efforts were put forth in order to induce them to throw the weight of their decision both to the patriot cause and also to that of the king. Consequently emissaries were sent amongst them. The prevalent impression was that they had a strong inclination towards the royalist cause, and that party took every precaution to cement their loyalty. Even the religious side of their natures was wrought upon.

The Americans early saw the advantage of decisive steps. In a letter from Joseph Hewes, John Penn, and William Hooper, the North Carolina delegates to the Continental Congress, to the members of the Provincial Congress, under date of December 1, 1775, occurs the admission that "in our attention to military preparations we have not lost sight of a means of safety to be effected by the power of the pulpit, reasoning and persuasion. We know the respect which the Regulators and Highlanders entertain for the clergy; they still feel the impressions of a religious education, and truths to them come with irresistible influence from the mouths of their spiritual pastors. * * * The Continental Congress have thought proper to direct us to employ two pious clergymen to make a tour through North Carolina in order to remove the prejudices which the minds of the Regulators and Highlanders may labor under with respect to the justice of the American controversy, and to obviate the religious scruples which Governor Tryon's heart-rending oath has implanted in their tender consciences. We are employed at present in quest of some persons who may be equal to this undertaking."*

The Regulators were divided in their sympathies, and it was impossible to find a Gaelic-speaking minister, clothed with authority, to go among the Highlanders. Even if such a personage could have been found, the effort would have been counteracted by the influence of John McLeod, their own minister. His sympathies, though not boldly expressed, were against the interests of the Thirteen Colonies, and on account of his suspicious actions was placed under arrest, but discharged May 11, 1776, by the Provincial Congress, in the following order:

---

*Ibid. Vol. VIII, p. XXIII.

"That the Rev. John McLeod, who was brought to this Congress on suspicion of his having acted inimical to the rights of America, be discharged from his further attendance."*

August 23, 1775, the Provincial Congress appointed, from among its members, Archibald Maclaine, Alexander McAlister, Farquhard Campbell, Robert Rowan, Thomas Wade, Alexander McKay, John Ashe, Samuel Spencer, Walter Gibson, William Kennon, and James Hepburn, "a committee to confer with the Gentlemen who have lately arrived from the Highlands in Scotland to settle in this Province, and to explain to them the Nature of our Unhappy Controversy with Great Britain, and to advise and urge them to unite with the other Inhabitants of America in defence of those rights which they derive from God and the Constitution."† ‡

No steps appear to have been taken by the Americans to organize the Highlanders into military companies, but rather their efforts were to enlist their sympathies. On the other hand, the royal governor, Josiah Martin, took steps towards enrolling them into active British service. In a letter to the earl of Dartmouth, under date of June 30, 1775, Martin declares he "could collect immediately among the emigrants from the Highlands of Scotland, who were settled here, and immoveably attached to His Majesty and His Government, that I am assured by the best authority I may compute at 3000 effective men," and begs permission "to raise a Battalion of a Thousand Highlanders here," and "I would most humbly beg leave to recommend Mr. Allen McDonald of Kingsborough to be Major, and Captain Alexd. McLeod of the Marines now on half pay to be first Captain, who besides being men of great worth, and good character, have most extensive influence over the Highlanders here, great part of which are of their own names and familys, and I should flatter myself that His Majesty would be graciously pleased to permit me to nominate some of the Subalterns of such a Battalion, not for pecuniary consideration, but for encouragement to some active and deserving young Highland Gentlemen who might be usefully employed in the speedy raising the proposed Battalion. Indeed I cannot help observing My Lord, that there are three of four Gentlemen of consideration here, of the name of McDonald, and a

---

*Ibid, Vol. X. p. 577. †Ibid, p. 173. ‡See Appendix, Note D.

Lieutenant Alexd. McLean late of the Regiment now on half pay, whom I should be happy to see appointed Captains in such a Battalion, being persuaded they would heartily promote and do credit to His Majesty's Service."*

November 12, 1775, the governor farther reports to the same that he can assure "your Lordship that the Scotch Highlanders here are generally and almost without exception staunch to Government," and that "Captain Alexr. McLeod, a Gentleman from the Highlands of Scotland and late an Officer in the Marines who has been settled in this Province about a year and is one of the Gentlemen I had the honor to recommend to your Lordship to be appointed a Captain in the Battalion of Highlanders, I proposed with his Majesty's permission to raise here found his way down to me at this place about three weeks ago and I learn from him that he is as well as his father in law, Mr. Allan McDonald, proposed by me for Major of the intended Corps moved by my encouragements have each raised a company of Highlanders since which a Major McDonald who came here some time ago from Boston under the orders from General Gage to raise Highlanders to form a Battalion to be commanded by Lieut. Coll. Allan McLean has made them proposals of being appointed Captains in that Corps, which they have accepted on the Condition that his Majesty does not approve my proposal of raising a Batallion of Highlanders and reserving to themselves the choice of appointments therein in case it shall meet with his Majesty's approbation in support of that measure. I shall now only presume to add that the taking away those Gentlemen from this Province will in a great measure if not totally dissolve the union of the Highlanders in it now held together by their influence, that those people in their absence may fall under the guidance of some person not attached like them to Government in this Colony at present but it will ever be maintained by such a regular military force as this established in it that will constantly reunite itself with the utmost facility and consequently may be always maintained upon the most respectable footing."†

The year 1775 witnessed the North Carolina patriots very alert. There were committees of safety in the various counties; and the Provincial Congress began its session at Hillsborough August 21st. Cumberland County was represented by Farquhard Campbell, Thomas Rutherford, Alexander McKay, Alexander

---

*Ibid, p. 45. †Ibid, p. 325.

McAlister and David Smith, Campbelton sent Joseph Hepburn. Among the members of this Congress having distinctly Highland names, the majority of whom doubtless were born in the Highlands, if not all, besides those already mentioned, were John Campbell and John Johnston from Bertie, Samuel Johnston of Chowan, Duncan Lamon of Edgecombe, John McNitt Alexander of Mecklenburg, Kenneth McKinzie of Martin, Jeremiah Frazier or Tyrell, William Graham of Tryon, and Archibald Maclaine of Wilmington. One of the acts of this Congress was to divide the state into military districts and the appointment of field officers of the Minute Men. For Cumberland county Thomas Rutherford was appointed colonel; Alexander McAlister, lieutenant colonel; Duncan McNeill, first major; Alexander McDonald, second major. One company of Minute Men was to be raised. This Act was passed on September 9th.

As the name of Farquhard Campbell often occurs in connection with the early stages of the Revolution, and quite frequently in the Colonial Records from 1771 to 1776, a brief notice of him may be of some interest. He was a gentleman of wealth, education and influence, and, at first, appeared to be warmly attached to the cause of liberty. As has been noticed he was a member of the Provincial Congress, and evinced much zeal in promoting the popular movement, and, as a visiting member from Cumberland county attended the meeting of the Safety Committee at Wilmington, on July 20, 1776. When Governor Martin abandoned his palace and retreated to Fort Johnston, and thence to an armed ship, it was ascertained that he visited Campbell at his residence. Not long afterwards the governor's secretary asked the Provincial Congress "to give Sanction and Safe Conduct to the removal of the most valuable Effects of Governor Martin on Board the Man of War and his Coach and Horses to Mr. Farquard Campbell's." When the request was submitted to that body, Mr. Campbell "expressed a sincere desire that the Coach and Horses should not be sent to his House in Cumberland and is amazed that such a proposal should have been made without his approbation or privity." On account of his positive disclaimer the Congress, by resolution exonerated him from any improper conduct, and that he had "conducted himself as an honest member of Society and a friend to the American Cause."*

He dealt treacherously with the governor as well as with Congress. The former, in a letter to the earl of Dartmouth, October 16, 1775, says:

"I have heard too My Lord with infinitely greater surprise and concern that the Scotch Highlanders on whom I had such firm reliance have declared themselves for neutrality, which I am informed is to be attributed to the influence of a certain Mr. Farquhard Campbell an ignorant man who has been settled from childhood in this Country, is an old Member of the Assembly and has imbibed all the American popular principles and prejudices. By the advice of some of his Countrymen I was induced after the receipt of your Lordship's letter No. 16 to communicate with this man on the alarming state of the Country and to sound his disposition in case of matters coming to extremity here, and he expressed to me such abhorence of the violences that had been done at Fort Johnston and in other instances and discovered so much jealousy and apprehension of the ill designs of the Leaders in Sedition here, giving me at the same time so strong assurances of his own loyalty and the good dispositions of his Countrymen that I unsuspecting his dissimulation and treachery was led to impart to him the encouragements I was authorized to hold out to his Majesty's loyal Subjects in this Colony who should stand forth in support of Government which he received with much seeming approbation and repeatedly assured me he would consult with the principles among his Countrymen without whose concurrence he could promise nothing of himself, and would acquaint me with their determinations. From the time of this conversation between us in July I heard nothing of Mr. Campbell until since the late Convention at Hillsborough, where he appeared in the character of a delegate from the County of Cumberland and there, according to my information, unasked and unsolicited and without provocation of any sort was guilty of the base Treachery of promulgating all I had said to him in confidential secrecy, which he had promised sacredly and inviolably to observe, and of the aggravating crime of falsehood in making additions of his own invention and declaring that he had rejected all my propositions."†

The governor again refers to him in his letter to the same, dated November 12, 1775:

"From Capt. McLeod, who seems to be a man of observation

---

*Ibid, p. 190. †Ibid, p. 266.

and intelligence, I gather that the inconsistency of Farquhard Campbell's conduct * * * has proceeded as much from jealousy of the Superior consequence of this Gentleman and his father in law with the Highlanders here as from any other motive. This schism is to be lamented from whatsoever cause arising, but I have no doubt that I shall be able to reconcile the interests of the parties whenever I have power to act and can meet them together."*

Finally he threw off the mask, or else had changed his views, and openly espoused the cause of his country's enemies. He was seized at his own house, while entertaining a party of royalists, and thrown into Halifax gaol. A committee of the Provincial Congress, on April 20, 1776, reported "that Farquhard Campbell disregarding the sacred Obligations he had voluntarily entered into to support the Liberty of America against all usurpations has Traitorously and insiduously endeavored to excite the Inhabitants of this Colony to take arms and levy war in order to assist the avowed enemies thereof. That when a prisoner on his parole of honor he gave intelligence of the force and intention of the American Army under Col. Caswell to the Enemy and advised them in what manner they might elude them."†

He was sent, with other prisoners, to Baltimore, and thence, on parole, to Fredericktown, where he behaved "with much resentment and haughtiness." On March 3, 1777, he appealed to Governor Caswell to be permitted to return home, offering to mortgage his estate for his good behavior.‡ Several years after the Revolution he was a member of the Senate of North Carolina.

The stormy days of discussion, excitement, and extensive preparations for war, in 1775, did not deter the Highlanders in Scotland from seeking a home in America. On October 21st, a body of one hundred and seventy-two Highlanders, including men, women and children arrived in the Cape Fear river, on board the George, and made application for lands near those already located by their relatives. The governor took his usual precautions with them, for in a letter to the earl of Dartmouth, dated November 12th, he says:

"On the most solemn assurances of their firm and unalterable loyalty and attachment to the King, and their readiness to lay

---
*Ibid, p. 326. †Ibid, p. 595. ‡Ibid, Vol. XI. p. 403.

down their lives in the support and defence of his Majesty's Government, I was induced to Grant their request on the Terms of their taking such lands in the proportions allowed by his Majesty's Royal Instructions, and subject to all the conditions prescribed by them whenever grants may be passed in due form, thinking it were advisable to attach these people to Government by granting as matter of favor and courtesy to them what I had not power to prevent than to leave them to possess themselves by violence of the King's lands, without owing or acknowledging any obligation for them, as it was only the means of securing these People against the seditions of the Rebels, but gaining so much strength to Government that is equally important at this time, without making any concessions injurious to the rights and interests of the Crown, or that it has effectual power to withhold."*

In the same letter is the further information that "a ship is this moment arrived from Scotland with upwards of one hundred and thirty Emigrants Men, Women and Children to whom I shall think it proper (after administering the Oath of Allegiance to the Men) to give permission to settle on the vacant lands of the Crown here on the same principles and conditions that I granted that indulgence to the Emigrants lately imported in the ship George."

Many of the emigrants appear to have been seized with the idea that all that was necessary was to land in America, and the avenues of affluence would be opened to them. Hence there were those who landed in a distressed condition. Such was the state of the last party that arrived before the Peace of 1783. There was "a Petition from sundry distressed Highlanders, lately arrived from Scotland, praying that they might be permitted to go to Cape Fear, in North Carolina, the place where they intended to settle," laid before the Virginia convention then being held at Williamsburgh, December 14, 1775. On the same day the convention gave orders to Colonel Woodford to "take the distressed Highlanders, with their families, under his protection, permit them to pass by land unmolested to Carolina, and supply them with such provisions as they may be in immediate want of."†

The early days of 1776 saw the culmination of the intrigues with the Scotch-Highlanders. The Americans realized that the

---

Ibid, p. 324.   †American Archives, 4th Series, Vol. IV, p. 84.

war party was in the ascendant, and consequently every movement was carefully watched. That the Americans felt bitterly towards them came from the fact that they were not only precipitating themselves into a quarrel of which they were not interested parties, but also exhibited ingratitude to their benefactors. Many of them came to the country not only poor and needy, but in actual distress.* They were helped with an open hand, and cared for with kindness and brotherly aid. Then they had not been long in the land, and the trouble so far had been to seek redress. Hence the Americans felt keenly the position taken by the Highlanders. On the other hand the Highlanders had viewed the matter from a different standpoint. They did not realize the craftiness of Governor Martin in compelling them to take the oath of allegiance, and they felt bound by what they considered was a voluntary act, and binding with all the sacredness of religion. They had ever been taught to keep their promises, and a liar was a greater criminal than a thief. Still they had every opportunity afforded them to learn the true status of affairs; independence had not yet been proclaimed; Washington was still beseiging Boston, and the Americans continued to petition the British throne for a redress of grievances.

That the action of the Highlanders was ill-advised, at that time, admits of no discussion. They failed to realize the condition of the country and the insuperable difficulties to overcome before making a junction with Sir Henry Clinton. What they expected to gain by their conduct is uncertain, and why they should march away a distance of one hundred miles, and then be transported by ships to a place they knew not where, thus leaving their wives and children to the mercies of those whom they had offended and driven to arms, made bitter enemies of, must ever remain unfathomable. It shows they were blinded and exhibited the want of even ordinary foresight. It also exhibited the reckless indifference of the responsible parties to the welfare of those they so successfully duped. It is no wonder that although nearly a century and a quarter have elapsed since the Highlanders unsheathed the claymore in the pine forests of North Carolina, not

---

*See Appendix, Note E.

a single person has shown the hardihood to applaud their action. On the other hand, although treated with the utmost charity, their bravery applauded, they have been condemned for their rude precipitancy, besides failing to see the changed condition of affairs, and resenting the injuries they had received from the House of Hanover that had harried their country and hanged their relatives on the murderous gallows-tree. Their course, however, in the end proved advantageous to them; for, after their disastrous defeat, they took an oath to remain peaceable, which the majority kept, and thus prevented them from being harrassed by the Americans, and, as loyal subjects of king George, the English army must respect their rights.

Agents were busily at work among the people preparing them for war. The most important of all was Allan MacDonald of Kingsborough. Early he came under the suspicion of the Committee of Safety at Wilmington. On the very day, July 3, 1775, he was in consultation with Governor Martin, its chairman was directed to write to him "to know from himself respecting the reports that circulate of his having an intention to raise Troops to support the arbitrary measures of the ministry against the Americans in this Colony, and whether he had not made an offer of his services to Governor Martin for that purpose."*

The influence of Kingsborough was supplemented by that of Major Donald MacDonald, who was sent direct from the army in Boston. He was then in his sixty-fifth year, had an extended experience in the army. He was in the Rising of 1745, and headed many of his own name. He now found many of these former companions who readily listened to his persuasions. All the emissaries sent represented they were only visiting their friends and relatives. They were all British officers, in the active service.

Partially in confirmation of the above may be cited a letter from Samuel Johnston of Edenton, dated July 21, 1775, written to the Committee at Wilmington:

"A vessel from New York to this place brought over two officers who left at the Bar to go to New Bern, they are both Highlanders, one named McDonnel the other McCloud. They pretend they are on a visit to some of their countrymen on your river, but

---

*North Carolina Colonial Records, Vol. X, p. 65.

THE HIGHLANDERS IN NORTH CAROLINA. 125

I think there is reason to suspect their errand of a base nature. The Committee of this town have wrote to New Bern to have them secured. Should they escape there I hope you will keep a good lookout for them."*

The vigorous campaign for 1776, in the Carolinas was determined upon in the fall of 1775, in deference to the oft repeated and urgent solicitations of the royal governors, and on account of the appeals made by Martin, the brunt of it fell upon North Carolina. He assured the home government that large numbers of the Highlanders and Regulators were ready to take up arms for the king.

The program, as arranged, was for Sir Henry Clinton, with a fleet of ships and seven corps of Irish Regulars, to be at the mouth of the Cape Fear early in the year 1776, and there form a junction with the Highlanders and other disaffected persons from the interior. Believing that Sir Henry Clinton's armament would arrive in January or early in February Martin made preparations for the revolt; for his "unwearied, persevering agent," Alexander MacLean brought written assurances from the principal persons to whom he had been directed, that between two and three thousand men would take the field at the governor's summons. Under this encouragement MacLean was sent again into the back country, with a commission dated January 10, 1776, authorizing Allan McDonald, Donald McDonald, Alexander McLeod, Donald McLeod, Alexander McLean, Allen Stewart, William Campbell, Alexander McDonald and Neal McArthur, of Cumberland and Anson counties, and seventeen other persons who resided in a belt of counties in middle Carolina, to raise and array all the king's loyal subjects, and to march them in a body to Brunswick by February 15th.†

Donald MacDonald was placed in command of this array and of all other forces in North Carolina with the rank of brigadier general, with Donald MacLeod next in rank. Upon receiving his orders, General MacDonald issued the following:

"*By His Excellency Brigadier-General Donald McDonald, Commander of His Majesty's Forces for the time being, in North Carolina:*

---
*Ibid, p, 117. †American Archives, 4th Series, Vol. IV. p, 981.

A MANIFESTO.

Whereas, I have received information that many of His Majesty's faithful subjects have been so far overcome by apprehension of danger, as to fly before His Majesty's Army as from the most inveterate enemy; to remove which, as far as lies in my power, I have thought it proper to publish this Manifesto, declaring that I shall take the proper steps to prevent any injury being done, either to the person or properties of His Majesty's subjects; and I do further declare it to be my determined resolution, that no violence shall be used to women and children, as viewing such outrages to be inconsistent with humanity, and as tending, in their consequences, to sully the arms of Britons and of Soldiers.

I, therefore, in His Majesty's name, generally invite every well-wisher to that form of Government under which they have so happily lived, and which, if justly considered, ought to be esteemed the best birth-right of Britons and Americans, to repair to His Majesty's Royal Standard, erected at Cross Creek, where they will meet with every possible civilty, and be ranked in the list of friends and fellow-Soldiers, engaged in the best and most glorious of all causes, supporting the rights and Constitution of their country. Those, therefore, who have been under the unhappy necessity of submitting to the mandates of Congress and Committees—those lawless, usurped, and arbitrary tribunals—will have an opportunity, (by joining the King's Army) to restore peace and tranquility to this distracted land—to open again the glorious streams of commerce—to partake of the blessings of inseparable from a regular administration of justice, and be again reinstated in the favorable opinion of their Sovereign.

Donald McDonald.

By His Excellency's command:
Kenn. McDonald, P. S."*

On February 5th General MacDonald issued another manifesto in which he declares it to be his "intention that no violation whatever shall be offered to women, children, or private property, to sully the arms of Britons or freemen, employed in the glorious and righteous cause of rescuing and delivering this country from the usurpation of rebellion, and that no cruelty whatever be offered against the laws of humanity, but what resistance shall make necessary; and that whatever provisions and other necessaries be taken for the troops, shall be paid for immediately; and in case any person, or persons, shall offer the least violence to the fami-

---

*Ibid, p, 982.

lies of such as will join the Royal Standard, such persons or persons, may depend that retaliation will be made; the horrors of such proceedings, it is hoped, will be avoided by all true Christians."*

Manifestos being the order of the day, Thomas Rutherford, erstwhile patriot, deriving his commission from the Provincial Congress, though having alienated himself, but signing himself colonel, also issues one in which he declares that this is "to command, enjoin, beseech, and require all His Majesty's faithful subjects within the County of Cumberland to repair to the King's Royal standard, at Cross Creek, on or before the 16th present, in order to join the King's army; otherwise, they must expect to fall under the melancholy consequences of a declared rebellion, and expose themselves to the just resentment of an injured, though gracious Sovereign."†

On February 1st General MacDonald set up the Royal Standard at Cross Creek, in the Public Square, and in order to cause the Highlanders all to respond with alacrity manifestos were issued and other means resorted to in order that the "loyal subjects of His Majesty" might take up arms, among which nightly balls were given, and the military spirit freely inculcated. When the day came the Highlanders were seen coming from near and from far, from the wide plantations on the river bottoms, and from the rude cabins in the depths of the lonely pine forests, with broadswords at their side, in tartan garments and feathered bonnet, and keeping step to the shrill music of the bag-pipe. There came, first of all, Clan MacDonald with Clan MacLeod near at hand, with lesser numbers of Clan MacKenzie, Clan MacRae, Clan MacLean, Clan MacKay, Clan MacLachlan, and still others,—variously estimated at from fifteen hundred to three thousand, including about two hundred others, principally Regulators. However, all who were capable of bearing arms did not respond to the summons, for some would not engage in a cause where their traditions and affections had no part. Many of them hid in the swamps and in the forests. On February 18th the Highland army took up its line of march for Wilmington and at evening encamped on the Cape Fear, four miles below Cross Creek.

---

*Ibid, p. 983. †Ibid, p. 1129.

The assembling of the Highland army aroused the entire country. The patriots, fully cognizant of what was transpiring, flew to arms, determined to crush the insurrection, and in less than a fortnight nearly nine thousand men had risen against the enemy, and almost all the rest were ready to turn out at a moment's notice. At the very first menace of danger, Brigadier General James Moore took the field at the head of his regiment, and on the 15th secured possession of Rockfish bridge, seven miles from Cross Creek, where he was joined by a recruit of sixty from the latter place.

On the 19th the royalists were paraded with a view to assail Moore on the following night; but he was thoroughly entrenched, and the bare suspicion of such a project was contemplated caused two companions of Cotton's corps to run off with their arms. On that day General MacDonald sent the following letter to General Moore:

"Sir: I herewith send the bearer, Donald Morrison, by advice of the Commissioners appointed by his Excellency Josiah Martin, and in behalf of the army now under my command, to propose terms to you as friends and countrymen. I must suppose you unacquainted with the Governor's proclamation, commanding all his Majesty's loyal subject to repair to the King's royal standard, else I should have imagined you would ere this have joined the King's army now engaged in his Majesty's service. I have therefore thought it proper to intimate to you, that in case you do not, by 12 o'clock to-morrow, join the royal standard, I must consider you as enemies, and take the necessary steps for the support of legal authority.

I beg leave to remind you of his Majesty's speech to his Parliament, wherein he offers to receive the misled with tenderness and mercy, from motives of humanity. I again beg of you to accept the proffered clemency. I make no doubt, but you will show the gentleman sent on this message every possible civilty; and you may depend in return, that all your officers and men, which may fall into our hands shall be treated with an equal degree of respect. I have the honor to be, in behalf of the army, Sir, Your most obedient humble servant,

Don. McDonald.

Head Quarters, Feb. 19, 1776.
His Excellency's Proclamation is herewith enclosed."

Brigadier General Moore's answer:

"Sir: Yours of this day I have received, in answer to which, I must inform you that the terms which you are pleased to say, in behalf of the army under your command, are offered to us as friends and countrymen, are such as neither my duty or inclination will permit me to accept, and which I must presume you too much of an officer to accept of me. You were very right when you supposed me unacquainted with the Governor's proclamation, but as the terms therein proposed are such as I hold incompatible with the freedom of Americans, it can be no rule of conduct for me. However, should I not hear farther from you before twelve o'clock to-morrow by which time I shall have an opportunity of consulting my officers here, and perhaps Col. Martin, who is in the neighborhood of Cross Creek, you may expect a more particular answer; meantime, you may be assured that the feelings of humanity will induce me to shew that civility to such of your people as may fall into our hands, as I am desirous should be observed towards those of ours, who may be unfortunate enough to fall into yours. I am, Sir, your most obedient and very humble servant,

James Moore.

Camp at Rockfish, Feb. 19, 1776."

General Moore, on the succeeding day sent the following to General MacDonald:

"Sir: Agreeable to my promise of yesterday, I have consulted the officers under my command respecting your letter, and am happy in finding them unanimous in opinion with me. We consider ourselves engaged in a cause the most glorious and honourable in the world, the defense of the liberties of mankind, in support of which we are determined to hazard everything dear and valuable and in tenderness to the deluded people under your command, permit me, Sir, through you to inform them, before it is too late, of the dangerous and destructive precipice on which they stand, and to remind them of the ungrateful return they are about to make for their favorable reception in this country. If this is not sufficient to recall them to the duty which they owe themselves and their posterity inform them that they are engaged in a cause in which they cannot succeed as not only the whole force of this country, but that of our neighboring provinces, is exerting and now actually in motion to suppress them, and which much end in their utter destruction. Desirous, however, of avoiding the effusion of human blood, I have thought proper to send you a test recommended by the Continental Congress, which if they will yet subscribe we are willing to receive them as friends and countrymen. Should this offer be rejected, I shall consider them as enemies to the constitutional liberties of America, and treat them accordingly.

I cannot conclude without reminding you, Sir, of the oath which you and some of your officers took at Newbern on your arrival to this country, which I imagine you will find is difficult to reconcile to your present conduct. I have no doubt that the bearer, Capt. James Walker, will be treated with proper civility and respect in your camp.

I am, Sir, your most obedient and very humble servant,

James Moore.

Camp at Rockfish, Feb. 20, 1776."

General MacDonald returned the following reply:

"Sir: I received your favor by Captain James Walker, and observed your declared sentiments of revolt, hostility and rebellion to the King, and to what I understand to be the constitution of the country. If I am mistaken future consequences must determine; but while I continue in my present sentiment, I shall consider myself embarked in a cause which must, in its consequences, extricate this country from anarchy and licentiousness. I cannot conceive that the Scottish emigrants, to whom I imagine you allude, can be under greater obligations to this country than to the King, under whose gracious and merciful government they alone could have been enabled to visit this western region: And I trust, Sir, it is in the womb of time to say, that they are not that deluded and ungrateful people which you would represent them to be. As a soldier in his Majesty's service, I must inform you, if you are to learn, that it is my duty to conquer, if I cannot reclaim, all those who may be hardy enough to take up arms against the best of masters, as of Kings. I have the honor to be, in behalf of the army under my command,

Sir, your most obedient servant,

Don. McDonald.

To the Commanding Officer at Rockfish."*

MacDonald realized that he was unable to put his threat into execution, for he was informed that the minute-men were gathering in swarms all around him; that Colonel Caswell, at the head of the minute men of Newbern, nearly eight hundred strong, was marching through Duplin county, to effect a junction with Moore, and that his communication with the war ships had been cut off.

---

*N. C. Colonial Records, Vol. XI, pp. 276-279.

Realizing the extremity of his danger, he resolved to avoid an engagement, and leave the army at Rockfish in his rear, and by celerity of movement, and crossing rivers at unsuspected places, to disengage himself from the larger bodies and fall upon the command of Caswell. Before marching he exhorted his men to fidelity, expressed bitter scorn for the "base cravens who had deserted the night before," and continued by saying:

"If any amongst you is so faint-hearted as not to serve with the resolution of conquering or dying, this is the time for such to declare themselves."

The speech was answered by a general huzza for the king; but from Cotton's corps about twenty laid down their arms. He decamped, with his army at midnight, crossed the Cape Fear, sunk his boats, and sent a party fifteen miles in advance to secure the bridge over South river, from Bladen into Hanover, pushing with rapid pace over swollen streams, rough hills, and deep morasses, hotly pursued by General Moore. Perceiving the purpose of the enemy General Moore detached Colonels Lillington and Ashe to reinforce Colonel Caswell, or if that could not be effected, then they were to occupy Widow Moore's Creek bridge.

Colonel Caswell designing the purpose of MacDonald changed his own course in order to intercept his march. On the 23rd the Highlanders thought to overtake him, and arrayed themselves in the order of battle, with eighty able-bodied men, armed with broad-swords, forming the center of the army; but Colonel Caswell being posted at Corbett's Ferry could not be reached for want of boats. The royalists were again in extreme danger; but at a point six miles higher up the Black river they succeeded in crossing in a broad shallow boat while MacLean and Fraser, left with a few men and a drum and a pipe, amused the corps of Caswell.

Colonel Lillington, on the 25th took post on the east side of Moore's Creek bridge; and on the next day Colonel Caswell reached the west side, threw up a slight embankment, and destroyed a part of the bridge. A royalist, who had been sent into his camp under pretext of summoning him to return to his allegiance, brought back the information that he had halted on the same side of the river as themselves, and could be assaulted with advantage. Colonel Caswell was not only a good woodman, but also a man of superior ability, and believing he had misled the enemy, marched his column to the east side of the stream, removed the planks from the bridge, and placed his men behind trees and such embankments as could be thrown up during the night. His force now amounted to a thousand men, consisting of the Newbern minute-men, the militia of Craven, Dobbs, Johnston, and Wake counties, and the detachment under Colonel Lillington. The men of the Neuse region, their officers wearing silver crescents upon their hats, inscribed with the words, "Liberty or Death," were in front. The situation of General MacDonald was again perilous, for while facing this army, General Moore, with his regulars was close upon his rear.

The royalists, expecting an easy victory, decided upon an immediate attack. General MacDonald was confined to his tent by sickness, and the command devolved upon Major Donald MacLeod, who began the march at one o'clock on the morning of the 27th; but owing to the time lost in passing an intervening morass, it was within an hour of daylight when they reached the west bank of the creek. They entered the ground without resistance. Seeing Colonel Caswell was on the opposite side they reduced their columns and formed their line of battle in the woods. Their rallying cry was, "King George and broadswords," and the signal for attack was three cheers, the drum to beat and the pipes to play. While it was still dark Major MacLeod, with a party of about forty advanced, and at the bridge was challenged by the sentinel, asking, "Who goes there?" He answered, "A friend." "A friend to whom?" "To the king." Upon this the sentinels bent their faces down to the ground. Major MacLeod thinking they might be some of his own command who had crossed the bridge, challenged them in Gaelic; but receiving no reply, fired his own piece, and ordered his party to fire also. All that remained of the bridge were the two logs, which had served for sleepers, permitting only two persons to pass at a time. Donald MacLeod and Captain John Campbell rushed forward and succeeded in getting over. The Highlanders who followed were shot down on the logs and fell into the muddy stream below. Major MacLeod was mortally wounded, but was seen to rise repeatedly from the ground, waving his sword and encouraging his men to come on, till twenty-six balls penetrated his body. Captain Campbell also was shot dead, and at that moment a party of militia, under Lieutenant Slocum, who had forded the creek and penetrated a swamp on its western bank, fell suddenly upon the rear of the royalists. The loss of their leader and the unexpected attack upon their rear threw them into confusion, when they broke and fled. The battle lasted but ten minutes. The royalists lost seventy killed and wounded, while the patriots had but two wounded, one of whcm recovered. The victory was lasting and complete. The Highland power was thoroughly broken. There fell into the hands of the Americans besides eight hundred and fifty prisoners, fifteen hundred rifles, all of them excellent pieces, three hundred and fifty guns and short bags, one hundred and fifty swords and dirks, two medicine chests, immediately from England, one valued at £300 sterling, thirteen wagons with horses, a box of Johannes and English guineas, amounting to about $75,000.

Some of the Highlanders escaped from the battlefield by breaking down their wagons and riding away, three upon a horse. Many who were taken confessed that they were forced and persuaded contrary to their inclinations into the service.* The soldiers taken were disarmed, and dismissed to their homes.

On the following day General MacDonald and nearly all the chief men were taken prisoners, amongst whom was MacDonald of Kingsborough and his son Alexander. A partial list of those apprehended is given in a report of the Committee of the Provincial Congress, reported April 20th and May 10th on the guilt of the Highland and Regulator officers then confined in Halifax gaol, finding the prisoners were of four different classes, viz.:

First, Prisoners who had served in Congress.

Second, Prisoners who had signed Tests or Associations.

Third, Prisoners who had been in arms without such circumstances.

---

*Ibid, Vol. X, p. 485.

Fourth, Prisoners under suspicious circumstances.

The Highlanders coming under the one or the other of these classes are given in the following order:

Farquhard Campbell, Cumberland county.
Alexander McKay, Capt. of 38 men, Cumberland county.
Alexander McDonald (Condrach), Major of a regiment.
Alexander Morrison, Captain of a company of 35 men.
Alexander MacDonald, son of Kingsborough, a volunteer, Anson county.
James MacDonald, Captain of a company of 25 men.
Alexander McLeod, Captain of a company of 32 men.
John MacDonald, Captain of a company of 40 men.
Alexander McLeod, Captain of a company of 16 men.
Murdoch McAskell, Captain of a company of 34 men.
Alexander McLeod, Captain of a company of 16 men.
Angus McDonald, Captain of a company of 30 men.
Neill McArthur, Freeholder of Cross Creek, Captain of a company of 55 men.
Francis Frazier, Adjutant to General MacDonald's Army.
John McLeod, of Cumberland county, Captain of company of 35 men.
John McKinzie, of Cumberland county, Captain of company of 43 men.
Kennith Macdonald, Aid-de-camp to General Macdonald.
Murdoch McLeod, of Anson county, Surgeon to General Macdonald's Army.
Donald McLeod, of Anson county, Lieutenant in Captain Morrison's Company.
Norman McLeod, of Anson county, Ensign in James McDonald's company.
John McLeod, of Anson county, Lieutenant in James McDonald's company.
Laughlin McKinnon, freeholder in Cumberland county, Lieutenant in Col. Rutherford's corps.
James Munroe, freeholder in Cumberland county, Lieutenant in Capt. McRay's company.
Donald Morrison, Ensign to Capt. Morrison's company.
John McLeod, Ensign to Capt. Morrison's company.
Archibald McEachern, Bladen county, Lieutenant to Capt. McArthur's company.
Rory McKinnen, freeholder Anson county, volunteer.
Donald McLeod, freeholder Cumberland county, Master to two Regiments, General McDonald's Army.

Donald Stuart, Quarter Master to Col. Rutherford's Regiment.
Allen Macdonald of Kingsborough, freeholder of Anson county, Col. Regiment.
Duncan St. Clair.
Daniel McDaniel, Lieutenant in Seymore York's company.
Alexander McRaw, freeholder Anson county, Capt. company 47 men.
Kenneth Stuart, Lieutenant Capt Stuart's company.
Collin McIver, Lieutenant Capt. Leggate's company.
Alexander Maclaine, Commissary to General Macdonald's Army.
Angus Campbell, Captain company 30 men.
Alexander Stuart, Captain company 30 men.
Hugh McDonald, Anson county, volunteer.
John McDonald, common soldier.
Daniel Cameron, common soldier.
Daniel McLean, freeholder, Cumberland county, Lieutenant to Angus Campbell's company.
Malcolm McNeill, recruiting agent for General Macdonald's Army, accused of using compulsion.*

The following is a list of the prisoners sent from North Carolina to Philadelphia, enclosed in a letter of April 22, 1776:

"1 His Excellency Donald McDonald Esqr Brigadier General of the Tory Army and Commander in Chief in North Carolina.
 2 Colonel Allen McDonald (of Kingsborough) first in Commission of Array and second in Command
 3 Alexander McDonald son of Kingsborough
 4 Major Alexander McDonald (Condrack)
 5 Capt Alexander McRay
 6 Capt John Leggate
 7 Capt James McDonald
 8 Capt Alexr. McLeod
 9 Capt Alexr. Morrison
10 Capt John McDonald
11 Capt Alexr. McLeod
12 Capt Murdoch McAskell
13 Capt Alexander McLeod
14 Capt Angus McDonald
15 Capt Neil McArthur†
16 Capt James Mens of the light horse.
17 Capt John McLeod

*Ibid, pp. 594-603.   †See Appendix, Note H.

18   Capt Thos. Wier
19   Capt John McKenzie
20   Lieut John Murchison
21   Kennith McDonald, Aid de Camp to Genl McDonald
22   Murdock McLeod, Surgeon
23   Adjutant General John Smith
24   Donald McLeod Quarter Master
25   John Bethune Chaplain
26   Farquhard Campbell late a delegate in the provincial Congress—Spy and Confidential Emissary of Governor Martin."*

Some of the prisoners were discharged soon after their arrest, by making and signing the proper oath, of which the following is taken from the Records:

"Oath of Malcolm McNeill and Joseph Smith. We Malcolm McNeil and Joseph Smith do Solemly Swear on the Holy Evangelists of Almighty God that we will not on any pretence whatsoever take up or bear Arms against the Inhabitants of the United States of America and that we will not disclose or make known any matters within our knowledge now carrying on within the United States and that we will not carry out more than fifty pounds of Gold & Silver in value to fifty pounds Carolina Currency. So help us God.

              Malcolm McNeill,
Halifax, 13th Augt., 1776. Joseph Smith."†

The North Carolina Provincial Congress on March 5, 1776, "Resolved, That Colonel Richard Caswell send, under a sufficient guard, Brigadier General Donald McDonald, taken at the battle of Moore's Creek Bridge, to the Town of Halifax, and there to have him committed a close prisoner in the jail of the said Town, until further orders."‡

The same Congress, held in Halifax April 5th, "Resolved, That General McDonald be admitted to his parole upon the following conditions: That he does not go without the limits of the Town of Halifax; that he does not directly or indirectly, while a prisoner, correspond with any person or persons who are or may be in opposition to American measures, or by any manner or means convey to them intelligence of any sort; that he take no draft, nor procure them to be taken by any one else, of any place or places in which he may be, while upon his parole, that shall

---

*Ibid, Vol. XI. p. 294.   †Ibid, Vol. X. p. 743.   ‡American Archives, Fourth Series, Vol. V, p. 69.

now, or may hereafter give information to our enemies which can be injurious to us, or the common cause of America; but that without equivocation, mental evasion, or secret reservation, he pay the most exact and faithful attention to the intent and meaning of these conditions, according to the rules and regulations of war; and that he every day appear between the hours of ten and twelve o'clock to the Officer of the Guard."*

On April 11th, the same parole was offered to Allan MacDonald of Kingsborough.†

'The Pennsylvania Committee of Safety, at its session in Philadelphia, held May 25, 1776, ordered the Highland prisoners, mentioned on page 219, naming each one separately to be "safely kept in close confinement until discharged by the honorable Congress or this Committee."‡ Four days later, General MacDonald addressed a letter to the Continental Congress, in which he said, "That he was, by a party of horsemen, upon the 28th day of February last, taken prisoner from sick quarters, eight miles from Widow Moor's Creek, where he lay dangerously ill, and carried to Colonel Caswell's camp, where General Moore then commanded, to whom he delivered his sword as prisoner of war, which General Moore was pleased to deliver back in a genteel manner before all his officers then present, according to the rules and customs of war practised in all nations; assuring him at the same time that he would be well treated, and his baggage and property delivered to him, &c. Having taken leave of General Moore and Colonel Caswell, Lieutenant-Colonel Bryant took him under his care; and after rummaging his baggage for papers, &c., conducted him to Newbern, from thence with his baggage to Halifax, where the Committee of Safety there thought proper to commit him to the common jail; his horses, saddles, and pistols, &c., taken from him, and never having committed any act of violence against the person or property of any man; that he remained in this jail near a month, until General Howe arrived there, who did him the honour to call upon him in jail; and he has reason to think that General Howe thought this treatment erroneous and without a precedent; that upon this representation to the Convention, General McDonald was, by order of the Convention, permitted, upon parole, to the limits of the town of Halifax, until the 25th of April last, when he was appointed to march, with the other gentlemen prisoners, escorted from the jail there to this place. General McDonald

---

*Ibid, Vol. V, p. 1317. †Ibid, p. 1320. ‡Ibid, Vol. VI, p. 663.

would wish to know what crime he has since been guilty of, deserving his being recommitted to the jail of Philadelphia, without his bedding or baggage, and his sword and his servant detained from him. The other gentlemen prisoners are in great want for their blankets and other necessaries.

Donald McDonald."*

The Continental Congress, on September 4th, "Resolved, That the proposal made by General Howe, as delivered by General Sullivan, of exchanging General Sullivan for General Prescot, and Lord Stirling for Brigadier-General, be complied with."†

This being communicated to General McDonald he addressed, to the Secretary of War the following:

"Philadelphia Gaol, September 6, 1776.

To the Secretary of War:

General McDonald's compliments to the Secretary of War. He is obliged to him for his polite information, that the Congress have been pleased to agree that Generals Prescott and McDonald shall be exchanged for the Generals Sullivan and Stirling. General McDonald is obliged to the Congress for the reference to the Board of War for his departure: The indulgence of eight or ten days will, he hopes, be sufficient to prepare him for his journey. His baggage will require a cart to carry it. He is not provided with horses—submits it to the Congress and Board how he may be conducted with safety to his place of destination, not doubting his servant will be permitted to go along with him, and that his sword may be returned to him, which he is informed the Commissary received from his servant on the 25th of May last.

General McDonald begs leave to acquaint the Secretary and the Board of War, for the information of Congress, that when he was brought prisoner from sick quarters to General Moore's camp, at Moore's Creek, upon the 28th of February last, General Moore treated him with respect to his rank and commission in the King of Great Britain's service. He would have given him a parole to return to his sick quarters, as his low state of health required it much at that time, but Colonel Caswell objected thereto, and had him conducted prisoner to Newbern, but gently treated all the way by Colonel Caswell and his officers.

From Newbern he was conducted by a guard of Horse to Halifax, and committed on his arrival, after forty-five miles journey the last day, in a sickly state of health, and immediately ushered into a common gaol, without bed or bedding, fire or candles,

---

Ibid, p. 613.   †*Ibid*, Fifth Series, Vol. II. p. 1330.

in a cold, long night, by Colonel Long, who did not appear to me to behave like a gentleman. That notwithstanding the promised protection for person and property he had from General Moore, a man called Longfield Cox, a wagonmaster to Colonel Caswell's army, seized upon his horse, saddle, pistols, and other arms, and violently detained the same by refusing to deliver them up to Colonel Bryan, who conducted him to Newbern. Colonel Long was pleased to detain his mare at Halifax when sent prisoner from thence to here. Sorry to dwell so long upon so disagreeable a subject."*

This letter was submitted to the Continental Congress on September 7th, when it "Resolved, That he be allowed four days to prepare for his journey; That a copy of that part of his Letter respecting his treatment in North Carolina, be sent to the Convention of that State."†

Notwithstanding General Sir William Howe had agreed to make the specified exchange of prisoners, yet in a letter addressed to Washington, September 21, 1776, he states:

"The exchange you propose of Brigadier-General Alexander, commonly called Lord Stirling, for Mr. McDonald, cannot take place, as he has only the rank of Major by my commission; but I shall readily send any Major in the enclosed list of prisoners that you will be pleased to name in exchange for him."‡

As Sir William Howe refused to recognize the rank conferred on General McDonald, by the governor of North Carolina, Washington was forced, September 23, to order his return, with the escort, to Philadelphia.|| But on the same day addressed Sir William Howe, in which he said:

"I had no doubt but Mr. McDonald's title would have been acknowledged, having understood that he received his commission from the hands of Governor Martin; nor can I consent to rank him as a Major till I have proper authority from Congress, to whom I shall state the matter upon your representation."|| That body, on September 30th, declared "That Mr. McDonald, having a commission of Brigadier-General from Governor Martin, be not exchanged for any officer under the rank of Brigadier-General in the service either of the United States or any of them."**

On the way from North Carolina to Philadelphia, while resting at Petersburg, May 2, 1776, Kingsborough indited the following letter:

---

*Ibid, p. 191. †Ibid, p. 1333. ‡Ibid, p. 437. ||Ibid, p. 464. **Ibid, p. 1383.

"Sir: Your kind favor I had by Mr. Ugin (?) with the Virginia money enclosed, which shall be paid if ever I retourn with thanks, if not I shall take to order payment. Colonel Eliot who came here to receive the prisoners Confined the General and me under a guard and sentries to a Roome; this he imputes to the Congress of North Carolina not getting Brigadier Lewes (who commands at Williamsburg) know of our being on parole by your permission when at Halifax. If any opportunity afford, it would add to our happiness to write something to the above purpose to some of the Congress here with directions (if such can be done) to forward said orders after us. I have also been depressed of the horse I held, and hath little chance of getting another. To walk on foot is what I never can do the length of Philadelphia. What you can do in the above different affairs will be adding to your former favors. Hoping you will pardon freedom wrote in a hurry. I am with real Esteem and respect
Honble Sir,
Your very obedt. Servt.
Allen MacDonald."*

June 28, 1776, Allen MacDonald of Kingsborough, was permitted, after signing a parole and word of honor to go to Reading, in Berks county.† At the same time the Committee of Safety

"Resolved, That such Prisoners from North Carolina as choose, may be permitted to write to their friends there; such letters to be inspected by this Committee; and the Jailer is to take care that all the paper delivered in to the Prisoners, be used in such Letters, or returned him."‡

The action of the Committee of Safety was approved by the Continental Congress on July 9th, by directing Kingsborough to be released on parole;‡ and on the 15th, his son Alexander was released on parole and allowed to reside with him.

Every attempt to exchange the prisoners was made on the part of the Americans, and as they appear to have been so unfortunate as to have no one to intercede for them among British officers, Kingsborough was permitted to go to New York and effect his own exchange, which he succeeded in doing during the month of November, 1777, and then proceeded to Halifax, Nova Scotia.‖

---

*North Carolina Colonial Records, Vol. XI. p. 295. †Am. Archives, 5th Series, Vol. I. p. 1291. ‡*Ibid*, p. 1570. ‖"Letter Book of Captain A. MacDonald," p. 387.

The Highland officers confined in prison became restive, and on October 31, 1776, presented a memorial, addressed to the North Carolina members of the Continental Congress, which at once met with the approval of William Hooper:

"Gentlemen: After a long separation of eight months from our Families & Friends, We the undersubscribers, Prisoners of war from North Carolina now in Philadelphia Prison, think ourselves justifiable at this period in applying to your Honours for permission to return to our Families; which indulgence we will promise on the Faith & honour of gentlemen not to abuse, by interfering in the present disputes, or aiding or assisting your enemies by word, writing, or action.

This request we have already laid before Congress who are willing to grant it, provided they shall have your approbation.

Hoping therefore, that you have no particular intention to distress us more than others whom you have treated with Indulgence, we flatter ourselves that your determinations will prove no obstruction to our Enlargement on the above terms; and have transmitted to you the enclosed Copy of the Resolve of Congress in our favor, which if you countenance; it will meet with the warmest acknowledgement of Gentn.

Your most obedt. humble Servts.,

Alexander Morison, Ferqd. Campbell, Alexr. Macleod, Alexr. McKay, James Macdonald, John McDonald, Murdoch Macleod, John Murchison, John Bethune, Neill McArthur, John Smith, Murdo MacCaskill, John McLeod, Alexr. McDonald, Angus McDonald, John Ligett."*

It was fully apparent to the Americans that so long as the leaders were prisoners there was no danger of another uprising among the Highlanders. This was fully tested by earl Cornwallis, who, after the battle of Guilford Courthouse, retreated towards the seaboard, stopping on the way at Cross Creek† hoping then to gain recruits from the Highlanders, but very few of whom responded to his call. In a letter addressed to Sir Henry Clinton, dated from his camp near Wilmington, April 10, 1781, he says:

"On my arrival there (Cross Creek), I found, to my great mortification, and contrary to all former accounts, that it was impossible to procure any considerable quantity of provisions, and

---

*N. C. Colonial Records, Vol. X. p. 888.   †See Appendix Note F.

that there was not four days' forage within twenty miles. The navigation of Cape Fear, with the hopes of which I had been flattered was totally impracticable, the distance from Wilmington by water being one hundred and fifty miles, the breadth of the river seldom exceeding one hundred yards, the banks generally high, and the inhabitants on each side almost universally hostile. Under these circumstances I determined to move immediately to Wilmington. By this measure the Highlanders have not had so much time as the people of the upper country, to prove the sincerity of their former professions of friendship. But, though appearances are rather more favorable among them, I confess they are not equal to my expectations."*

The Americans did not rest matters simply by confining the officers, but every precaution was taken to overawe them, not only by their parole, which nearly all implicitly obeyed, but also by armed force, for some militia was at once stationed at Cross Creek, which remained there until the Provincial Congress, on November 21, 1776, ordered it discharged.† General Charles Lee, who had taken charge of the Southern Department, on June 6, 1776, ordered Brigadier-General Lewis to take "as large a body of the regulars as can possibly be spared to march to Cross Creek, in North Carolina."‡

Notwithstanding the fact that many of the Highlanders who had been in the battle of Moore's Creek Bridge afterwards engaged in the service with the Americans, the community was regarded with suspicion, and that not without some cause. On July 28, 1777, it was reported that there were movements among the royalists that caused the patriots to be in arms and watch the Highlanders at Cross Creek. On August 3rd it was again reported that there were a hundred in arms with others coming.‖

As might be anticipated the poor Highlanders also were subjected to fear and oppression. They remained at heart, true to their first love. In June, 1776, a report was circulated among them that a company of light horse was coming into the settle-

---

*"Earl Cornwallis' Answer to Sir Henry Clinton," p. 10. †N. C. Colonial Records, Vol. XI. p. 927. ‡Am. Archives, Fourth Series, Vol. VI, p. 721. ‖N. C. Colonial Records, Vol. XI. pp. 546, 555.

ment, and every one thought he was the man wanted, and hence all hurried to the swamps and other fastnesses in the forest.*

From the poor Highland women, who had lost father, husband, brother in battle, or whose menfolk were imprisoned in the gaol at Halifax, there arose such a wail of distress as to call forth the attention of the Provincial Congress, which at once put forth a proclamation, and ordered it translated into the "Erse tongue," in which it was declared that they "warred not with those helpless females, but sympathized with them in their sorrow," and recommended them to the compassion of all, and to the "bounty of those who had aught to spare from their necessities."

One of the remarkable things, and one which cannot be accounted for, is, that although the North Carolina Highland emigrants were deeply religious, yet no clergyman accompanied them to the shores of America, until 1770, when Reverend John McLeod came direct from Scotland and ministered to them for some time; and they were entirely without a minister prior to 1757, when Reverend James Campbell commenced to preach for them, and continued in active work until 1770. He was the first ordained minister who took up his abode among the Presbyterian settlements in North Carolina. He pursued his labors among the outspreading neighborhoods in what are now Cumberland and Robeson counties. This worthy man was born in Campbelton, on the peninsula of Kintyre, in Argyleshire, Scotland. Of his early history but little is known, and by far too little of his pioneer labors has been preserved. About the year 1730 he emigrated to America, landing at Philadelphia. His attention having been turned to his countrymen on the Cape Fear, he removed to North Carolina, and took up his residence on the left bank of the above river, a few miles north of Cross Creek. He died in 1781. His preaching was in harmony with the tenets of his people, being presbyterian. He had three regular congregations on the Sabbath, besides irregular preaching, as occasion demanded. For some ten years he preached on the southwest side of the river at a place called "Roger's meeting-house." Here Hector McNeill ("Bluff Hector") and

---

* *Ibid*, p. 829.

Alexander McAlister acted as elders. About 1758 he began to preach at the "Barbacue Church,"—the building not erected until about the year 1765. It was at this church where Flora MacDonald worshipped. The first elders of this church were Gilbert Clark, Duncan Buie, Archibald Buie, and Donald Cameron.

Another of the preaching stations was at a place now known

BARBACUE CHURCH, WHERE FLORA MACDONALD WORSHIPPED.

as "Long Street." The building was erected about 1766. The first elders were Malcolm Smith, Archibald McKay and Archibald Ray.

There came, in the same ship, from Scotland, with Reverend John McLeod, a large number of Highland families, all of whom settled upon the upper and lower Little Rivers, in Cumberland county. After several years' labor, proving himself a man of genuine piety, great worth, and popular eloquence, he left America, with a view of returning to his native land; having never been heard of afterwards, it was thought that he found a watery grave.

With the exception of the Reverend John McLeod, it is not known that Reverend James Campbell had any ministerial brother residing in Cumberland or the adjoining counties, who could assist him in preaching to the Gaels. Although McAden preached in Duplin county, he was unable to render assistance because he was unfamiliar with the language of the Highlanders.

CHAPTER VI.

HIGHLANDERS IN GEORGIA.

The second distinctive and permanent settlement of Highland Scotch in the territory now constituting the United States of America was that in what was first called New Inverness on the Alatamaha river in Georgia, but now known as Darien, in McIntosh County. It was established under the genius of James Oglethorpe, an English general and philanthropist, who, in the year 1728, began to take active legislative support in behalf of the debtor classes, which culminated in the erection of the colony of Georgia, and incidentally to the formation of a settlement of Highlanders.

There was a yearly average in Great Britain of four thousand unhappy men immured in prison for the misfortune of being poor. A small debt exposed a person to a perpetuity of imprisonment; and one indiscreet contract often resulted in imprisonment for life. The sorrows hidden within the prison walls of Fleet and Marshalsea touched the heart of Oglethorpe—a man of merciful disposition and heroic mind—who was then in the full activity of middle life. His benevolent zeal persevered until he restored multitudes, who had long been in confinement for debt, and were now helpless and strangers in the land of their birth. Nor was this all: for them and the persecuted Protestants he planned an asylum in America, where former poverty would be no reproach, and where the simplicity of piety could indulge in the spirit of devotion without fear of persecution or rebuke.

The first active step taken by Oglethorpe, in his benevolent designs was to move, in the British House of Commons, that a committee be appointed "to inquire into the state of the gaols of the kingdom, and to report the same and their opinion thereupon to the House." Of this committee consisting of ninety-six per-

sons, embracing some of the first men in England, Oglethorpe was made chairman. They were eulogized by Thompson, in his poem on Winter, as
"The generous band,
Who, touched with human woe, redressive searched
Into the horrors of the gloomy gaol."
In the abodes of crime, and of misfortune, the committee beheld all that the poet depicted: "The freeborn Briton to the dungeon chained," and "Lives crushed out by secret, barbarous ways, that for their country would have toiled and bled." One of Britain's authors was moved to indite: "No modern nation has ever enacted or inflicted greater legal severities upon insolvent debtors than England."*

While the report of the committee did honor to their humanity, yet it was the moving spirit of Oglethorpe that prompted efforts to combine present relief with permanent benefits, by which honest but unfortunate industry could be protected, and the poor enabled to reap the fruit of their toils, which now wrung out their lives with bitter and unrequited labor. On June 9, 1732, a charter was procured from the king, incorporating a body by name and style of the Trustees for Establishing the Colony of Georgia in America. Among its many provisions was the declaration that "all and every person born within the said province shall have and enjoy all liberties, franchises and immunities of free denizens, as if abiding and born within Great Britain." It further ordained that there should be liberty of conscience, and free exercise of religion to all, except Papists. The patrons, by their own request, were restrained from receiving any grant of lands, or any emoluments whatever.

The charter had in view the settling of poor but unfortunate people on lands now waste and desolate, and also the interposing of the colony as a barrier between the French, Spanish and Indians on the south and west and the other English colonies on the north. Oglethorpe expressed the purpose of the colonizing scheme, in the following language:

"These trustees not only give land to the unhappy who go

---
*Graham's " History of United States," Vol. II, p. 179.

thither; but are also empowered to receive the voluntary contributions of charitable persons to enable them to furnish the poor adventurers with all necessaries for the expense of the voyage, occupying the land, and supporting them till they find themselves comfortably settled. So that now the unfortunate will not be obliged to bind themselves to a long servitude to pay for their passage; for they may be carried gratis into a land of liberty and plenty, where they immediately find themselves in possession of a competent estate, in a happier climate than they knew before; and they are unfortunate, indeed, if here they cannot forget their sorrow."*

Subsidiary to this it was designed to make Georgia a silk, wine, oil and drug-growing colony. It was calculated that the mother country would be relieved of a large body of indigent people and unfortunate debtors, and, at the same time, assist the commerce of Great Britain, increase home industries, and relieve, to an appreciative extent, the impost on foreign productions. Extravagant expectations were formed of the capabilities of Georgia by the enthusiastic friends of the movement. It was to rival Virginia and South Carolina, and at once to take the first rank in the list of provinces depending on the British crown. Its beauties and greatness were lauded by poets, statesmen and divines. It attracted attention throughout Europe, and to that promised land there pressed forward Swiss, German, Scotch and English alike. The benevolence of England was aroused, and the charities of an opulent nation began to flow towards the new plantation. The House of Parliament granted £10,000, which was augmented, by private subscription, to £36,000.

Oglethorpe had implicit faith in the enterprise, and with the first shipload, on board the Ann, he sailed from Gravesend November 17, 1732, and arrived at the bar, outside of the port of Charleston, South Carolina, January 13, 1733. Having accepted of a hearty welcome, he weighed anchor, and sailed directly for Port Royal; and while his colony was landing at Beaufort, he ascended the boundary river of Georgia, and selected the site for his chief town on the high bluff, where now is the city of Savannah. Having established his town, he then selected a command-

---

*"Georgia Historical Collections," Vol. I, p. 58.

ing height on the Ogeechee river, where he built a fortification and named it Fort Argyle, in honor of the friend and patron of his early years.

Within a period of five years over a thousand persons had been sent over on the Trustee's account; several freeholders, with their servants, had also taken up lands; and to them and to others also, settling in the province, over fifty-seven thousand acres had been granted. Besides forts and minor villages there had been laid out and settled the principal towns of Augusta, Ebenezer, Savannah, New Inverness, and Frederica. The colonists were of different nationalities, widely variant in character, religion and government. There were to be seen the depressed Briton from London; the hardy Gael from the Highlands of Scotland; the solemn Moravian from Herrnhut; the phlegmatic German from Salzburg in Bavaria; the reflecting Swiss from the mountainous and pastoral Grisons; the mercurial peasant from sunny Italy, and the Jew from Portugal.

The settlements were made deliberately and with a view of resisting any possible encroachments of Spain. It was a matter of protection that the Highlanders were induced to emigrate, and their assignment to the dangerous and outlying district, exposed to Spanish forays or invasions, is sufficient proof that their warlike qualities were greatly desired. Experience also taught Oglethorpe that the useless poor in England did not change their characters by emigration.

In company with a retinue of Indian chiefs, Oglethorpe returned to England on board the Aldborough man-of-war, where he arrived on June 16, 1734, after a passage of a little more than a month. His return created quite a sensation; complimentary verses were bestowed upon him, and his name was established among men of large views and energetic action as a distinguished benefactor of mankind. Among many things that engrossed his attention was to provide a bulwark against inroads that might be made by savages and dangers from the Spanish settlements; so he turned his eyes, as already noted, to the Highlands of Scotland. In order to secure a sufficient number of Highlanders a commission was granted to Lieutenant Hugh Mackay and George Dunbar to proceed to the Highlands and "raise 100 Men free or servants and for that purpose allowed to them the free passage of ten servants over and above the 100. They farther allowed them to take 50 Head of Women and Children and agreed with Mr. Simmonds to send a ship about, which he w'd not do unless they agreed for 130 Men Heads certain. This may have led the trust into the mistake That they were to raise only 130."*

The enterprising commissioners, using such methods as were customary to the country, soon collected the required number within the immediate vicinity of Inverness. They first enlisted the interest and consent of some of the chief gentlemen, and as they were unused to labor, they were not only permitted but required also to bring each a scrvant capable of supporting him. These gentlemen were not reckless adventurers, or reduced emigrants forced by necessity, or exiled by insolvency and want; but men of pronounced character, and especially selected for their approved military qualities, many of whom came from the glen of Stralbdean, about nine miles distant from Inverness. They were commanded by officers most highly connected in the Highlands. Their political sympathies were with the exiled house of Stuart, and having been more or less implicated in the rising of 1715, they found themselves objects of jealousy and suspicion, and thus circumstanced seized the opportunity to seek an asylum in America and obtain that unmolested quietude which was denied them in their native glens.

These people being deeply religious selected for their pastor, Reverend John MacLeod, a native of Skye, who belonged to the Dunvegan family of MacLeods. He was well recommended by his clerical brethren, and sustained a good examination before the presbytery of Edinburgh, previous to his ordination and commission, October 13, 1735. He was appointed by the directors of the Society in Scotland for Propagating Christian Knowledge (from whom he was to receive his annual stipend of £50) "not only to officiate as minister of the Gospel to the Highland families going

---

*Oglethorpe's letter to the Trustees, Feb. 13, 1736, in " Georgia Hist. Coll.," Vol. III, p. 10.

hither," and others who might be inclined to the Presbyterian form of worship, but "also to use his utmost endeavors for propagating Christian knowledge among natives in the colony."

The Trustees were greatly rejoiced to find that they had secured so valuable an acquisition to their colony, and that they could settle such a bold and hardy race on the banks of their southern boundary, and thus establish a new town on the Florida frontier. The town council of Inverness, in order to express their regard for Oglethorpe, on account of his kind offers to the Highlanders, conferred on him the honor of a burgess of the town, through his proxy, Captain George Dunbar.

Besides the military band, others, among whom were Mac-Kays, Bailies, Dunbars, and Cuthberts, applied for large tracts of land to people with their own servants; most of them going over themselves to Georgia, and finally settling there for life.

Of the Highlanders, some of them paid their passage and that of one out of two servants, while others paid passage for their servants and took the benefit of the trust passage for themselves. Some, having large families, wanted farther assistance for servants, which was acceded to by Captain Dunbar, who gave them the passage of four servants, which was his right, for having raised forty of the one hundred men. Of the whole number the Trustees paid for one hundred and forty-six, some of whom became indentured servants to the Trust. On October 20, 1735, one hundred and sixty-three were mustered before Provost Hassock at Inverness. One of the number ran away before the ship sailed, and two others were set on shore because they would neither pay their passage nor indent as servants to the Trust.

These pioneers, who were to carve their own fortunes and become a defense for the colony of Georgia, sailed from Inverness, October 18, 1735, on board the Prince of Wales, commanded by Captain George Dunbar, one of their own countrymen. They made a remarkably quick trip, attended by no accidents, and in January, 1736, sailed into Tybee Road, and at once the officer in charge set about sending the emigrants to their destination. All who so desired, at their own expense, were permitted to go up to Savannah and Joseph's Town. On account of a deficiency in boats, all could not be removed at once. Seven days after their arrival sixty-one were sent away, and on February 4th forty-six more proceeded to their settlement on the Alatamaha,—all of whom being under the charge of Hugh MacKay. Thus the advanced station, the post of danger, was guarded by a bold and hardy race; brave and robust by nature, virtuous by inclination, inured to fatigue and willing to labor:

"To distant climes, a dreary scene, they go,
Where wild Altama murmurs to their woe,
Far different these from all that charmed before,
The various terrors of that distant shore;
Those matted woods where birds forget to sing,
But silent bats in drowsy clusters cling;
Those poisonous fields with rank luxuriance crown'd,
Where the dark scorpion gathers death around,
Where at each step the stranger fears to wake
The rattling terrors of the vengeful snake,
Where crouching tigers wait their hapless prey,
And savage men, more murderous still than they.
Far different these from every former scene."
—Goldsmith.

On their first landing at Savannah, some of the people from South Carolina endeavored to discourage them by saying that the Spaniards would shoot them as they stood upon the ground where they contemplated erecting their homes. "Why then," said the Highlanders in reply, "we will beat them out of their fort and shall have houses ready built to live in." The spot designated for their town is located twenty miles northwest from St. Simons and ten above Frederica, and situated on the mainland, close to a branch of the Alatamaha river, on a bluff twenty feet high, then surrounded on all sides with woods. The soil is a brackish sand. Formerly Fort King George, garrisoned by an independent company, stood within a mile and a half of the new town, but had been abandoned and destroyed on account of a want of supplies and communication with Carolina. The village was called New Inverness, in honor of the city they had left in Scotland; while the surrounding district was named Darien, on account of the settlement attempted on the Isthmus of Darien, in 1698-1701. Under the direction of Hugh MacKay, who proved himself to be an excellent officer and a man of executive ability, by the middle of February they had constructed a fort consisting of two bastions and two half bastions, which was so strong that forty men could maintain it against three hundred, and on it placed four pieces, which, afterwards was so enlarged as to demand twelve cannon; built a guardhouse, storehouse, a chapel, and huts for the people. One of the men dying, the rest joined and built a house for the widow.

In the meantime Oglethorpe had sailed from London on board the Symonds, accompanied by the London Merchant, with additional emigrants, and arrived in the Tybee Road a short time after the Highlanders had left. He had never met them, and desiring to understand their ways and to make as favorable an impression on them as possible, he retained Captain Dunbar to go with him to the Highlanders and to instruct him fully in their customs. On February 22d he left St. Simons and rowing up the Alatamaha after three hours, reached the Highland settlement. Upon seeing the boat approaching, the Highlanders marched out to meet him, and made a most manly appearance in their plaids, with claymores, targets and fire-arms. Captain MacKay invited Oglethorpe to lie in his tent, where there was a bed with sheets —a rarity as yet in that part of the world. He excused himself, choosing to lie at the guard-fire, wrapped in his plaid, for he had on the Highland garb. Captain MacKay and the other gentlemen did the same, though the night was cold.

Oglethorpe had previously taken the precaution, lest the Highlanders might be apprehensive of an attack by the Spaniards, Indians, or other enemies, while their houses were in process of construction, to send Captain James McPherson, who commanded the rangers upon the Savannah, overland to support them. This troop arrived while Oglethorpe was yet present. Soon after they were visited by the Indians, who were attracted by their costume, and ever after retained an admiration for them, which was enhanced by the Highlanders entering into their wild sports, and joining them in the chase. In order to connect the new settlement with direct land communication with the other colonists, Oglethorpe, in March, directed Hugh MacKay, with a detachment of twelve rangers, to conduct Walter Augustin, who ran a traverse line from Savannah by Fort Argyle to Darien, in order to locate a roadway.

It was during Oglethorpe's first trip to the Highland settlement that he encamped on Cumberland island, and on the extreme western point, which commands the passage of boats from the southward, marked out a fort to be called St. Andrews, and gave Captain Hugh MacKay orders to build it. The work commenced immediately, thirty Highlanders being employed in the labor. On March 26th Oglethorpe, visiting the place, was astonished to find the fort in such an advanced stage of completion; the ditch was dug, the parapet was raised with wood and earth on the land side, and the small wood was cleared fifty yards round the fort. This seemed to be the more extraordinary because MacKay had no engineer, nor any other assistance in that way, except the directions originally given. Besides it was very difficult to raise the works, the ground being a loose sand. They were forced to lay the trees and sand alternately,—the trees preventing the sand from falling, and the sand the wood from fire. He returned thanks to the Highlanders and offered to take any of them back to their settlement, but all refused so long as there was any danger from the Spaniards, in whose vicinity they were now stationed. But two of them, having families at Darien, he ordered along with him.

The Highlanders were not wholly engaged in military pursuits, for, to a great extent, they were engaged in making their settlement permanent. They engaged in the cultivation of Indian corn and potatoes; learned to cut and saw timber, and laid out farms upon which they lived. For a frontier settlement, constantly menaced, all was accomplished that could be reasonably expected. In the woods they found ripe oranges and game, such as the wild turkey, buffalo and deer, in abundance. But peace and prosperity were not their allotted portion, for their lines were now cast in troubled waters. The first year witnessed an appeal to arms and a struggle with the Spaniards, which eventually resulted in a disaster to the Highlanders. Deeds of heroism were now enacted, fully in keeping with the tenor of the race.

The Spaniards, who had their main force at St. Augustine, were more or less aggressive, which kept the advanced posts in a state of alarm. John Mohr MacIntosh, who had seen service in Scotland, was directed by Oglethorpe to instruct the Highlanders in their military duty, and under his direction they were daily exercised. Hugh MacKay, with a company, had been directed to the immediate command of Oglethorpe.

Disputes early arose between the English colonists and the Spaniards regarding the frontier line between the two nationalities, and loud complaints were made by the latter on account of being harrassed by Indians. Oglethorpe took steps to restrain the Indians, and to the Spaniards sent friendly messengers, who were immediately seized and confined and at once took measures against the colonists. A Spanish warship sailed by St. Simon's island and passed Fort St. Andrews, but was not fired upon by the Highlanders because she answered their signals. She made her way back to St. Augustine when the report gained currency that the whole coast was covered with war boats armed with cannon. On June 8th the colonists were again threatened by a Spanish vessel which came close to Fort St. Andrews before she was discovered; but when challenged rowed away with the utmost precipitation. On board this boat was Don Ignatio with a detachment of the Spanish garrison, and as many boatmen and Indians as the launch could hold. It was at this time that a Highland lad named Fraser distinguished himself. Oglethorpe in endeavoring to meet the Spaniards by a flag of truce, or else obtain a conference with them, but unable to accomplish either, and being about to withdraw, saw the boy, whom he had sent forward, returning through the woods, driving before him a tall man with a musket on his shoulder, two pistols stuck in his girdle, and further armed with both a long and short sword. Coming up to Oglethorpe the lad said: "Here, sir; I have caught a Spaniard for you." The man was found to have in his possession a letter from Oglethorpe's imprisoned messengers which imparted certain information that proved to be of great value.

The imprisoned messengers were ultimately released and sent back in a launch with commissioners to treat with Oglethorpe.

In order to make a favorable impression on the Spaniards, the Highlanders, under Ensign MacKay, were ordered out. June 19th, Ensign MacKay arrived on board the man-of-war Hawk, then just off from Amelia island, with the Highlanders, and a detachment of the independent company, in their regimentals, who lined one side of the ship, while the Highlanders, with their claymores, targets, plaids, etc., did the same on the other side. The commissioners were very handsomely entertained on board the war vessel, and after dinner messages in writing were exchanged. While this hilarity and peace protestations were being indulged, an Indian brought the news that forty Spaniards and some Indians had fallen upon a party of the Creek nation who, then depending upon the general peace between the Indians, Spanish and English, without suspicion, and consequently without guard, were surrounded and surprised, several killed and others taken, two of whom, being boys, were murdered by dashing out their brains.

To the people of New Iverness the year 1737 does not appear to have been a propitious one. Pioneers were compelled to endure hardships of which they had little dreamed, and the Highland settlement was no exception to the rule. The record preserved for this year is exceedingly meagre and consists almost wholly in the sworn statement of Alexander Monroe, who deserted the colony in 1740. In the latter year he deposed that at Darien, where he arrived in 1736 with his wife and child, he had cleared, fenced in and planted five acres of land, built a good house in the town, and made other improvements, such as gardening, etc.; that he was never able to support his family by cultivation, though he planted the said five acres three years and had good crops, and that he never heard of any white man being able to gain a living by planting; that in 1737 the people were reduced to such distress for want of provisions, having neither corn, peas, rice, potatoes, nor bread-kind of any sort, nor fish, nor flesh of any kind in store; that they were forced to go in a body, with John Mohr MacIntosh at the head, to Frederica and there make a demand on the Trust's agent for a supply; that they were relieved by Captain Gascoigne of the Hawk, who spared them two barrels of flour, and one barrel of beef; and further, he launches an indictment against John Mohr MacIntosh, who had charge of the Trust's store at Darien, for giving the better class of food to his own hogs while the people were forced to take that which was rotten.*

While this statement of Monroe may possibly be true in the main, and that there was actual suffering, yet it must be borne in mind that the Highlanders were there living in a changed condition. The labor, climate, soil, products, etc., were all new to them, and to the changed circumstances the time had been too short for them to adapt themselves; nor is it probable that five acres were enough for their subsistence. The feeding of cattle, which was soon after adopted, would give them a larger field of industry.

Nor was this all. Inevitable war fell upon the people; for we learn that the troop of Highland rangers, under Captain MacKay, held Fort St. Andrews "with thirty men, when the Spaniards attempted the invasion of this Province with a great number of men in the year 1737."† Drawing the men away from the settlement would necessarily cause more or less suffering and disarrangement of affairs.

The record for the year 1738 is more extensive, although somewhat contradictory, and exhibits a strong element of dissention. Oglethorpe admitted the difficulties under which the people labored, ascribing them to the Spanish alarms, but reports that John Mohr MacIntosh, pursuant to orders from the Trust, had disposed of a part of the servants to the free-holders of Darien, which encouragement had enabled the settlement to continue.

"The women were a dead charge to the Trust, excepting a few who mended the Cloaths, dressed the Victuals and washed the Linnen of the Trustees Men Servants. Some of the Soldiers who were Highlanders desiring to marry Women, I gave them leave upon their discharging the Trustees from all future Charges arising from them."‡

---

*Georgia Hist. Society, Vol. II, p. 115. †*Ibid*, Vol. III, p. 114. Oglethorpe to H. Verelst, May 6, 1741. ‡Oglethorpe to H. Verelst, Dec. 21, 1738, Georgia Hist. Society, Vol. III p. 67.

The difficulties appear also to have arisen from the fact that the free-holders were either unable or else unwilling—which is the more likely—to perform manual labor. They labored under the want of a sufficient number of servants until they had procured some who had been indentured to the Trust for passage from Scotland.

The Reverend John MacLeod, who abandoned the colony in 1741, made oath that in the year 1738 they found by experience that the produce from the land did not answer the expense of time and labor, and the voice of the people of Darien was to abandon their improvements, and settle to the northward, where they could be free from the restraints which rendered incapable of subsisting themselves and families.* The declaration of Alexander Monroe is still more explicit:

"That in December, 1738, the said inhabitants of Darien finding that from their first settling in Georgia, their labors turned to no account, that their wants were daily growing on them, and being weary of apprehension, they came to a resolution to depute two men, chosen from amongst them, to go to Charleston, in South Carolina, and there to make application to the government, in order to obtain a grant of lands to which the whole settlement of Darien to a man were to remove altogether, the said John McIntosh More excepted; but that it being agreed among them, first to acquaint the said Colonel with their intentions, and their reasons for such resolutions, John McIntosh L. (Lynvilge) was employed by the said free-holders to lay the same before him, who returned them an answer 'that they should have credit for provisions, with two cows and three calves, and a breeding mare if they would continue on their plantations.' That the people with the view of these helps, and hoping for the further favor and countenance of the said Colonel, and being loth to leave their little all behind them, and begin the world in a strange place, were willing to make out a livelihood in the colony; but whilst they were in expectation of these things, this deponent being at his plantation, two miles from the town, in Dec., 1738, he received a letter from Ronald McDonald, which was sent by order of the said McIntosh More, and brought to this deponent by William, son of the said McIntosh, ordering him, the said deponent, immediately to come himself, and bring William Monro along with

---

*Georgia Hist. Society, Vol. II, p. 113.

him to town, and advising him that, 'if he did so, he would be made a man of, but, that if he did not, he would be ruined forever.' That this deponent coming away without loss of time, he got to the said McIntosh More's house about nine of the clock that night, where he found several of the inhabitants together, and where the said McIntosh More did tell this deponent, 'that if he would sign a paper, which he then offered him, that the said Colonel would give him cattle and servants from time to time, and that he would be a good friend to as many as would sign the said paper, but that they would see what would become of those that would not sign it, for that the people of Savannah would be all ruined, who opposed the said Colonel in it.' That this deponent did not know the contents of the said paper, but seeing that some before him had signed it, his hopes on one side, and fears on the other, made him sign it also. That upon his conversing with some of the people, after leaving the house, he was acquainted with the contents and design of said paper, which this deponent believes to be the petition from the eighteen, which the trustees have printed, and that very night he became sensible of the wrong he had done; and that his conscience did thereupon accuse him, and does yet."*

The phrase "being weary of oppression" has reference to the accusation against Captain Hugh MacKay, who was alleged to have "exercised an illegal power there, such as judging in all causes, directing and ordering all things according to his will, as did the said McIntosh More, by which many unjust and illegal things were done. That not only the servants of the said freeholders of Darien were ordered to be tied up and whipt; but also this deponent, and Donald Clark, who themselves were free-holders, were taken into custody, and bound with ropes, and threatened to be sent to Frederica to Mr. Horton, and there punished by him; this deponent, once for refusing to cry 'All's well,' when he was an out-sentry, he having before advised them of the danger of so doing, lest the voice should direct the Indians to fire upon the sentry, as they had done the night before, and again for drumming with his fingers on the side of his house, it being pretended that he had alarmed the town. That upon account of these, and many other oppressions, the free-holders applied to Mr. Oglethorpe for a court of justice to be erected, and proper magistrates in Darien, as in other towns in Georgia, that they might have justice done among themselves, when he gave them for an-

---

*Georgia Hist. Coll. Vol. II, p. 116.

swer, 'that he would acquaint the trustees with it'; but that this deponent heard no more of it."*

One of the fundamental regulations of the Trustees was the prohibition of African slavery in Georgia. However, they had instituted a system of servitude which indentured both male and female to individuals, or the Trustees, for a period of from four to fourteen years. On arriving in Georgia, their services were sold for the term of indenture, or apportioned to the inhabitants by the magistrates, as their necessities required. The sum which they brought when thus bid off varied from £2 to £6, besides an annual tax of £1 for five years to defray the expense of their voyage. Negro slavery was agitated in Savannah, and on December 9, 1738, a petition was addressed to the Trustees, signed by one hundred and sixteen, and among other things asked was the introduction of Negro slavery. On January 3, 1739, a counter petition was drawn up and signed by the Highlanders at Darien. On March 13th the Saltzburghers of Ebenezer signed a similar petition in which they strongly disapproved of the introduction of slave labor into the colony. Likewise the people of Frederica prepared a petition, but desisted from sending it, upon an assurance that their apprehensions of the introduction of Negroes were entirely needless. Many artifices were resorted to in order to gain over the Highlanders and have them petition for Negro slaves. Failing in this letters were written to them from England endeavoring to intimidate them into a compliance. These counter petitions strengthened the Trustees in their resolution. It is a noticeable fact, and worthy of record, that at the outbreak of the American Revolution the Highlanders of Darien again protested against African slavery.

Those persons dissatisfied with the state of affairs increased in numbers and gradually grew more rancorous. It is not supposable that they could have bettered the condition under the circumstances. Historians have been universal in their praise of Oglethorpe, and in all probability no one could have given a better administration. His word has been taken without question.

---

*Ibid.

He declared that "Darien hath been one of the Settlements where the People have been most industrious as those of Savannah have been most idle. The Trustees have had several Servants there who under the direction of Mr. Moore McIntosh have not only earned their bread but have provided the Trust with such Quantities of sawed stuff as hath saved them a great sum of money. Those Servants cannot be put under the direction of anybody at Frederica nor any one that does not understand the Highland language. The Woods fit for sawing are near Darien and the Trustees engaged not to separate the Highlanders. They are very useful under their own Chiefs and no where else. It is very necessary therefore to allow Mr. Mackintosh for the overseeing the Trust's Servants at Darien."*

That such was the actual condition of affairs in 1739 there is no doubt. However, a partial truth may change the appearance. George Philp, who at Savannah in 1740, declared that for the same year the people "are as incapable of improving their lands and raising produces as the people in the northern division, as appears from the very small quantity of Indian corn which hitherto had been the chief and almost only produce of the province, some few potatoes excepted; and as a proof of which, that he was in the south in May last, when the season for planting was over, and much less was done at Frederica than in former years; and that the people in Darien did inform him, that they had not of their own produce to carry to market, even in the year 1739, which was the most plentiful year they ever saw there, nor indeed any preceding year; nor had they (the people of Darien) bread-kind of their own raising, sufficient for the use of their families, from one crop to another, as themselves, or some of them, did tell this deponent; and further, the said people of Darien were, in May last, repining at their servants being near out of their time, because the little stock of money they carried over with them was exhausted in cultivation which did not bring them a return; and they were thereby rendered quite unable to plant their lands, or help themselves anyway."†

It was one of the agreements made by the Trust that assistance should be given the colonists. Hence Oglethorpe speaks of "the £58 delivered to Mr. McIntosh at Darien, it was to support the Inhabitants of Darien with cloathing and delivered to the Trustees' Store there, for which the Individuals are indebted to

---

*Oglethorpe to the Trustees, Oct. 20, 1739. Georgia Hist. Coll., Vol. III, p. 90. †Georgia Hist. Coll., Vol. II, p. 119.

the Trust. Part of it was paid in discharge of service done to the Trustees in building, Part is still due and some do pay and are ready to pay."*

The active war with Spain commenced by the murder of two unarmed Highlanders on Amelia Island, who had gone into the woods for fuel. It was November 14, 1739, that a party of Spaniards landed on the island and skulked in the woods. Francis Brooks, who commanded a scout boat, heard reports of musketry, and at once signaled the fort, when a lieutenant's squad marched out and found the murdered Highlanders with their heads cut off and cruelly mangled. The Spaniards fled with so much precipitation that the squad could not overtake them, though they pursued rapidly. Immediately Oglethorpe began to collect around him his inadequate forces for the invasion of Florida. In January, 1740, he received orders to make hostile movements against Florida, with the assurance that Admiral Vernon should co-operate with him. Oglethorpe took immediate action, drove in the Spanish outposts and invaded Florida, having learned from a deserter that St. Augustine was in want of provisions. South Carolina rendered assistance; and its regiment reached Darien the first of May, where it was joined by Oglethorpe's favorite corps, the Highlanders, ninety strong, commanded by Captain John Mohr McIntosh and Lieutenant MacKay. They were ordered, accompanied by an Indian force, to proceed by land, at once, to Cow-ford (afterwards Jacksonville), upon the St. Johns. With four hundred of his regiment, Oglethorpe, on May 3d, left Frederica, in boats, and on the 9th reached the Cow-ford. The Carolina regiment and the Highlanders having failed to make the expected junction at that point, Oglethorpe, who would brook no delay, immediately proceeded against Fort Diego, which surrendered on the 10th, and garrisoned it with sixty men under Lieutenant Dunbar. With the remainder he returned to the Cow-ford, and there met the Carolina regiment and McIntosh's Highlanders. Here Oglethorpe massed nine hundred soldiers and eleven hun-

---

*Oglethorpe to H. Verelst, Dec. 29, 1739. Georgia Hist. Coll., Vol. III, p. 96.

dred Indians, and marched the whole force against Fort Moosa, which was built of stone, and situated less than two miles from St. Augustine, which the Spaniards evacuated without offering resistance. Having burned the gates, and made three breaches in the walls, Oglethorpe then proceeded to reconnoitre the town and castle. Assisted by some ships of war lying at anchor off St. Augustine bar, he determined to blockade the town. For this purpose he left Colonel Palmer, with ninety-five Highlanders and fifty-two Indians, at Fort Moosa, with instructions to scour the woods and intercept all supplies for the enemy; and, for safety, encamp every night at different places. This was the only party left to guard the land side. The Carolina regiment was sent to occupy a point of land called Point Quartel, about a mile distant from the castle; while he himself with his regiment and the greater part of the Indians embarked in boats, and landed on the Island of Anastatia, where he erected batteries and commenced a bombardment of the town. The operations of the beseigers beginning to relax, the Spanish commander sent a party of six hundred to surprise Colonel Palmer at Fort Moosa. The Spaniards had noted that for five nights Colonel Palmer had made Fort Moosa his resting place. They came in boats with muffled oars at the dead of night, and landed unheard and undiscovered. The Indians, who were relied on by Palmer, were watching the land side, but never looked towards the water.

Captain MacIntosh had remonstrated with Colonel Palmer for remaining at Fort Moosa more than one night, until it produced an alienation between them. The only thing then left for MacIntosh was to make his company sleep on their arms. At the first alarm they were in rank, and as the Spanish infantry approached in three columns they were met with a Highland shout.

The contest was unequal, and although the Highlanders rallied to the support of MacIntosh, their leader, and fought with desperation, yet thirty-six of them fell dead or wounded at the first charge. When Colonel Palmer saw the overwhelming force that assaulted his command, he directed the rangers without the wall to fly; but, refusing to follow them, he paid the debt of his obstinacy with his blood.

The surprise at Fort Moosa led to the failure of Oglethorpe's expedition. John Mohr MacIntosh was a prisoner, and as Oglethorpe had no officer to exchange for him, he was sent to Spain, where he was detained several years—his fate unknown to his family—and when he did return to his family it was with a broken constitution and soon to die, leaving his children to such destiny as might await them, without friends, in the wilds of America, for the one who could assist them—General Oglethorpe—was to be recalled, in preparation to meet the Highland Rising of 1745, when he, too, was doomed to suffer degradation from the duke of Cumberland, and injury to his military reputation.

It was the same regiment of Spaniards that two years later was brought from Cuba to lead in all enterprises that again was destined to meet the remnant of those Highlanders, but both the scene and the result were different. It was in the light of day, and blood and slaughter, but not victory awaited them.

The conduct of the eldest son of John Mohr MacIntosh is worthy of mention. He was named after his grand uncle, the celebrated Old Borlum (General William MacIntosh), who commanded a division of the Highlanders in the Rising of 1715. William was not quite fourteen years of age when his father left Darien for Florida. He wished to accompany the army, but his father refused. Determined not to be thwarted in his purpose, he overtook the army at Barrington. He was sent back the next day under an armed guard. Taking a small boat, he ferried up to Clarke's Bluff, on the south side of the Alatamaha, intending to keep in the rear until the troops had crossed the St. Mary's river. He soon fell in with seven Indians, who knew him, for Darien had become a great rendezvous for them, and were greatly attached to the Highlanders, partly on account of their wild manners, their manly sports and their costume, somewhat resembling their own. They caressed the boy, and heartily entered into his views. They followed the advancing troops and informed him of all that transpired in his father's camp, yet carefully concealing his presence among them until after the passage of the St. Mary's, where, with much triumph, led him to his father and said "that he was a young warrior and would fight; that the Great Spirit would watch over his life, for he loved young warriors." He followed his father until he saw him fall at Fort Moosa, covered with wounds, which so transfixed him with horror, that he was not aroused to action until a Spanish officer laid hold of his plaid. Light and as elastic as a steel bow, he slipped from under his grasp, and made his escape with the wreck of the corps.

Those who escaped the massacre went over in a boat to Point Quartel. Some of the Chickasaw Indians, who also had escaped, met a Spaniard, cut off his head and presented it to Oglethorpe. With abhorence he rejected it, calling them barbarian dogs and bidding them begone. As might be expected, the Chickasaws were offended and deserted him. A party of Creeks brought four Spanish prisoners to Oglethorpe, who informed him that St. Augustine had been reinforced by seven hundren men and a large supply of provisions. The second day after the Fort Moosa affair, the Carolina* regiment deserted, the colonel leading the rout; nor did he arrest his flight until darkness overtook him, thirty miles from St. Augustine. Other circumstances operating against him, Oglethorpe commenced his retreat from Florida and reached Frederica July 10, 1740.

The inhabitants of Darien continued to live in huts that were tight and warm. Prior to 1740 they had been very industrious in planting, besides being largely engaged in driving cattle for the regiment; but having engaged in the invasion of Florida, little could be done at home, where their families remained. One writer† declared that "the people live very comfortably, with great unanimity. I know of no other settlement in this colony more desirable, except Ebenezer." The settlement was greatly decimated on account of the number killed and taken prisoners at Fort Moosa. This gave great discontent on the part of those who already felt aggrieved against the Trust.

The discontent among many of the colonists, some of whom were influential, again broke out in 1741, some of whom went to Savannah, October 7th, to consider the best method of presenting their grievances. They resolved to send an agent to England

---

*See Appendix, Note H. †Thomas Jones, dated Savannah, Sept. 18, 1740 Georgia Hist. Coll., Vol. I, p. 200.

to represent their case to the proper authorities, "in order to the effectual settling and establishing of the said province, and to remove all those grievances and hardships we now labor under." The person selected as agent was Thomas Stevens, the son of the president of Georgia, who had resided there about four years, and who, it was thought, from his connection with the president, would give great weight to the proceedings. Mr. Stevens sailed for England on March 26, 1742, presented his petition to parliament, which was considered together with the answer of the Trustees; which resulted in Mr. Stevens being brought to the bar of the House of Commons, and upon his knees, before the assembled counsellors of Great Britain, was reprimanded for his conduct, and then discharged, on paying his fees.

A list of the people who signed the petition and counter petions affords a good criterion of the class represented at Darien, living there before and after the battle of Moosa. Among the complainants may be found the names of:

James Campbell, Thomas Fraser, Patrick Grahame, John Grahame, John McDonald, Peter McKay, Benjamin McIntosh, John McIntosh, Daniel McKay, Farquhar McGuilvery, Daniel McDonald, Rev. John McLeod, Alexander Monro, John McIntire, Owen McLeod, Alexander Rose, Donald Stewart.

It is not certain that all the above were residents of Darien. Among those who signed the petition in favor of the Trust, and denominated the body of the people, and distinctly stated to be living at Darien, are the names of:

John Mackintosh Moore, John Mackintosh Lynvilge, Ronald McDonald, Hugh Morrison, John McDonald, John Maclean, John Mackintosh, son of L., John Mackintosh Bain, John McKay, Daniel Clark, first, Alexander Clarke, Donald Clark, third, Joseph Burges, Donald Clark, second, Archibald McBain, Alexander Munro, William Munro, John Cuthbert.

During the autumn of 1741, Reverend John McLeod abandoned his Highland charge at Darien, went to South Carolina and settled at Edisto. In an oath taken November 12, 1741, he represents the people of Darien to be in a deplorable condition. Oglethorpe, in his letter to the Trustees,* evidently did not think

---

*Dated April 28 1741. Georgia Hist. Coll., Vol. III, p. 113.

Mr. McLeod was the man really fit for his position, for he says: "We want here some men fit for schoolmasters, one at Frederica and one at Darien, also a sedate and sober minister, one of some experience in the world and whose first heat of youth is over."

The long-threatened invasion of Carolina and Georgia by the Spaniards sailed from Havana, consisting of a great fleet, among which were two half galleys, carrying one hundred and twenty men each and an eighteen-pound gun. A part of the fleet, on June 20th, was seen off the harbor of St. Simons, and the next day in Cumberland Sound. Oglethorpe dispatched two companies in three boats to the relief of Fort William, on Cumberland island, which were forced to fight their way through the fire from the Spanish galleys. Soon after thirty-two sail came to anchor off the bar, with the Spanish colors flying, and there remained five days. They landed five hundred men at Gascoin's bluff, on July 5th. Oglethorpe blew up Fort William, spiked the guns and signalled his ships to run up to Frederica, and with his land forces retired to the same place, where he arrived July 6th. The day following the enemy were within a mile of Frederica. When this news was brought to Oglethorpe he took the first horse he found and with the Highland company, having ordered sixty men of the regiment to follow, he set off on a gallop to meet the Spaniards, whom he found to be one hundred and seventy strong, including forty-five Indians. With his Indian Rangers and ten Highlanders, who outran the rest of the company, he immediately attacked and defeated the Spaniards. After pursuing them a mile, he halted his troops and posted them to advantage in the woods, leaving two companies of his regiment with the Highlanders and Indians to guard the way, and then returned to Frederica to await further movements of the enemy. Finding no immediate movement on the part of his foes, Oglethorpe, with the whole force then at Frederica, except such as were absolutely necessary to man the batteries, returned to the late field of action, and when about half way met two platoons of his troops, with the great body of his Indians, who declared they had been broken by the whole Spanish force, which assailed them in the woods; and the enemy were now in pursuit, and would soon be upon them. Notwithstanding this disheartening report, Oglethorpe continued his march, and to his great satisfaction, found that Lieutenants Southerland and MacKay, with the Highlanders alone, had defeated the enemy, consisting of six hundred men, and killed more of them than their own force numbered. At first the Spanish forces overwhelmed the colonists by their superior numbers, when the veteran troops became seized with a panic. They made a precipitate retreat, the Highlanders following reluctantly in the rear. After passing through a defile, LieutenantMacKay communicated to his friend, Lieutenant Southerland, who commanded the rear guard, composed also of Highlanders, the feelings of his corps, and agreeing to drop behind as soon as the whole had passed the defile. They returned through the brush and took post at the two points of the crescent in the road. Four Indians remained with them. Scarcely had they concealed themselves in the woods, when the Spanish grenadier regiment, the *elite* of their troops, advanced into the defile, where, seeing the footprints of the rapid retreat of the broken troops, and observing their right was covered by an open morass, and their left, as they supposed, by an impracticable wall of brushwood, and a border of dry white sand, they stacked their arms and sat down to partake of refreshments, believing that the contest for the day was over. Southerland and MacKay, who, from their hiding places, had anxiously watched their movements, now from either end of the line raised the Highland cap upon a sword, the signal for the work of death to begin. Immediately the Highlanders poured in upon the unsuspecting enemy a well delivered and most deadly fire. Volley succeeded volley, and the sand was soon strewed with the dead and the dying. Terror and dismay seized the Spaniards, and making no resistance attempted to fly along the marsh. A few of their officers attempted, though in vain, to re-form their broken ranks; discipline was gone; orders were unheeded; safety alone was sought; and, when, with a Highland shout of triumph, the hidden foe burst among them with levelled musket and flashing claymore, the panic stricken Spaniards fled in every direction; some to the marsh, where they mired and were taken; others along the defile, where they were met by the claymore, and still others into the thicket, where they became entangled and perished; and a few succeeded in escaping to their camp. Barba was taken, though mortally wounded. Among the killed were a captain, lieutenant, two sergeants, two drummers and one hundred and sixty privates, and a captain and nineteen men taken prisoners. This feat of arms was as brilliant as it was successful. Oglethorpe, with the two platoons, did not reach the scene of action, since called the "Bloody Marsh," until the victory was won. To show his sense of the services rendered, he promoted the brave young officers who had gained it on the very field of their valor. But he rested only for a few minutes, waiting for the marines and the reserve of the regiment to come up; and then pursued the retreating enemy to within a mile and a half of their camp. During the night the foe retreated within the ruins of the fort, and under the protection of their cannon. A few days later the Spaniards became so alarmed on the appearance of three vessels off the bar that they immediately set fire to the fort and precipitately embarked their troops, abandoning in their hurry and confusion, several cannon, a quantity of military stores, and even leaving unburied some of the men who had just died of their wounds.

The massacre of Fort Moosa was more than doubly avenged, and that on the same Spanish regiment that was then victorious. On the present occasion they had set out from their camp with the determination to show no quarter. In the action William MacIntosh, now sixteen years of age, was conspicuous. No shout rose higher, and no sword waved quicker than his on that day. The tract of land which surrounded the field of action was afterwards granted to him.

A brief sketch of Ensign John Stuart will not be out of place in this record and connection. During the Spanish invasion he was stationed at Fort William, and there gained an honorable reputation in holding it against the enemy. Afterwards he became the celebrated Captain Stuart and father of Sir John Stuart, the victor over General Ranier, at the battle of Maida, in Calabria.

In 1757 Captain Stuart was taken prisoner at Fort Loudon, in the Cherokee country, and whose life was saved by his friend, Attakullakulla. This ancient chief had remembered Captain Stuart when he was a young Highland officer under General Oglethorpe, although years had rolled away. The Indians were now filled with revenge at the treachery of Governor Littleton, of Carolina, on account of the imprisonment and death of the chiefs of twenty towns; yet no actions of others could extinguish, in this generous and high-minded man, the friendship of other years. The dangers of that day, the thousand wiles and accidents Captain Stuart escaped from, made him renowned among the Indians, and centered on him the affections and confidence of the southern tribes. It was the same Colonel John Stuart, of the Revolutionary War, who, from Pensacola, directed at will the movements of the Cherokees, Creeks, Chickasaws and Choctaws, against all, save Georgia. That state suffered but little from Indian aggression during the War for Independence. Nor was that feeling extinct among the Creeks for a period of fifty years, or until they believed that the people of Oglethorpe had passed away.

The year 1743 opened with fresh alarms of a new invasion, jointly of the French and Spanish. The Governor of Cuba offered to invade Georgia and Carolina, with ten thousand men, most of whom were then in Havanna. Oglethorpe, with his greatly reduced force, was left alone to bear the burden of defending Georgia. Believing that a sudden blow would enhance his prospects, he took his measures, and accordingly, on Saturday, February 26, 1743, the detachment destined for Florida, consisting of a portion of the Highlanders, rangers and regulars, appeared under arms at Frederica, and on March 9th, landed in Florida. He advanced upon St. Augustine, and used every device to decoy them into an ambush, but even failed to provoke the garrison. Having no cannon with him, he returned to Frederica, without the loss of a man. This expedition was attended with great toil, fatigue and privation, but borne cheerfully. A few slight eruptive efforts were made, but each party kept its own borders, and the slight conflicts in America were lost in the universal conflagration in Europe.

The Highlanders had borne more than their share of the burdens of war, and had lost heavily. Their families had shared in their privations. The majority had remained loyal to Oglethorpe, and proved that in every emergency they could be depended on. In later years the losses were partially supplied by accessions from their countrymen.

With all the advantages that Georgia offered and the inducements held out to emigrants, the growth was very slow. In 1761 the whole number of white inhabitants amounted to but sixty-one hundred. However, in 1773, or twelve years later, it had leaped to eighteen thousand white and fifteen thousand black. The reasons assigned for this increase were the great inducements held out to people to come and settle where they could get new and good lands at a moderate cost, with plenty of good range for cattle, horses and hogs, and where they would not be so pent up and confined as in the more thickly settled provinces.

The MacIntoshes had ever been foremost, and in the attempt to consolidate Georgia with Carolina they were prominent in their opposition to the scheme.

Forty years in America had endeared the Highlanders of Darien to the fortunes of their adopted country. The children knew of none other, save as they heard it from the lips of their parents. Free in their inclinations, and with their environments it is not surprising that they should become imbued with the principles of the American Revolution. Their foremost leader, who gained imperishable renown, was Lachlan MacIntosh, son of John Mor. His brother, William, also took a very active part, and made great sacrifices. At one time he was pursued beyond the Alatamaha and his negroes taken from him.

To what extent the Darien Highlanders espoused the cause of Great Britain would be difficult to fathom, but in all probability to no appreciable extent. The records exhibit that there were some royalists there, although when under British sway may have been such as a matter of protection, which was not uncommon throughout the Southern States. The record is exceedingly brief. On May 20, 1780, Charles McDonald, justice of peace for St. Andrew's parish (embracing Darien), signed the address to the King. Sir James Wright, royal governor of Georgia, writing to lord George Germain, dated February 16, 1782, says:

"Yesterday my Lord I Received Intelligence that two Partys of about 140 in the whole were gone over the Ogechee Ferry towards the Alatamaha River & had been in St. Andrews Parish (a Scotch settlement) & there Murdered 12 or 13 Loyal Subjects."*

The Highlanders were among the first to take action, and had no fears of the calamities of war. The military spirit of their ancestors showed no deterioration in their constitutions. During the second week in January, 1775, a district congress was held by the inhabitants of St. Andrew's Parish (now Darien), at which a series of resolutions were passed, embodying, with great force and earnestness, the views of the freeholders of that large and flourishing district. These resolutions, six in number, expressed first, their approbation of "the unparalleled moderation, the decent, but firm and manly, conduct of the loyal and brave people of Boston and Massachusetts Bay, to preserve their liberty;" their approval of "all the resolutions of the Grand American Congress," and their hearty and "cheerful accession to the association entered into by them, as the wisest and most moderate measure that could be adopted." The second resolution condemned the closing of the land offices, to the great detriment of Colonial growtn, and to the injury of the industrious poor, declaring "that all encouragement should be given to the poor of every nation by every generous American." The third, animadverted upon the ministerial mandates which prevented colonial assemblies from passing such laws as the general exigencies of the provinces required, an especial grievance, as they affirmed, "in this young colony, where our internal police is not yet well settled." The fourth condemned the practice of making colonial officers dependent for salaries on Great Britain, "thus making them independent of the people, who should support them according to their usefulness and behavior." The fifth resolution declares "our disapprobation and abhorrence of the unnatural practice of slavery in America," and their purpose to urge "the manumission of our slaves in this colony, upon the most safe and equitable footing

---
*Georgia Hist. Coll., Vol. III, p. 370.

for the masters and themselves." And, lastly, they thereby chose delegates to represent the parish in a provincial congress, and instruct them to urge the appointment of two delegates to the Continental Congress, to be held in Philadelphia, in May.

Appended to these resolutions were the following articles of agreement or association:

"Being persuaded that the salvation of the rights and liberties of America depend, under God, on the firm union of the inhabitants in its vigorous prosecution of the measures necessary for its safety, and convinced of the necessity of preventing the anarchy and confusion which attend the dissolution of the powers of government, we, the freemen, freeholders, and inhabitants of the province of Georgia, being greatly alarmed at the avowed design of the Ministry to raise a revenue in America, and shocked by the bloody scene now acting in the Massachusetts Bay, do, in the most solemn manner, resolve never to become slaves; and do associate, under all the ties of religion, honor and love of country, to adopt and endeavor to carry into execution, whatever may be recommended by the Continental Congress, or resolved upon by our Provincial Convention that shall be appointed, for the purpose of preserving our Constitution, and opposing the execution of the several arbitrary and oppressive acts of the British Parliament, until a reconciliation between Great Britain and America, on constitutional principles, which we most ardently desire, can be obtained; and that we will in all things follow the advice of our general committee, to be appointed, respecting the purposes aforesaid, the preservation of peace and good order, and the safety of individuals and private property."

Among the names appended to these resolutions there may be selected such as:

Lach. McIntosh, Charles McDonald, John McIntosh, Samuel McClelland, Jno. McCulloch, William McCullough, John McClelland, Seth McCullough.

On July 4, 1775, the Provincial Congress met at Tondee's Long Room, Savannah. Every parish and district was represented. St. Andrew's parish sent:

Jonathan Cochran, William Jones, Peter Tarlin, Lachlan McIntosh, William McIntosh, George Threadcroft, John Wesent, Roderick McIntosh, John Witherspoon, George McIntosh, Allen Stuart, John McIntosh, Raymond Demere.

The resolutions adopted by these hardy patriots were sacredly kept. Their deeds, however, partake more of personal narration, and only their heroic defense need be mentioned. The following narration should not escape special notice:

On the last of February, 1776, the Scarborough, Hinchinbroke, St. John, and two large transports, with soldiers, then lying at Tybee, came up the river and anchored at five fathoms. On March 2nd, two of the vessels sailed up the channel of Back river, The Hinchinbroke, in attempting to go round Hutchinson's island, and so come down upon the shipping from above, grounded at the west end of the island, opposite Brampton. During the night there landed from the first vessel, between two and three hundred troops, under the command of Majors Grant and Maitland, and silently marched across Hutchinson's island, and through collusion with the captains were embarked by four A. M., in the merchant vessels which lay near the store on that island. The morning of the 3rd revealing the close proximity of the enemy caused great indignation among the people. Two companies of riflemen, under Major Habersham, immediately attacked the grounded vessel and drove every man from its deck. By nine o'clock it became known that troops had been secreted on board the merchantmen, which news created intense excitement, and three hundred men, under Colonel McIntosh, were marched to Yamacraw Bluff, opposite the shipping, and there threw up a hasty breast-work, through which they trained three four-pounders to bear upon the vessels. Anxious, however, to avoid bloodshed, Lieutenant Daniel Roberts, of the St. John's Rangers, and Mr. Raymond Demere, of St. Andrew's Parish, solicited, and were permitted by the commanding officer, to go on board and demand a surrender of Rice and his people, who, with his boat's crew, had been forcibly detained. Although, on a mission of peace, no sooner had they reached the vessel, on board of which was Captain Barclay and Major Grant, than they were seized and detained as prisoners. The people on shore, after waiting a sufficient length of time, hailed the vessel, through a speaking-trumpet, and demanded the return of all who were detained on board; but receiving only insulting replies, they discharged two four-pounders at the vessel; whereupon they solicited that the people should send on board two men in whom they most confided, and with them they agreed to negotiate. Twelve of the Rangers, led by Captain Screven, of the St. John's Rangers, and Captain Baker, were immediately rowed under the stern of the vessel and there peremptorily demanded the deputies. Incensed by insulting language, Captain Baker fired a shot, which immediately drew on his boat a discharge of swivels and small arms. The batteries then opened, which was briskly answered for the space of four hours. The next step was to set fire to the vessels, the first being the Inverness, which drifted upon the brig Nelly, which was soon in flames. The officers and soldiers fled from the vessels, in the utmost precipitation across the low marshes and half-drained rice-fields, several being killed by the grape shot played upon them. As the deputies were still held prisoners, the Council of Safety, on March 6th, put under arrest all the members of the Royal Council then in Savannah, besides menacing the ships at Tybee. An exchange was not effected until the 27th."

As already stated, Darien experienced some of the vicissitudes of war. On April 18, 1778, a small army, under Colonel Elbert, embarked on the galleys Washington, Lee and Bullock, and by 10 o'clock next morning, near Frederica, had captured the brigantine Hinchinbroke, the sloop Rebecca and a prize brig, which had spread terror on the coast.

In 1779 the parishes of St. John, St. Andrew and St. James were erected into one county, under the name of Liberty.

In March, 1780, the royal governor, Sir James Wright, attempted to re-establish the old government, and issued writs returnable May 5. Robert Baillie and James Spalding were returned from St. Andrew's parish.

The settlement of Darien practically remained a pure Highland one until the close of the Revolution. The people proved themselves faithful and loyal to the best interests of the commonwealth, and equal to such exigencies as befell them. While disasters awaited them and fierce ordeals were passed through, yet fortune eventually smiled upon them.

CHAPTER VII.

Captain Lauchlan Campbell's New York Colony.

The fruitful soil of America, together with the prospects of a home and an independent living, was peculiarly adapted to awaken noble aspirations in the breasts of those who were interested in the welfare of that class whose condition needed a radical enlargement. Among this class of Nature's noblemen there is no name deserving of more praise than that of Lauchlan Campbell. Although his name, as well as the migration of his infant colony, has gone out of Islay ken, where he was born, yet his story has been fairly well preserved in the annals of the province of New York. It was first publicly made known by William Smith, in his "History of New York."

Lauchlan Campbell was possessed of a high sense of honor and a good understanding; was active, loyal, of a military disposition, and, withal, strong philanthropic inclinations. By placing implicit confidence in the royal governors of New York, he fell a victim to their roguery, deception and heartlessness, which ultimately crushed him and left him almost penniless. The story has been set forth in the following memorial, prepared by his son:

"Memorial of Lieutenant Campbell to the Lords of Trade. To the Right Honourable the Lords Commissioners of Trade, &c. Memorial of Lieut. Donald Campbell of the Province of New York Plantation. Humbly Showeth,

That in the year 1734 Colonel Cosby being then Governor of the Province of New York by and with the advice and assent of his Council published a printed Advertisement for encouraging the Resort of Protestants from Europe to settle upon the Northern Frontier of the said Province (in the route from Fort Edward to Crown Point) promising to each family two hundred acres of unimproved land out of 100,000 acres purchased from the Indians, without any fee or expences whatsoever, except a very moderate charge for surveying & liable only to the King's Quit

Rent of one shilling and nine pence farthing per hundred acres, which settlement would at that time have been of the utmost utility to the Province & these proposals were looked upon as so advantageous, that they could not fail of having a proper effect.

That these Proposals in 1737, falling into the hands of Captain Lauchlin Campbell of the Island of Isla, he the same year went over to North America, and passing through the Province of Pennsilvania where he rejected many considerable offers that were made him, he proceeded to New York, where, tho' Governor Cosby was deceased, George Clarke Esqr. then Governor, assured him no part of the lands were as yet granted; importuned him & two or three persons that went over with him to go up and visit the lands, which they did, and were very kindly received and greatly caressed by the Indians. On his return to New York he received the most solemn promises that he should have a thousand acres for every family that he brought over, and that each family should have according to their number from five hundred to one hundred and fifty acres, but declined making any Grant till the Families arrived, because, according to the Constitution of that Government, the names of the settlers were to be inserted in that Grant. Captain Campbell accordingly returned to Isla, and brought from thence at a very large expense, his own Family and Thirty other Families, making in all, one hundred and fifty-three Souls. He went again to visit the lands, received all possible respect and kindness from the Government, who proposed an old Fort Anna to be repaired, to cover the new settlers from the French Indians. At the same time, the People of New York proposed to maintain the people already brought, till Captain Campbell could return and bring more, alledging that it would be for the interest of the Infant Colony to settle upon the lands in a large Body; that, covered by the Fort, and assisted by the Indians, they might be less liable to the Incursions of Enemies.

That to keep up the spirit of the undertaking, Governor Clarke, by a writing bearing date the 4th day of December, 1738, declared his having promised Captain Campbell thirty thousand acres of land at Wood Creek, free of charges, except the expence of surveying & the King's Quit Rent in consideration of his having already brought over thirty families who according to their respective numbers in each family, were to have from one hundred and fifty to five hundred acres. Encouraged by this declaration, he departed in the same month for Isla, and in August, 1739, brought over Forty Families more, and under the Faith of the said promises made a third voyage, from which he returned in November, 1740, bringing with him thirteen Families the whole making eighty-three Families, composed of Four Hundred and Twenty Three Persons, all sincere and loyal Protestants, and very capable of forming a respectable Frontier for the security of the Province, But after all these perilous and expensive voyages, and tho' there wanted but Seventeen Families to complete the number for which he had undertaken, he found no longer the same countenance or protection but on the contrary it was insinuated to him that he could have no land either for himself or the people, but upon conditions in direct violation of the Faith of Government, and detrimental to the interests of those who upon his assurances had accompanied him into America. The people also were reduced to demand separate Grants for themselves, which upon large promises some of them did, yet more of them never had so much as a foot of land, and many listed themselves to join the Expedition to Cuba.

That Captain Campbell having disposed of his whole Fortune in the Island of Isla, expended the far greatest part of it from his confidence in these fallacious promises found himself at length constrained to employ the little he had left in the purchase of a small farm seventy miles north of New York for the subsistence of himself and his Family consisting of three sons and three daughters. He went over again into Scotland in 1745, and having the command of a Company of the Argyleshire men, served with Reputation under his Royal Highness the Duke, against the Rebels. He went back to America in 1747 and not longer after died of a broken heart, leaving behind him the six children before mentioned of whom your Memoralist is the eldest, in very narrow and distressed circumstances."

All these facts are briefly commemorated by Mr. Smith in his History of the Colony of New York, page 179, where are some severe, though just strictures on the behavior of those in power towards him and the families he brought with him, and the loss the Province sustained by such behavior towards them.

That at the Commencement of the present War, your Memoralist and both his brothers following their Father's principles in hopes of better Fortune entered into the Army & served in the Forty Second, Forty Eighth and Sixtieth Regiments of Foot during the whole War, at the close of which your Memoralist and his brother George were reduced as Lieutenants upon half pay, and their youngest Brother still continues in the service; the small Farm purchased by their father being the sole support of themselves and three sisters till they were able to provide for themselves in the manner before mentioned, and their sisters are now married & settled in the Province of New York.

That after the conclusion of the Peace, your Memorialist considering the number of Families dispersed through the Province which came over with his Father, and finding in them a general disposition to settle with him on the lands originally promised them, if they could be obtained, in the month of February, 1763, petitioned Governor Monckton for the said lands but was able only to procure a Grant of ten thousand acres, (for obtaining which, he disbursed in Patent and other fees, the sum of two hundred Guineas), the people in Power alledging that land was now at a far greater value than at the time of your Memoralist's Father's coming into the Province, and even this upon the common condition of settling ten Families upon the said lands and paying a Quit Rent to the Crown. Part however of the People who had promised to settle with your Memoralist in case he had prevailed, were drawn to petition for lands to themselves, which they obtained, tho' they never could get one foot of land before, which provision of lands as your Memoralist apprehends, ought in Equity to be considered as an obligation on the Province to perform, so far as the number of those Families goes, the Conditions stipulated with his Father, as those Families never had come into & consequently could not now be remaining in the Province, if he had not persuaded them to accompany him, & been at a very large expence in transporting them thither.

That there are still very many of these Families who have no land and would willingly settle with your Memoralist. That there are numbers of non commissioned Officers and Soldiers of the Regiments disbanded in North America who notwithstanding His Majesty's gracious Intentions are from many causes too long to trouble your Lordship with at present without any settlement provided for them, and that there are also many Families of loyal Protestants in the Islands and other parts of North Britain which might be induced by reasonable proposals and a **certainty of their** being fulfilled, to remove into the said Province, which would add greatly to the strength, security and opulence thereof, and be in all respects faithful and serviceable subjects to His Majesty.

That the premisses considered, particularly the long scene of hardships to which your Memoralist's Family has been exposed, for Twenty Six years, in consideration of his own and his Brothers' services, & the perils to which they have been exposed during the long and fatiguing War, and the Prospect he still has of contributing to the settlement of His Majesty's unimproved country, your Memoralist humbly prays that Your Lordships would direct the Government of New York to grant to him the said One Hundred thousand Acres, upon his undertaking to settle One Hundred or One Hundred and Fifty Families upon the same within the space of Three years or such other Recompence or Relief as upon mature Deliberation on the Hardships and Sufferings which his Father and his Family have for so many years endured, & their merits, in respect to the Province of New York which might be incontestably proved, if it was not universally acknowledged, may in your great Wisdom be thought to deserve.

And your Memorialist; &c., &c., &c.*

May, 1764."

It was the policy of the home government to settle as rapidly as possible the wild lands; not so much for the purpose of benefiting the emigrant as it was to enhance the king's exchequer. The royal governors apparently held out great inducements to the settlers, but the sequel always showed that a species of blackmail or tribute must be paid by the purchasers before the lands were granted. The governor was one thing to the higher authorities, but far different to those from whom he could reap advantage. The seeming disinterested motives may be thus illustrated:

Under date of New York, July 26, 1736, George Clarke, lieutenant governor of New York, writes to the duke of Newcastle, in which he says, it was principally

"To augment his Majesty's Quit rents that I projected a Scheme to settle the Mohacks Country in this Province, which I have the pleasure to hear from Ireland and Holland is like to succeed. The scheme is to give grants gratis of an hundred thousand acres of land to the first five hundred protestant familys that come from Europe in two hundred acres to a family, these being settled will draw thousands after them, for both the situation and quantity of the Land are much preferable to any in Pensilvania, the only Northern Colony to which the Europeans resort, and the Quit rents less. Governor Cosby sent home the proposals last Summer under the Seal of the Province, and under his and the Council's hands, but it did not reach Dublin till the last day of March; had it come there two months sooner I am assured by a letter which I lately received, directed to Governor Cosby, that we should have had two ships belonging to this place (then lying there) loaded with people but next year we hope to

---

*" Documentary and Colonial History of New York," Vol. VII, p. 630.
Should 1763 be read for 1764?

have many both from thence and Germany. When the Mohocks Country is settled we shall have nothing to fear from Canada."*

The same, writing to the Lords of Trade, under date of New York, June 15, 1739, says:

"The lands whereon the French propose to settle were purchased from Indian proprietors (who have all along been subject to and under the protection of the Crown of England) by one Godfrey Dellius and granted to him by patent under the seal of this province in the year 1696, which grant was afterwards resumed by act of Assembly whereby they became vested in the Crown; on part of these lands I proposed to settle some Scotch Highland familys who came hither last year, and they would have been now actually settled there, if the Assembly would have assisted them, for they are poor and want help; however as I have promised them lands gratis, some of them about three weeks ago went to view that part of the Country, and if they like the lands I hope they will accept my offer (if the report of the French designs do not discourage them:) depending upon the voluntary assistance of the people of Albany whose more immediate interest it is to encourage their settlement in that part of the country."†

That Captain Campbell would have secured the lands there can be no question had he complied with Governor Clarke's demands, although said demands were contrary to the agreement. Private faith and public honor demanded the fair execution of the project, which had been so expensive to the undertaker, and would have added greatly to the benefit of the colony. The governor would not make the grant unless he should have his fees and a share of the land.

The quit rent in the province of New York was fixed at two shillings six pence for every one hundred acres. The fees for a grant of a thousand acres were as follows: To the governor, $31.25; secretary of state, $10; clerk of the council, $10 to $15; receiver general, $14.37; attorney general, $7.50; making a total of about $75, besides the cost of survey. This amount does not appear to be large for the number of acres, yet it must be considered that land was plenty, but money very scarce. There were thousands of substantial men who would have found it exceedingly difficult to raise the amount in question.

---

*Ibid, p. 72. †Ibid, Vol. VI, p. 145.

It is possible that Captain Campbell could not have paid this extortion even if he had been so disposed; but being high-spirited, he resolutely refused his consent. The governor, still pretending to be very anxious to aid the emigrants, recommended the legislature of the province to grant them assistance; but, as usual, the latter was at war with the governor, and refused to vote money to the Highlanders, which they suspected, with good reason, the latter would be required to pay to the colonial officers for fees.

Not yet discouraged, Captain Campbell determined to exhaust every resource that justice might be done to him. His next step was to appeal to the legislature for redress, but it was in vain; then he made an application to the Board of Trade, in England, which had the power to rectify the wrong. Here he had so many difficulties to contend with that he was forced to leave the colonists to themselves, who soon after separated. But all his efforts proved abortive.

The petition of Lieutenant Donald Campbell, though courteously expressed, and eminently just, was rejected. It was claimed that the orders of the English government positively forbade the granting of over a thousand acres to any one person; yet that thousand acres was denied him.

The injustice accorded to Captain Campbell was more or less notorious throughout the province. It was generally felt there had been bad treatment, and there was now a disposition on the part of the colonial authorities to give some relief to his sons and daughters. Accordingly, on November 11, 1763, a grant of ten thousand acres, in the present township of Greenwich, Washington county, New York, was made to the three brothers, Donald, George and James, their three sisters and four other persons, three of whom were also named Campbell.

The final success of the Campbell family in obtaining redress inspired others who had belonged to the colony to petition for a similar recompense for their hardships and losses. They succeeded in obtaining a grant of forty-seven thousand, four hundred and fifty acres, located in the present township of Argyle, and a small part of Fort Edward and Greenwich, in the same county.

On March 2, 1764, Alexander McNaughton and one hundred and six others of the original Campbell emigrants and their descendants, petitioned for one thousand acres to be granted to each of them

"To be laid out in a single tract between the head of South bay and Kingsbury, and reaching east towards New Hampshire and westwardly to the mountains in Warren county. The committee of the council to whom this petition was referred reported May 21, 1764, that the tract proposed be granted, which was adopted, the council specifying the amount of land each individual of the petitioners should receive, making two hundred acres the least and six hundred the most that anyone should obtain. Five men were appointed as trustees, to divide and distribute the land as directed. The same instrument incorporated the tract into a township, to be called Argyle, and should have a supervisor, treasurer, collector, two assessors, two overseers of highways, two overseers of the poor and six constables, to be elected annually by the inhabitants on the first day of May. The patent, similar to all others of that period, was subject to the following conditions:

An annual quit rent of two shillings and six pence sterling on every one hundred acres, and all mines of gold and silver, and all pine trees suitable for masts for the royal navy, namely, all which were twenty-four inches from the ground, reserved to the crown."*

The land thus granted lies in the central part of Washington county, with a broken surface in the west and great elevations and ridges in the east. The soil is rich and the whole well watered.

The trustees were vested with the power to execute title deeds to such of the grantees, should they claim the lands, the first of which were issued during the winter and spring of 1764-5 by Duncan Reid, of the city of New York, *gentleman;* Peter Middleton, of same city, *physician;* Archibald Campbell, of same city, *merchant;* Alexander McNaughton,† of Orange county, *farmer;* and Neil Gillaspie, of Ulster county, *farmer,* of the one part, and the grantees of the other part.

---
*On record in library at Albany in "Patents," Vol. IV, pp. 3-17. †See Appendix, Note I.

While the application for the grant was yet pending, the petitioners greatly exalted over their future prospects, evolved a grand scheme for the survey of the prospective lands, which should include a stately street from the banks of the Hudson river on the east through the tract, upon which each family should have a town lot, where he might not only enjoy the protection of near neighbors, but also have that companionship of which the Highlander is so particularly fond. In the rear of these town lots were to be the farms, which in time were to be occupied by tenants. The surveyors, Archibald Campbell, of Raritan, New Jersey, and Christopher Yates, of Schenectady, who began their labors June 19, 1764, were instructed to lay off the land as planned, the street to extend from east to west, twenty-four rods wide and extending through the width of the grant as near the center as practicable, and to set aside a glebe lot for the benefit of the school master and the minister. North and south of the street, and bordering on it, the surveyors laid off lots running back one hundred and eighty rods, varying in width so as to contain from twenty to sixty acres. These lots were numbered, making in all one hundred and forty-one, seventy-two being on the south side of the street, and the remainder on the north. The farms were also numbered, also making one hundred and forty-one.

In the plan no allowance had been made for the rugged nature of the country, and consequently the magnificent street was located over hills whose proportions prevented its use as a public highway, while some of the lots were uninhabitable.

The following is a list of the grantees, the number of the lot and its contents being set opposite the name:

Lot.	Name.	Acres.	Lot.	Name.	Acres.
1.	Catharine Campbell	250	10.	Mary Anderson	300
2.	Elizabeth Cargill	250	11.	Archibald McNeil	300
3.	Allan McDonald	300	12.	Dougall McAlpine	300
4.	Neil Gillaspie	450	13.	David Lindsey	250
5.	Mary Campbell	350	14.	Elizabeth Campbell	300
6.	Duncan McKerwan	350	15.	Ann McDuffie	350
7.	Ann McAnthony	250	16.	Donald McDougall	300
8.	Mary McGowne	300	17.	Archibald McGowne	300
9.	Catherine McLean	300	18.	Eleanor Thompson	300

Lot.	Name.	Acres.	Lot.	Name.	Acres.
19.	Duncan McDuffie	350	44.	Dunçan McArthur	450
20.	Duncan Reid	600	45.	John Torrey	300
21.	John McDuffie	250	46.	Malcolm Campbell	300
22.	Dougall McKallor	550	47.	Florence McKenzie	200
23.	Daniel Johnson	350	48.	John McKenzie	300
24.	Archibald Campbell	250	49.	Jane Cargill	250
25.	William Hunter	300	50.	John McGowan	300
26.	Duncan Campbell	300	59.	John McEwen	500
27.	Elizabeth Fraser	200	60.	John McDonald	300
28.	Alexander Campbell	350	61.	James McDonald	400
	Glebe lot	500	62.	Mary Belton	300
29.	Daniel Clark	350	72.	Rachael Nevin	300
43.	Elizabeth Campbell	300	73.	James Cargill	400

Lots 29, 43, 44, 50, and 62 are partly in the present limits of the township of Greenwich, and the other lots, from 29 to 73, not above enumerated, are wholly in that township and in Salem. The following lots are located north of the street:

Lot.	Name.	Acres.	Lot.	Name.	Acres.
74.	John Cargill	300	97.	Charles McAllister	300
75.	Duncan McDougall	300	98.	William Graham	300
76.	Alexander Christie	350	99.	Hugh McDougall	300
77.	Alex. Montgomery	600	100.	James Campbell	300
78.	Marian Campbell	250	101.	George McKenzie	400
79.	John Gilchrist	300	102.	John McCarter	400
80.	Agnes McDougall	300	103.	Morgan McNeil	250
81.	Duncan McGuire	500	104.	Malcolm McDuffie	550
82.	Edward McKallor	500	105.	Florence McVarick	300
83.	Alexander Gilchrist	300	106.	Archibald McEwen	300
84.	Archibald McCullom	350	107.	Neil McDonald	500
85.	Archibald McCore	300	108.	James Gillis	500
86.	John McCarter	350	109.	Archibald McDougall	450
87.	Neil Shaw	600	110.	Marian McEwen	200
88.	Duncan Campbell	300	111.	Patrick McArthur	350
89.	Roger McNeil	300	112.	John McGowne, Jr.	250
90.	Elizabeth Ray	200	113.	John Shaw, Sr.	300
91.	James Nutt	300	114.	Angus Graham	300
92.	Donald McDuffie	350	115.	Edward McCoy	300
93.	George Campbell	300	116.	Duncan Campbell, Jr.	300
94.	Jane Widrow	300	117.	Jenette Ferguson	250
95.	John McDougall	400	118.	Hugh McElroy	200
96.	Archibald McCarter	300	119.	Dougall Thompson	400

Lot.	Name.	Acres.	Lot.	Name.	Acres.
120.	Mary Graham	300	126.	Mary Anderson	300
121.	Robert McAlpine	300	127.	Donald McMullin	450
122.	Duncan Taylor	600	130.	John Shaw, Sr.	300
123.	Elizabeth Caldwell	250	131.	Duncan Lindsey	300
124.	William Clark	350	132.	Donald Shaw	
124.	William Clark	350			
125.	Barbara McAllister	300	133.	John Campbell	300

Each of the foregoing had a "street lot," with a corresponding number, as before mentioned, which contained one-tenth of the area of the farm lots; that is, a lot of two hundred acres had a "street lot" of twenty acres, and so on.

Ten lots comprehended between Nos. 127 and 146 are now within the township of Fort Edward. The number of these lots and the persons to whom granted were as follows, varying in area from 250 to 500 acres:

Lot 128, Duncan Shaw; 129, Alex. McDougall; 134, John McArthur; 135, John McIntyre; 136, Catharine McIlfender; 137, Mary Hammel; 138, Duncan Gilchrist; 139, John McIntyre; 140, Mary McLeod; 141, David Torrey.

The lots originally belonging to Argyle township, but now forming a part of Greenwich, were numbered and allotted as follows:

Lot.	Name.	Acres.	Lot.	Name.	Acres.
30.	Angus McDougall	300	67.	Catharine McCarter	250
31.	Donald McIntyre	350	68.	Margaret Gilchrist	250
32.	Alexander McNachten	600	42.	John McGuire	400
33.	John McCore	300	43.	Elizabeth McNeil	200
34.	William Fraser	350	44.	Duncan McArthur	450
35.	Mary Campbell	250	29.	Daniel Clark	250
36.	Duncan Campbell, Sr.	450	50.	John McGowan, Sr.	300
37.	Neil McFadden	300	55.	Ann Campbell	300
38.	Mary Torry	250	56.	Archibald McCullom	350
39.	Margaret McAllister	250	57.	Alexander McArthur	250
40.	Robert Campbell, Jr.	450	58.	Alex. McDonald	250
41.	Catharine Shaw	250	59.	John McEwen	500
51.	Charles McArthur	350	62.	Mary Baine	300
52.	Duncan McFadden	300	63.	Margaret Cargyle	300
53.	Roger Reed	300	64.	Neil McEachern	450
54.	John McCarter	300	69.	Hannah McEwen	400
65.	Hugh Montgomery	300	70.	John Reid	450
66.	Isabella Livingston	250	71.	Archibald Nevin	350

Many of the grantees immediately took possession of the lands alloted to them; but others never took advantage of their claims, which, for a time, were left unoccupied, and then passed into the hands of others, who generally were left in undisputed possession. This state of affairs, in connection with the large size of the lots, had the effect of retarding the growth of that district.

Before the arrival of the settlers, a desperado, named Rogers, had taken possession of a part of the lands on the Batten Kill. He warned the people off, making various threats; but the Highlanders knowing their titles were perfect, disregarded the menace, and set about industriously clearing up their lands and erecting their houses. One day, when Archibald Livingston was away, his wife was forcibly carried off by Rogers, and set down outside the limits of the claim, who also proceeded to remove the furniture from the premises. He was arrested by Roger Reid, the constable, and brought before Alexander McNaughton, the justice, which constituted the first civil process ever served in that county. Rogers did not submit peaceably to be taken, but defended himself with a gun, which Joseph McCracken seized, and in his endeavor to wrest it from the hands of the ruffian, he burst the buttons from off the waist-bands of his pantaloons, which, as he did not wear suspenders, slipped over his feet. The little son of Rogers, fully taking in the situation, ran up and bit McCracken, which, however, did not cause him to desist from his purpose. Rogers was conveyed to Albany, after which all trace of him has been lost.

The township of Argyle, embracing what is now both Argyle and Fort Edward, was organized in 1771. The record of the first meeting bears date April 2, 1771, and was called for the purpose of regulating laws and choosing officers. It was called by virtue of the grant in the Argyle patent. The officers elected were: supervisor, Duncan Campbell, who continued until 1781, and was then succeeded by Roger Reid; town clerk, Archibald Brown, succeeded in 1775 by Edward Patterson, who, in turn, was succeeded in 1778 by John McNeil, and he by Duncan Gilchrist, in 1780; collector, Roger Reid, succeeded in 1778 by Duncan Mc-

Arthur, and the latter in 1781 by Alexander Gilchrist; assessors, Archibald Campbell and Neal Shaw; constables, John Offery, John McNiel; poor-masters, James Gilles, Archibald McNiel; road-masters, Duncan Lindsey, Archibald Campbell; fence viewers, Duncan McArthur, John Gilchrist.

The following extracts from township records are not without interest:

1772.—"All men from sixteen to sixty years old to work on the roads this year. Fences must be four feet and a half high."

1776.—"Duncan Reid is to be constable for the south part of the patent and Alexander Gillis for the north part; George Kilmore and James Beatty for masters. John Johnson was chosen a justice of the peace."

1781.—"Alexander McDougall and Duncan Lindsey were elected tithing men."

In order to make the laws more efficient, on March 12, 1772, the county of Charlotte was struck off from Albany, which was the actual beginning of the present county of Washington. As Charlotte county had been named for the consort of George III. and as his troops had devastated it during the Revolution, the title was not an agreeable one, so the state legislature on April 2, 1784, changed it to Washington, thus giving it the most honored appellation known in the annals of American history.

For several years after 1764 the colony on the east, and in what is now Hebron township, was augmented by a number of discharged Highland soldiers, mostly of the 77th Regiment, who settled on both sides of the line of the township. It is a noticeable fact that in every case these settlers were Scotch Highlanders. They had in all probability been attracted to this spot partly by the settlement of the colony of Captain Lachlan Campbell, and partly by that of the Scotch-Irish at New Perth (Salem), which has been noted already in its proper connection. These additional settlers took up their claims, owing to a proclamation made by the king, in October, 1763, offering land in America, without fees, to all such officers and soldiers who had served on that continent, and who desired to establish their homes there.

Nothing shows more clearly than this proclamation the lofty position of an officer in the British service at that time as compared with a private. A field officer received four thousand acres; a captain three thousand; a lieutenant, or other subaltern commissioned officer, two thousand; a non-commissioned officer, whether sergeant or corporal, dropped to two hundred acres, while the poor private was put off with fifty acres. Fifty acres of wild land, on the hill-sides of Washington County, was not an extravagant reward for seven years' service amidst all the dangers and horrors of French and Indian warfare.

Many of these grants were sold by the soldiers to their countrymen. Their method of exchange was very simple. The corporal and private would meet by the roadside, or at a neighboring ale-house, and after greeting each other, the American land would immediately be the subject for barter. The private, who may be called Sandy, knew his fifty acres was not worth the sea-voyage, while Corporal Donald, having already two hundred, might find it profitable to emigrate, provided he could add other tracts. After the preliminaries and the haggling had been gone through with, Donald would draw out his long leather purse and count down the amount, saying:

"There, mon; there's your siller."

The worthy Sandy would then dive into some hidden recess of his garments and bring forth his parchment, signed in the name of the king by "Henry Moore, baronet, our captain-general and governor-in-chief, in and over our province of New York, and the lands depending thereon, in America, chancellor and vice-admiral of the same." This document would be promptly handed to the purchaser, with the declaration,

"An' there's your land, corporal."

Many of the soldiers never claimed their lands, which were eventually settled by squatters, some of whom remained thereon so long that they or their heirs became the lawful owners.

The famous controversy concerning the "New Hampshire grants," affected the Highland settlers; but the more exciting events of the wrangle took place outside the limits of Washington county, and consequently the Highland settlement. This controversy, which was carried on with acrimonious and warlike contention, arose over New York's officials' claim to the possession of all the land north of the Massachusetts line lying west of the Connecticut river. In 1751 both the governors of New York and New Hampshire presented their respective claims to the territory in dispute to the Lords of Trade in London. The matter was finally adjusted in 1782, by New York yielding her claim.

In 1771 there were riots near the southern boundary of Hebron township, which commenced by the forcible expulsion of Donald McIntire and others from their lands, perpetrated by Robert Cochran and his associates. On October 29th, same year, another serious riot took place. A warrant was issued for the offenders by Alexander McNaughton, justice of the peace, residing in Argyle. Charles Hutchison, formerly a corporal in Montgomery's Highlanders, testified that Ethan Allen (afterwards famous), and eight others, on the above date, came to his residence, situated four miles north of New Perth, and began to demolish it. Hutchison requested them to stop, but they declared that they would make a burnt offering to the gods of this world by burning the logs of that house. Allen and another man held clubs over Hutchison's head, ordered him to leave the locality, and declared that, in case he returned, he should be worse treated. Eight or nine other families were driven from their homes, in that locality, at the same time, all of whom fled to New Perth, where they were hospitably received. The lands held by these exiled families had been wholly improved by themselves. They were driven out by Allen and his associates because they were determined that no one should build under a New York title east of the line they had established as the western boundary.

Bold Ethan Allen was neither to be arrested nor intimidated by a constable's warrant. Governor Tryon of New York offered twenty pounds reward for the arrest of the rioters, which was as inefficient as esquire McNaughton's warrant.

The county of Washington was largely settled by people from the New England states. The breaking out of the Revolutionary War found these people loyal to the cause of the patriots. The Highland settlements were somewhat divided, but the greater part allied themselves with the cause of their adopted country.

Those who espoused the cause of the king, on account of the atrocities committed by the Indians, were forced to flee, and never returned save in marauding bands. There were a few, however, who kept very quiet, and were allowed to remain unmolested.

There were no distinctive Highland companies either in the British or Continental service from this settlement. A company of royalists was secretly formed at Fort Edwards, under David Jones (remembered only as being the betrothed of the lovely but unfortunate Jane McCrea), and these joined the British forces. There were five companies from the county that formed the regiment under Colonel Williams, one of which was commanded by Captain Charles Hutchison, the Highland corporal whom Ethan Allen had mobbed in 1771. In this company of fifty-two men it may be reasonably supposed that the greater number were the sons of the emigrants of Captain Lauchlan Campbell.

The committee of Charlotte county, in September 21, 1775, recommended to the Provincial Congress, that the following named persons, living in Argyle, should be thus commissioned: Alexander Campbell, captain; Samuel Pain, first lieutenant; Peter Gilchrist, second lieutenant; and John McDougall, ensign.

Captain Joseph McCracken, on the arrival of Burgoyne, built a fort at New Perth, which was finished on July 26th, and called Salem Fort.

Donald, son of Captain Lauchlan Campbell, espoused the cause of the people, but his two brothers sided with the British. Soon after all these passed out of the district, and their whereabouts became unknown.

The bitter feelings engendered by the war was also felt in the Highland settlement, as may be instanced in the following circumstance preserved by S. D. W. Bloodgood:*

"When Burgoyne found that his boats were not safe, and were in fact much nearer the main body of our army than his own, it became necessary to land his provisions, of which he had already been short for many weeks, in order to prevent his being actually starved into submission. This was done under a heavy fire from our troops. On one of these occasions a person by

---
*The Sexagenary, p. 110.

name of Mr. ——, well known at Salem, and a foreigner by birth, and who had at the very time a son in the British army, crossed the river at De Ruyter's, with a person by name of McNeil; they went in a canoe, and arriving opposite to the place intended, crossed over to the western bank, on which a redoubt called Fort Lawrence had been placed. They crawled up the bank with their arms in their hands, and peeping over the upper edge, they saw a man in a blanket coat loading a cart. They instantly raised their guns to fire, an action more savage than commendable. At the moment the man turned so as to be more plainly seen, when old M—— said to his companion, 'Now that's my own son Hughy; but I'm dom'd for a' that if I sill not gie him a shot.' He then actually fired at his own son, as the person really proved to be, but happily without effect. Having heard the noise made by their conversation and the cocking of the pieces, which the nearness of his position rendered perfectly practicable, he ran round the cart, and the ball lodged in the felly of the wheel. The report drew the attention of the neighboring guards, and the two marauders were driven from their lurking place. While retreating with all possible speed, McNeil was wounded in the shoulder, and, if alive, carries the wound about with him to this day. Had the ball struck the old Scotchman, it is questionable whether any one would have considered it more than even handed justice commending the chalice to his own lips."

A map of Washington County would show that it was on the war path that led to some terrible conflicts related in American history. Occupying a part of the territory between the Hudson and the northern lakes, it had borne the feet of warlike Hurons, Iroquois, Canadians, New Yorkers, New Englanders, French, English, Continentals and Hessians, who proceeded in their mission of destruction and vengeance. As the district occupied by the Highlanders was close to the line of Burgoyne's march, it experienced the realities of war and the tomahawk of the merciless savage. How terrible was the work of the ruthless savage, and how shocking the fate of those in his pathway, has been graphically related by Arthur Reid, a native of the township of Argyle, who received the account from an aunt, who was fully cognizant of all the facts. The following is a condensed account:

During the latter part of the summer of 1777, a scouting party of Indians, consisting of eight, received either a real or supposed injury from some white persons at New Perth (now

Salem), for which they sought revenge. While prowling around the temporary fort, they were observed and fired upon, and one of their number killed. In the presence of a prisoner, a white man,* the remaining seven declared their purpose to sacrifice the first white family that should come in their way. This party belonged to a large body of Indians which had been assembled by General Burgoyne, the British commander, then encamped not far distant in a northerly direction from Crown Point. In order to inspire the Indians with courage General Burgoyne considered it expedient, in compliance with their custom, to give them a war-feast, at which they indulged in the most extravagant manœuvres, gesticulations, and exulting vociferations, such as lying in ambush, and displaying their rude armored devices, and dancing, and whooping, and screaming, and brandishing their tomahawks and scalping knives.

The particular band, above mentioned, was in command of an Iroquois chief, who, from his bloodthirsty nature, was called Le Loup, the wolf,—bold, fiercely revengeful, and well adapted to lead a party bent on committing atrocities. Le Loup and his band left New Perth *en route* to the place where the van of Burgoyne's army was encamped. The family of Duncan McArthur, consisting of himself, wife and four children, lived on the direct route. Approaching the clearing upon which the dwelling stood, the Indians halted in order to make preparations for their fiendish design. Every precaution was taken, even to enhancing their naturally ferocious appearance by painting their faces, necks and shoulders with a thick coat of vermilion. The party next moved forward with stealthy steps to the very edge of the forest, where again they halted in order to mature the final plan of attack.

Fortunately for the McArthur family, on that day, two neighbors had come for the purpose of assisting in the breaking of a horse, and, when the Indians saw them, and also the three

---

*Samuel Standish, who was present at the time of the murder of Jane McCrea, and afterwards gave the account to Jared Sparks, who records it in his "Life of Arnold." See "Library of American Biography," Vol. III, Chap. VII.

buildings, which they mistook for residences, they became disconcerted. They decided as there were three men present, and the same number of houses, there must also be three families.

The Indians withdrew exasperated, but none the less determined to seek vengeance. With elastic step, and in single file they pressed forward, and an hour later came to another clearing, in the midst of which stood a dwelling, occupied by the family of John Allen, consisting of five persons, viz., himself and wife and three children. Temporarily with them at the time were Mrs. Allen's sister, two negroes and a negress. John Allen was notoriously in sympathy with the purposes of the British king. When the Indians steathily crept to the edge of the clearing they observed the white men busily engaged reaping the wheat harvest. They decided to wait until the reapers retired for dinner. Their white prisoner begged to be spared from witnessing the scene about to be enacted. This request was finally granted, and one of the Indians remained with him as a guard, while the others went forward to execute their purpose.

When the family had become seated at the table the Indians burst upon them with a fearful yell. When the neighbors came they found the body of John Allen a few rods from the house. Apparently he had escaped through a back door, but had been overtaken and shot down. Nearer the house, but in the same direction, were the bodies of Mrs. Allen, her sister, and the youngest child, all tomahawked and scalped. The other two children were found hidden in a bed, but also tomahawked and scalped. One of the negroes was found in the doorway, his body gashed and mutilated in a horrible manner. From the wounds inflicted on his body it was thought he had made a desperate resistance. The position of the remaining two has not been distinctly recollected.

George Kilmore, father of Mrs. Allen and owner of the negroes, who lived three miles distant, becoming anxious on account of the prolonged absence of his daughter and servants, on the Sunday following, sent a negro boy on an errand of inquiry. As the boy approached the house, the keen-scented horse, which he was riding, stopped and refused to go farther. After much difficulty he was urged forward until his rider got a view of the awful scene. The news brought by the boy spread rapidly, and the terror-stricken families fled to various points for protection, many of whom went to Fort Edward. After Burgoyne had been hemmed in, the families cautiously returned to their former homes.

From Friday afternoon, July 25th, until Sunday morning following, the whereabouts of Le Loup and his band cannot be determined. But on that morning they made their appearance on the brow of the hill north of Fort Edward, and then and there a shocking tragedy was enacted, which thoroughly aroused the people, and formed quite an element in the overthrow and surrender of Burgoyne's army. It was the massacre of Miss Jane McCrea, a lovely, amiable and intelligent lady. This tragedy at once drew the attention of all America. She fell under the blow of the savage Le Loup, and the next instant he flung down his gun, seized her long, luxuriant hair with one hand, with the other passed the scalping knife around nearly the whole head, and, with a yell of triumph, tore the beautiful but ghastly trophy from his victim's head.

It is a work of superogation to say that the Highland settlers of Argyle were strongly imbued with religious sentiments. That question has already been fully commented on. The colony early manifested its disposition to build churches where they might worship. The first of these houses were humble in their pretensions, but fully in keeping with a pioneer settlement in the wilderness. Their faith was the same as that promulgated by the Scotch-Irish in the adjoining neighborhood, and were visited by the pastor of the older settlement. They do not appear to have sustained a regular pastor until after the Peace of 1783.

CHAPTER VIII.

HIGHLAND SETTLEMENT ON THE MOHAWK.

Sir William Johnson thoroughly gained the good graces of the Iroquois Indians, and by the part he took against the French at Crown Point and Lake George, in 1755, added to his reputation at home and abroad. For his services to the Crown he was made a baronet and voted £5000 by the British parliament, besides being paid £600 per annum as Indian agent, which he retained until his death in 1774. He also received a grant of one hundred thousand acres of land north of the Mohawk. In 1743 he built Fort Johnson, a stone dwelling, on the same side of the river, in what is now Montgomery county. A few miles farther north, in 1764, he built Johnson Hall, a wooden structure, and there entertained his Indian bands and white tenants, with rude magnificence, surrounded by his mistresses, both white and red. He had dreams of feudal power, and set about to realize it. The land granted to him by the king, he had previously secured from the Mohawks, over whom he had gained an influence greater than that ever possessed heretofore or since by a white man over an Indian tribe. The tract of land thus gained was long known as "Kingsland," or the "Royal Grant." The king had bound Sir William to him by a feudal tenure of a yearly rental of two shillings and six pence for each and every one hundred acres. In the same manner Sir William bound to himself his tenants to whom he granted leases. In order to secure the greatest obedience he deemed it necessary to secure such tenants as differed from the people near him in manners, language, and religion, and that class trained to whom the strictest personal dependence was perfectly familiar. In all this he was highly favored. He turned his eyes to the Highlands of Scotland, and without trouble, owing to the dissatisfied condition of the people and their desire to emigrate, he secured as many colonists as he desired, all of whom were of the Roman Catholic faith. The agents having secured the requisite number, embarked, during the month of August, 1773, for America.

A journal of the period states that "three gentlemen of the name of Macdonell, with their families, and 400 Highlanders from the counties (!) of Glengarry, Glenmorison, Urquhart, and Strathglass lately embarked for America, having obtained a grant of land in Albany."*

This extract appears to have been copied from the *Courant* of August 28th, which stated they had "lately embarked for America." This would place their arrival on the Mohawk some time during the latter part of the following September, or first of October. The three gentlemen above referred to were Macdonell of Aberchalder, Leek, and Collachie, and also another, Macdonell of Scotas. Their fortunes had been shattered in "the 45," and in order to mend them were willing to settle in America. They made their homes in what was then Tryon county, about thirty miles from Albany, then called Kingsborough, where now is the thriving town of Gloversville. To certain families tracts were allotted varying from one hundred to five hundred acres, all subjected to the feudal system.

Having reached the places assigned them the Highlanders first felled the trees and made their rude huts of logs. Then the forest was cleared and the crops planted amid the stumps. The country was rough, but the people did not murmur. Their wants were few and simple. The grain they reaped was carried on horseback along Indian trails to the landlord's mills. Their women became accustomed to severe outdoor employment, but they possessed an indomitable spirit, and bore their hardships bravely, as became their race. The quiet life of the people promised to become permanent. They became deeply attached to the interests of Sir William Johnson, who, by consummate tact soon gained a mastery over them. He would have them assemble at Johnson Hall that they might make merry; encourage them in Highland games, and invite them to Indian councils. Their meth-

---

*Gentleman's Magazine, Sept. 30, 1773.

ods of farming were improved under his supervision; superior breeds of stock sought for, and fruit trees planted. But Sir William, in reality, was not with them long; for, in the autumn of 1773, he visited England, returning in the succeeding spring, and dying suddenly at Johnson Hall on June 24th, following.

Troubles were rising beneath all the peaceful circumstances enjoyed by the Highlanders, destined to become severe and oppressive under the attitude of Johnson's son and son-in-law who were men of far less ability and tact than their father. The spirit of democracy penetrated the valley of the Mohawk, and open threats of opposition began to be heard. The Acts of the Albany Congress of 1774 opened the eyes of the people to the possibilities of strength by united efforts. Just as the spirit of independence reached bold utterance Sir William died. He was succeeded in his title, and a part of his estates by his son John. The dreams of Sir William vanished, and his plans failed in the hands of his weak, arrogant, degenerate son. Sir John hesitated, temporized, broke his parole, fled to Canada, returned to ravage the lands of his countrymen, and ended by being driven across the border.

The death of Sir William made Sir John commandant of the militia of the Province of New York. Colonel Guy Johnson became superintendent of Indian affairs, with Colonel Daniel Claus, Sir William's son-in-law, for assistant. The notorious Thayendanegea (Joseph Brant) became secretary to Guy Johnson. Nothing but evil could be predicated of such a combination; and Sir John was not slow to take advantage of his position, when the war cloud was ready to burst. As early as March 16, 1775, decisive action was taken, when the grand jury, judges, justices, and others of Tryon county, to the number of thirty-three, among whom was Sir John, signed a document, expressive of their disapprobation of the act of the people of Boston for the "outrageous and unjustifiable act on the private property of the India Company," and of their resolution "to bear faith and true allegiance to their lawful Sovereign King George the Third."* It is a noticeable feature that not one of the names of Highlanders appears on

---

*Am. Archives, Fourth Series, Vol. II. p. 151.

the paper. This would indicate that they were not a factor in the civil government of the county.

On May 18, 1775, the Committee of Palatine District, Tryon county, addressed the Albany Committee of Safety, in which they affirm:

"This County has, for a series of years, been ruled by one family, the different branches of which are still strenuous in dissuading people from coming into Congressional measures, and even have, last week, at a numerous meeting of the Mohawk District, appeared with all their dependants armed to oppose the people considering of their grievances; their number being so large, and the people unarmed, struck terror into most of them, and they dispersed. We are informed that Johnson-Hall is fortifying by placing a parcel of swivel-guns round the same, and that Colonel Johnson has had parts of his regiment of Militia under arms yesterday, no doubt with a design to prevent the friends of liberty from publishing their attachment to the cause to the world. Besides which we are told that about one hundred and fifty Highlanders, (Roman Catholicks) in and about Johnstown, are armed and ready to march upon the like occasion."*

In order to allay the feelings engendered against them Guy Johnson, on May 18th, wrote to the Committee of Schenectady declaring "my duty is to promote peace,"† and on the 20th to the Magistrates of Palatine, making the covert threat "that if the Indians find their council fire disturbed, and their superintendent insulted, they will take a dreadful revenge.‡ The last letter thoroughly aroused the Committee of Tryon county, and on the 21st stated, among other things:

"That Colonel Johnson's conduct in raising fortifications round his house, keeping a number of Indians and armed men constantly about him, and stopping and searching travelers upon the King's highway, and stopping our communication with Albany, is very alarming to this County, and is highly arbitrary, illegal, oppressive, and unwarrantable; and confirms us in our fears, that his design is to keep us in awe, and oblige us to submit to a state of Slavery."‖

On the 23rd the Albany Committee warned Guy Johnson that his interference with the rights of travelers would no longer

---

*Ibid, p. 637. †Ibid, p. 638. ‡Ibid, p. 661. ‖Ibid, p. 665.

be tolerated.* So flagrant had been the conduct of the Johnsons that a sub-committee of the city and county of Albany addressed a communication on the subject to the Provincial Congress of New York.† On June 2nd the Tryon County Committee addressed Guy Johnson, in which they affirm "it is no more our duty than inclination to protect you in the discharge of your province," but will not "pass over in silence the interruption which the people of the Mohawk District met in their meeting," "and the inhuman treatment of a man whose only crime was being faithful to his employers."‡ The tension became still more strained between the Johnsons and patriots during the summer.

The Dutch and German population was chiefly in sympathy with the cause of America, as were the people generally, in that region, who did not come under the direct influence of the Johnsons. The inhabitants deposed Alexander White, the Sheriff of Tryon county, who had, from the first, made himself obnoxious. The first shot, in the war west of the Hudson, was fired by Alexander White. On some trifling pretext he arrested a patriot by the name of John Fonda, and committed him to prison. His friends, to the number of fifty, went to the jail and released him; and from the prison they proceeded to the sheriff's lodgings and demanded his surrender. He discharged a pistol at the leader, but without effect. Immediately some forty muskets were discharged at the sheriff, with the effect only to cause a slight wound in the breast. The doors of the house were broken open, and just then Sir John Johnson fired a gun at the hall, which was the signal for his retainers and Highland partisans to rally in arms. As they could muster a force of five hundred men in a short time, the party deemed it prudent to disperse.‖

The royalists became more open and bolder in their course, throwing every impediment in the way of the Safety Committee of Tryon county, and causing embarrassments in every way their ingenuity could devise. They called public meetings themselves, as well as to interfere with those of their neighbors; all of which

---

*Ibid, p. 672. †Ibid, p. 712. ‡Ibid, p. 880. ‖Stone's Life of Brant, Vol. I, p. 106.

caused mutual exasperation, and the engendering of hostile feelings between friends, who now ranged themselves with the opposing parties.

On October 26th the Tryon County Committee submitted a series of questions for Sir John Johnson to answer.* These questions, with Sir John's answers, were embodied by the Committee in a letter to the Provincial Congress of New York, under date of October 28th, as follows:

"As we found our duty and particular reasons to inquire or rather desire Sir John Johnson's absolute opinion and intention of the three following articles, viz:

1. Whether he would allow that his tenants may form themselves into Companies, according to the regulations of our Continental Congress, to the defence of our Country's cause;
2. Whether he would be willing himself also to assist personally in the same purpose;
3. Whether he pretendeth a prerogative to our County Court-House and Jail, and would hinder or interrupt the Committee of our County to make use of the said publick houses for our want and service in our common cause;

We have, therefore, from our meeting held yesterday, sent three members of our Committee with the afore-mentioned questions contained in a letter to him directed, and received of Sir John, thereupon, the following answer:

1. That he thinks our requests very unreasonable, as he never had denied the use of either Court-House or Jail to anybody, nor would yet deny it for the use which these houses have been built for; but he looks upon the Court-House and Jail at Johnstown to be his property till he is paid seven hundred Pounds —which being out of his pocket for the building of the same.
2. In regard of embodying his tenants into Companies, he never did forbid them, neither should do it, as they may use their pleasure; but we might save ourselves that trouble, he being sure they would not.
3. Concerning himself he declared, that before he would sign any association, or would lift his hand up against his King, he would rather suffer that his head shall be cut off. Further, he replied, that if we would make any unlawful use of the Jail, he would oppose it; and also mentions that there have many unfair means been used for signing the Association, and uniting the peo-

---

*Am. Archives, Fourth Series, Vol. III. p. 1194.

ple; for he was informed by credible gentlemen in New-York, that they were obliged to unite, otherwise they could not live there. And that he was also informed, by good authority, that likewise two-thirds of the Canajoharie and German Flatts people have been forced to sign; and, by his opinion, the Boston people are open rebels, and the other Colonies have joined them.

Our Deputies replied to his expressions of forcing the people to sign in our County; that his authority spared the truth, and it appears by itself rediculous that one-third should have forced two-thirds to sign. On the contrary, they would prove that it was offered to any one, after signing, that the regretters could any time have their names crossed, upon their requests.

We thought proper to refer these particular inimical declarations to your House, and would be very glad to get your opinion and advice, for our further directions. Please, also, to remember what we mentioned to you in our former letters, of the inimical and provoking behaviour of the tenants of said Sir John, which they still continue, under the authority of said Sir John."*

The attitude of Sir John had become such that the Continental Congress deemed it best, on December 30th to order General Schuyler "to take the most speedy and effective measures for securing the said Arms and Military Stores, and for disarming the said Tories, and apprehending their chiefs."† The action of Congress was none too hasty; for in a letter from Governor William Tryon of New York to the earl of Dartmouth, under date of January 5, 1776, he encloses the following addressed to himself:

"Sir: I hope the occasion and intention of this letter will plead my excuse for the liberty I take in introducing to your Excellency the bearer hereof Captain Allen McDonell who will inform you of many particulars that cannot at this time with safety be committed to writing. The distracted & convulsed State this unhappy country is now worked up to, and the situation that I am in here, together with the many Obligations our family owe to the best of Sovereigns induces me to fall upon a plan that may I hope be of service to my country, the propriety of which I entirely submit to Your Excellency's better judgment, depending on that friendship which you have been pleased to honour me with for your advice on and Representation to his Majesty of what we propose. Having consulted with all my friends in this quarter, among whom are many old and good Officers, most of whom have

---

*Ibid, p. 1245. †Ibid, p. 1963.

a good deal of interests in their respective neighborhoods, and have now a great number of men ready to compleat the plan—We must however not think of stirring till we have a support, & supply of money, necessaries to enable us to carry our design into execution, all of which Mr. McDonell who will inform you of everything that has been done in Canada that has come to our knowledge. As I find by the papers you are soon to sail for England I despair of having the pleasure to pay my respect to you but most sincerely wish you an Agreeable Voyage and a happy sight of Your family & friends. I am,
   Your Excellency's most obedient
        humble Servant,
        John Johnson."*

General Schuyler immediately took active steps to carry out the orders of Congress, and on January 23, 1776, made a very lengthy and detailed report to that body.† Although he had no troops to carry into execution the orders of Congress, he asked for seven hundred militia, yet by the time he reached Caughnawaga, there were nearly three thousand men, including the Tryon county militia. Arriving at Schenectady, he addressed, on January 16th, a letter to Sir John Johnson, requesting him to meet him on the next day, promising safe conduct for him and such person as might attend him. They met at the time appointed sixteen miles beyond Schenectady, Sir John being accompanied by some of the leading Highlanders and two or three others, to whom General Schuyler delivered his terms. After some difficulty, in which the Mohawk Indians figured as peacemakers, Sir John Johnson and Allan McDonell (Collachie) signed a paper agreeing "upon his word and honor immediately deliver up all cannon, arms, and other military stores, of what kind soever, which may be in his own possession," or that he may have delivered to others, or that he knows to be concealed; that "having given his parole of honour not to take up arms against America," "he consents not to go to the westward of the German-Flats and Kingsland (Highlanders') District," but to every other part to the southward he expects the privilege of going; agreed that the Highlanders shall, "without

---

*Documentary and Colonial History of New York, Vol. VIII, p. 651.
†Am. Archives, Fourth Series, Vol. IV, pp. 818-829.

any kind of exception, immediately deliver up all arms in their possession, of what kind soever," and from among them any six prisoners may be taken, but the same must be maintained agreeable to their respective rank.

On Friday the 19th General Schulyer marched to Johnstown, and in the afternoon the arms and military stores in Sir John's possession were delivered up. On the next day, at noon, General Schuyler drew his men up in the street, "and the Highlanders, between two and three hundred, marched to the front, where they grounded their arms;" when they were dismissed "with an exhortation, pointing out the only conduct which could insure them protection." On the 21st, at Cagnuage, General Schuyler wrote to Sir John as follows:

JOHNSON HALL.

"Although it is a well known fact that all the Scotch (Highlanders) people that yesterday surrendered arms, had not broadswords when they came to the country, yet many of them had, and most of them were possessed of dirks; and as none have been given up of either, I will charitably believe that it was rather inattention than a wilful omission. Whether it was the former or the latter must be ascertained by their immediate compliance with that part of the treaty which requires that all arms, of what kind soever, shall be delivered up.

After having been informed by you, at our first interview, that the Scotch people meant to defend thmselves, I was not a little surprised that no ammunition was delivered up, and that you had none to furnish them with. These observations were immediately made by others as well as me. I was too apprehensive of the consequences which might have been fatal to those people, to take notice of it on the spot. I shall, however, expect an eclaircissement on this subject, and beg that you and Mr. McDonell will give it me as soon as may be."

Governor Tryon reported to the earl of Dartmouth, February 7th, that General Schuyler "marched to Johnson Hall the 24th of last month, where Sr John had mustered near Six hundred men, from his Tenants and neighbours, the majority highlanders, after disarming them and taking four pieces of artillery, ammunition and many Prisoners, with 360 Guineas from Sr John's Desk, they compelled him to enter into a Bond in 1600 pound Sterling not to aid the King's Service, or to remove within a limited district from his house."*

The six of the chiefs of the Highland clan of the McDonells made prisoners were, Allan McDonell, sen. (Collachie), Allan McDonell, Jur., Alexander McDonell, Ronald McDonell, Archibald McDonell, and John McDonell, all of whom were sent to Reading, Pennsyvania, with their three servants, and later to Lancaster.†

Had Sir John obeyed his parole, it would have saved him his vast estates, the Highlanders their homes, the effusion of blood, and the savage cruelty which his leadership engendered. Being incapable of forecasting the future, he broke his parole of honor, plunged headlong into the conflict, and dragged his followers into the horrors of war. General Schuyler wrote him, March 12, 1776, stating that the evidence had been placed in his hands that he had been exciting the Indians to hostility, and promising to defer taking steps until a more minute inquiry could be made he begged Sir John "to be present when it was made," which would be on the following Monday.

Sir John's actions were such that it became necessary to use stringent measures. General Schuyler, on May 14th, issued his instructions to Colonel Elias Dayton, who was to proceed to Johnstown, "and give notice to the Highlanders, who live in the vicinity of the town, to repair to it; and when any number are collected

---
*Documentary and Colonial History of New York, Vol. VIII, p. 663.
†See Appendix, Note J.

there, you will send off their baggage, infirm women and children, in wagons." Sir John was to be taken prisoner, carefully guarded and brought to Albany, but "he is by no means to experience the least ill-treatment in his own person, or those of his family."* General Schuyler had previously written (May 10th) to Sir John intimating that he had "acted contrary to the sacred engagements you lay under to me, and through me to the publick," and have "ordered you a close prisoner, and sent down to Albany."† The reason assigned for the removal of the Highlanders as stated by General Schuyler to Sir John was that "the elder Mr. McDonald (Allan of Collachie), a chief of that part of the clan of his name now in Tryon County, has applied to Congress that those people with their families may be moved from thence and subsisted."‡
To this Sir John replied as follows:

"Johnson Hall, May 18, 1776.

Sir: On my return from Fort Hunter yesterday, I received your letter by express acquainting me that the elder Mr. McDonald had desired to have all the clan of his name in the County of Tryon, removed and subsisted. I know none of that clan but such as are my tenants, and have been, for near two years supported by me with every necessary, by which means they have contracted a debt of near two thousand pounds, which they are in a likely way to discharge, if left in peace. As they are under no obligations to Mr. McDonald, they refuse to comply witn his extraordinary request; therefore beg there may be no troops sent to conduct them to Albany, otherwise they will look upon it as a total breach of the treaty agreed to at Johnstown. Mrs. McDonald showed me a letter from her husband, written since he applied to the Congress for leave to return to their families, in which he mentions that he was told by the Congress that it depended entirely upon you; he then desired that their families might be brought down to them, but never mentioned anything with regard to moving my tenants from hence, as matters he had no right to treat of. Mrs. McDonald requested that I would inform you that neither herself nor any of the other families would choose to go down.

I am, sir, your very humble servant,

John Johnson."||

---

*Am. Archives, Fourth Series, Vol. VI, p. 447.   †*Ibid*, p. 643.   ‡*Ibid*, p. 642. ||*Ibid*, p. 644.

Colonel Dayton arrived at Johnstown May 19th, and as he says, in his report to General John Sullivan, he immediately sent "a letter to Sir John Johnson, informing him that I had arrived with a body of troops to guard the Highlanders to Albany, and desired that he would fix a time for their assembling. When these gentlemen came to Johnson Hall they were informed by Lady Johnson that Sir John Johnson had received General Schuyler's letter by the express; that he had consulted the Highlanders upon the contents, and that they had unanimously resolved not to deliver themselves as prisoners, but to go another way, and that Sir John Johnson had determined to go with them. She added that, that if they were pursued they were determined to make an opposition, and had it in their power, in some measure."*

The approach of Colonel Dayton's command caused great commotion among the inhabitans of Johnstown and vicinity. Sir John determined to decamp, take with him as many followers as possible, and travel through the woods to Canada. Lieutenant James Gray, of the 42nd Highlanders, helped to raise the faithful bodyguard, and all having assembled at the house of Allen McDonell of Collachie started through the woods. The party consisted of three Indians from an adjacent village to serve as guides, one hundred and thirty Highlanders, and one hundred and twenty others.† The appearance of Colonel Dayton was more sudden than Sir John anticipated. Having but a brief period for their preparation, the party was but illy prepared for their flight. He did not know whether or not the royalists were in possession of Lake Champlain, therefore the fugitives did not dare to venture on that route to Montreal; so they were obliged to strike deeper into the forests between the headwaters of the Hudson and the St. Lawrence. Their provisions soon were exhausted; their feet soon became sore from the rough travelling; and several were left in the wilderness to be picked up and brought in by the Indians who were afterwards sent out for that purpose. After nineteen days of great hardships the party arrived in Montreal in a pitiable con-

---

*Ibid, p. 511. †Documentary and Colonial History of New York, Vol. VIII, p. 683.

dition, having endured as much suffering as seemed possible for human nature to undergo.

Sir John Johnson and his Highlanders, unwittingly, paid the highest possible compliment to the kindness and good intentions of the patriots, when they deserted their families and left them to face the foe. When the flight was brought to the attention of General Schuyler, he wrote to Colonel Dayton, May 27, in which he says:

"I am favored with a letter from Mr. Caldwell, in which he suggests the propriety of suffering such Highlanders to remain at their habitations as have not fled. I enter fully into his idea; but prudence dictates that this should be done under certain restrictions. These people have been taught to consider us in politicks in the same light that Papists consider Protestants in a religious relation, viz: that no faith is to be kept with either. I do not, therefore, think it prudent to suffer any of the men to remain, unless a competent number of hostages are given, at least five out of a hundred, on condition of being put to death if those that remain should take up arms, or in any wise assist the enemies of our country. A small body of troops * * may keep them in awe; but if an equal body of the enemy should appear, the balance as to numbers, by the junction of those left, would be against us. I am, however, so well aware of the absurdity of judging with precision in these matters at the distance we are from one another, that prudence obliges me to leave these matters to your judgment, to act as circumstances may occur."*

Lady Johnson, wife of Sir John, was taken to Albany and there held as a hostage until the following December when she was permitted to go to New York, then in the hands of the British. Nothing is related of any of the Highlanders being taken at that time to Albany, but appear to have been left in peaceable possession of their lands.

As might have been, and perhaps was, anticipated, the Highland settlement became the source of information and the base of supplies for the enemy. Spies and messengers came and went, finding there a welcome reception. The trail leading from there and along the Sacandaga and through the Adirondack woods,

---

*Am. Archives, Fourth Series, Vol. VI. p. 647.

soon became a beaten path from its constant use. The Highland women gave unstintingly of their supplies, and opened their houses as places of retreat. Here were planned the swift attacks upon the unwary settlers farther to the south and west. Agents of the king were active everywhere, and the Highland homes became one of the resting places for refugees on their way to Canada. This state of affairs could not be concealed from the Americans, who, none too soon, came to view the whole neighborhood as a nest of treason. Military force could not be employed against women and children (for from time to time nearly all the men had left), but they could be removed where they would do but little harm. General Schuyler discussed the matter with General Herkimer and the Tryon County Committee, when it was decided to remove of those who remained "to the number of four hundred." A movement of this description could not be kept a secret, especially when the troops were put in motion. In March, 1777, General Schuyler had permitted both Alexander and John MacDonald to visit their families. Taking the alarm, on the approach of the troops, in May, they ran off to Canada, taking with them the residue of the Highlanders, together with a few of the German neighbors. The journey was a very long and tedious one, and very painful for the aged, the women, and the children. They were used to hardships and bore their sufferings without complaint. It was an exodus of a people, whose very existence was almost forgotten, and on the very lands they cleared and cultivated there is not a single tradition concerning them.

From papers still in existence, preserved in Series B, Vol. 158, p. 351, of the Haldeman Papers, it would appear that some of the families, previous to the exodus, had been secured, as noted in the two following petitions, both written in either 1779 or 1780, date not given although first is simply dated "27th July," and second endorsed "27th July":

"To His Excellency General Haldimand, General and Commander in Chief of all His Majesty's Forces in Canada and the Frontiers thereof,

The memorial of John and Alexander Macdonell, Captains in the King's Royal Regiment of New York, humbly sheweth,

That your Memorialist, John Macdonell's, family are at present detained by the rebels in the County of Tryon, within the Province of New York, destitute of every support but such as they may receive from the few friends to Government in said quarters, in which situation they have been since 1777.

And your Memorialist, Alexander Macdonell, on behalf of his brother, Captain Allan Macdonell, of the Eighty-Fourth Regiment: that the family of his said brother have been detained by the Rebels in and about Albany since the year 1775, and that unless it was for the assistance they have met with from Mr. James Ellice, of Schenectady, merchant, they must have perished.

Your Memorialists therefore humbly pray Your Excellency will be graciously pleased to take the distressed situation of said families into consideration, and to grant that a flag be sent to demand them in exchange, or otherwise direct towards obtaining their releasement, as Your Excellency in your wisdom shall see fit, and your Memorialists will ever pray as in duty bound.

John Macdonell,
Alexander Macdonell."

"To the Honourable Sir John Johnson, Lieutenant-Colonel Commander of the King's Royal Regiment of New York.

The humbel petition of sundry soldiers of said Regiment sheweth,—

That your humble petitioners, whose names are hereunto subscribed, have families in different places of the Counties of Albany and Tryon, who have been and are daily ill-treated by the enemies of Government.

Therefore we do humbly pray that Your Honour would be pleased to procure permission for them to come to Canada,

And your petitioners will ever pray.

John McGlenny, Thomas Ross, Alexander Cameron, Frederick Goose, Wm. Urchad (Urquhart?), Duncan McIntire, Andrew Mileross, Donald McCarter, Allen Grant, Hugh Chisholm, Angus Grant, John McDonald, Alex. Ferguson, Thomas Taylor, William Cameron, George Murdoff, William Chession (Chisholm), John Christy, Daniel Campbell, Donald Ross, Donald Chissem, Roderick McDonald, Alexander Grant.

The names and number of each family intended in the written petition:—

	Name of Family	Consisting of	No
1,	Duncan McIntyre's	Wife, Sister and Child	3
2,	John Christy's	Wife and 3 Children	4
3,	George Mordoff's	" and 6 "	7
4,	Daniel Campbell's	" and 5 "	6

	Name of Family	Consisting of	No
5,	Andrew Milross'	Wife	1
6,	William Urghad's	Wife and 3 "	4
7,	Donald McCarter's	" and 3 "	4
8,	Donald Ross'	" and 1 Child	2
9,	Allan Grant's	" and 1 "	2
10,	William Chissim's	" and 1 "	2
11,	Donald Chissim's	" and 2 Children	3
12,	Hugh Chissims	" and 5 "	6
13,	Roderick McDonald's	" and 4 "	5
14,	Angus Grant's	" and 5 "	6
15,	Alexander Grant's	" and 4 "	5
16,	Donald Grant's	" and 4 "	5
17,	John McDonald's	Wife	1
18,	John McGlenny's	" and 2 "	3
19,	Alexander Ferguson's	" and 5 "	6
20,	Thomas Ross'	" and 4 "	5
21,	Thomas Taylor's	" and 1 Child	2
22,	Alexander Cameron's	" and 3 Children	4
23,	William Cameron's	" and 3 "	4
24,	Frederick Goose's	" and 4 "	5"

Mrs. Helen MacDonell, wife of Allan, the chief, was apprehended and sent to Schenectady, and in 1780 managed to escape, and made her way to New York. Before she was taken, and while her husband was still a prisoner of war, she appears to have been the chief person who had charge of the settlement, after the men had fled with Sir John Johnson. A letter of hers has been preserved, which is not only interesting, but throws some light on the action of the Highlanders. It is addressed to Major Jellis Fonda, at Caughnawaga.

"Sir: Some time ago I wrote you a letter, much to this purpose, concerning the Inhabitants of this Bush being made prisoners. There was no such thing then in agitation as you was pleased to observe in your letter to me this morning. Mr. Billie Laird came amongst the people to give them warning to go in to sign, and swear. To this they will never consent, being already prisoners of General Schuyler. His Excellency was pleased by your proclamation, directing every one of them to return to their farms, and that they should be no more troubled nor molested during the war. To this they agreed, and have not done anything against the country, nor intend to, if let alone. If not, they will lose their lives before being taken prisoners again. They begged the favour of me to write to Major Fonda and the gentlemen of the committee to this purpose. They blame neither the one nor the other of you gentlemen, but those ill-natured fellows amongst them that get up an excitement about nothing, in order to ingratiate themselves in your favour. They were of very great hurt to your cause since May last, through violence and ignorance. I do not know what the consequences would have been to them long ago, if not prevented. Only think what daily provocation does.

Jenny joins me in compliments to Mrs. Fonda.

I am, Sir,
Your humble servant,
Callachie, 15th March, 1777.   Helen McDonell."*

Immediately on the arrival of Sir John Johnson in Montreal, with his party who fled from Johnstown, he was commissioned a Colonel in the British service. At once he set about to organize a regiment composed of those who had accompanied him, and other refugees who had followed their example. This regiment was called the "King's Royal Regiment of New York," but by Americans was known as "The Royal Greens," probably because the facings of their uniforms were of that color. In the formation of the regiment he was instructed that the officers of the corps were to be divided in such a manner as to assist those who were distressed by the war; but there were to be no pluralities of officers,— a practice then common in the British army.

In this regiment, Butler's Rangers, and the Eighty-Fourth, or Royal Highland Emigrant Regiment also then raised, the Highland gentlemen who had, in 1773, emigrated to Tryon county, received commissions, as well as those who had previously had joined the ranks. After the war proper returns of the officers were made, and from these the following tables have been extracted. The number of private soldiers of the same name are in proportion.

---

*Sir John Johnson's Orderly Book, p. LXXXII.

HIGHLAND SETTLEMENT ON THE MOHAWK. 213

"First Battalion King's Royal Regiment of New York."

Rank	Name	Place of Nativity	Service	Remarks
Captain..	Alexander Macdonell... (Aberchalder)	Scotland.	8 yrs.	200 acres of land in fee simple, under Sir John Johnson, at yearly annual rent of £6 per 100.
Captain..	Angus Macdonell.......	Scotland.	25 yrs.	Ensign in 60th Regt., 8th July, 1760; Lieut. in do. Dec. 27, 1770; sold out on account of bad health, May 22, 1775. Had no lands.
Captain..	John Macdonell......... (Scotas)	Scotland.	8 yrs.	Had landed property, 500 acres, purchased and began to improve in April, 1774.
Captain..	Archibald Macdonell.... (Leek)	Scotland.	8 yrs.	Merchant; had no lands.
Captain.. Lieut.....	Allan Macdonell........ (Leek)	Scotland.	8 yrs.	Held 200 acres in fee simple, under Sir John, at £6 per 100 acres.
Lieut.....	Hugh Macdonell........ (Aberchalder)	Scotland.	7 yrs.	Son of Captain Macdonell
Ensign...	Miles Macdonell........ (Scotas)	Scotland.	3 yrs.	Son of Captain John Macdonell.

Second Battalion King's Royal Regiment of New York.

Rank	Name	Place of Nativity	Service	Remarks
Captain..	James Macdonell.......	Scotland.	8 yrs.	Held —— acres in fee simple, under Sir John, at £6 per 100 acres.
Lieut.....	Ronald Macdonell...... (Leek)	Scotland.	3 yrs.	Farmer.

CORPS OF BUTLER'S RANGERS, COMMANDED BY LIEUTENANT-COLONEL JOHN BUTLER.

Rank	Name	Place of Nativity	Service	Remarks
Captain..	John Macdonell......... (Aberchalder)	Invernessshire Scotland.	9 yrs.	Came to America with his father and other Highlanders in 1773, settled in Tryon County, near Johnstown, in the Province of New York; entered His Majesty's Service as a Subaltern Officer, June 14, 1775, in the 84th or Royal Highland Emigrants.
First Lieut.	Alexander Macdonell.... (Collachie)	Invernessshire Scotland.	7 yrs.	Came to America with his father and other Highland Emigrants in 1773, settled in Tryon County, near Johnstown, in the Province of New York; entered His Majesty's Service as a Volunteer in the 84th or Royal Highland Emigrants.
Second Lieut.	Chichester Macdonell... (Aberchalder)	Invernessshire Scotland.	6 yrs.	Came to America with his father and other Highland Emigrants in 1773, and settled near Johnstown; entered His Majesty's Service as a Volunteer in the King's Royal Regiment of New York in the year 1778.

EIGHTY-FOURTH OR ROYAL HIGHLAND EMIGRANT REGIMENT.

Rank	Name	Place of Nativity	Service	Remarks
Captain..	Allan Macdonell....... (Collachie)			Prisoner at Lancaster in Pennsylvania.
Lieut....	Ronald Macdonell.....		40 yrs.	
Lieut....	Arch'd Macdonell......		8 yrs	

SEVENTY-FIRST REGIMENT.

Rank	Name	Place of Nativity	Service	Remarks
Lieut....	Angus Macdonell......	....	.....	..................."*

In the month of January, following his flight into Canada, Sir John Johnson found his way into the city of New York. From that time he became one of the most bitter and virulent foes of his countrymen engaged in the contest, and repeatedly became the scourge of his former neighbors—in all of which his Highland retainers bore a prominent part. In savage cruelty, together with Butler's Rangers, they outrivalled their Indian allies. The aged, the infirm, helpless women, and the innocent babe in the cradle, alike perished before them. In all this the MacDonells were among the foremost. Such warfare met the approval of the British Cabinet, and officers felt no compunction in relating their achievements. Colonel Guy Johnson writing to lord George Germain, November 11, 1779, not only speaks of the result of his conference with Sir John Johnson, but further remarks that "there appeared little prospect of effecting anything beyond harrassing the frontiers with detached partys."† In all probability none of the official reports related the atrocities perpetrated under the direction of the minor officers.

Although "The Royal Greens" were largely composed of the Mohawk Highlanders, and especially all who decamped from Johnstown with Sir John Johnson, and Butler's Rangers had a fair percentage of the same, it is not necessary to enter into a detailed account of their achievements, because neither was essentially Highlanders. Their movements were not always in a body, and the essential share borne by the Highlanders have not been recorded in the papers that have been preserved. Individual deeds have been narrated, some of which are here given.

The Royal Greens and Butler's Rangers formed a part of the expedition under Colonel Barry St. Leger that was sent against Fort Schuyler in order to create a diversion in favor of General

---
*Macdonell's Sketches of Glengarry in Canada, p. 22. †Documentary and Colonial History of New York, Vol. VIII, p. 779.

Burgoyne's army then on its march towards Albany. In order to relieve Fort Schuyler (Stanwix) General Herkimer with a force of eight hundred was dispatched and, on the way, met the army of St. Leger near Oriskany, August 6, 1777. On the 3rd St. Leger encamped before Fort Stanwix, his force numbering sixteen hundred, eight hundred of whom were Indians. Proper precautions were not taken by General Herkimer, while every advantage was enforced by his wary enemy. He fell into an ambuscade, and a desperate conflict ensued. During the conflict Colonel Butler attempted a *ruse-de guerre,* by sending, from the direction of the fort, a detachment of The Royal Greens, disguised as American troops, in expectation that they might be received as reenforcements from the garrison. They were first noticed by Lieutenant Jacob Sammons, who at once notified Captain Jacob Gardenier; but the quick eye of the latter had detected the ruse. The Greens continued to advance until hailed by Gardenier, at which moment one of his own men observing an acquaintance in the opposing ranks, and supposing them to be friends, ran to meet him, and presented his hand. The credulous fellow was dragged into their lines and notified that he was a prisoner.

"He did not yield without a struggle; during which Gardenier, watching the action and the result, sprang forward, and with a blow from his spear levelled the captor to the dust and liberated his man. Others of the foe instantly set upon him, of whom he slew the second and wounded the third. Three of the disguised Greens now sprang upon him, and one of his spurs becoming entangled in their clothes, he was thrown to the ground. Still, contending, however, with almost super-human strength, both of his thighs were transfixed to the earth by the bayonets of two of his assailants, while the third presented a bayonet to his breast, as if to thrust him through. Seizing the bayonet with his left hand, by a sudden wrench he brought its owner down upon himself, where he held him as a shield against the arms of the others, until one of his own men, Adam Miller, observing the struggle, flew to the rescue. As the assailants turned upon their new adversary, Gardenier rose upon his seat; and although his hand was severely lacerated by grasping the bayonet which had been drawn through it, he seized his spear lying by his side, and quick as lightning planted it to the barb in the side of the assailant with whom he had been clenched. The man fell and expired—proving to be

Lieutenant McDonald, one of the loyalist officers from Tryon county."*

This was John McDonald, who had been held as a hostage by General Schuyler, and when permitted to return home, helped run off the remainder of the Highlanders to Canada, as previously noticed. June 19, 1777, he was appointed captain Lieutenant in The Royal Greens.† During the engagement thirty of The Royal Greens fell near the body of McDonald. The loss of Herkimer was two hundred killed, exclusive of the wounded and prisoners. The royalist loss was never given, but known to be heavy. The Indians lost nearly a hundred warriors among whom were sachems held in great favor. The Americans retained possession of the field owing to the sortie made by the garrison of Fort Schuyler on the camp of St. Leger. On the 22nd St. Leger receiving alarming reports of the advance of General Arnold suddenly decamped from before Fort Schuyler, leaving his baggage behind him. Indians, belonging to the expedition followed in the rear, tomahawking and scalping the stragglers; and when the army did not run fast enough, they accelerated the speed by giving their war cries and fresh alarms, thus adding increased terror to the demoralized troops. Of all the men that Butler took with him, when he arrived in Quebec he could muster but fifty. The Royal Greens also showed their numbers greatly decimated.

Among the prisoners taken by the Americans was Captain Angus McDonell of The Royal Greens. ‡ For greater security he was transferred to the southern portion of the State. On October 12th following, at Kingston, he gave the following parole to the authorities:

"I, Angus McDonell, lieutenant in the 60th or Royal American regiment, now a prisoner to the United States of America and enlarged on my parole, do promise upon my word of honor that I will continue within one mile of the house of Jacobus Hardenburgh, and in the town of Hurley, in the county of Ulster; and that I will not do any act, matter or thing whatsoever against the interests of America; and further, that I will remove hereafter to such place as the governor of the state of New York or the presi-

---

*Stone's Life of Joseph Brant, Vol. I, p. 238.   †Johnson's Orderly Book, p. 57.   *Ibid, p. 59.

dent of the Council of Safety of the said state shall direct, and that I will observe this my parole until released, exchanged or otherwise ordered.

Angus McDonell."

The following year Captain Angus McDonald and Allen McDonald, ensign in the same company were transferred to Reading, Pennsylvania. The former was probably released or exchanged for he was with the regiment when it was disbanded at the close

THE VALLEY OF WYOMING.

of the War. What became of the latter is unknown. Probably neither of them were Sir John Johnson's tenants.

The next movement of special importance relates to the melancholy story of Wyoming, immortalized in verse by Thomas Campbell in his "Gertrude of Wyoming." Towards the close of June 1778 the British officers at Niagara determined to strike a blow at Wyoming, in Pennsylvania. For this purpose an expedition of about three hundred white men under Colonel John

Butler, together with about five hundred Indians, marched for the scene of action. Just what part the McDonells took in the Massacre of Wyoming is not known, nor is it positive any were present; but belonging to Butler's Rangers it is fair to assume that all such participated in those heartrending scenes which have been so often related. It was a terrible day and night for that lovely valley, and its beauty was suddenly changed into horror and desolation. The Massacre of Wyoming stands out in bold relief as one of the darkest pictures in the whole panorama of the Revolution.

While this scene was being enacted, active preparations were pushed by Alexander McDonald for a descent on the New York frontiers. It was the same Alexander who has been previously mentioned as having been permitted to return to the Johnstown settlement, and then assisted in helping the remaining Highland families escape to Canada. He was a man of enterprise and activity, and by his energy he collected three hundred royalists and Indians and fell with great fury upon the frontiers, Houses were burned, and such of the people as fell into his hands were either killed or made prisoners. One example of the blood thirsty character of this man is given by Sims, in his "Trappers of New York," as follows:

"On the morning of October 25, 1781, a large body of the enemy under Maj. Ross, entered Johnstown with several prisoners, and not a little plunder; among which was a number of human scalps taken the afternoon and night previous, in settlements in and adjoining the Mohawk valley; to which was added the scalp of Hugh McMonts, a constable, who was surprised and killed as they entered Johnstown. In the course of the day the troops from the garrisons near and militia from the surrounding country, rallied under the active and daring Willett, and gave the enemy battle on the Hall farm, in which the latter were finally defeated with loss, and made good their retreat into Canada. Young Scarsborough was then in the nine months' service, and while the action was going on, himself and one Crosset left the Johnstown fort, where they were on garrison duty, to join in the fight, less than two miles distant. Between the Hall and woods they soon found themselves engaged. Crosset after shooting down one or two, received a bullet through one hand, but winding a handkerchief around it he continued the fight under cover of a hemlock stump. He was shot down and killed there, and his companion surrounded and made prisoner by a party of Scotch (Highlanders) troops commanded by Captain McDonald. When Scarsborough was captured, Capt. McDonald was not present, but the moment he saw him he ordered his men to shoot him down. Several refused; but three, shall I call them men? obeyed the dastardly order, and yet he possibly would have survived his wounds, had not the miscreant in authority cut him down with his own broadsword. The sword was caught in its first descent, and the valiant captain drew it out, cutting the hand nearly in two."*

This was the same McDonald who, in 1779, figured in the battle of the Chemung, together with Sir John and Guy Johnson and Walter N. Butler.

Just what part the Mohawk Highlanders, if any, had in the Massacre of Cherry Valley on October 11, 1778, may not be known. The leaders were Walter N. Butler, son of Colonel John Butler, who was captain of a company of Rangers, and the monster Brant.

Owing to the frequent depredations made by the Indians, the Royal Greens, Butler's Rangers, and the independent company of Alexander McDonald, upon the frontiers, destroying the innocent and helpless as well as those who might be found in arms, Congress voted that an expedition should be sent into the Indian country. Washington detached a division from the army under General John Sullivan to lay waste that country. The instructions were obeyed, and Sullivan did not cease until he found no more to lay waste. The only resistance he met with that was of any moment was on August 29, 1779, when the enemy hoping to ambuscade the army of Sullivan, brought on the battle of Chemung, near the present site of Elmira. There were about three hundred royalists under Colonel John Butler and Captain Alexander McDonald, assisting Joseph Brant who commanded the Indians. The defeat was so overwhelming that the royalists and Indians, in a demoralized condition sought shelter under the walls of Fort Niagara.

The lower Mohawk Valley having experienced the calamities of border wars was yet to feel the full measures of suffering. On

---

*Ibid, p. 56.

Sunday, May 21, 1780, Sir John Johnson with some British troops, a detachment of Royal Greens, and about two hundred Indians and Tories, at dead of night fell unexpectedly on Johnstown, the home of his youth. Families were killed and scalped, the houses pillaged and then burned. Instances of daring and heroism in withstanding the invaders have been recorded.

Sir John's next achievement was in the fall of the same year, when he descended with fire and sword into the rich settlements along the Schoharie. He was overtaken by the American force at Klock's Field and put to flight.

Sir John Johnson with the Royal Greens, principally his former tenants and retainers, appear to have been especially stimulated with hate against the people of their former homes who did not sympathize with their views. In the summer of 1781 another expedition was secretly planned against Johnstown, and executed with silent celerity. The expedition consisted of four companies of the Second battalion of Sir John's regiment of Royal Greens, Butler's Rangers and two hundred Indians, numbering in all about one thousand men, under the command of Major Ross. He was defeated at the battle of Johnstown on October 25th. The army of Major Ross, for four days in the wilderness, on their advance had been living on only a half pound of horse flesh per man per day; yet they were so hotly pursued by the Americans that they were forced to trot off a distance of thirty miles before they stopped,—during a part of the distance they were compelled to sustain a running fight. They crossed Canada Creek late in the afternoon, where Walter N. Butler attempted to rally the men. He was shot through the head by an Oneida Indian, who was with the Americans. When Captain Butler fell his troops fled in the utmost confusion, and continued their flight through the night. Without food and even without blankets they had eighty miles to traverse through the dreary and pathless wilderness.

On August 6, 1781, Donald McDonald, one of the Highlanders who had fled from Johnstown, made an attempt upon Shell's Bush, about four miles north of the present village of Herkimer, at the head of sixty-six Indians and Tories. John Christian Shell had built a block-house of his own, which was large and substantial, and well calculated to withstand a seige. The first story had no windows, but furnished with loopholes which could be used to shoot through by muskets. The second story projected over the first, so that the garrison could fire upon an advancing enemy, or cast missles upon their heads. The owner had a family of six sons, the youngest two were twins, and only eight years old. Most of his neighbors had taken refuge in Fort Dayton; but this settler refused to leave his home. When Donald McDonald and his party arrived at Shell's Bush his brother with his sons were at work in the field; and the children, unfortunately were so widely separated from their father, as to fall into the hands of the enemy.

"Shell and his other boys succeeded in reaching their castle, and barricading the ponderous door. And then commenced the battle. The beseiged were well armed, and all behaved with admirable bravery; but none more bravely than Shell's wife, who loaded the pieces as her husband and sons discharged them. The battle commenced at two o'clock, and continued until dark. Several attempts were made by McDonald to set fire to the castle, but without success; and his forces were repeatedly driven back by the galling fire they received. McDonald at length procured a crow-bar and attempted to force the door; but while thus engaged he received a shot in the leg from Shell's Blunderbuss, which put him *hors du combat*. None of his men being sufficiently near at the moment to rescue him, Shell, quick as lightning, opened the door, and drew him within the walls a prisoner. The misfortune of Shell and his garrison was, that their ammunition began to run low; but McDonald was very amply provided, and to save his own life, he surrendered his cartridges to the garrison to fire upon his comrades. Several of the enemy having been killed and others wounded, they now drew off for a respite. Shell and his troops, moreover, needed a little breathing time; and feeling assured that, so long as he had the commanding officer of the beseigers in his possession, the enemy would hardly attempt to burn the citadel, he ceased firing. He then went up stairs, and sang the hymn which was a favorite of Luther during the perils and afflictions of the Great Reformer in his controversies with the Pope. While thus engaged the enemy likewise ceased firing. But they soon after rallied again to the fight, and made a desperate effort to carry the fortress by assault. Rushing up to the walls, five of them thrust the muzzles of their guns through the loop-holes, but had no sooner done so, than Mrs. Shell, seizing an axe, by quick and well directed blows ruined every musket thus thrust through the walls, by bending the barrels. A few more well-directed shots by Shell and his sons once more drove the assailants back. Shell thereupon ran up to the second story, just in the twilight, and calling out to his wife with a loud voice, informed her that Captain Small was approaching from Fort Dayton with succors. In yet louder notes he then exclaimed—'Captain Small march your company round upon this side of the house. Captain Getman, you had better wheel your men off to the left, and come up upon that side.' There were of course no troops approaching; but the directions of Shell were given with such precision, and such apparent earnestness and sincerity, that the stratagem succeeded, and the enemy immediately fled to the woods, taking away the twin-lads as prisoners. Setting the best provisions they had before their reluctant guest, Shell and his family lost no time in repairing to Fort Dayton, which they reached in saftey—leaving McDonald in the quiet possession of the castle he had been striving to capture in vain. Some two or three of McDonald's Indians lingered about the premises to ascertain the fate of their leader; and finding that Shell and his family had evacuated the post, ventured in to visit him. Not being able to remove him, however, on taking themselves off, they charged their wounded leader to inform Shell, that if he would be kind to him, (McDonald,) they would take good care of his (Shell's) captive boys. McDonald was the next day removed to the fort by Captain Small, where his leg was amputated; but the blood could not be stanched, and he died within a few hours. The lads were carried away into Canada. The loss of the enemy on the ground was eleven killed and six wounded. The boys, who were rescued after the war, reported that they took twelve of their wounded away with them, nine of whom died before they arrived in Canada. McDonald wore a silver-mounted tomahawk, which was taken from him by Shell. It was marked by thirty scalp-notches, showing that few Indians could have been more industrious than himself in gathering that description of military trophies."*

The close of the Revolution found the First Battalion of the King's Regiment of New York stationed at Isle aux Noix and Carleton Island with their wives and children to the number of one thousand four hundred and sixty-two. The following is a list of the officers of both Battalions at the close of the War:

---

*Stone's Life of Joseph Brant, Vol. II, p. 164.

"Return of the Officers of the late First Battalion, King's Royal Regiment of New York."

Rank	Names	Place of Nativity	Length of Service	Former Situations and Remarks
Lt...... Col...... Com ... Lt......	Sir John Johnson..... Bart	America.	8 yrs.	Succeeded his father, the late Sir Wm. Johnson, as a Maj. Gen. of the Northern Dis. of the Prov. of New York; was in possession of nearly 200,000 acres of valuable land, lost in consequence of the rebellion.
Maj......	James Gray..........	Scotland.	26 yrs.	Ensign in Lord London's Regt., 1745; Lieut. and Capt. in ye 42nd till after taking the Havannah, at which time he sold out. Had some landed property, part of which is secured to his son, ye remnant lost in consequence of the rebellion.
Capt.....	Angus McDonell.....	Scotland.	25 yrs.	Ensign in 60th Regt. July 8th, 1760; Lieut. in same regt., 27th Dec., 1770. Sold out on account of bad state of health, 22nd May, 1775. Had no lands.
Capt.....	John Munro.........	Scotland.	8 yrs.	Had considerable landed property, lost in consequence of ye Rebellion, and served in last war in America.
Capt.....	Patrick Daly.........	Ireland..	9 yrs.	Lieut. in the 84th Regt. at the Siege of Quebec, 1775-76.
Capt.....	Richard Duncan.....	Scotland.	13 yrs.	Five years Ensign in the 55th Regiment.
Capt.....	Sam'l. Anderson.....	America.	8 yrs.	Had landed property, and served in last war in America.
Capt.....	John McDonell.......	Scotland.	8 yrs.	Had landed property, 500 acres, purchased and began to improve in April, 1774.
Capt	Alex McDonell......	Scotland.	8 yrs.	200 acres of land in fee simple, under Sir John Johnson, Bart., ye annual rent of £6 per 100.

"RETURN OF THE OFFICERS OF THE LATE FIRST BATTALION, KING'S ROYAL REGIMENT OF NEW YORK,"—Continued.

Rank	Names	Place of Nativity	Length of Service	Former Situations and Remarks
Capt.	Arch. McDonell	Scotland.	8 yrs.	Merchant. No lands.
Capt. Lt.	Allan McDonell	Scotland.	8 yrs.	Held 200 acres of land under Sir John Johnson, at £6 per 100.
Lt.	Mal. McMartin	Scotland.	8 yrs.	Held 100 acres of land under Sir John Johnson, at £6.
Lt.	Peter Everett	America.	7 yrs.	Had some landed property.
Lt.	John Prentiss	America.	9 yrs.	A volunteer at the Siege of Quebec, 1775-76.
Lt.	Hugh McDonell	Scotland.	7 yrs.	Son of Capt. McDonell.
Lt.	John F. Holland	America.	5 yrs.	Son of Major Holland, Surveyor-General, Province of Quebec.
Lt.	William Coffin	America.	3 yrs.	Son of Mr. Coffin, merchant, late of Boston.
Lt.	Jacob Farrand	America.	7 yrs.	Nephew to Major Gray.
Lt.	William Claus	America.	7 yrs.	Son of Col. Claus, deputy agent Indian Affairs.
Lt.	Hugh Munro	America.	6 yrs.	Son of Capt. John Munro.
Lt.	Joseph Anderson	America.	6 yrs.	Son of Capt. Sam'l. Anderson.
Lt.	Thomas Smith	Ireland.	4 yrs.	Son of Dr. Smith.
Ens.	John Connolly	Ireland.	2 yrs.	Private Gentleman.
Ens.	Jacob Glen	America.	3 yrs.	Son of John Glen, Esq., of Schenectady. Had considerable landed property.
Ens.	Miles McDonell	Scotland.	3 yrs.	Son of Capt. John McDonell.
Ens.	Eben'r Anderson	America	6 yrs.	Son of Capt. Sam'l. Anderson.
Ens.	Duncan Cameron	Scotland.	14 yrs.	In service last war preceding this one.
Ens.	John Mann	America.	8 yrs.	Private Gentleman.
Ens.	Francis McCarthy	Ireland.	28 yrs.	Formerly Sergeant in the 34th Regiment.
Ens.	John Valentine	America.	24 yrs.	18 years in 55th and 62nd Regiments.
Ch'p.	John Doty	America.	8 yrs.	Formerly minister of the Gospel at Schenectady.
Adj't.	James Valentine	Ireland.	4 yrs.	Son of Ens. John Valentine.
Q. M.	Isaac Mann	America.	8 yrs.	Merchant.
Surg.	Charles Austin	England.	22 yrs.	14 years in hospital work.
M'te	James Stewart	Scotland.	14 yrs.	Surgeon's mate in the 42nd Regt. the war before last.

"Return of the Officers of the Late Second Battalion, King's Royal Regiment of New York."

Rank	Names	Place of Nativity	Length of Service	Former Situations and Remarks
Maj.....	Robert Leake........	England..	7 yrs.	Had some landed property, etc., lost in consequence of the rebellion.
Capt.....	Thos. Gummesell....	England.	8 yrs.	Formerly Merchant in New York.
Capt.....	Jacob Maurer........	Foreign'r	28 yrs.	Served in ye army in the 60th Regt., from 1756 to 1763, afterwards in the Quarter-Master General's Dept.
Capt.....	Wm. Morrison.......	Scotland.	8 yrs.	Was lieut., 19th June, 1776, in 1st Batt.; Capt., 15th Nov., 1781, in the 2nd Batt.
Capt.....	James McDonell.....	Scotland.	8 yrs.	Held 200 acres of land in fee simple, under Sir John Johnson, at £6 per 100.
Capt.....	Geo. Singleton.......	Ireland..	8 yrs.	Formerly merchant.
Capt.....	Wm. Redf'd Crawford	America.	8 yrs.	Held lands under Sir John Johnson.
Capt.....	—Byrns	Ireland..	8 yrs.	Held lands under Sir John Johnson.
Capt.....	—Lepscomb..........	England.	7 yrs.	Midshipman Royal Navy.
Capt.....	—McKenzie	Scotland.	8 yrs.	Held lands under Sir John Johnson.
Lt........	Patrick Langan......	Ireland..	7 yrs.	Private Gentleman.
Lt........	Walter Sutherland...	Scotland.	10 yrs.	Soldier and non-commissioned officer in 26th Regt; ensign, 17th Oct., 1779, in 1st Batt., lieut., Nov., 1781, in 2nd Batt.
Lt........	William McKay......	Scotland.	15 yrs.	7 years volunteer and sergeant in 21st Regt.
Lt........	Neal Robertson......	Scotland.	8 yrs.	Merchant.
Lt........	Henry Young........	America.	8 yrs.	Farmer.
Lt........	John Howard........	Ireland..	13 yrs.	Farmer; served 6 years last war, from 1755 to 1761, as soldier and non-commissioned officer in 28th Regt.

"Return of the Officers of the Late Second Battalion, King's Royal Regiment of New York,"—Continued.

Rank	Names	Place of Nativity	Length of Service	Former Situations and Remarks
Lt......	Jeremiah French.....	America.	7 yrs.	Farmer.
Lt......	Phil. P. Lansingh....	America.	4 yrs.	High Sheriff, Charlot County.
Lt......	Hazelt'n Spencer.....	America.	7 yrs.	Farmer.
Lt......	Oliver Church.......	America.	7 yrs.	Farmer.
Lt......	William Fraser	Scotland.	7 yrs.	Farmer.
Lt......	Christian Wher......	Foreign'r	7 yrs.	Farmer.
Ens......	Alex. McKenzie....	N.Britain	4 yrs.	Farmer.
Ens......	Ron. McDonell.....	N.Britain	3 yrs.	Farmer.
Ens......	—Hay.............	America.	3 yrs.	Son of Gov. Hay at Detroit.
Ens......	Samuel McKay......	America.	3 yrs.	Son of the late Capt. McKay.
Ens......	Timothy Thompson..	America.	3 yrs.	Private Gentleman.
Ens......	John McKay........	America.	3 yrs.	Son of the late Capt. McKay.
Ens......	—Johnson...........	Ireland..	2 yrs.	Nephew of the late Sir Wm. Johnson, Bart.
Ens......	—Crawford..........	America.	4 yrs.	Son of Capt. Crawford.
Ch'p....	John Stuart.........	America.	3 yrs.	Missionary for the Mohawk Indians at Fort Hunter.
Adjt.....	—Fraser.............	Scotland.	10 yrs.	7 years soldier and non-commissioned officer in 34th Regiment.
Q. M....	—Dies..............	America.	7 yrs.	Farmer.
Surg....	R. Kerr............	Scotland.	3 yrs.	Assistant Surgeon."*

The officers and men of the First Battalion, with their families, settled in a body in the first five townships west of the boundary line of the Province of Quebec, being the present townships of Lancaster, Charlottenburgh, Cornwall, Osnabruck and Williamsburgh; while those of the Second Battalion went farther west to the Bay of Quinte, in the counties of Lennox and Prince Edward. Each soldier received a certificate entitling him to land; of which the following is a copy:

"His Majesty's Provincial Regiment, called the King's Royal

---

*Macdonell's Sketches of Glengarry, p. 47.

Regiment of New York, whereof Sir John Johnson, Knight and Baronet is Lieutenant-Colonel, Commandant.

These are to certify that the Bearer hereof, Donald McDonell, soldier in Capt. Angus McDonell's Company, of the aforesaid Regiment, born in the Parish of Killmoneneoack, in the County of Inverness, aged thirty-five years, has served honestly and faithfully in the said regiment Seven Years; and in consequence of His Majesty's Order for Disbanding the said Regiment, he is hereby discharged, is entitled, by His Majesty's late Order, to the Portion of Land allotted to each soldier of His Provincial Corps, who wishes to become a Settler in this Province, He having first received all just demands of Pay, Cloathing, &c., from his entry into the said Regiment, to the Date of his Discharge, as appears from his Receipt on the back hereof.

Given under my Hand and Seal at Arms, at Montreal, this twenty-fourth Day of December, 1783.

John Johnson."

"I, Donald McDonell, private soldier, do acknowledge that I have received all my Cloathing, Pay, Arrears of Pay, and all Demands whatsoever, from the time of my Inlisting in the Regiment and Company mentioned on the other Side to this present Day of my Discharge, as witness my Hand this 24th day of December, 1783.

Donald McDonell."*

There appears to have been some difficulty in according to the men the amount of land each should possess, as may be inferred from the petition of Colonel John Butler on behalf of The Royal Greens and his corps of Rangers. The Order in Council, October 22 1788 allowed them the same as that allotted to the members of the Royal Highland Emigrants.† Ultimately each soldier received one hundred acres on the river front, besides two hundred at a remote distance. If married he was entitled to fifty acres more, an additional fifty for every child, Each child, on coming of age, was entitled to a further grant of two hundred acres.

It is not the purpose to follow these people into their future homes, for this would be later than the Peace of 1783. Let it suffice to say that their lands were divided by lot, and into the wilderness they went, and there cleared the forests, erected their shanties out of round logs, to a height of eight feet, with a room not exceeding twenty by fifteen feet.

---

*Ibid, p. 51. †See Appendix, Note K.

HIGHLAND SETTLEMENT ON THE MOHAWK. 229

These people were pre-eminently social and attached to the manners and customs of their fathers. In Scotland the people would gather in one of their huts during the long winter nights and listen to the tales of Ossian and Fingal. So also they would gather in their huts and listen to the best reciter of tales. Often the long nights would be turned into a recital of the sufferings they endured during their flight into Canada from Johnstown; and also of their privations during the long course of the war. It required no imagination to picture their hardships, nor was it necessary to indulge in exaggeration. Many of the women, through the wilderness, carried their children on their backs, the greater part of the distance, while the men were burdened with their arms and such goods as were deemed necessary. They endured perils by land and by water; and their food often consisted of the flesh of dogs and horses, and the roots of trees. Gradually some of these story tellers varied their tale, and, perhaps, believed in the glosses.

A good story has gained extensive currency, and has been variously told, on Donald Grant. He was born at Crasky, Glenmoriston, Scotland, and was one of the heroes who sheltered prince Charles in the cave of Corombian, when wandering about, life in hand, after the battle of Culloden, before he succeeded in effecting his escape to the Outer Hebrides. Donald, with others, settled in Glengarry, a thousand acres having been allotted to him. This old warrior, having seen much service, knew well the country between Johnstown and Canada. He took charge of one of the parties of refugees in their journey from Schenectady to Canada. Donald lived to a good old age and was treated with much consideration by all, especially those whom he had led to their new homes. It was well known that he could spin a good story equal to the best. As years went on, the number of Donald's party rapidly increased, as he told it to open-mouthed listeners, constantly enlarging on the perils and hardships of the journey. A Highland officer, who had served in Canada for some years, was returning home ,and, passing through Glengarry, spent a few days with Alexander Macdonell, priest at St. Raphael's. Having expressed his desire to meet some of the veterans of the war, so that he might hear their tales and rehearse them in Scotland, that they might know how their kinsmen in Canada had fought and suffered for the Crown, the priest, amongst others, took him to see old Donald Grant. The opportunity was too good to be lost, and Donald told the general in Gaelic the whole story, omitting no details; giving an account of the number of men, women and children he had brought with him, their perils and their escapes, their hardships borne with heroic devotion; how, when on the verge of starvation, they had boiled their moccassins and eaten them; how they had encountered the enemy, the wild beasts and Indians, beaten all off and landed the multitude safely in Glengarry. The General listened with respectful attention, and at the termination of the narrative, wishing to say something pleasant, observed: "Why, dear me, Donald, your exploits seem almost to have equalled even those of Moses himself when leading the children of Israel through the Wilderness from Egypt to the Land of Promise." Up jumped old Donald. "Moses," exclaimed the veteran with an unmistakable air of contempt, and adding a double expletive that need not here be repeated, "Compare ME to Moses! Why, Moses took forty years in his vain attempts to lead his men over a much shorter distance, and through a mere trifling wilderness in comparison with mine, and he never did reach his destination, and lost half his army in the Red Sea. I brought my people here without the loss of a single man."

It has been noted that the Highlanders who settled on the Mohawk, on the lands of Sir William Johnson, were Roman Catholics. Sir William, nor his son and successor, Sir John Johnson, took any steps to procure them a religious teacher in the principles of their faith. They were not so provided until after the Revolution, and then only when they were settled on the lands that had been allotted to them. In 1785, the people themselves took the proper steps to secure such an one,—and one who was able to speak the Gaelic, for many of them were ignorant of the English language. In the month of September, 1786, the ship "McDonald," from Greenock, brought Reverend Alexander McDonell, Scotus, with five hundred emigrants from Knoydart, who settled with their kinsfolk in Glengarry, Canada.

CHAPTER IX.

THE GLENALADALE HIGHLANDERS OF PRINCE EDWARD ISLAND.

Highlanders had penetrated into the wilds of Ontario, Nova Scotia and Prince Edward Island before they had formed any distinctive settlements of their own. Some of these belonged to the disbanded regiments, but the bulk had come into the country, either through the spirit of adventure, or else to better their condition, and establish homes that would be free from usurpation, oppression, and persecution. It cannot be said that any portion of Canada, at that period, was an inviting field. The Highland settlement that bears the honor of being the first in British North America is that on Prince Edward Island, on the north coast at the head of Tracadie Bay, almost due north of Charlottetown. This settlement was due to John Macdonald, Eighth of Glenaladale, of the family of Clanranald.

John Macdonald was but a child at the date of the battle of Culloden. When of sufficient age he was sent to Ratisbon, Germany, to be educated, where he went through a complete course in the branches of learning as taught in the seminary. Returning to his country he was considered to be one of the most finished and accomplished gentlemen of his generation. But events led him to change his prospects in life. In 1770 a violent persecution against the Roman Catholics broke out in the island of South Uist. Alexander Macdonald, First of Boisdale, also of the house of Clanranald, abandoned the religion of his forbears, and like all new converts was over zealous for his new found faith, and at once attempted to compel all his tenants to follow his example. After many acts of oppression, he summoned all his tenants to hear a paper read to them in their native tongue, containing a renunciation of their religion, and a promise, under oath, never more to hold communication with a catholic priest. The alternative was to sign the paper or lose their lands and homes. At once the people unanimously decided to starve rather than submit. The next step of Boisdale was to take his gold headed cane and drive his tenants before him, like a flock of sheep, to the protestant church. Boisdale failed to realize that conditions had changed in the Highlands; but, even if his methods had smacked of originality, he would have been placed in a far better light. To attempt to imitate the example of another may win applause, but if defeated contempt is the lot.

The history of *Creideamh a bhata bhuidhe*, or the religion of the yellow stick, is such an interesting episode in West Highland story as not to be out of place in this connection. Hector MacLean, Fifth of Coll, who held the estates from 1559 to 1593, became convinced of the truths of the principles of the Reformation, and decided that his tenants should think likewise. He passed over to the island of Rum, and as his tenants came out of the Catholic church he held his cane straight out and said in Gaelic,— "Those who pass the stick to the Kirk are very good tenants, and those who go on the other side may go out of my island." This stick remained in the family until 1868, when it mysteriously disappeared. Mrs. Hamilton Dundas, daughter of Hugh, Fifteenth of Coll, in a letter dated March 26, 1898, describing the stick says, "There was the crest on the top and initials either H. McL. or L. McL. in very flourishing writing engraved on a band or oval below the top. It was a polished, yellow brown malacca stick, much taller than an ordinary walking stick. I seem to recollect that it had two gold rimmed eyelet holes for a cord and tassle."

John Macdonald of Glenaladale, having heard of the proceedings, went to visit the people, and was so touched by their pitiable condition, that he formed the resolution of expatriating himself, and going off at their head to America. He sold out his estates to his counsin Alexander Macdonald of Borrodale, and before the close of 1771, he purchased a tract of forty thousand acres on St. John's Island (now Prince Edward Island), to which he took out about two hundred of his persecuted fellow catholics from South Uist, in the year 1772.

Whatever may have been the trials endured by these people,

what ship they sailed in, how the land was allotted, if at all given to the public, has not come under the author's observation. Certain facts concerning Glenaladale have been advertised. His first wife was Miss Gordon of Baldornie, and his second, Marjory Macdonald of Ghernish, and had issue, Donald who emigrated with him, William, drowned on the coast of Ireland, John, Roderick and Flora. He died in 1811, and was buried on the Island at the Scotch Fort.

Glenaladale early took up arms against the colonists, and having raised a company from among his people, he became a Captain in the Royal Highland Emigrants, or 84th. That he was a man of energy and pluck will appear from the following daring enterprise. During the Revolution, an American man-of-war came to the coast of Nova Scotia, near a port where Glenaladale was on detachment duty, with a small portion of his men. A part of the crew of the warship having landed for the purpose of plundering the people, Glenaladale, with his handful of men, boarded the vessel, cut down those who had been left in charge, hoisted sail, and brought her as a prize triumphantly into the harbor of Halifax. He there got a reinforcement, marched back to his former post, and took the whole crew, composed of Americans and French. As regards his miltary virtues and abilities Major John Small, of the 2nd Battalion of the Royal Highland Emigrants, to which he was attached, writing to the English government, said of him,—

"The activity and unabating zeal of Captain John Macdonald of Glenaladale in bringing an excellent company into the field is his least recommendation, being acknowledged by all who know him to be one of the most accomplished men and best officers of his rank in his Majesty's service."

Slight information may be gained of his connection with the Royal Highland Emigrant Regiment from the "Letter-Book" of Captain Alexander McDonald, of the same regiment. In embodying that regiment he was among the very earliest and readiest. Just why he should have exhibited so much feeling against the Americans whose country he had never seen and who had never harmed him in the least , does not appear. Captain Mc-

Donald, writing from Halifax, September 1, 1775, to Colonel Allan MacLean, says,—

"What Men that are on the Island of St. Johns (Prince Edward's) are already Engaged with Glenaladall who is now here with me, also young Mcdonald, with whom he came, he will Write to you by this opportunity and from the Contents of his Letter I will Leave you to Judge what sort of a Man he is."

By the same letter, "young Mcdonald" had been sent "to ye Island of St. John," unquestionably for the purpose of raising the Highlanders. His great zeal is revealed in a letter from Captain Alexander McDonald to Major Small, dated at Halifax, November 15, 1775:

"Mr. McDonald of Glenaladale staid behind at Newfoundland and by the Last accounts from him he and one Lt Fizgerald had Six and thirty men. I dont doubt by this time his having as many more, he is determined to make out his Number Cost what it will, and I hope you will make out a Commission in his brother Donald's name, * * * "poor Glenaladall I am afraid is Lost as there is no account of him since a small Schooner Arrived which brought an account of his having Six & thirty men then and if he should Not be Lost he is unavoidably ruined in his Means."

The last reference is in a letter to Colonel Allan MacLean, dated at Halifax June 5, 1776:

Glen a la Del is an Ornament to any Corps that he goes into and if the Regiment is not established it had been telling him 300 Guineas that he had never heard of it. On Account of his Affairs upon the Island of St. John's and in Scotland where he was preparing to go to settle his Business when he received the Proposals."

The British government offered Glenaladale the governorship of Prince Edward Island, but owing to the oath of allegiance necessary at the time, he, being a catholic, was obliged to decline the office.

CHAPTER X.

HIGHLAND SETTLEMENT IN PICTOU, NOVA SCOTIA.

"What noble courage must their hearts have fired,
How great the ardor which their souls inspired,
Who leaving far beyond their native plain
Have sought a home beyond the western main;
And braved the perils of the stormy seas
In search of wealth, of freedom, and of ease.
Oh, none can tell, but those who sadly share,
The bosom's anguish, and its wild despair,
What dire distress awaits the hardy bands,
That venture first on bleak and desert lands;
How great the pain, the danger and the toil
Which mark the first rude culture of the soil.
When looking round, the lonely settler sees
His home amid a wilderness of trees;
How sinks his heart in those deep solitudes,
Where not a voice upon his ear intrudes;
Where solemn silence all the waste pervades,
Heightening the horror of its gloomy shades;
Save where the sturdy woodman's strokes resound
That strew the fallen forest on the ground."
—*H. Glodsmith.*

The second settlement of Highlanders in British America was at Pictou, Nova Scotia. The stream of Scottish emigration which flowed in after years, not only over the county of Pictou, but also over the greater portion of eastern Nova Scotia, Cape Breton, Prince Edward Island, and even the upper provinces of Canada, was largely due to this settlement; for these emigrants, in after years, communicated with their friends and induced them to take up their abode in the new country. The stream once started did not take long to deepen and widen.

A company of gentlemen, the majority of whom lived in Philadelphia, received a grant of land in Nova Scotia. Some of the shares passed into the hands of the celebrated Dr. John Witherspoon and John Pagan, a merchant of Greenock, Scotland. These two men appear to have jointly been engaged in promoting emigration to the older colonies. Pagan owned a ship called *Hector*, which was engaged in carrying passengers across the Atlantic. In 1770 she landed Scottish emigrants in Boston. In order to carry out the original obligations of the grant, the proprietors offered liberal inducements for the settlement of it. An agent, named John Ross, was employed, with whom it was agreed that each settler should have a free passage from Scotland, a farm, and a year's free provisions. Ross sailed for Scotland on board the Hector, and on his arrival proceeded to the Highlands, where he painted in glowing colors a picture of the land and the advantages offered. The Highlanders knew nothing of the difficulties awaiting them in a land covered over with a dense unbroken forest, and, tempted by the prospect of owning splendid farms, they were imposed upon, and many agreed to cast their lot on the western side of the Atlantic. The Hector was the vessel that should convey them, with John Spears as master, James Orr being first mate, and John Anderson second. The vessel called first at Greenock, where three families and five young men were taken on board. From there she sailed for Lochbroom, in Ross-shire, where she received thirty-three families and twenty-five single men, having all told about two hundred souls.

On July 1, 1773, this band bade adieu to friends, home, and country and started for a land they knew naught of. But few had ever crossed the ocean. Just as the ship was starting a piper named John McKay came on board who had not paid his passage; the captain ordered him ashore, but the strains of the national instrument so affected those on board that they interceded to have him allowed to accompany them, and offered to share their own rations with him, in exchange for his music, during the passage. Their request was granted, and his performance aided in no small degree to cheer the pilgrims in their long voyage of eleven weeks, in a miserable hulk, across the Atlantic. The band of emigrants kept up their spirits, as best they could, by song, pipe music, dancing, wrestling, and other amusements, during the long and painful voyage. The Hector was an old Dutch ship, and a slow sailer. It was so rotten that the passengers could pick the wood out of the sides with their fingers. They met with a severe gale off the Newfoundland coast, and were driven back so far that it required two weeks to recover the lost distance. The accommodations on board were wretched and the provisions of inferior quality. Small-pox and dysentery broke out among the passengers. Eighteen, most of whom were children, died and were committed to the deep. The former disease was brought on board by a mother and child, both of whom lived to an advanced age. Owing to the voyage being prolonged, the stock of provisions and water became low; the remnant of food left consisted mostly of salt meat, which, with the scarcity of water, added greatly to their sufferings. The oatcake, carried by them, became mouldy, so that much of it was thrown away before they thought such a long passage was before them; but, fortunately for them, Hugh Macleod, more prudent than the rest, gathered into a bag these despised scraps, and during the last few days of the voyage, all were glad to avail themselves of this refuse food.

At last, all the troubles and dangers of the voyage having been surmounted, on September 15th, the Hector dropped anchor, opposite where the town of Pictou now stands. Previous to the arrival of the vessel, the sparsely inhabited country had been somewhat disturbed by the Indians. Word had been received that the Hector was on the way to that region with Highland emigrants. The whites warned the Indians that the Highlanders were coming—the same men they had seen at the taking of Quebec. When the Hector appeared, according to the fashion of that time, her sides were painted in imitation of gunports, which induced the impression that she was a man-of-war. Though the Highland dress was then proscribed at home, this emigrant band, carefully preserving and fondly cherising the national costume, carried it along with them, and, in celebration of their arrival, many of the younger men donned themselves in their kilts, with *Sgian Dubh* and the claymore. Just as the vessel dropped anchor, the piper blew up his pipes with might and main, and its thrilling sounds then first startling the denizens of the endless forest, caused the Indians to fly in terror, and were not again seen there for quite an interval. After the terror of the Indians had subsided, they returned to cultivate the friendship of the Highlanders, and proved to be of great assistance. From them they learned to make and use snowshoes, to call moose, and acquired the art of woodcraft. Often too from them they received provisions. They never gave them any trouble, and generally showed real kindness.

The first care of the emigrants was to provide for the sick. The wife of Hugh Macleod had just died of smallpox, and the body was sent ashore and buried. Several were sick, and others dying. The resident settlers did all within their power to alleviate the sufferers; and with the supply of fresh provisions most of the sick rapidly recovered, but some died on board the vessel.

However great may have been the expectation of these poor creatures on the eve of their leaving Scotland, their hopes almost deserted them by the sight that met their view as they crowded on the deck of the vessel to see their future homes. The primeval forest before them was unbroken, save a few patches on the shore between Brown's Point and the head of the harbor, which had been cleared by the few people who had preceded them. They were landed without the provisions promised them, and without shelter of any kind, and were only able, with the help of the earlier settlers, to erect camps of the rudest and most primitive description, to shelter their sick, their wives and children from the elements. Their feelings of disappointment were most bitter, when they compared the actual facts with the free farms and the comfort promised them by the emigration agent. Although glad to be freed from the pest-house of the ship, yet they were so overcome by their disappointment that many of them sat down and wept bitterly. The previous settlers could not promise food for one-third of those who had arrived on board the Hector, and what provisions were there soon became exhausted, and the season was too late to raise another crop. To make matters still worse, they were sent three miles into the forest, so that they could not even take advantage, with the same ease, of any fish that might be caught in the harbor. These men were unskilled, and the work of cutting down the gigantic trees, and clearing up the land appeared to them to be a hopeless task. They were naturally afraid of the Indians and the wild beasts; and without roads or paths through the forest, they were frightened to move, doubtful about being lost in the wilderness.

Under circumstances, such as above narrated, it is not surprising that the people refused to settle on the company's land. In consequence of this, when the supplies did arrive, the agents refused to give them any. To add still further to the difficulties, there arose a jealously between them and the older settlers; Ross quarrelled with the company, and ultimately he left the new-comers to their fate. The few who had a little money with them bought food of the agents, while others, less fortunate, exchanged clothing for provisions; but the majority had absolutely nothing to buy with; and what little the others could purchase was soon devoured. Driven to extremity they insisted on having the supplies that had been sent to them. They were positively refused, and now determined on force in order to save the colony from starvation. Donald McDonald and Colin Douglass went to the store seized the agents, tied them, took their guns from them, which they hid at a distance. Then they carefully measured the articles, took account of what each man received, that the same might be paid for, in case they should ever become able. They then left, leaving behind them Roderick McKay, a man of great energy and determination, a leader among them, who was to liberate the agents—Robert Patterson and Dr. Harris—as soon as the others could get to a safe distance, when he released them and informed them where their guns might be found, and then got out of the way himself.

Intelligence was at once dispatched to Halifax that the Highlanders were in rebellion, from whence orders were sent to Captain Thomas Archibald of Truro, to march his company of militia to Pictou to suppress and pacify the rebels; but to his honor, be it said, he pointedly refused, and made reply, "I will do no such thing; I know the Highlanders, and if they are fairly treated there will be no trouble with them." Correct representations of the case were sent to Halifax, and as lord William Campbell, whose term as governor had just expired, was still there, and interesting himself on behalf of the colony as his countrymen, he secured orders for the provisions. Robert Patterson, in after years, admitted that the Highlanders, who had arrived in poverty, paid him every farthing with which he had trusted them, notwithstanding the fact that they had been so badly treated.

Difficulties hemming them in on every hand, with rigorous winter approaching, the majority removed to Truro, and places adjacent, to obtain by their labor food for their families. A few settled at Londonderry, some went to Halifax, and still others to Windsor and Cornwallis. In, these settlements, the fathers mothers, and even the children were forced to bind themselves, virtually as slaves, that they might have subsistence. Those who remained,—seventy in number—lived in small huts, covered over only with the bark and branches of trees to shelter them from the bitter cold of winter, enduring incredible hardships. To procure food for their families, they must trudge eighty miles to Truro, through cold and snow and a trackless forest, and there obtaining a bushel or two of potatoes, and a little flour, in exchange for their labor, they had to return, carrying the supply either on their backs, or else dragging it behind them on handsleds. The way was beset with dangers such as the climbing of steep hills, the descending of high banks, crossing of brooks on the trunk of a single tree, the sinking in wet or boggy ground, and the camping out at night without shelter. Even the potatoes with which they were supplied were of an inferior grade, being soft, and such as is usually fed to cattle. Sometimes the cold was so piercing that the potatoes froze to their backs.

Many instances have been related of the privations of this period, some of which are here subjoined. Hugh Fraser, after having exhausted every means of procuring food for his family, resorted to the expedient of cutting down a birch tree and boiling the buds, which he gave them to eat. He then went to a heap, where one of the first settlers had buried some potatoes, and took out some, intending to inform the owner. Before he did so, some of the neighbors maliciously reported him, but the proprietor simply remarked that he thanked God he had them there for the poor old man's family. On another occasion when the father and

HIGHLAND SETTLEMENT IN PICTOU.   241

eldest son had gone to Truro for provisions, everything in the shape of food being exhausted, except an old hen, which the mother finally killed, for the younger children. She boiled it in salt water for the benefit of the salt, with a quantiy of herbs, the nature of which she was totally ignorant. A few days later the hen's nest was found with ten eggs in it. Two young men set off for Halifax, so weak from want of food, that they could scarcely travel, and when they reached Gay's River, were nearly ready to give up. However they saw there a fine lot of trout, hanging by a rod, on a bush. They hesitated to take them, thinking they might belong to the Indians who would overtake and kill them. They therefore left them, but returned, when the pains of hunger prevailed. Afterwards they discovered that they had been caught by two sportsmen, neither of whom would carry them. Alexander Fraser, then only sixteen, carried his sister on his back to Truro, while the only food he had for the whole journey was the tale of an eel. On another occasion the supply of potatoes, which had been brought a long distance for seed and planted, were dug up by the family and some of the splits eaten. The remembrance of these days sank deep into the minds of that generation, and long after, the narration of the scenes and cruel hardships through which they had to pass, beguiled the winter's night as they sat by their comfortable firesides.

During the first winter, the first death among the emigrants was a child of Donald McDonald, and the first birth was a son of Alexander Fraser, named David, afterwards Captain Fraser. When the following spring opened they set to work to improve their condition. They sought out suitable spots on which to settle, judging the land by the kind and variety of trees produced. They explored the different rivers, and finding the soil near their banks to be the most fertile, and capable of being more easily improved than the higher lands, they settled upon it. Difficulties were thrown in the way of getting their grant. The first grant obtained was to Donald Cameron, who had been a soldier in the Fraser Highlanders at the taking of Quebec. His lot was situated at the Albion Mines. This grant is dated February 8, 1775, and besides the condition of the king's quit rent, contains the following:

"That the grantee, his heirs or assigns, shall clear and work, within three years, three acres for every fifty granted, in that part of the land which he shall judge most convenient and advantageous, or clear and drain three acres of swampy or sunken ground, or drain three acres of marsh, if any such be within the bounds of this grant, or put and keep on his lands, within three years from the date hereof, three neat cattle, to be continued upon the land until three acres for every fifty be fully cleared and improved. But if no part of the said tract be fit for present cultivation, without manuring and improving the same, then this grantee, his heirs and assigns shall be obliged, within three years from the date hereof, to erect on some part of said land a dwelling house, to contain twenty feet in length by sixteen feet in breadth, and to put on said land three neat cattle for every fifty acres, or if the said grantee, his heirs or assigns, shall, within three years, after the passing of this grant, begin to employ thereon, and so continue to work for three years then next ensuing, in digging any stone quarry or any other mine, one good and able hand for every one hundred acres of such tract, it shall be accounted a sufficient seeding, planting, cultivation and improvement, and every three acres which shall be cleared and worked as aforesaid; and every three acres which shall be cleared and drained as aforesaid, shall be accounted a sufficient seeding, planting cultivation and improvement, to save for ever from forfeiture fifty acres in every part of the tract hereby granted."

All were not so fortunate as to secure their grants early. As late as January 22, 1781, in a petition to the government, they complained that a grant had been often promised but never received; but finally, on August 26, 1783, the promise was fulfilled. It contains the names of forty-four persons, some of whom were not passengers on board the Hector; conveying the lands on which they were located, the size of the lots being regulated by the number in the family. The following is a list of grantees, with the number of acres received and notices of situation of their lots:

ON WEST RIVER: David Stewart, 300 acres; John McKenzie, 500; Hugh Fraser, 400; William McLellan, —; James McDonald, 200; James McLellan, 100; Charles Blaikie, 300, and in another division 250 acres, 550 in all; Robert Patterson, 300, and in an after division 500 in all; James McCabe, 300; Alex. Cameron, —.

ON MIDDLE RIVER, EAST SIDE: Alex. Fraser, 100 acres; Alex. Ross, Jr., 100; John Smith, 350; Robert Marshall, 350; James McCulloch, 240; Alex, Ross, 300; Alex. Fraser, Jr., 100; John Crockett, 500; Simon Fraser, 500; Donald McDonald, 350; David Urquhart, 250; Kenneth Fraser, 450; James McLeod, 150.

ON EAST RIVER, EAST SIDE: Walter Murray, 280 acres, and 70 acres in after division; James McKay, 70; Donald McKay, Jr., 80; John Sutherland, 180, and 70 in after division; Rod. McKay, Sr., 300, and in after division, 50; James Hays, —; Hugh McKay, 100; Alex. McKay, 100; Heirs of Donald McLellan, 260; Hugh Fraser, 400, and in after division, 100; Wm. McLeod, 80; John McLellan, 200; Thomas Turnbull, 220, in after division, 180; Wm. McLeod, 210, and in after division, 60; Alex. McLean, —; Colin McKenzie, 370.

ON EAST RIVER, WEST SIDE: Donald Cameron, 100 acres; James Grant, 400; Colin McKay, 400; Wm. McKay, 550; Donald Cameron, 100; Donald McKay, Sr., 450; Donald Cameron, a gore lot; Anthony Culton, 500.

The following is a list of passengers that arrived on board the Hector, originally drawn up, about 1837, by William McKenzie, Loch Broom, Novia Scotia:

SHIPPED AT GLASGOW: a Mr. Scott and family; George Morrison and family, from Banff, settled on west side of Barnys River; John Patterson, prominent in the settlement; George McConnell, settled on West River; Andrew Main and family, settled at Noel; Andrew Wesley; Charles Fraser, settled at Cornwallis; John Stewart.

FROM INVERNESSHIRE: Wiliam McKay, wife and four children, settled on East River; Roderick McKay, wife and daughter, settled on East River; Colin McKay and family, on East River; Hugh Fraser, wife and three children, on McLellans Brook; Donald Cameron and family, on East River; Donald McDonald, wife and two children, on Middle River; Colin Douglass, wife and three children, two of the latter lost on the Hector, on Middle River; Hugh Fraser and family, on West River; Alex.

Fraser, wife and five children; James Grant and family, East River; Donald Munroe, settled in Halifax, and Donald Mc——.

FROM LOCH BROOM: John Ross, Agent, history unknown; Alexander Cameron, wife and two children, settled at Loch Broom; Alex. Ross and wife, advanced in life; Alex Ross and Family, on Middle River; Colin McKenzie and Family, on East River; John Munroe and family; Kenneth McRitchie and family; William McKenzie, at Loch Broom; John McGregor; John McLellan, on McLellans Brook; William McLellan, on West River; Alexander McLean, East River; Alexander Falconer, Hopewell; Donald McKay, East River; Archibald Chisholm, East River; Charles Matheson; Robert Sim, removed to New Brunswick; Alexander McKenzie and Thomas Fraser, From Sutherlandshire; Kenneth Fraser and family, Middle River; William Fraser and family; James Murray and family, Londonderry; David Urquhart and family, Londonderry; Walter Murray and family, Merigomish; James McLeod and wife, Middle River; Hugh McLeod, wife, and three daughters, the wife died as the vessel arrived, West River; Alexander McLeod, wife, and three sons, one of the last died in the harbor, and the father drowned in the Shubenacadie; John McKay and family, Schubenacadie; Philip McLeod and family; Donald McKenzie and family, Shubenacadie(?); Alexander McKenzie and family; John Sutherland and family; William Matheson, wife and son, first settled at Londonderry, then at Rogers Hill; Donald Grant; Donald Graham; John McKay, piper; William McKay, worked for an old settler named McCabe, and took his name; John Sutherland, first at Windsor, and then on Sutherland river; Angus McKenzie, first at Windsor, and finally on Green Hill.

Some interesting facts have been gathered concerning the history of these emigrants, Roderick McKay, who took up land on the East River, was born in Beauly, and before leaving his native country gained a local admiration by rescuing some whiskey from the officers who had seized it, and for the offence was lodged in jail in Inverness. He soon ingratiated himself into the good

HIGHLAND SETTLEMENT IN PICTOU.   245

graces of the jailer, and had no difficulty in sending him for some ale and whiskey. The jailer returning, advanced into the cell with both hands full. Roderick stepped behind him, passed out the door, locked it, and brought off the key. In Halifax he added to his reputation. An officer was paying some attention to a female inmate of his house which did not meet the approbation of Roderick, and meeting them together upbraided him for his conduct, when the latter drew his sword and struck him a cruel blow on the head. Telling the officer he would meet him within an hour, he had his wound dressed, and securing a stick stood before his antagonist. The officer again drew his sword and in the melee, Roderick disarmed him and well repaid him for his cowardly assault. Alexander Fraser, who settled on Middle River, although too young to serve in the Rising of the Forty Five had three brothers at Culloden, of whom two were killed. He was in comfortable circumstances, when he left what he thought was a Saxon oppression, which determined him to seek freedom in America. His horses and cart were seized by guagers, with some whiskey which they were carrying, and taken to Inverness. During the night, the stable boy, a relative of Fraser, took out the horses and cart, and driving across country delivered them to the owner, who lost no time in taking them to another part of the country and disposed of them. He was the last to engage a passage in the Hector. Alexander Cameron who gave the name to Loch Broom, after that of his native parish was not quite eighteen at the Rising of the Forty Five. His brothers followed prince Charles, and he was drawn by the crowd that followed the prince to Culloden. When he returned to his charge, it was to meet an angry master who attempted to chastize him. Cameron ran with his master in pursuit. The latter finding him too nimble, stooped down to pick up a stone to throw at him, and in doing so wounded himself with his dirk in the leg, so that he was obliged to remain some time in hiding, lest he should be taken as having been at Culloden, by the soldiers who were scouring the country, killing any wounded stragglers from the field. The eldest son of James Grant who settled on East

River, did not emigrate with the family, but is believed to have emigrated afterwards, and was the grandfather of General U. S. Grant.

As has already been intimated, amidst all the discouragements and disappointments, the Highlanders used every means in their power to supply the wants of their families. They rapidly learned from the Indians and their neighbors. The former taught them the secrets of the forests and they soon became skilled in hunting the moose, and from the latter they became adepts in making staves, which were sent in small vessels to the older colonies, and in exchange were supplied with necessaries. But the population rather decreased, for a return made January 1, 1775, showed the entire population to be but seventy-eight, consisting of twenty-three men, fourteen women, twenty-one boys and twenty-girls. The produce raised in 1775, was two hundred and sixty-nine bushels of wheat, thirteen of rye, fifty-six of peas, thirty-six of barley, one hundred of oats, and three hundred and forty pounds of flax. The farm stock consisted of thirteen oxen, thirteen cows, fifteen young neat cattle, twenty-five sheep and one swine. They manufactured seventeen thousand feet of boards. While the improvement was somewhat marked, the supply was not sufficient; and the same weary journeys must be taken to Truro for necessaries. The moose, and the fish in the rivers, gave them a supply of meat, and they soon learned to make sugar from the sap of the maple tree. They learned to dig a large supply of clams in the autumn, heap the same on the shore, and cover with sand.

Scarcely had these people become able to supply themselves, when they were again tried by the arrival of a class poorer than themselves. Inducements having been held out by the proprietors of Prince Edward Island to parties in Scotland, to settle their land, John Smith and Wellwood Waugh, living at Lockerbie, in Dumfriesshire, sold out their property and chartered a small vessel to carry thither their families, and all others that would accompany them. They arrived at Three Rivers, in the year 1774, followed by others a few months later. They commenced operations on the Island with fair prospects of success, when they were almost overwhelmed by a plague of mice. These animals swarmed everywhere, consuming everything eatable, even to the potatoes in the ground; and for eighteen months the settlers experinced all the miseries of a famine, having for several months only what lobsters or shell-fish they could gather on the sea-shore. The winter brought them to such a state of weakness that they were unable to convey food a reasonable distance, even when they had means to buy it. In this pitiable condition they heard that the Pictou people were beginning to prosper and had provisions to spare. They sent one of their number David Stewart to make inquiry. One of the settlers, who had come from one of the older colonies, brought with him some negro slaves, and when the messenger arrived had just returned from Truro to sell one of them, and brought home with him some provisions, the proceeds of the sale of the negro. The agent was cheerful in spite of his troubles; and withal was something of a wag. On his return to the Island the people gathered around him to hear the news. "What kind of a place is Pictou?" inquired one. "Oh, an awful place. Why, I was staying with a man who was just eating the last of his nigger;" and as the people were reduced themselves they did not hesitate to believe the tale. Receiving correct information, fifteen of the families went to Pictou, where, for a time, they fared little better, but afterwards became prosperous and happy. Had it not been for a French settlement a few miles distant the people of Lockerbie would have perished during the winter. For supplies, principally of potatoes, they exchanged the clothing they had brought from Scotland, until they barely had enough for themselves. John Smith who was one of the leaders removed to Truro, and Waugh left the Island for Pictou, having only a bucket of clams to support his family on the way.

The American Revolution effected that distant colony. The people had received most of the supplies from the States, which was paid for in fish, fur, and lumber. This trade was at once cut off and the people, at first, felt it severely. Even salt could only be obtained by boiling down sea water. The selection of Halifax as the chief depot for the British navy promoted the business interests for that region of country. As large sums of money were expended there, the district shared in the prosperity. While prices for various kinds of lumber rapidly increased, and the Pictou colony was greatly advantaged thereby, still they found it difficult to obtain British goods, of which they were in need until 1779, when John Patterson went to Scotland and purchased a supply. The War had the effect to divide the colony of Pictou. Not only the Highlanders but all others from Scotland were loyally attached to the British government; while the earlier settlers, who were from the States, were loyally attached to the American cause, with the exception of Robert Patterson. Although the Americans were so situated as to be unable to take up arms, yet they manifested their sympathy in harmless ways, as in the refusal of tea, and the more permanent method of naming their sons after those who were prominent in the theatre of war. At times the feeling became quite violent, in so much so that the circular addressed to the magistrates in the Province was sent to Pictou, requiring these officers "to be watchful and attentive to the behaviour of the people in your county, and that you will apprehend any person or persons who shall be guilty of any opposition to the King's authority and Government, and send them properly guarded to Halifax." The inhabitants were not only required to take the oath of allegiance, but the magistrates were compelled to send a list of all who so complied as well as those who refused. Robert Patterson, who had been made a magistrate in 1774, was very zealous in carrying out this order. He even started for Halifax, intending to get copies of the oath required, for the purpose of imposing it on the inhabitants. When he reached Truro one of the Archibalds discovered his mission and presenting a pistol, used its persuasive influence to induce him immediately to return home. So officious did Patterson become that his sons several times were obliged to hide him in the woods, taking him to Fraser's Point for that purpose.

Many occurrences relating to the War effected the Province, the County of Pictou, and indirectly the Highlanders, though not in a marked degree. The first special occurrence, was probably during the spring of 1776, when an American privateer captured a vessel at Merigomish, loaded with a valuable cargo of West India produce. The vessel was immediately got to sea. The news of the capture was immediately circulated, and presuming the privateer would enter the harbor of Pictou, the inhabitants collected with every old musket and fowling piece to resist the enemy. —The next incident was the capture of Captain Lowden's vessel in the harbor in 1777, variously reported to have been the work of Americans from Machias, Maine, and also by Americans from Pictou and Truro. In all probability the latter were in the plot. The vessel had been loading with timber for the British market. The captain was invited to the house of Wellwood Waugh, and went without suspicion, leaving the vessel in charge of the mate. During the visit he was surrounded and informed that he was a prisoner, and commanded to deliver up his arms. In the meantime an armed party proceeded to the vessel, which was easily secured. As the crew came on deck they were made prisoners and confined in the forecastle. Some of the captors took a boat belonging to the ship and went to the shop of Roderick McKay some distance up East River, and plundered it of tools, iron, &c. In the meantime Roderick and his brother Donald had boarded the vessel and were also made prisoners. When night came the captors celebrated the event by a carousal. When well under the influence of liquor, Roderick proposed to his brother to take the ship, the plan being to make a sudden rush up the cabin stairs to the deck; that he would seize the sentry and pitch him overboard, while Donald should stand with an axe over the companionway and not allow any of them to come up. Donald was a quiet, peaceable man, and opposed to the effusion of blood and refused to take part in the scheme. The McKays were released and the vessel sailed for Bay Verte, not knowing that the Americans had retired from the place. The vessel fell into the hands of a man-of-war, and the captors took to the woods, where, it is supposed, many of them perished. All of Waugh's goods were seized, by the officers of the war-vessel, and sold, and he was forced to leave. This affair caused the American sympathizers to leave the settlement moving eastward, and without selling their farms.

American privateers were frequently off the coast, but had little effect on Pictou. One of the passengers of the Hector who had removed to Halifax and there married, came to Pictou by land, but sent his baggage on a vessel. She was captured and he lost all. A privateer came into the harbor, the alarm was given, and the people assembled to repel the invader. An American living in the settlement, went on board the vessel and urged the commander to leave because there were only a few Scotch settlers commencing in the woods, and not yet possessing anything worth taking away. In consequence of his representations the vessel put out to sea.— The wreck of the Malignant excited some attention at Pictou, near the close of the war. She was a man-of-war bound to Quebec, and late in the fall was wrecked at a place since known as Malignant Cove. The crew came to Pictou and staid through the winter, being provided for through the efforts of Robert Patterson.

The cause of the greatest alarm during the War was a large gathering of Indians at Fraser's Point in 1779. In that year some Indians, in the interest of the Americans, having plundered the inhabitants at Miramichi, a British man-of-war seized sixteen of them of whom twelve were carried to Quebec as hostages, and from there, afterwards, brought to Halifax. Several hundred Indians, for quite a number of days were in council, the design of which was believed to join in the war against the English. The settlers were greatly alarmed, but the Indians quietly dispersed. Most of the Highlanders that emigrated on board the Hector were very ignorant. Only a few could read and books among them were unknown. The Lockerbie settlers were much more intelligent in religion and in everything else. They brought with them from Scotland a few religious books, some of which were lost on Prince Edward Island, but those preserved were carefully read. In 1779 John Patterson brought a supply of books from Scotland, among which was a lot of the New England Primer, which was distributed among the young.

The people were all religiously inclined, and some very devout. All were desirous of religious ordinances. They would meet at the regular hour on the Sabbath, Robert Marshall holding

HIGHLAND SETTLEMENT IN PICTOU. 251

what was called a religious teaching for the English, and Colin Douglass doing the same in Gaelic. The exercises consisted of praise, prayer and the reading of the Scriptures and religious books. They were visited once or twice by Reverend David Smith of Londonderry, and Reverend Daniel Cock of Truro came among them several times. As the people considered themselves under the ministry of the latter, they went on foot to Truro to be present at his communions, and carried their children thither on their backs to be baptized by him. These people had so little English that they could scarcely understand any sermon in that language. This may be judged from an incident that occurred some years later. A Highlander, living in Truro, attended Mr. Cock's service. The latter one day took for his text the words, "Fools make a mock of sin." The former bore the sermon patiently, but said afterward, "Mr. Cock's needn't have talked so about moccasins; Mr. McGregor wore them many a time."

The people were also visited by itinerant preachers, the most important of whom was Henry Alline. In his journal, under date of July 25, 1782, he says:

"Got to a place called Picto, where I had no thought of making any stay, but finding the spirit to attend my preaching, I staid there thirteen days and preached in all the different parts of the settlement, I found four Christians in this place, who were greatly revived and rejoiced that the Gospel was sent among them."— Reverend James Bennet, missionary of the Church of England, in 1775, visited the eastern borders of the Province, and in 1780 visited Pictou and Tatamagouche, and on his return lost his way in the woods.

The Peace of 1783 brought in an influx of settlers mostly from the Highlands, with some who had served in the Revolution against the Americans. This added strength gave more solidity to the settlement. Although considerable prosperity had been attained the added numbers brought increased wealth. Among the fresh arrivals came Reverend James McGregor, in 1786, and under his administration the religious tone was developed, and the state of society enhanced.

CHAPTER XI.

First Highland Regiments in America.

The conflict known as THE FRENCH AND INDIAN WAR, which began in 1754, forced the English colonies to join in a common cause. The time had come for the final struggle between France and England for colonial supremacy in America. The principal cause for the war was brought on by the conflicting territorial claims of the two nations. Mutual encroachments were made by both parties on the other's territory, in consequence of which both nations prepared for war. The English ministry decided to make their chief efforts against the French in that quarter where the aggressions took place, and for this purpose dispatched thither two bodies of troops. The first division, of which the 42nd Highlanders formed a part, under the command of Lieutenant-General Sir James Abercromby, set sail in March, 1756, and landed in June following.

The Highland regiments that landed in America and took part in the conflict were the 42nd or Royal Highland Regiment, but better known as "The Black Watch" (*Am Freiceadan Dubh*), the 77th or Montgomery's Highlanders, and the Old 78th, or Fraser's Highlanders.

The Black Watch, socalled from the sombre appearance of their dress was embodied, as the 43rd Regiment, May, 1740, having been composed largely of the independent companies raised in 1729. When Oglethorpe's regiment, the 42nd was reduced in 1749, the Black Watch received its number, which ever since, it has retained. From 1749 to 1756 the regiment was stationed in Ireland, and between them and the inhabitants of the districts, where quartered, the utmost cordiality existed. Previous to the departure of the regiment from Ireland to America, officers with parties had been sent to Scotland for recruits. So success-

FIRST HIGHLAND REGIMENTS IN AMERICA.

ful were they, that in the month of June, seven hundred embarked at Greenock for America. The officers of the regiment were as follows:

Rank	Name	Commission	Rank	Name	Commission
Colonel..	Lord John Murray...	Apr. 25, 1745	Lieut....	John Graham........	Jan. 25, 1756
Lieut. Colonel..	Francis Grant.......	Dec. 17, 1755	Lieut....	Hugh McPherson....	" 26, 1756
			Lieut....	Alexander Turnbull..	" 27, 1756
Major....	Duncan Campbell, Inveraw...	Dec. 17, 1755	Lieut....	Alexander Campbell.	" 28, 1756
			Lieut....	Alexander McIntosh.	" 29, 1756
Capt....	Gordon Graham.....	June 3, 1752	Lieut....	James Gray.........	" 30, 1756
Capt....	John Read...........	do.	Lieut....	William Baillie.....	" 31, 1756
Capt....	John McNeile........	Dec. 16, 1752	Lieut....	Hugh Arnott........	Apr. 9, 1756
Capt....	Alan Campbell.......	Mar. 15, 1755	Lieut....	John Sutherland......	" 10, 1756
Capt....	Thomas Græme Duchray......	Feb. 16, 1756	Lieut....	John Small.........	" 11, 1756
Capt....	James Abercromby, Son of Glassa...	do.	Lieut....	Archibald Campbell..	May 5, 1756
			Ensign..	James Campbell......	Jan. 24, 1756
Capt....	John Campbell, Strachur.......	Apr. 9, 1756	Ensign..	Archibald Lamont...	" 25, 1756
Capt.- Lieut....	John Campbell, sr....	Feb. 16, 1756	Ensign..	Duncan Campbell....	" 26, 1756
			Ensign..	George McLagan....	" 27, 1756
Lieut....	William Grant.......	May 22, 1746	Ensign..	Patrick Balneaves....	" 28, 1756
Lieut....	Robert Gray........	Aug. 7, 1747	Ensign..	Patrick Stuart.......	" 29, 1756
Lieut....	John Campbell.......	May 16, 1748	Ensign..	Norman McLeod.....	" 30, 1756
Lieut....	George Farquharson.	Mar. 29, 1750	Ensign..	George Campbell...	" 31, 1756
Lieut....	Colin Campbell......	Feb. 9, 1751	Ensign..	Donald Campbell....	May 5, 1756
Lieut....	James Campbell......	June 3, 1752	Chaplain	Adam Ferguson......	Apr. 30, 1746
Lieut....	Sir James Cockburn, B't.......	Mar. 15, 1755	Adjutant	James Grant.........	June 26, 1751
			Q. M....	John Graham........	Feb. 19, 1756
Lieut....	Kenneth Tolme......	Jan. 23, 1756	Surgeon.	David Hepburn.....	June 26, 1751
Lieut....	James Grant.........	" 24, 1756			

The regiment known as Montgomery's Highlanders (77th) took its name from its commander, Archibald Montgomery, son of the earl of Eglinton. Being very popular among the Highlanders, Montgomery very soon raised the requisite body of men, who were formed into thirteen companies of one hundred and five rank and file each; making in all fourteen hundred and sixty effective men, including sixty-five sergeants and thirty pipers and drummers. The Colonel's commission was dated January 4, 1757, and those of the other officers one day later than his senior in rank. They are thus recorded:

Lieut.-Colonel commanding, Archibald Montgomery; majors, James Grant of Ballindalloch and Alexander Campbell; captains, John Sinclair, Hugh Mackenzie, John Gordon, Alexander Mackenzie, William Macdonald, George Munro, Robert Mackenzie, Allan Maclean, James Robertson, Allan Cameron; captain-lieut., Alexander Mackintosh; lieutenants, Charles Farquharson, Nichol Sutherland, Donald Macdonald, William Mackenzie, Robert Mackenzie, Henry Munro, Archibald Robertson, Duncan Bayne, James Duff, Colin Campbell, James Grant, Alexander Macdonald, Joseph Grant, Robert Grant, Cosmo Martin, John Macnab, Hugh Gordon, Alexander Macdonald, Donald Campbell, Hugh Montgomery, James Maclean, Alexander Campbell, John Campbell, James Macpherson, Archibald Macvicar; ensigns: Alexander Grant, William Haggart, Lewis Houston, Ronald Mackinnon, George Munro, Alexander Mackenzie, John Maclachlane, William Maclean, James Grant, John Macdonald, Archibald Crawford, James Bain, Allan Stewart; chaplain: Henry Munro; adjutant: Donald Stewart; quarter-master: Alexander Montgomery; surgeon: Allan Stewart.

The regiment embarked at Greenock for Halifax immediately on its organization.

Fraser's Highlanders, or the 78th Regiment was organized by Simon Fraser, son of the notorious lord Lovat who was executed by the English government for the part he acted in the Rising of the Forty-five. Although his estates had been seized by the Crown, and not possessing a foot of land, so great was the influence of clanship, that in a few weeks he raised eight hundred men, to whom were added upwards of six hundred more by the gentlemen of the country and those who had obtained commissions. In point of the number of companies and men, the battalion was precisely the same as Montgomery's Highlanders. The list of officers, whose commissions are dated January 5, 1757, is as follows:

Lieut.-col. commandant: Simon Fraser; majors: James Clephane and John Campbell of Dunoon; captains: John Mac-

FIRST HIGHLAND REGIMENTS IN AMERICA. 255

pherson, brother of Cluny, John Campbell of Ballimore, Simon Fraser of Inverallochy, Donald Macdonald, brother of Clanranald, John Macdonell of Lochgarry, Alexander Cameron of Dungallon, Thomas Ross of Culrossie, Thomas Fraser of Strui, Alexander Fraser of Culduthel, Sir Henry Seton of Abercorn and Culbeg, James Fraser of Belladrum; capt.-Lieut.: Simon Fraser; lieutenants: Alexander Macleod, Hugh Cameron, Ronald Macdonell, son of Keppoch, Charles Macdonell, from Glengarry, Roderick Macneil of Barra, William Macdonell, Archibald Campbell, son of Glenlyon, John Fraser of Balnain, Hector Macdonald, brother of Boisdale, Allan Stewart, son of Innernaheil, John Fraser, Alexander Macdonald, son of Boisdale, Alexander Fraser, Alexander Campbell of Aross, John Douglas, John Nairn, Arthur Rose, Alexander Fraser, John Macdonell of Leeks, Cosmo Gordon, David Baillie, Charles Stewart, Ewen Cameron, Allan Cameron, John Cuthbert, Simon Fraser, Archibald Macallister, James Murray, Alexander Fraser, Donald Cameron, son of Fassifern; ensigns: John Chisolm, Simon Fraser, Malcolm Fraser, Hugh Fraser, Robert Menzies, John Fraser of Errogie, James Mackenzie, Donald Macneil, Henry Munro, Alexander Gregorson, Ardtornish, James Henderson, John Campbell; chaplain: Robert Macpherson; adjutant: Hugh Fraser; quarter-master: John Fraser; surgeon: John Maclean.

"The uniform of the regiment was the full Highland dress with musket and broad-sword, to which many of the soldiers added the dirk at their own expense, and a purse of badger's or otter's skin. The bonnet was raised or cocked on one side, with a slight bend inclining down to the right ear, over which were suspended two or more black feathers. Eagle's or hawk's feathers were usually worn by the gentlemen, in the Highlands, while the bonnets of the common people were ornamented with a bunch of the distinguishing mark of the clan or district. The ostrich feathers in the bonnets of the soldiers were a modern addition of that period."*

The regiment was quickly marched to Greenock, where it embarked, in company with Montgomery's Highlanders, and landed at Halifax in June 1757, where it remained till it formed a junction with the expedition against Louisbourg. The regi-

---
*Stewart's Sketches of the Highlanders, Vol. II, p. 66.

ment was quartered between Canada and Nova Scotia till the conclusion of the war. On all occasions they sustained a uniform character for unshaken firmness, incorruptible probity and a strict regard to their duties. The men were always anxious to conceal their misdemeanors from the *Caipal Mohr,* as they called the chaplain, from his large size.

When The Black Watch landed in New York they attracted much notice, particularly on the part of the Indians, who, on the march of the regiment to Albany, flocked from all quarters to see strangers, whom, from the somewhat similarity of dress, they believed to be of the same extraction with themselves, and therefore considered them to be brothers.

HIGHLAND OFFICER.

During the whole of 1756 the regiment remained inactive in Albany. The winter and spring of 1757 they were drilled and disciplined for bush-fighting and sharpshooting, a species of warfare then necessary and for which they were well fitted, being in general good marksmen, and expert in the management of their arms.

In the month of June, 1757, lord Loudon, who had been appointed commander-in-chief of the army in North America, with the 22d, 42d, 44th, 48th, 2d and 4th battalions of the 60th, together with six hundred Rangers, making in all five thousand and three hundred men, embarked for Halifax, where his force was increased to ten thousand and five hundred men by the addition of five regiments lately arrived from England, which included Fraser's and Montgomery's Highlanders. When on the eve of his departure for an attack on Louisburg, information was received that the Brest fleet, consisting of seventeen sail of the line, besides frigates, had arrived in the harbor of that fortress. Letters, which had been captured in a vessel bound from Louisburg to France, revealed that the force was too great to be encountered. Lord Loudon abandoned the enterprise and soon after returned to New York taking with him the Highlanders and four other regiments.

By the addition of three new companies and the junction of seven hundred recruits "The Black Watch" or 42nd, was now augmented to upwards of thirteen hundred men, all Highlanders, for at that period, none others were admitted.

During the absence of lord Loudon, Montcalm, the French commander, was very active, and collecting all his disposable forces, including Indians, and a large train of artillery, amounting in all to more than eight thousand men, laid seige to Fort William Henry, under the command of Colonel Munro. Some six miles distant was Fort Edward, garrisoned by four thousand men under General Webb. The seige was conducted with great vigor and within six days Colonel Munro surrendered, conditioned on not serving again for eighteen months, and allowed to march out of the fort with their arms and two field pieces. As soon as they were without the gate the Indians fell upon them and committed all sorts of outrages and barbarities,—the Frech being unable to restrain them.

Thus terminated the campaign of 1757 in America, undistinguished by any act which might compensate for the loss of territory or the sacrifice of lives. With an inferior force the French had been successful at every point, and besides having obtained complete control of Lakes George and Champlain, the destruction of Oswego gave the dominion of those lakes, which are connected with the St. Lawrence, to the Mississippi, thus opening a direct communication between Canada and the southwest.

Lord Loudon having been recalled, the command of the army again devolved on General James Abercromby. Determined to wipe off the disgrace of former campaigns, the new ministry, which had just come into power, fitted out, in 1758, a great naval and military force consisting of fifty-two thousand men. To the military staff were added Major-General Amherst, and Brigadier-General's Wolfe, Townsend and Murray. Three expeditions were proposed: the first to renew the attempt on Louisburg; the second directed against Ticonderoga and Crown Point, and the third against Fort du Quesne.

General Abercromby took command, in person, of the expedition against Ticonderoga, with a force of fifteen thousand three hundred and ninety men, of whom over six thousand were regulars, the rest being provincials, besides a train of artillery. Among the regulars must be reckoned the 42d Highlanders. Ticonderoga, situated on a point of land between Lake George and Lake Champlain is surrounded on three sides by water, and on one-half of the fourth by a morass. The remaining part of the fort was protected by high entrenchments, supported and flanked by three batteries, and the whole front of that which was accessible intersected by deep traverses, and blocked up with felled trees, with their branches turned outwards, and their points sharpened.

On July 5th the army struck their tents at daybreak, and in nine hundred small boats and one hundred and thirty-five whale-boats, with artillery mounted on rafts, embarked on Lake George. The fleet in stately procession, bright with banners and cheered by martial music, moved down the beautiful lake, beaming with hope and pride. The solemn forests were broken by the echoes of the happy soldiery. There was no one to molest them, and victory was their one desire. Over the broader expanse they passed to the first narrows, witnessing the mountains rising from the water's edge, the dark forest, and the picturesque loveliness of the scene. Long afterwards General John Stark recounted that when they had halted at Sabbathday Point at twilight, lord Howe, reclining in his tent on a bearskin, and bent on winning a hero's name, questioned him closely as to the position of Ticonderoga and the fittest modes of attack.

After remaining five hours at their resting place, the army, an hour before midnight, moved once more down the lake, and by nine the next morning, disembarked on the west side, in a cove sheltered by a point which still keeps the name of Lord Howe. The troops were formed into two parallel columns and marched on the enemy's advanced posts, which were abandoned without a shot. The march was continued in the same order, but the guides proving ignorant, the columns came in contact, and were thrown into confusion. A detachment of the enemy which had also become bewildered in the woods, fell in with the right column, at the head of which was lord Howe, and during the skirmish which ensued, Howe was killed. Abercromby ordered the army to march back to the landing place.

Montcalm, ever alert, was ready to receive the English army. On July 6th he called in all his parties, and when united amounted to two thousand eight hundred French and four hundred and fifty Canadians. On the 7th the whole army toiled incredibly in strengthening their defenses. On the same evening De Levi returned from the projected expedition against the Mohawks, bringing with him four hundred chosen men. On the morning of the 8th, the drums of the French beat to arms, that the troops, now thirty-six hundred and fifty in number, might know their stations and resume their work.

The strongest regiment in the army of Abercrombie was the 42nd Highlanders, fully equipped, in their native dress. The officers wore a narrow gold braiding round their tunics, all other lace being laid aside to make them less conspicuous to the French and Canadian riflemen. The sergeants wore silver lace on their coats, and carried the Lochaber axe, the head of which was fitted for hewing, hooking or spearing an enemy, or such other work as might be found before the ramparts of Ticonderoga. Many of the men had been out in the Rising of the Forty-five.

When Abercrombie received information from some prisoners that De Levi was about to reinforce Montcalm, he determined, if possible to strike a blow before a junction could be effected. Report also having reached him that the entrenchments were still unfinished, and might be assaulted with prospects of success, he immediately made the necessary dispositions for attack. The British commander, remaining far behind during the action, put the army in motion, on the 8th, the regulars advancing through the openings of the provincials, and taking the lead. The pickets were followed by the grenadiers, supported by the battalions and reserve, which last consisted of the Highlanders and 55th regiment, advanced with great alacrity towards the entrenchments, which they found much more formidable than they expected. As the British advanced, Montcalm, who stood just within the trenches, threw off his coat for the sunny work of the July afternoon, and forbade a musket to be fired until he had given the order. When the British drew very near, in three principal columns, to attack simultaneously the left, the center, and the right, they became entangled among the rubbish and broken into disorder by clambering over logs and projecting limbs. The quick eye of Montcalm saw the most effective moment had come, and giving the word of command, a sudden and incessant fire of swivels and small arms mowed down brave officers and men by hundreds. The intrepidity of the English made the carnage terrible. With the greatest vivacity the attacks were continued all the afternoon. Wherever the French appeared to be weak, Montcalm immediately strengthened them. Regiment after regiment was hurled against the beseiged, only to be hurled back with the loss of half their number.

The Scottish Highlanders, held in the reserve, from the very first were impatient of the restraint; but when they saw the column fall back, unable longer to control themselves, and emulous of sharing the danger, broke away and pushed forward to the front, and with their broadswords and Lochaber axes endeavored to cut through the abattis and chevaux-de-frize. For three hours the Highlanders struggled without the least appearance of discouragement. After a long and deadly struggle they penetrated the exterior defences and reached the breastwork; having no scaling ladders, they attempted to gain the summit by mounting on each others shoulders and partly by fixing their feet in holes they made with their swords, axes and bayonets in the face of the work, but no sooner did a man appear on top than he was hurled down by the defending troops. Captain John Campbell, with a few men, at length forced their way over the breastwork, but were immediately dispatched with the bayonet.

While the Highlanders and grenadiers were fighting without faltering and without confusion on the French left, the columns which had attacked the center and right, at about five o'clock, concentrated themselves at a point between the two; but De Levi advanced from the right and Montcalm brought up the reserve. At six the two parties nearest the water turned desperately against the center, and being repulsed, made a last effort on the left, where, becoming bewildered, the English fired on an advanced party of their own, producing hopeless dejection.

The British general, during the confusion of battle cowered safely at the saw-mills, and when his presence was needed to rally the fugitives, was nowhere to be found. The second in command, unable to seize the opportunity, gave no commands. The Highlanders persevered in their undertaking and did not relinquish their labors until they received the third order to retreat, when they withdrew, unmolested, and carrying with them the whole of their wounded.

The loss sustained by the 42nd was as follows: eight officers, nine sergeants and two hundred and ninety-seven men killed; and seventeen officers, ten sergeants and three hundred and six soldiers wounded. The officers killed were Major Duncan Campbell of Inveraw, Captain John Campbell, Lieutenants George Farquharson, Hugh MacPherson, William Baillie, and John Sutherlànd; Ensigns Patrick Stewart of Bonskied and George Rattray. The wounded were Captains Gordon Graham, Thomas Graham of Duchray, John Campbell of Strachur, James Stewart of Urrad, James Murray; Lieutenants James Grant, Robert Gray, John Campbell of Melford, William Grant, John Graham, brother of Duchray, Alexander Campbell, Alexander Mackintosh, Archibald Campbell, David Miller, Patrick Balneaves; and Ensigns John Smith and Peter Grant.

The intrepid conduct of the Highlanders, in the storming of Ticonderoga, was made the topic of universal panegyric throughout the whole of Great Britain, the public prints teeming with honorable mention of, and testimonies to their bravery. Among these General Stewart copies* the two following:

"With a mixture of esteem, grief and envy (says an officer of the 55th, lord Howe's regiment), I consider the great loss and immortal glory acquired by the Scots Highlanders in the late bloody affair. Impatient for orders, they rushed forward to the entrenchments, which many of them actually mounted. They appeared like lions, breaking from their chains. Their intrepidity was rather animated than damped by seeing their comrades fall on every side. I have only to say of them, that they seemed more anxious to revenge the cause of their deceased friends, than careful to avoid the same fate. By their assistance, we expect soon to give a good account of the enemy and of ourselves. There is much harmony and friendship between us." "The attack (says Lieutenant William Grant of the 42nd) began a little past one in the afternoon, and, about two, the fire became general on both sides, which was exceedingly heavy, and without any intermission, insomuch that the oldest soldier present never saw so furious and incessant a fire. The affair at Fontenoy was nothing to it. I saw both. We labored under insurmountable difficulties. The enemy's breastwork was about nine or ten feet high, upon the top of which they had plenty of wall pieces fixed, and which was well lined in the inside with small arms. But the difficult access to their lines was what gave them the fatal advantage over us. They took care to cut down monstrous large oak trees, which covered all the ground from the foot of their breastwork about the distance of a cannon shot every way in their front. This not only broke our ranks, and made it impossible for us to keep our order, but put it entirely out of our power to advance till we cut our way through. I have seen men behave with courage and resolution before now, but so much determined bravery can hardly be equalled in any part of the history of ancient Rome. Even those that were mortally wounded cried aloud to their companions, not to mind or lose a thought upon them, but to follow their officers, and to mind the honor of their country. Nay, their ardor was such, that it was difficult to bring them off. They paid dearly for their intrepidity. The remains of the regiment had the honor to cover the retreat of the army, and brought off the wounded, as we did at Fontenoy. When shall we have so fine a regiment again? I hope we shall be allowed to recruit."

The English outnumbered the French four-fold, and with

---

*Sketches of the Highlanders, Vol. I, p. 289.

their artillery, which was near at hand, could have forced a passage. "Had I to besiege Ticonderoga," said Montcalm, "I would ask for but six mortars and two pieces of artillery." But Abercrombie, that evening, hurried the army to the landing place, with such precipitancy, that but for the alertness of Colonel Bradstreet, it would at once have rushed in a mass into the boats. On the morning of the 9th the army embarked and Abercrombie did not rest until he had placed the lake between himself and Montcalm, and even then he sent the artillery and ammunition to Albany for safety.

The expedition against Louisburg, under Major-General Jeffrey Amherst, set sail from Halifax on May 28, 1758. It was joined by the fleet under Admiral Boscawen. The formidable armament consisted of twenty-five sail of the line, eighteen frigates, and a number of bomb and fire ships, with the Royals, 15th, 17th, 22nd, 28th, 35th, 40th, 45th, 47th, 48th, 58th, the 2d and 3d battalions of the 60th, 78th Highlanders, and New England Rangers,—in all, thirteen thousand and nine men. On June 2nd the vessels anchored in Garbarus Bay, seven miles from Louisburg. The garrison, under the Chevalier Ducour, consisted of twenty-five hundred regulars, six hundred militia, and four hundred Canadians and Indians. The harbor was protected by six ships of the line and five frigates, three of the latter being sunk at its mouth. The English ships were six days on the coast before a landing could be attempted, on account of a heavy surf continually rolling with such violence, that no boat could approach the shore. The violence of the surf having somewhat abated, a landing was effected on June 8th. The troops were disposed for landing in three divisions. That on the left, which was destined for the real attack, commanded by Brigadier General Wolfe, was composed of the grenadiers and light infantry, and the 78th, or Fraser's Highlanders. While the boats containing this division were being rowed ashore, the other two divisions on the right and center, commanded by Brigadier Generals Whitmore and Lawrence, made a show of landing, in order to divide and distract the enemy. The landing place was occupied by two thousand men entrenched behind a battery of eight pieces of cannon and swivels. The enemy wisely reserved their fire till the boats were close to the shore, and then directed their discharge of cannon and musketry with considerable execution. The surf aided the fire. Many of the boats were upset or dashed to pieces on the rocks, and numbers of the men were killed or drowned before land was reached. Captain Baillie and Lieutenant Cuthbert of the Highlanders, Lieutenant Nicholson of Amherts, and thirty-eight men were killed. Notwithstanding the great disadvantages, nothing could stop the troops when led by such a general as Wolfe. Some of the light infantry and Highlanders were first ashore, and drove all before them. The rest followed, and soon pursued the enemy to a distance of two miles, when they were checked by the canonading from the town.

In this engagement the French lost seventeen pieces of cannon, two mortars, and fourteen swivels, besides seventy-three prisoners. The cannonading from the town enabled Wolfe to prove the range of the enemy's guns, and to judge of the exact distance at which he might make his camp for investing the town. The regiments then took post at the positions assigned them. For some days operations went on slowly. The sea was so rough that the landing of stores from the fleet was much retarded; and it was not until the 11th that the six pounder field pieces were landed. Six days later a squadron was fairly blown out to sea by the tempest. By the 24th the chief engineer had thirteen twenty-four pounders in position against the place. The first operation was to secure a point called Lighthouse Battery, the guns from which could play upon the ships and on the batteries on the opposite side of the harbor. On the 12th this point was captured by Wolfe at the head of his gallant Fraser's and flank companies, with but little loss. On the 25th, the fire from this post silenced the island battery immediately opposite. An incessant fire, however, was kept up from the other batteries and shipping of the enemy. On July 9th the enemy made a sortie on General Lawrence's brigade, but were quickly repulsed. In this affair, the earl of Dundonald was killed. There were twenty other casualties. The French captain who led the attack, with seventeen of his men, was also killed.

FIRST HIGHLAND REGIMENTS IN AMERICA. 265

On the 16th, Wolfe pushed forward some grenadiers and Highlanders, and took possession of the hills in front of the Lighthouse battery, where a lodgement was made under a fire from the town and the ships. On the 21st one of the French ships was set on fire by a bombshell and blew up, and the fire being communicated to two others, they were burned to the water's edge. The fate of the town was now almost decided, the enemy's fire nearly silenced and the fortifications shattered to the ground. All that now remained in the reduction was to get possession of the harbor, by taking or burning the two ships of the line which remained. For this purpose the admiral, on the night of July 25th sent six hundred seamen in boats, with orders to take, or burn, the two ships of the line that remained in the harbor, resolving if they succeeded to send in some of his larger vessels to bombard the town. This enterprise was successfully executed by the seamen under Captains Laforey and Balfour, in the face of a terrible fire of cannon and musketry. One of the ships was set on fire and the other towed off. On the 26th the town surrendered; the garrison and seamen amounted to five thousand six hundred and thirty-seven, besides one hundred and twenty pieces of cannon, eighteen mortars, seven thousand five hundred stand of arms, eleven colors, and eleven ships of war. The total loss of the English army and fleet, during the siege amounted to five hundred and twenty-five. Besides Captain Baillie and Lieutenant Cuthbert the Highlanders lost Lieutenant J. Alexander Fraser and James Murray, killed; Captain Donald MacDonald, Lieutenant Alexander Campbell (Barcaldine) and John MacDonald, wounded; and sixty-seven rank and file killed and wounded.

The third expedition was against Fort du Quesne, undertaken by Brigadier General John Forbes. Although the point of attack was less formidable and the enemy inferior in numbers to those at either Ticonderoga or Louisburg, yet the difficulties were greater, owing to the great extent of country to be traversed, through woods without roads, over mountains and through almost impassable morasses. The army consisted of six thousand two hundred and thirty-eight men, composed of Montgomery's

Highlanders, twelve hundred and eighty-four strong, five hundred and fifty-five of the Royal Americans, and four thousand four hundred provincials. Among the latter were the two Virginia regiments, nineteen hundred strong, under the command of Washington. Yet vast as were the preparations of the army, Forbes never would have seen the Ohio had it not been for the genius of Washington, although then but twenty-six years of age.

The army took up its line of march from Philadelphia in July, and did not reach Raystown until the month of September, when they were still ninety miles distant from Fort du Quesne. It was Washington's earnest advice that the army should advance with celerity along Braddock's road; but other advice prevailed, and the army commemorated its march by moving slowly and constructing a new route to the Ohio. Thus the summer was frittered away. While Washington's forces joined the main army, Boquet was detached with two thousand men to take post at Loyal Hanna, fifty miles in advance. Here intelligence was received that the French garrison consisted of but eight hundred men, of whom three hundred were Indians. The vainglory of Boquet, without the consent or knowledge of his superior officer urged him to send forward a party of four hundred Highlanders and a company of Virginians under Major James Grant to reconnoitre. Major Grant divided his troops, and when near the fort, advanced with pipes playing and drums beating, as if he was on a visit to a friendly town. The enemy did not wait to be attacked, but instantly marched out of their works and invited the conflict. The Highlanders threw off their coats and charged sword in hand. At first the French gave way, but rallied and surrounded the detachment on all sides. Being concealed in the thick foliage, their heavy and destructive fire could not be returned with any effect. Major Grant was taken in an attempt to force into the woods, where he observed the thickest of the fire. On losing their commander, and so many officers killed and wounded, the Highlanders dispersed, and were only saved from utter ruin by the provincials. Only one hundred and fifty of the Highlanders succeeded in making their way back to Loyal Hanna.

In this battle, fought September 14, 1758, two hundred and thirty-one Highlander's were killed and wounded. The officers killed were Captain William Macdonald and George Munro; Lieutenants Alexander Mackenzie, William Mackenzie, Robert Mackenzie, Colin Campbell, and Alexander Macdonald; and the wounded were Captain Hugh Mackenzie, Lieutenants Alexander Macdonald, Archibald Robertson, Henry Munro, and Ensigns John Macdonald and Alexander Grant.

General Forbes did not reach Loyal Hanna until November 5th, and there a council of war determined that no farther advance should be made for that season. But Washington had plead that owing to his long intimacy with these woods, and his familiarity with the difficulties and all the passes should be allowed the responsibility of commanding the first party. This having been denied him, he prevailed on the commander to be allowed to make a second advance. His brigade was of provincials, and they toiled cheerfully by his side, infusing his own spirit into the men he commanded. Over the hills white with snow, his troops poorly fed and poorly clothed toiled onward. His movements were rapid: on November 15th he was at Chestnut Ridge; and the 17th at Bushy Run. As he drew near Fort du Quesne, the disheartened garrison, about five hundred in number, set fire to the fort, and by the light of the conflagration, descended the Ohio. On the 25th Washington could point out to the army the junction of the rivers, and entering the fortress, they planted the British colors on the deserted ruins. As the banner of England floated over the Ohio, the place was with one voice named Pittsburg, in honor of the great English premier William Pitt.

The troops under Washington were accompanied by a body of Highlanders. On the morning of November 25th, the army advanced with the provincials in the front. They entered upon an Indian path, "Upon each side of which a number of stakes, with the bark peeled off, were stuck into the earth, and upon each stake was fixed the head and kilt of a Highlander who had been killed or taken prisoner at Grant's defeat. The provincials, being front, obtained the first view of these horrible spectacles, which it may readily be believed, excited no kindly feelings in their breasts.

They passed along, however, without any manifestation of their violent wrath. But as soon as the Highlanders came in sight of the remains of their countrymen, a slight buzz was heard in their ranks, which rapidly swelled and grew louder and louder. Exasperated not only by the barbarous outrages upon the persons of their unfortunate fellow soldiers who had fallen only a few days before, but maddened by the insult which was conveyed by the exhibition of their kilts, and which they well understood, as they had long been nicknamed the 'petticoat warriors' by the Indians, their wrath knew no bounds. Directly a rapid and violent tramping was heard, and immediately the whole corps of the Highlanders, with their muskets abandoned, and broad swords drawn, rushed by the provincials, foaming with rage, and resembling, as Captain Craighead coarsely expressed it, 'mad boars engaged in battle,' swearing vengeance and extermination upon the French troops who had permitted such outrages. Their march was now hastened—the whole army moved forward after the Highlanders, and when they arrived somewhere about where the canal now passes, the Fort was discovered to be in flames, and the last of the boats, with the flying Frenchmen, were seen passing down the Ohio by Smoky Island. Great was the disappointment of the exasperated Highlanders at the escape of the French, and their wrath subsided into a sullen and relentless desire for vengeance."*

The Highlanders passed the winter of 1758 in Pittsburg, and in May following marched to the assistance of General Amherst in his proceedings at Ticonderoga, Crown Point and the Lakes.

Before the heroic action of The Black Watch at Ticonderoga was known in England, a warrant was issued conferring upon the regiment the title of Royal, so that it became known also by the name of 42d Royal Highland Regiment, and letters were issued to raise a second battalion. So successful were the recruiting officers that within three months, seven companies, each one hundred and twenty men strong were embodied at Perth in October 1758. Although Highlanders only were admitted, yet two officers, anxious to obtain commissions, enlisted eighteen Irishmen, several of whom were O'Donnels, O'Lachlans, O'Briens, &c. The O was changed to Mac, and the Milesians passed muster as true Macdonels, Maclachlans, and Macbriars, without being questioned.

The second battalion immediately embarked at Greenock for

---

*The Olden Time, Vol. I, p. 181.

the West Indies, under the convoy of the Ludlow Castle; and after the reduction of Guadaloupe, it was transferred to New York, and in July, 1759, was combined with the first battalion, in order to engage in the operations then projected against the French settlements in Canada. General Wolfe was to proceed up the St. Lawrence and besiege Quebec. General Amherst, who had succeeded Abercromby as commander-in-chief, was to attempt the reduction of Ticonderoga and Crown Point, and then effect a junction with General Wolfe before Quebec. Brigadier General John Prideaux was to proceed against the French fort near the falls of Niagara, the most important post of all French America.

The army first put in motion was that under Amherst, which assembled at Fort Edward on June 19th. It included the 42nd and Montgomery's Highlanders, and when afterwards joined by the second battalion of the 42nd, numbered fourteen thousand five hundred men. On the 21st, preceded by The Black Watch the army moved forward and encamped on Lake George, where, during the previous year, the army rested prior to the attack on Ticonderoga. Considerable time was spent in preparations for assaulting this formidable post, but on seeing the preparations made by the English generals for a siege, the French set fire to the magazines and buildings, and retired to Crown Point.

The plan of campaign on the part of the French appeared to have been to embarrass Amherst by retarding the advance of his army, but not to hazard any considerable engagement, nor to allow themselves to be so completely invested as to cut off all retreat. The main object of their tactics was so to delay the advance of the English that the season for action on the Lakes would pass away without showing any decisive advantage on the part of the invaders, whilst their own forces could be gradually concentrated, and thus arrest the progress of Amherst down the St. Lawrence.

On taking possession of Ticonderoga, which effectually covered the frontiers of New York, General Amherst proceeded to repair the fortifications; and, while superintending this work, was indefatigable in preparing batteaux and other vessels for conveying his troops, and obtaining the superiority on the Lakes.

Meanwhile the French abandoned Crown Point and retired to Isle aux Noix, on the northern extremity of Lake Champlain. General Amherst moved forward and took possession of the fort which the French had abandoned, and the second battalion of the 42nd was ordered up. Having gained a naval superiority on Lake Champlain the army went into winter quarters at Crown Point.

The main undertaking of the campaign was the reduction of Quebec, by far the most difficult operation, where General Wolfe was expected to perform an important part with not more than seven thousand effective men. The movement commenced at Sandy Hook, Tuesday May 8, 1759 when the expedition set sail for Louisburg, under convoy of the Nightingale, the fleet consisting of about twenty-eight sail, the greater part of which was to take in the troops from Nova Scotia, and the rest having on board Fraser's Highlanders. They arrived at Louisburg on the 17th. and there remained until June 4th, when the fleet again set sail, consisting of one hundred and fifty vessels, twenty-two of which were ships of the line. They entered the St. Lawrence on the 13th, and on the 23rd anchored near Isle aux Coudres. On the 26th, the whole armament arrived off the Isle of Orleans, and the next day disembarked. Montcalm depended largely on the natural position of the city of Quebec for defence, although he neglected nothing for his security. Every landing-place was intrenched and protected. At midnight on the 28th a fleet of fire-ships came down the tide, but was grappled by the British soldiers and towed them free of the shipping. Point Levi, on the night of the 29th was occupied, and batteries constructed, from which red-hot balls were discharged, demolishing the lower town of Quebec and injuring the upper. But the citadel and every avenue from the river to the cliff were too strongly entrenched for an assault.

General Wolfe, enterprising, daring, was eager for battle. Perceiving that the eastern bank of the Montmorenci was higher than the position of Montcalm, on July 9th he crossed the north channel and encamped there; but not a spot on the line of the Montmorenci was left unprotected by the vigilant Montcalm.

General Wolfe planned that two brigades should ford the Montmorenci at the proper time of the tide, while Monckton's regiments should cross the St. Lawrence in boats from Point Levi. The signal was given and the advance made in the face of shot and shell. Those who got first on shore, not waiting for support, ran hastily towards the entrenchments, and were repulsed in such disorder that they could not again come into line. Wolfe was compelled to order a retreat. Intrepidity and discipline could not overcome the heavy fire of a well protected enemy. In that assault, which occurred on July 31st, Wolfe lost four hundred in killed.

General Murray was next sent with twelve hundred men, above the town, to destroy the French ships and open communicacation with General Amherst. They learned that Niagara had surrendered and that Ticonderoga and Crown Point had been abandoned. But General Wolfe looked in vain for General Amherst. The commander-in-chief, opposed by no more than three thousand men, was loitering at Crown Point; nor was even a messenger received from him. The heroic Wolfe was left to struggle alone against odds and difficulties which every hour made more appalling. Every one able to bear arms was in the field fighting for their homes, their language, and their religion. Old men of seventy and boys of fifteen fired at the English detachments from the edges of the woods.

The feeble frame of General Wolfe, disabled by fever, began to sink under the fearful strain. He laid before his chief officers three desperate methods of attacking Montcalm, all of which they opposed, but proposed to convey five thousand men above the town, and thus draw Montcalm from his intrenchments. General Wolfe acquiesced and prepared to carry it into effect. On the 5th and 6th of September he marched the army from Point Levi, and embarked in transports, resolving to land at the point that ever since has borne his name, and take the enemy by surprise. Every officer knew his appointed duty, when at one o'clock on the morning of the 13th, about half the army glided down with the tide. When the cove was reached, General Wolfe and the troops with him leaped ashore, and clambered up the steep hill, holding by the roots and boughs of the maple, spruce and ash trees, that covered the declivity, and with but little difficulty dispersed the picket which guarded the height. At daybreak General Wolfe, with his battalions, stood on the plains of Abraham. When the news was carried to Montcalm, he said, "They have at last got to the weak side of this miserable garrison; we must give battle, and crush them before mid-day." Before ten o'clock the two opposing armies were ranged in each other's presence. The English, five thousand strong, were all regulars, perfect in discipline, terrible in their fearless enthusiasm, and commanded by a man whom they obeyed with confidence and admiration. Montcalm had but five weak battalions of two thousand men, mingled with disorderly peasantry. The French with three and the English with two small pieces of artillery cannonaded each other for nearly an hour.

Montcalm led the French army impetuously to the attack. The ill-disciplined companies broke by their precipitation and the unevenness of the ground, fired by platoons without unity. The English received the shock with calmness, reserving their fire until the enemy were within forty yards, when they began a regular, rapid firing. Montcalm was everywhere, braving dangers, though wounded, cheered others by his example. The Canadians flinching from the hot fire, gave way when General Wolfe placing himself at the head of two regiments, charged with bayonets. General Wolfe was wounded three times, the third time mortally. "Support me," he cried to an officer near him; "let not my brave fellows see me drop." He was carried to the rear. "They run, they run," cried the officer on whom he leaned. "Who run?" asked Wolfe, as his life was fast ebbing. "The French," replied the officer, "give way everywhere." "What," cried the dying hero, "do they run already? Go, one of you, to Colonel Burton; bid him march Webb's regiment with all speed to Charles River to cut off the fugitives." "Now, God be praised, I die happy," were the last words be uttered. The heroic Montcalm, struck by a musket ball, continued in the engagement, till attempting to rally a body of fugitive Canadians, was mortally wounded. On September 17th, the city surrendered.

The rapid sketch thus given does not represent the part taken by Fraser's Highlanders. Fortunately Lieutenant Malcolm Fraser kept a journal, and from it the following is gleaned: June 30th, the Highlanders with Kennedy's or the 43rd, crossed the river and joined the 15th, or Amhersts', with some Rangers, marched to Point Levi, having numerous skirmishes on the way. Captain Campbell posted his company in St. Joseph's church, and there fired a volley upon an assaulting party. On Sunday, July 1st, the regiment was cannonaded by some floating batteries, losing four killed and eight wounded. On the 9th, before daylight, the Highlanders struck tents at Point Levi, and marched out of sight of the town. On the 11th three men were wounded by the fire of the great guns from the city. On the 21st, it was reported that fourteen privates of Fraser's Highlanders were wounded by the Royal Americans, having, in the dark, mistaken them for the enemy. On the night of July 24th, Colonel Fraser, with a detachment of about three hundred and fifty men of his regiment, marched down the river, in order to take up such prisoners and cattle as might be found. Lieutenant Alexander Fraser, Jr., returned to the camp with the information that Colonel Fraser had been wounded by a shot from some Canadians in ambush; and the same shot wounded Captain MacPherson; both of whom returned that day to camp. On the 27th the detachment returned bringing three women and one man prisoners, and almost two hundred cattle. July 31st Fraser's and Amherst's regiments embarked in boats at Point Levi and landed on the Montmorenci, where, on that day, General Wolfe fought the battle of Beauport Flats, in which he lost seven hundred killed and wounded. His retreat was covered by the Highlanders, without receiving any hurt, although exposed to a battery of two cannons which kept a very brisk fire upon them. The regiment went to the island of Orleans, and on August 1st to Point Levi. On Wednesday, August 15th, Captain John MacDonell, seven subalterns, eight sergeants, eight corporals and one hundred and forty-four men of

Fraser's regiment, crossed from Point Levi to the Island of Orleans and lodged in the church of St. Peter's, and the next day marched to the east end of the island, and on the 17th crossed to St. Joachim, where they met with slight resistance. They fortified the Priest's house, and were not reinforced until the 23rd, and then all marched to attack the village, which was captured, with "a few prisoners taken, all of whom the barbarous Captain Montgomery, who commanded us, ordered to be butchered in a most inhuman and cruel manner. . . . After this skirmish we set about burning the houses with great success, setting all in flames till we came to the church of St. Anne's, where we put up for this night, and were joined by Captain Ross, with about one hundred and twenty men of his company." The work of devastation continued the following day, until the forces reached Ange Gardien. August 28, Captain MacDonell with Captain Ross took post at Chateau Richer. September 1st, Chateau Richer was burned, and the force marched to Montmorenci, burning all the houses on the way. On the 2nd the Highlanders returned to their camp at Point Levi. Captain Alexander Cameron of Dungallon died on the 3rd. On the 4th Captain Alexander Fraser of Culduthell arrived with a fourteenth company to the regiment. On the 6th a detachment of six hundred Highlanders with the 15th and 43rd regiments, marched five miles above Point Levi and then crossed the river in crowded vessels, but for several days remained mostly on board the ships. On September 17th, the Highlanders landed at Wolfe's Cove, with the rest of the army, and were soon on the plains of Abraham. When the main body of the French commenced to retreat "our regiment were then ordered by Brigadier General Murray to draw their swords and pursue them; which I dare say increased their panic but saved many of their lives. * * * In advancing we passed over a great many dead and wounded (French regulars mostly) lying in the front of our regiment, who,—I mean the Highlanders—to do them justice behaved extremely well all day, as did the whole of the army. After pursuing the French to the very gates of the town, our regiment was ordered to form fronting the town, on the ground whereon the French formed first. At this time the rest of the army came up in good order. General Murray having then put himself at the head of our regiment ordered them to face to the left and march thro' the bush of wood, towards the General Hospital, when they got a great gun or two to play upon us from the town, which however did no damage, but we had a few men killed and officers wounded by some skulking fellows, with small arms, from the bushes and behind the houses in the suburbs of St. Louis and St. John's. After marching a short way through the bush, Brigadier Murray thought proper to order us to return again to the high road leading from Porte St. Louis, to the heights of Abraham, where the battle was fought, and after marching till we got clear of the bushes, we were ordered to turn to the right, and go along the edge of them towards the bank at the descent between us and the General Hospital, under which we understood there was a body of the enemy who, no sooner saw us, than they began firing on us from the bushes and from the bank; we soon dispossessed them from the bushes, and from thence kept firing for about a quarter of an hour on those under cover of the bank; but, as they exceeded us greatly in numbers, they killed and wounded a great many of our men, and killed two officers, which obliged us to retire a little, and form again, when the 58th Regiment with the 2nd Battalion of Royal Americans having come up to our assistance, all three making about five hundred men, advanced against the enemy and drove them first down to the great meadow between the hospital and town and afterwards over the river St. Charles. It was at this time and while in the bushes that our regiment suffered most; Lieutenant Roderick, McNeill of Barra, and Alexander McDonell, and John McDonell, and John McPherson, volunteer, with many of our men, were killed before we were reinforced; and Captain Thomas Ross having gone down with about one hundred men of the 3rd Regiment to the meadow, after the enemy, when they were out of reach, ordered me up to desire those on the height would wait till he would come up and join them, which I did, but before Mr. Ross could get up, he unfortunately was mortally wounded. * * * We had of our regiment three officers killed and ten wounded, one of whom Captain Simon Fraser, afterwards died. Lieutenant Archibald Campbell was thought to have been mortally wounded, but to the surprise of most people recovered, Captain John McDonell thro' both thighs; Lieut. Ronald McDonell thro' the knee; Lieutenant Alexander Campbell thro' the leg; Lieutenant Douglas thro' the arm, who died of this wound soon afterwards; Ensign Gregorson, Ensign McKenzie and Lieutenant Alexander Fraser, all slightly, I received a contusion in the right shoulder or rather breast, before the action become general, which pained me a good deal, but it did not disable me from my duty then, or afterwards.

The detachment of our regiment consisted, at our marching from Point Levi, of six hundred men, besides commissioned and non commissioned officers; but of these, two officers and about sixty men were left on board for want of boats, and an officer and about thirty men left at the landing place; besides a few left sick on board, so that we had about five hundred men in the action. We suffered in men and officers more than any three regiments in the field. We were commanded by Captain John Campbell; the Colonel and Captain McPherson having been unfortunately wounded on the 25th July, of which they were not yet fully recovered. We lay on our arms all the night of the 13th September."

On the 14th the Highlanders pitched their tents on the battlefield, within reach of the guns of the town. On the following day they were ordered to camp near the wood, at a greater distance from the town. Here, within five hundred yards of the town, they commenced to make redoubts. After the surrender of Quebec the Highlanders marched into the city and there took up their quarters. On February 13, 1760, in an engagement with the French at Point Levi, Lieutenant McNeil was killed, and some of the soldiers wounded. March 18th Captain Donald McDonald, with some detachments, in all five hundred men, attacked the French posts at St. Augustin, and without loss took eighty prisoners, and that night returned to Quebec.

Scurvy, occasioned by salt provisions and cold, made fierce work in the garrison, and in the army scarce a man was free from it. On April 30th a return of Fraser's Highlanders, in the garrison at Quebec, showed three hundred and fourteen fit for duty, five hundred and eighty sick, and one hundred and six dead since September 18, 1759.

April 27th, the French under De Levi, in strong force advanced against the English, the latter being forced to withdraw within the walls of Quebec. Fraser's Highlanders was one of the detachments sent to cover the retreat of the army, which was effected without loss. At half-past six, the next morning General Murray marched out and formed his army on the heights of

Abraham. The left wing was under Colonel Simon Fraser composed of the Highlanders, the 43rd, and the 23rd Welsh Fusiliers. The Highlanders were exposed to a galling fire from the bushes in front and flank and were forced to fall back; and every regiment made the best of its way into the city. The British loss was two hundred and fifty-seven killed and seven hundred and sixty-one wounded.

The Highlanders had about four hundred men in the field, nearly one-half of whom had that day, of their own accord, come out of the hospital. Among the killed were Captain Donald Macdonald, Lieutenant Cosmo Gordon and fifty-five non-commissioned officers, pipers and privates; their wounded were Colonel Fraser, Captains John Campbell of Dunoon, Alexander Fraser, Alexander MacLeod, Charles Macdonell; Lieutenants Archibald Campbell, son of Glenlyon, Charles Stewart, Hector Macdonald, John Macbean, Alexander Fraser, senior, Alexander Campbell, John Nairn, Arthur Rose, Alexander Fraser, junior, Simon Fraser, senior, Archibald McAlister, Alexander Fraser, John Chisholm, Simon Fraser, junior, Malcolm Fraser, and Donald McNeil; Ensigns Henry Munro, Robert Menzies, Duncan Cameron, of Fassifern, William Robertson, Alexander Gregorson and Malcolm Fraser, and one hundred and twenty-nine non-commissioned officers and privates.

Lieutenant Charles Stewart, engaged in the Rising of the Forty-Five, in Stewart of Appin's regiment, was severely wounded at Culloden. As he lay in his quarters after the battle on the heights of Abraham, speaking to some brother officers on the recent actions, he exclaimed, "From April battles, and Murray generals, good Lord deliver me!" alluding to his wound at Culloden, where the vanquished blamed lord George Murray for fighting on the best field in the country for regular troops, cavalry and artillery; and likewise alluding to his present wound, and to General Murray's conduct in marching out of a garrison to attack an enemy, more than treble his numbers, in an open field, where their whole strength could be brought to act. No time was lost in repeating to the general what the wounded officer had said; but Murray, who was a man of humor and of a generous mind, on the following morning called on his subordinate, and heartily wished him better deliverance in the next battle, when he hoped to give him occasion to pray in a different manner.

On the night of the battle De Levi opened trenches within six hundred yards of the walls of the city, and proceeded to besiege the city, while General Murray made preparations for defence. On May 1st the largest of the English blockhouses accidentally blew up, injuring Captain Cameron. On the 17th the French suddenly abandoned their entrenchments. Lord Murray pursued but was unable to overtake them. He formed a junction, in September with General Amherst.

General Amherst had been notified of the intended siege of Quebec by De Levi; but only persevered in the tardy plans which he had formed. Canada now presented no difficulties only such as General Amherst might create. The country was suffering from four years of scarcity, a disheartened, starving peasantry, and the feeble remains of five or six battalions wasted by incredible hardships. Colonel Haviland proceeded from Crown Point and took the deserted fort at Isle aux Noix. Colonel Haldimand, with the grenadiers, light infantry and a battalion of The Black Watch, took post at the bottom of the lake. General Amherst led the main body of ten thousand men by way of Oswego; why, no one can tell. The labor of going there was much greater than going direct to Montreal. After toiling to Oswego, he proceeded cautiously down the St. Lawrence, treating the people humanely, and without the loss of life, save while passing the rapids, he met, on September 7th, the army of lord Murray before Montreal, the latter on his way up from Quebec, intimidated the people and amused himself by burning villages and harrying Canadians. On the 8th Colonel Haviland joined the forces. Thus the three armies came together in overwhelming strength, to take an open town of a few hundred inhabitants who were ready to surrender on the first appearance of the English.

The Black Watch, or Royal Highlanders remained in America until the close of the year 1761. The officers were Lieutenant Colonel Francis Grant; Majors, Gordon Graham and John Reid; Captains, John McNeil, Allan Campbell, Thomas Græme, James

Stewart, James Murray, Thomas Stirling, William Murray, John Stuart, Alexander Reid, William Grant, David Haldane, Archibald Campbell, John Campbell, Kenneth Tolmie, William Cockburne; Captain-Lieutenant, James Grant; Lieutenants, John Graham, Alexander Turnbull, Alexander McIntosh, James Gray, John Small, Archibald Campbell, James Campbell, Archibald Lamont, David Mills, Simon Blair, David Barclay, Alexander Mackay, Robert Menzies, Patrick Balneaves, John Campbell, senior, John Robertson, John Grant, George Leslie, Duncan Campbell, Adam Stuart, George Grant, James McIntosh, John Smith, Peter Grant, Simon Fraser, Alexander Farquharson, John Campbell, junior, William Brown, Thomas Fletcher, Elbert Herring, John Leith, Archibald Campbell, Alexander Donaldson, Archibald Campbell, Patrick Sinclair, John Gregor, Lewis Grant, Archibald Campbell, John Graham, Allan Grant, Archibald McNab; Ensigns, Charles Menzies, John Charles St. Clair, Neil McLean, Thomas Cunison, Alexander Gregor, William Grant, George Campbell, Nathaniel McCulloch, Daniel Robertson, John Sutherland, Charles Grant, Samuel Stull, James Douglass, Thomas Scott, Charles Graham, James Robertson, Patrick Murray, Lewis Grant; Chaplain, Lauchlan Johnston; Adjutants, Alexander Donaldson, John Gregor; Quarter-Masters, John Graham, Adam Stewart; Surgeons, David Hepburn, Robert Drummond.

At the close of the year 1761 The Black Watch, with ten other regiments, among which was Montgomery's Highlanders, embarked for Barbadoes, there to join an armament against Martinique and Havanna. After the surrender of Havanna, the first battalion of the 42nd, and Montgomery's Highlanders embarked for New York, which they reached in the end of October, 1762. Before leaving Cuba, all the men of the second battalion of the 42nd, fit for service were consolidated with the first, and the remainder shipped to Scotland, where they were reduced the follownig year.

The 42nd, or The Black Watch was stationed at Albany till the summer of 1763 when they, with a detachment of Montgomery's Highlanders and another of the 60th, under command of Colonel Henry Boquet, were sent to the relief of Fort Pitt, then beseiged by the Indians. This expedition consisting of nine hundred and fifty-six men, with its convoy, reached Fort Bedford, July 25, 1763. The whole country in that region was aroused by the depredations of the Indians. On the 28th Boquet moved his army out of Fort Bedford and marched to Fort Ligonier, where he left his train, and proceeded with pack-horses. Before them lay a dangerous defile, several miles in length, commanded the whole distance by high and craggy hills. On August 5th, when within half a mile of Bushy-Run, about one o'clock in the afternoon, after a harrassing march of seventeen miles, they were suddenly attacked by the Indians; but two companies of the 42nd Highlanders drove them from their ambuscade. When the pursuit ceased, the savages returned. These savages fought like men contending for their homes, and their hunting grounds. To them it was a crisis which they were forced to meet. Again the Highlanders charged them with fixed bayonets; but as soon as they were driven from one post they appeared at another, and at last entirely surrounded the English, and would have entirely cut them off had it not been for the cool behavior of the troops and the good manœuvering of the commander. Night came on, and the English remainded on a ridge of land, commodious for a camp, except for the total want of water. The next morning the army found itself still in a critical position. If they advanced to give battle, then their convoy and wounded would fall a prey to the enemy; if they remained quiet, they would be picked off one by one, and thus miserably perish. Boquet took advantage of the resolute intrepidity of the savages by feigning a retreat. The red men hurried to the charge, when two companies concealed for the purpose fell upon their flank; others turned and met them in front; and the Indians yielding to the irresistible shock, were utterly routed.

The victory was dearly bought, for Colonel Boquet, in killed and wounded, in the two days action, lost about one-fourth of his men, and almost all his horses. He was obliged to destroy his stores, and was hardly able to carry his wounded. That night the English encamped at Bushy Run, and four days later were at Fort Pitt. In the skirmishing and fighting, during the march, the 42nd, or The Black Watch, lost Lieutenants John Graham and James

Mackintosh, one sergeant and twenty-six rank and file killed; and Captain John Graham of Duchray, Lieutenant Duncan Campbell, two serjeants, two drummers, and thirty rank and file, wounded. Of Montgomery's Highlanders one drummer and five privates were killed; and Lieutenant Donald Campbell and volunteer John Peebles, three serjeants and seven privates wounded.

The 42nd regiment passed the winter at Fort Pitt, and during the summer of 1764, eight companies were sent with the army of Boquet against the Ohio Indians. After a harrassing warfare the

OLD BLOCK-HOUSE, FORT DUQUESNE.

Indians sued for peace. Notwithstanding the labors of a march of many hundred miles among dense forests, during which they experienced the extremes of heat and cold, the Highlanders did not lose a single man from fatigue or exhaustion. The army returned to Fort Pitt in January, 1765, during very severe weather. Three men died of sickness, and on their arrival at Fort Pitt only nineteen men were under the surgeon's charge. The regiment was now in better quarters than it had been for years. It was greatly reduced in numbers, from its long service, the nature and variety of its hardships, amidst the torrid heat of the West Indies, the rigorous winters of New York and Ohio, and the fatalities on the field of battle.

The regiment remained in Pennsylvania until the month of July, 1767, when it embarked at Philadelphia for Ireland. Such of the men who preferred to remain in America were permitted to join other regiments. These volunteers were so numerous, that, along with those who had been previously sent home disabled, and others discharged and settled in America, the regiment that returned was very small in proportion of that which had left Scotland.

The 42nd Royal Highlanders, or The Black Watch, made a very favorable impression in America. The *Virginia Gazette*, July 30, 1767, published an article from which the following extracts have been taken:

"Last Sunday evening, the Royal Highland Regiment embarked for Ireland, which regiment, since its arrival in America, has been distinguished for having undergone most amazing fatigues, made long and frequent marches through an unhospitable country, bearing excessive heat and severe cold with alacrity and cheerfulness, frequently encamping in deep snow, such as those that inhabit the interior parts of this province do not see, and which only those who inhabit the most northern parts of Europe can have any idea of, continually exposed in camp and on their marches to the alarms of a savage enemy, who, in all their attempts, were forced to fly. * * * And, in a particular manner, the freemen of this and the neighboring provinces have most sincerely to thank them for that resolution and bravery with which they, under Colonel Boquet, and a small number of Royal Americans, defeated the enemy, and ensured to us peace and security from a savage foe; and, along with our blessings for these benefits, they have our thanks for that decorum in behavior which they maintained during their stay in this city, giving an example that the most amiable behavior in civil life is no way inconsistent with the character of the good soldier; and for their loyalty, fidelity, and orderly behavior, they have every wish of the people for health, honor, and a pleasant voyage."

The loss sustained by the regiment during the seven years it was employed in America and the West Indies was as follows:

FIRST HIGHLAND REGIMENTS IN AMERICA. 283

	Killed						Wounded					
	Fed. Officers	Captains	Subalterns	Serjeants	Drummers	Privates	Fed. Officers	Captains	Subalterns	Serjeants	Drummers	Privates
Ticonderoga, July 7, 1758...	1	1	6	9	...	267	...	5	12	10	...	306
Martinique, January, 1759..	...	...	...	...	...	8	...	...	1	2	...	22
Guadaloupe, February and March, 1759............	...	...	1	1	...	25	...	...	4	3	...	57
General Amherst's Expedition to the Lakes, July and August, 1759.......	...	...	...	...	...	3	...	...	...	1	...	4
Martinique, January and February, 1762.........	...	1	1	1	...	12	1	1	7	3	1	72
Havanna, June and July, 1762, both battalions...	...	...	...	...	1	3	...	...	...	...	1	4
Expedition under Colonel Boquet, August, 1763...	...	1	1	1	...	26	..	1	1	2	2	30
Second Expedition under Boquet, in 1764 and 1765	...	...	...	...	...	7	...	...	...	1	...	9
Total in the Seven Years' War................	1	3	9	12	1	381	1	7	25	22	4	504

Comparing the loss sustained by the 42nd in the field with that of other corps, it has generally been less than theirs, except at the defeat at Ticonderoga. The officers who served in the corps attributed the comparative loss to the celerity of their attack and the use of the broadsword, which the enemy could never withstand.

Of the officers who were in the regiment in 1759 seven rose to be general officers, viz., Francis Grant of Grant, John Reid of Strathloch, Allan Campbell of Glenure, James Murray, son of lord George Murray, John Campbell of Strachur, Thomas Stirling of Ardoch, and John Small. Those who became field officers were, Gordon Graham, Duncan Campbell of Inneraw, Thomas Graham of Duchray, John Graham his brother, William Murray of Lintrose, William Grant, James Abercromby of Glassa, James Abercromby junior, Robert Grant, James Grant, Alexander Turnbull of Strathcathro, Alexander Donaldson, Thomas Fletcher of Landertis, Donald Robertson, Duncan Campbell, Alexander Maclean and James Eddington. A corp of officers, respectable in their persons, character and rank in private society, was of itself sufficient to secure esteem and lead a regiment where every man was a soldier.

It has already been noticed that in the spring of 1760, the thought of General Amherst was wholly engrossed on the conquest of Canada. He was appealed to for protection against the Cherokees who were committing cruelties, in their renewed warfare against the settlements. In April he detached, from the central army, that had conquered Ohio, Colonel Montgomery with six hundred Highlanders of his own regiment and six hundred Royal Americans to strike a blow at the Cherokees and then return. The force embarked at New York, and by the end of April was in Carolina. At Ninety-six, near the end of May, the army was joined by many gentlemen of distinction, as volunteers, besides seven hundred Carolina rangers, which constituted the principal strength of the country. On June 1st, the army crossed Twelve-mile River; and leaving their tents standing on advantageous ground, at eight in the evening moved onward through the woods to surprise Estatoe, about twenty miles from the camp. On the way Montgomery surprised Little Keowee and put every man to the sword, sparing only women and children. Early the next morning they reached Estatoe only to find it abandoned, except by a few who could not escape. The place was reduced to ashes, as was Sugar Town, and every other settlement in the lower nation destroyed. For years, the half-charred rafters of their houses might be seen on the desolate hill-sides. "I could not help pitying them a little," wrote Major Grant; "their villages were agreeably situated; their houses neatly built; there were everywhere astonishing magazines of corn, which were all consumed." The surprise in every town was almost equal, for the whole was the work of only a few hours; the Indians had no time to save what they valued most; but left for the pillagers money and watches, wampum and furs. About sixty Cherokees were killed; forty, chiefly women and children, were made prisoners; but the warriors had generally escaped to the mountains.

Meanwhile Fort Prince George had been closely invested, and

Montgomery marched to its relief. From this place he dispatched two friendly chiefs to the middle settlements, to offer terms of peace, and orders were sent to Fort Loudon to bring about accommodations for the upper towns. The Indians would not listen to any overtures, so Montgomery was constrained to march against them. The most difficult part of the service was now to be performed; for the country to be passed through was covered by dark thickets, numerous deep ravines, and high river banks; where a small number of men might distress and even wear out the best appointed army.

Colonel Montgomery began his march June 24, 1760, and at night encamped at the old town of Oconnee. The next evening he arrived at the War-Woman's Creek; and on the 26th, crossed the Blue Montains, and made his encampment at the deserted town of Stecoe. The army trod the rugged defiles, which were as dangerous as men had ever penetrated, with fearless alacrity, and the Highlanders were refreshed by coming into the presence of the mountains. "What may be Montgomery's fate in the Cherokee country," wrote Washington, "I cannot so readily determine. It seems he has made a prosperous beginning, having penetrated into the heart of the country, and he is now advancing his troops in high health and spirits to the relief of Fort Loudon. But let him be wary. He has a crafty, subtle enemy to deal with, that may give him most trouble when he least expects it."*

The morning of the 27th found the whole army early on the march to the town of Etchowee, the nearest of the Cherokee settlements, and eighteen miles distant. When within five miles of the town, the army was attacked in a most advantageous position for the Indians. It was a low valley, in which the bushes were so thick that the soldiers could see scarcely three yards before them; and through this valley flowed a muddy river, with steep clay banks. Captain Morrison, in command of a company of rangers, was in the advance. When he entered the ravine, the Indians emerged from their ambush, and, raising the war-whoop, darted from covert to covert, at the same time firing at the whites. Cap-

---

*Spark's Writings of Washington, Vol. II, p. 332.

tain Morrison was immediately shot down, and his men closely engaged. The Highlanders and provincials drove the enemy from their lurking-places, and, returning to their yells three huzzas and three waves of their bonnets and hats, they chased them from height and hollow. The army passed the river at the ford; and, protected by it on their right, and by a flanking party on the left, treading a path, at times so narrow as to be obliged to march in Indian file, fired upon from both front and rear, they were not collected at Etchowee until midnight; after a loss of twenty killed and seventy-six wounded. Of these, the Highlanders had one serjeant, and six privates killed, and Captain Sutherland, Lieutenants Macmaster and Mackinnon, and Assistant-Surgeon Munro, and one serjeant, one piper, and twenty-four rank and file wounded.

"Several soldiers of this (Montgomery's) and other regiments fell into the hands of the Indians, being taken in an ambush. Allan Macpherson, one of these soldiers, witnessing the miserable fate of several of his fellow-prisoners, who had been tortured to death by the Indians, and seeing them preparing to commence the same operations upon himself, made signs that he had something to communicate. An interpreter was brought. Macpherson told them, that, provided his life was spared for a few minutes, he would communicate the secret of an extraordinary medicine, which, if applied to the skin, would cause it to resist the strongest blow of a tomahawk, or sword, and that, if they would allow him to go to the woods with a guard, to collect the plants proper for this medicine, he would prepare it, and allow the experiment to be tried on his own neck by the strongest and most expert warrior among them. This story easily gained upon the superstititious credulity of the Indians, and the request of the Highlander was instantly complied with. Being sent into the woods, he soon returned with such plants as he chose to pick up. Having boiled these herbs, he rubbed his neck with their juice, and laying his head upon a log of wood, desired the strongest man among them to strike at his neck with his tomahawk, when he would find he could not make the smallest impression. An Indian, levelling a blow with all his might, cut with such force, that the head flew off to a distance of several yards. The Indians were fixed in amazement at their own credulity, and the address with which the prisoner had escaped the lingering death prepared for him; but, instead of being enraged at this escape of their victim, they were so pleased with his ingenuity that they refrained from inflicting farther cruelties on the remaining prisoners."*

Only for one day did Colonel Montgomery rest in the heart of the Alleghanies. On the following night, deceiving the Indians by kindling lights at Etchowee, the army retreated, and, marching twenty-five miles, never halted, till it came to War-Woman's Creek. On the 30th, it crossed the Oconnee Mountain, and on July 1st reached Fort Prince George, and soon after returned to New York.

The retreat of Colonel Montgomery was the knell of the famished Fort Loudon, situated on the borders of the Cherokee country. The garrison was forced to capitulate to the Indians, who agreed to escort the men in safety to another fort. They were, however, made the victims of treachery; for the day after their departure a body of savages waylaid them, killed some, and captured others, whom they took back to Fort Loudon.

The expedition of Montgomery but served to inflame the Indians. July 11th the General Assembly represented their inability to prevent the ravages made by the savages on the back settlements, and by unanimous vote entreated the lieutenant governor "to use the most pressing instances with Colonel Montgomery not to depart with the king's troops, as it might be attended with the most pernicious consequences." Montgomery, warned that he was but giving the Cherokees room to boast among the other tribes, of their having obliged the English army to retreat, not only from the mountains, but also from the province, shunned the path of duty, and leaving four companies of the Royal Scots, sailed for Halifax by way of New York, coldly writing "I cannot help the people's fears." Afterwards, in the House of Commons, he acted as one who thought the Americans factious in peace and feeble in war.

In 1761 the Montgomery Highlanders were in the expedition against Dominique, and the following year against Martinique and Havanna. At the end of October were again in New York. Before the return of the six companies to New York, the two com-

---

*Stewart's Sketches of the Highlanders, Vol. II, p. 61.

panies that had been sent against the Indians in 1761, were sent, with a small force, to retake St. John's, New Foundland, which was occupied by a French force. The English army consisted of the flank companies of the Royals, a detachment of the 45th, two companies of Fraser's Highlanders, a small party of provincials, besides Montgomery's. The army landed on September 12, 1762, seven miles northward of St. John's. On the 17th the French surrendered. Of Montgomery's Highlanders, Captain Mackenzie and four privates were killed, and two privates wounded. After this service the two companies joined the regiment at New York and there passed the winter. As already noticed a detachment was with Colonel Boquet to the relief of Fort Pitt in 1763. After the termination of hostilities an offer was made to the officers and men either to settle in America, or return to their own country. Those who remained obtained a grant of land in accordance to their rank.*

The following table shows the number of killed and wounded of Montgomery's Highlanders during the war:—

	Killed				Wounded			
	Officers	Serjeants	Drummers and Pipers	Rank and File	Officers	Serjeants	Drummers and Pipers	Rank and File
Fort du Quesne, Sept. 11, 1758	7	3	2	92	9	7	3	201
Little Keowe, June 1, 1760	...	...	...	2	...	...	...	...
Etchowee, June 27, 1760	...	2	...	6	4	1	1	24
Martinique, 1761	1	...	...	4	1	1	...	26
Havanna, 1762	1	...	...	2	...	...	...	6
St. John's, September, 1762	1	...	...	4	...	...	...	2
On Passage to West Indies	1	...	...	...	...	...	...	...
Total during the war	11	5	2	110	14	9	4	259

After the surrender of Montreal, Fraser's Highlanders were not called into action, until the fall of 1762, when the two companies were with the exepdition under Colonel William Amherst, against St. John's, Newfoundland. In this service Captain Mac-

*See Appendix, Note L.

FIRST HIGHLAND REGIMENTS IN AMERICA. 289

donell was mortally wounded, three rank and file killed, and seven wounded. At the conclusion of the war, a number of the officers and men having expressed a desire to remain in America, had their wishes granted, and an allowance of land granted them. The rest returned to Scotland and were discharged.

The following is a return of the killed and wounded of Fraser's Highlanders during the war from 1756 to 1763:—

	Killed						Wounded					
	Fd. Officers	Captains	Subalterns	Serjeants	Drummers and Pipers	Rank and File	Fd. Officers	Captains	Subalterns	Serjeants	Drummers	Rank and File
Louisburg, July 1758	...	1	3	...	...	17	...	1	2	...	...	41
Montmorency, Sept. 2, 1759	...	...	2	...	1	18	1	2	3	...	...	85
Heights of Abraham, Sept. 13, 1759	...	1	2	1	...	14	...	2	8	7	...	131
Quebec, April, 1760	...	1	3	3	1	51	1	4	22	10	...	119
St. John's, Sept. 1762	...	1	...	...	...	3	...	...	...	...	...	7
Total during the war	...	4	10	4	2	103	2	9	35	17	...	383

Whatever may be said of the 42nd, or The Black Watch, concerning its soldierly bearing may also be applied to both Montgomery's and Fraser's regiments. Both officers and men were from the same people, having the same manners, customs, language and aspirations. The officers were from among the best families, and the soldiers respected and loved those who commanded them.

For three years after the fall of Montreal the war between France and England lingered on the ocean. The Treaty of Paris was signed February 10, 1763, which gave to England all the French possessions in America eastward of the Mississippi from its source to the river Iberville, and thence through Lakes Maurepas and Pontchartrain to the Gulf of Mexico. Spain, with whom England had been at war, at the same time ceded East and West Florida to the English Crown. France was obliged to cede to Spain all that vast territory west of the Mississippi, known as the province of Louisiana. The Treaty deprived France of all her possessions in North America. To the genius of William Pitt must be ascribed the conquest of Canada and the deprivation of France of her possessions in the New World.

The acquisition of Canada, by keen sighted observers, was regarded as a source of danger to England. As early as the year 1748, the Swedish traveller Kalm, having described in vivid language the commercial oppression under which the colonists were suffering, added these remarkable words:

"I have been told, not only by native Americans, but by English emigrants publicly, that within thirty or fifty years the English colonies in North America may constitute a separate state entirely independent of England. But as this whole country towards the sea is unguarded, and on the frontier is kept uneasy by the French, these dangerous neighbors are the reason why the love of these colonies for their metropolis does not utterly decline. The English government has, therefore, reason to regard the French in North America as the chief power which urges their colonies to submission."*

On the definite surrender of Canada, Choiseul said to those around him, "We have caught them at last"; his eager hopes anticipating an early struggle of America for independence. The French ministers consoled themselves for the Peace of Paris by the reflection that the loss of Canada was a sure prelude to the independence of the colonies. Vergennes, the sagacious and experienced ambassador, then at Constantinople, a grave, laborious man, remarkable for a calm temper and moderation of character, predicted to an English traveller, with striking accuracy, the events that would occur. "England," he said, "will soon repent of having removed the only check that could keep her colonies in awe. They stand no longer in need of her protection. She will call on them to contribute towards supporting the burdens they have helped to bring on her, and they will answer by striking off all dependence."

It is not to be presumed that Englishmen were wholly blind to this danger. There were advocates who maintained that it

---

*Pinkerton's Travels, Vol. XIII.

would be wiser to restore Canada and retain Guadaloupe, with perhaps Martinico and St. Lucia. This view was supported with distinguished ability in an anonymous paper, said to have been written by William Burke, the friend and kinsman of the great orator. The views therein set forth were said to have been countenanced by lord Hardwicke. The tide of English opinion was, however, very strongly in the opposite direction.

CHAPTER XII.

Scotch Hostility to America.

The causes which led to the American Revolution have been set forth in works pertaining to that event, and fully amplified by those desiring to give a special treatise on the subject. Briefly to rehearse them, the following may be pointed out: The general cause was the right of arbitrary government over the colonies claimed by the British parliament. So far as the claim was concerned as a theory, but little was said, but when it was put in force an opposition at once arose. The people had long been taught to act and think upon the principle of eternal right, which had a tendency to mould them in a channel that looked towards independence. The character of George III. was such as to irritate the people. He was stubborn and without the least conception of human rights; nor could he conceive of a magnanimous project, or appreciate the value of civil liberty. His notions of government were despotic, and around him, for advisers, he preferred those as incompetent and as illiberal as himself. Such a king could not deal with a people who had learned freedom, and had the highest conceptions of human rights. The British parliament, composed almost entirely of the ruling class, shared the views of their master, and servilely did his bidding, by passing a number of acts destructive of colonial liberty. The first of these was a strenuous attempt to enforce in 1761 THE IMPORTATION ACT, which gave to petty constables the authority to enter any and every place where they might suspect goods upon which a duty had not been levied. In 1763 and 1764 the English ministers attempted to enforce the law requiring the payment of duties on sugar and molasses. In vain did the people try to show that under the British constitution taxation and representation were inseparable. Nevertheless English vessels were sent to hover around American ports, and soon succeeded in paralyzing the trade with the West Indies.

The close of the French and Indian war gave to England a renewed opportunity to tax America. The national debt had increased from £52,092,238 in 1727 to £138,865,430 in 1763. The ministers began to urge that the expenses of the war ought to be borne by the colonies. The Americans contended, that they had aided England as much as she had aided them; that the cession of Canada had amply remunerated England for all her losses; and, further, the colonies did not dread the payment of money, but feared that their liberties might be subverted. Early in March 1765, the English parliament, passed the celebrated STAMP ACT, which provided that every note, bond, deed, mortgage, lease, licence, all legal documents of every description, every colonial pamphlet, almanac, and newspaper, after the first day of the following November, should be on paper furnished by the British government, the stamp cost being from one cent to thirty dollars. When the news of the passage of this act was brought to America the excitement was intense, and action was resolved on by the colonies. The act was not formally repealed until March 18, 1766. On June 29, 1767, another act was passed to tax America. On October 1, 1768, seven hundred troops, sent from Halifax, marched with fixed bayonets into Boston, and quartered themselves in the State House. In February 1769 parliament declared the people of Massachusetts rebels, and the governor was directed to arrest those deemed guilty of treason, and send them to England for trial. In the city of New York, in 1770, the soldiers wantonly cut down a liberty pole, which had for several years stood in the park. The most serious affray occurred on March 5th, in Boston between a party of citizens and some soldiers, in which three citizens were shot down and several wounded. This massacre inflamed the city with a blaze of excitement. On that day lord North succeeded in having all the dutes repealed except that on tea; and that tax, in 1773, was attempted to be enforced by a stratagem. On the evening of December 16th, the tea, in the three tea-ships, then in Boston harbor, was thrown overboard, by fifty men disguised as Indians. Parliament, instead of using legal means, hastened to find revenge. On March 31, 1774, it was enacted that Boston port should be closed.

The final act which brought on the Revolution was the firing upon the seventy minute men, who were standing still at Lexington, by the English soldiers under Major Pitcairn, on April 19, 1775, sixteen of the patriots fell dead or wounded. The first gun of the Revolution fired the entire country, and in a few days Boston was besieged by the militia twenty thousand strong. Events passed rapidly, wrongs upon wrongs were perpetrated, until, finally, on July 4, 1776, the Declaration of Independence was published to the world. By this act all hope of reconciliation was at an end. Whatever concessions might be made by England, her own acts had caused an impassable gulf.

America had done all within her power to avert the impending storm. Her petitions had been spurned from the foot of the English throne. Even the illustrious Dr. Franklin, venerable in years, was forced to listen to a vile diatribe against him delivered by the coarse and brutal Wedderburn, while members of the Privy Council who were present, with the single exception of lord North, "lost all dignity and all self-respect. They laughed aloud at each sarcastic sally of Wedderburn. 'The indecency of their behaviour,' in the words of Shelburne, 'exceeded, as is agreed on all hands, that of any committee of elections;' and Fox, in a speech which he made as late as 1803, reminded the House how on that memorable occasion 'all men tossed up their hats and clapped their hands in boundless delight at Mr. Wedderburn's speech.' "*

George III., his ministers and his parliament hurled the country headlong into war, and that against the judgment of her wisest men, and her best interests. To say the least the war was not popular in England. The wisest statesmen in both Houses of Parliament plead for reconciliation, but their efforts fell on callous ears. The ruling class was seized with the one idea of humbling America. They preferred to listen to such men as Major James Grant,—the same who allowed his men, (as has been already narrated) to be scandalously slaughtered before Fort du Quesne, and had made himself offensive in South Carolina under Colonel Montgomery. This braggart asserted, in the House of Commons, "amidst the loudest cheering, that he knew the Americans very well, and was certain they would not fight; 'that they

---

*Lecky's History of England, Vol. IV. p. 151.

were not soldiers and never could be made so, being naturally pusillanimous and incapable of discipline; that a very slight force would be more than sufficient for their complete reduction'; and he fortified his statement by repeating their peculiar expressions, and ridiculing their religious enthusiasm, manners and ways of living, greatly to the entertainment of the house."*

The great Pitt, then earl of Chatham, in his famous speech in January 1775, declared:

"The spirit which resists your taxation in America is the same that formerly opposed loans, benevolences, and ship-money in England. * * * This glorious spirit of Whiggism animates three millions in America who prefer poverty with liberty to gilded chains and sordid affluence, and who will die in defence of their rights as freemen. * * * For myself, I must declare that in all my reading and observation—and history has been my favorite study; I have read Thucydides, and have studied and admired the master states of the world—that for solidity of reasoning, force of sagacity, and wisdom of conclusion under such a complication of difficult circumstances, no nation or body of men can stand in preference to the General Congress at Philadelphia. * * * All attempts to impose servitude upon such men, to establish despotism over such a mighty continental nation, must be vain, must be fatal. We shall be forced ultimately to retreat. Let us retreat while we can, not when we must."

In accordance with these sentiments Chatham withdrew his eldest son from the army rather than suffer him to be engaged in the war. Lord Effingham, finding his regiment was to serve against the Americans, threw up his commission and renounced the profession for which he had been trained and loved, as the only means of escaping the obligation of fighting against the cause of freedom. Admiral Keppel, one of the most gallant officers in the British navy, expressed his readiness to serve against the ancient enemies of England, but asked to be released from employment against the Americans. It is said that Amherst refused to command the army against the Americans. In 1776 it was openly debated in parliament whether British officers ought to serve their sovereign against the Americans, and no less a person than General Conway leaned decidedly to the negative, and compared the

---

*Bancroft's History United States, Vol. VI, p. 136; American Archives, Fourth Series, Vol. I, p. 1543.

case to that of French officers who were employed in the Massacre of St. Bartholomew. Just after the battle of Bunker Hill, the duke of Richmond declared in parliament that he "did not think that the Americans were in rebellion, but that they were resisting acts of the most unexampled cruelty and oppression." The Corporation of London, in 1775, drew up an address strongly approving of the resistance of the Americans, and similar addresses were expressed by other towns. A great meeting in London, and also the guild of merchants in Dublin, returned thanks to lord Effingham for his recent conduct. When Montgomery fell at the head of the American troops before Quebec, he was eulogized in the British parliament.

The merchants of Bristol, September 27, 1775, held a meeting and passed resolutions deprecating the war, and calling upon the king to put a stop to it. The Lord Mayor, Aldermen, and Livery of London, September 29th, issued an address to the Electors of Great Britain, against carrying on the war. A meeting of the merchants and traders of London was held October 5th, and moved an address to the king "relative to the unhappy dispute between Great Britain and her American Colonies," and that he should "cause hostilities to cease." The principal citizens, manufacturers and traders of the city of Coventry, October 10th, addressed the sovereign beseeching him "to stop the effusion of blood, to recommend to your Parliament to consider, with all due attention, the petition from America lately offered to be presented to the throne." The mayor and burgesses of Nottingham, October 20th, petitioned the king in which they declared that "the first object of our desires and wishes is the return of peace and cordial union with our American fellow-subjects," and humbly requested him to "suspend those hostilities, which, we fear, can have no other than a fatal issue." This was followed by an address of the inhabitants of the same city, in which the king was asked to "stay the hand of war, and recall into the bosom of peace and grateful subjection your American subjects, by a restoration of those measures which long experience has shown to be productive of the greatest advantages to this late united and flourishing Empire." The petition of the free burgesses, traders and inhabitants of Newcastle-upon-Tyne declared that "in the present unnatural war with our American brethren, we have seen neither provocation nor object; nor is it, in our humble apprehension, consonant with the rights of humanity, sound policy, or the Constitution of our Country." A very great majority of the gentlemen, clergy and freeholders of the county of Berks signed an address, November 7th, to the king in which it was declared that "the disorders have arisen from a complaint (plausible at least) of one right violated; and we can never be brought to imagine that the true remedy for such disorders consists in an attack on all other rights, and an attempt to drive the people either to unconstitutional submission or absolute despair." The gentlemen, merchants, freemen and inhabitants of the city of Worcester also addressed the king and besought him to adopt such measures as shall "seem most expedient for putting a stop to the further effusion of blood, for reconciling Great Britain and her Colonies, for reuniting the affections of your now divided people, and for establishing, on a permanent foundation, the peace, commerce, and prosperity of all your Majesty's Dominions."

It is a fact, worthy of special notice, that in both England and Ireland there was a complete absence of alacrity and enthusiasm in enlisting for the army and navy. This was the chief reason why George III. turned to the petty German princes who trafficked in human chattels. There people were seized in their homes, or while working the field, and sold to England at so much per head. On account of the great difficulty in England in obtaining voluntary recruits for the American war, the press-gang was resorted to, and in 1776, was especially fierce. In less than a month eight hundred men were seized in London alone, and several lives were lost in the scuffles that took place. The press-gang would hang about the prison-gates, and seize criminals whose sentences had expired and force them into the army.

"It soon occurred to the government that able-bodied criminals might be more usefully employed in the coercion of the revolted colonists, and there is reason to believe that large numbers of criminals of all but the worst category, passed at this time into the English army and navy. In estimating the light in which British soldiers were regarded in America, and in estimating the violence and misconduct of which British soldiers were sometimes guilty, this fact must not be forgotten." In Ireland criminals were released from their prisons on condition of enlisting in the army or navy.*

The regular press-gang was not confined to England, and it formed one of the grievances of the American colonists. One of the most terrible riots ever known in New England, was caused, in 1747, by this nefarious practice, under the sanction of Admiral Knowles. An English vessel was burnt, and English officers were seized and imprisoned by the crowd; the governor was obliged to flee to the castle; the sub-sheriffs were impounded in the stocks; the militia refused to act against the people; and the admiral was compelled to release his captives. Resistance, in America, was shown in many subsequent attempts to impress the people.

The king and his ministers felt it was necessary to sustain the acts of parliament in the American war by having addresses sent to the king upholding him in the course he was pursuing. Hence emissaries were sent throughout the kingdom who cajoled the ignorant into signing such papers. The general sentiment of the people cannot be estimated by the number of addresses for they were obtained by the influence of the ministers of state. Every magistrate depending upon the favor of the crown could and would exert his influence as directed. Hence there were numerous addresses sent to the king approving the course he was bent upon. When it is considered that the government had the advantage of more than fifty thousand places and pensions at its disposal, the immense lever for securing addresses is readily seen. From no section of the country, however, were these addresses so numerous as from Scotland.

It is one of the most singular things in history that the people of Scotland should have been so hostile to the Americans, and so forward in expressing their approbation of the attitude of George III. and his ministers. The Americans had in no wise ever harmed them or crossed their path. The emigrants from Scotland had been received with open arms by the people. If any had been mistreated, it was by the appointees of the crown. With

---

*Leeky's History of England, Vol. IV. p. 346

scarcely an exception the whole political representation in both Houses of Parliament supported lord North, and were bitterly opposed to the Americans. Lecky has tried to soften the matter by throwing the blame on the servile leaders who did not represent the real sentiment of the people:

"Scotland, however, is one of the very few instances in history, of a nation whose political representation was so grossly defective as not merely to distort but absolutely to conceal its opinions. It was habitually looked upon as the most servile and corrupt portion of the British Empire; and the eminent liberalism and the very superior political qualities of its people seem to have been scarcely suspected to the very eve of the Reform Bill of 1832. That something of that liberalism existed at the outbreak of the American war, may, I think, be inferred from the very significant fact that the Government were unable to obtain addresses in their favor either from Edinburgh or Glasgow. The country, however, was judged mainly by its representatives, and it was regarded as far more hostile to the American cause than either England or Ireland."*

A very able editor writing at the time has observed:

"It must however be acknowledge, that an unusual apathy with respect to public affairs, seemed to prevail with the people, in general, of this country; of which a stronger proof needs not to be given, that than which will probably recur to every body's memory, that the accounts of many of the late military actions, as well as of political procedings of no less importance, were received with as much indifference, and canvassed with as much coolness and unconcern, as if they had happened between two nations with whom they were scarcely connected. We must except from all these observations, the people of North Britain (Scotland), who, almost to a man, so far as they could be described or distinguished under any particular denomination, not only applauded, but proffered life and fortune in support of the present measures."†

The list of addresses sent from Scotland to the king against the Colonies is a long one,—unbroken by any remonstrance or correction. It embraces those sent by the provost, magistrates, and common (or town) council of Aberbrothock, Aberdeen, Annan, Ayr, Burnt-Island, Dundee, Edinburgh, Forfar, Forres, Inverness, Irvine, Kirkaldy, Linlithgow, Lochmaben, Montrose, Nairn,

---

*History of England, Vol. IV, p. 338.   †Annual Register, 1776, p. 39.

Peebles, Perth, Renfrew, Rutherglen, and Stirling; by the magistrates and town council of Brechine, Inverary, St. Andrews, Selkirk, Jedburgh, Kirkcudbright, Kirkwall, and Paisley; by the magistrates, town council and all the principal inhabitants of Fortrose; by the provost, magistrates, council, burgesses and inhabitants of Elgin; by the chief magistrates of Dunfermline, Inverkeiting and Culross; by the magistrates, common council, burgesses, and inhabitants of Dumfries; by the lord provost, magistrates, town council and deacons of craft of Lanark; by the magistrates, incorporated societies, and principal inhabitants of the town and port of Leith; by the principal inhabitants of Perth; by the gentlemen, clergy, merchants, manufacturers, incorporated trades and principal inhabitants of Dundee; by the deacon convenier, deacons of fourteen incorporated trades and other members of trades houses of Glasgow; by the magistrates, council and incorporations of Cupar in Fife, and Dumbarton; by the freeholders of the county of Argyle and Berwick; by the noblemen, gentlemen and freeholders of the counties of Aberdeen and Fife; by the noblemen, gentlemen, freeholders and others of the county of Linlithgow; by the noblemen and gentlemen of the county of Roxburgh; by the noblemen, justices of the peace, freeholders, and commissioners of supply of the counties of Perth and Caithness; by the noblemen, freeholders, justices of the peace, and commissioners of the land-tax of the counties of Banff and Elgin; by the freeholders and justices of the peace of the county of Dumbarton; by the gentlemen, justices of the peace, clergy, freeholders and committee of supply of the county of Clackmanan; by the gentlemen, justices of the peace and commissioners of land tax of the counties of Kincardine, Lanark and Renfrew; by the freeholders, justices of the peace and commissioners of supply of the counties of Kinross and Orkney; by the justices of the peace, freeholders and commissioners of land tax of the county of Peebles; by the gentlemen, freeholders, justices of the peace and commissioners of supply of the county of Nairn; by the gentlemen, heretors, freeholders and clergy of the counties of Ross and Cromarty; by the General Assembly of the Church of Scotland; by the ministers and elders of the provincial synod of Angus and Mearns;

also of the synod of Glasgow and Ayr; by the provincial synod of Dumfries, and by the ministers of the presbytery of Irvine.

The list ascribes but eight of the addresses to the Highlands. This does not signify that they were any the less loyal to the pretentions of George III. The probability is that the people generally stood ready to follow their leaders, and these latter exerted themselves against the colonists. The addresses that were proffered, emanating from the Highlands, in chronological order, may be thus summarized: The freeholders of Argyleshire, on October 17, 1775, met at Inverary with Robert Campbell presiding, and through their representative in Parliament, Colonel Livingston, presented their "humble Address" to the king, in which they refer to their predecessors who had "suffered early and greatly in the cause of liberty" and now judge it incumbent upon themselves "to express our sense of the blessings we enjoy under your Majesty's mild and constitutional Government; and, at the same time, to declare our abhorrence of the unnatural rebellion of our deluded fellow-subjects in America, which, we apprehend, is encouraged and fomented by several discontented and turbulent persons at home." They earnestly desire that the measures adopted by parliament may be "vigorously prosecuted;" "and we beg leave to assure your Majesty, that, in support of such measures, we are ready to risk our lives and fortunes."

The address of the magistrates, town council, and all the principal inhabitants of Fortrose, is without date, but probably during the month of October of the same year. They met with Colonel Hector Munro, their representative in parliament, presiding, and addressing the king declared their "loyal affection" to his person; are "filled with a just sense of the many blessings" they enjoy, and "beg leave to approach the throne, and express our indignation at, and abhorrence of, the measures adopted by our unhappy and deluded fellow-subjects in America, in direct opposition to law and justice, and to every rational idea of civilization;" "with still greater indignation, if possble, we behold this rebellious disposition, which so fatally obtains on the other side of the Atlantic, fomented and cherished by a set of men in Great Britain;" that the "deluded children may quickly return to their duty," and if not, "we hope your Majesty will direct such vigorous, speedy, and effectual measures to be pursued, as may bring them to a due sense of their error."

The provost, magistrates and town council of Nairn met November 6, 1775, and addressed their "Most Gracious Sovereign" as his "most faithful subjects" and it was their "indispensable duty" to testify their "loyalty and attachment;" they were "deeply sensible of the many blessings" they enjoyed; they viewed with "horror and detestation" the "audacious attempts that have been made to alienate the affections of your subjects." "Weak as our utmost efforts may be deemed, and limited our powers, each heart and hand devoted to your service will, with the most ardent zeal, contribute in promoting such measures as may be now thought necessary for re-establishing the violated rights of the British Legislature, and bringing back to order and allegiance your Majesty's deluded and unhappy subjects in America."

On the same day, the same class of men at Inverness made their address as "dutiful and loyal subjects," and declared "the many blessings" they enjoyed; and expressed their "utmost detestation and abhorrence of that spirit of rebellion which has unhapily broke forth among your Majesty's subjects in America," and "the greatest sorrow we behold the seditious designs of discontented and factious men so far attended with success as to seduce your infatuated and deluded subjects in the colonies from their allegiance and duty," and they declared their "determined resolution of supporting your Majesty's Government, to the utmost of our power, against all attempts that may be made to disturb it, either at home or abroad."

The following day, or November 7th, the gentlemen, freeholders, justices of the peace, and commissioners of supply of the county of Nairn, met in the city of Nairn, and addressed their "Most Gracious Sovereign," declaring themselves the "most dutiful and loyal subjects," and it was their "indispensable duty" "to declare our abhorrence of the present unnatural rebellion carried on by many of your infatuated subjects in America." "With profound humility we profess our unalterable attachment to your

Majesty's person and family, and our most cordial approbation of the early measures adopted for giving a check to the first dawnings of disobedience. This county, in the late war, sent out many of its sons to defend your Majesty's ungrateful colonies against the invasion of foreign enemies, and they will now, when called upon, be equally ready to repel all the attempts of the traitorous and disaffected, against the dignity of your crown, and the just rights of the supreme Legislature of Great Britain."

The gentlemen, heretors, freeholders, and clergy of the Counties of Ross and Cromarty assembled at Dingwall, November 23, 1775, and also addressed their "Most Gracious Sovereign" as the "most faithful and loyal subjects," acknowledging "the protection we are blessed with in the enjoyment of our liberties," it is "with an inexpressible concern we behold many of our fellow-subjects in America, incited and supported by factions and designing men at home," and that "we shall have no hesitation in convincing your rebellious and deluded subjects in America, that with the same cheerfulness we so profusely spilled our blood in the last war, in defending them against their and our natural enemies, we are now ready to shed it, if necessary, in bringing them back to a just sense of their duty and allegiance to your Majesty, and their subordination to the Mother Country."

The magistrates and town council of Inverary met on November 28, 1775, and to their "Most Gracious Sovereign" they were also the "most dutiful and loyal subjects," and further "enjoyed all the blessings of the best Government the wisdom of man ever devised, we have seen with indignation, the malignant breath of disappointed faction, by prostituting the sacred sounds of liberty, too successful in blowing the sparks of a temporary discontent into the flames of a rebellion in your Majesty's Colonies, that we from our souls abhor;" and they desired to be applied "such forcive remedies to the affected parts, as shall be necessary to restore that union and dependency of the whole on the legislative power."

At Thurso, December 6, 1775, there met the noblemen, gentlemen, freeholders, justices of the peace and commissioners of supply of the county of Caithness, and in an address to their

"Most Gracious Sovereign" declared themselves also to be the "most dutiful and loyal subjects;" they approved the "lenient measures" which had hitherto been taken in America by parliament, "and that they will support with their lives and fortunes, the vigorous exertions which they forsee may soon be necessary to subdue a rebellion premeditated, unprovoked, and that is every day becoming more general, untainted by the vices that too often accompany affluence, our people have been inured to industry, sobriety, and, when engaged in your Majesty's service, have been distinguished for an exact obedience to discipline, and a faithful discharge of duty; and we hope, if called forth to action in one combined corps, it will be their highest ambition to merit a favorable report to your Majesty from their superior officers. At the same time, it is our most ardent prayer to Almighty God, that the eyes of our deluded fellow-subjects in America may soon be opened, to see whether it is safe to trust in a Congress unconstitutionally assembled, in a band of officers unconstitutionally appointed, or in a British King and Parliament whose combined powers have indeed often restrained the licentiousness, but never invaded the rational liberties of mankind."

A survey of the addresses indicates that they were composed by one person, or else modelled from the same formula. All had the same source of inspiration. This, however, does not militate against the moral effect of those uttering them. So far as Scotland is concerned, it must be regarded as a fair representation of the sentiment of the people. While only an insignificant part of the Highlands gave their humble petitions, yet the subsequent acts must be the criterion from which a judgment must be formed.

It is possible that some of the loyal addresses were accelerated by the prohibition placed on Scotch emigration to America. Early in September, 1775, Henry Dundas, lord-advocate for Scotland, urged the board of customs to issue orders to all inferior custom houses enjoining them to grant no clearances for America of any ship which had more than the common complement of hands on board. On September 23, 1775, Archibald Cockburn, sheriff deputy of Edinburgh, issued the following order:

"Whereas a letter was received by me some time ago, from His Majesty's Advocate for Scotland, intimating that, on account

---
*See Appendix, Note M.

of the present rebellion in America, it was proper a stop should
be put for the present to emigrations to that Country, and that
the necessary directions were left at the different sea-ports in
Scotland to that purpose; I think it my duty, in obedience to his
Lordship's requisition contained in that letter, to take this publick
method of notifying to such of the inhabitants within my jurisdiction, if any such there be, who have formed resolutions to themselves of leaving this Country, and going in quest of settlements
in America, that they aught not to put themselves to the unnecessary trouble and expense of preparing for a removal of their habitations, which they will not, so far as it lies in my power to prevent, be permitted to effectuate."

The British government had every assurance of the undivided support of all Scotland in its attempt to subjugate
America. It also put a strong dependence in enlisting in the
army such Highlanders as had emigrated, and especially those
who had belonged to the 42nd, Fraser's, and Montgomery's regiments, but remained in the country after the peace of 1763. This
alone would make a very unfavorable impression on the minds of
Americans. But when to this is added the efforts of British officers to organize the emigrants from the Highlands into a special
regiment, as early as Novemeber, 1775, the rising of the Highlanders both in North Carolina and on the Mohawk, the enlisting
of emigrants on board vessels before landing and sailing by
Boston to join their regiments at Halifax, and on the passage
listening to the booming of the cannon at Bunker Hill; and the
further fact that both the 42nd and Fraser's Highlanders were
ordered to embark at Greenock for America, five days before the
battle of Lexington, it is not a matter of surprise that a strong
resentment should be aroused in the breasts of many of the most
devoted to the cause of the Revolution.

The feeling engendered by the acts of Scotland towards
those engaged in the struggle for human liberty crops out in the
original draft of the Declaration of Independence as laid before
Congress July 1, 1776. In the memorable paper appeared the
following sentence: "At this very time, too, they are permitting
their chief magistrate to send over, not only soldiers of our common blood, but Scotch and foreign mercenaries to invade and

destroy us." The word "Scotch" was struck out, on motion of Dr. John Witherspoon, himself a native of Scotland; and subsequently the whole sentence was deleted.

The sentence was not strictly true, for there were thousands of Americans of Scotch ancestry, but principally Lowland. There were also thousands of Americans, true to the principles of the Revolution, of Highland extraction. If the sentence had been strictly true, it would have served no purpose, even if none were alienated thereby. But, the records show that in the American army there were men who rendered distinguished services who were born in the Highlands; and others, from the Lowlands, rendered services of the highest value in their civil capacities.

The armies of the Colonies had no regiments or companies composed of Highland Scotch, or even of that extraction, although their names abound scattered through a very large percentage of the organized forces. The only effort* which appears to have been made in that direction rests on two petitions by Donald McLeod. The first was directed to the Committee for the City and County of New York, dated at New York, June 7, 1775:

"That your petitioner, from a deep sense of the favors conferred on himself, as well as those shown to many of his countrymen when in great distress after their arrival into this once happy city, is moved by a voluntary spirit of liberty to offer himself in the manner and form following, viz: That your said petitioner understands that a great many Companies are now on foot to be raised for the defence of our liberties in this once happy land, which he thinks to be a very proper maxim for the furtherance of our rights and liberty; that your said petitioner (although he has nothing to recommend himself but the variety of calling himself a Highlander, from North-Britain) flatters himself that if this honorable Committee were to grant him a commission, under their hand and seal, that he could, without difficulty, raise one hundred Scotch Highlanders in this City and the neighboring Provinces, provided they were to be put in the Highland dress, and under pay during their service in defence of our liberties. Therefore, may it please your Honors to take this petition under your serious consideration; and should your Honors think proper

---
*See Appendix, Note N.

to confer the honor upon him as to have the command of a Highland Company, under the circumstances proposed, your petitioner assures you that no person shall or will be more willing to accept of the offer than your humble petitioner."

On the following day Donald McLeod sent a petition, couched in the following language to the Congress for the Colony of New York:

"That yesterday your said petitioner presented a petition before this honorable body, and as to the contents of which he begs leave to give reference. That since, a ship arrived from Scotland, with a number of Highlanders passengers. That your petitioner talked to them this morning, and after informing them of the present state of this as well as the neighboring Colonies, they all seemed to be very desirous to form themselves into companies, with the proviso of having liberty to wear their own country dress, commonly called the Highland habit, and moreover to be under pay for the time they are in the service for the protection of the liberties of this once happy country, but by all means to be under the command of Highland officers, as some of them cannot speak the English language. That the said Highlanders are already furnished with guns, swords, pistols, and Highland dirks, which, in case of occasion, is very necessary, as all the above articles are at this time very difficult to be had. Therefore may it please your Honors to take all and singular the premises under your serious and immediate consideration; and as your petitioner wants an answer as soon as possible, he further prays that as soon as they think it meet, he may be advised. And your petitioner, is in duty bound, shall ever pray."

This petition was presented during the formative state of the army, and when the colonies were in a state of anarchy. Congress had not yet assumed control of the army, although on the very eve of it. With an empire to found and defend, the continental Congress had not at its disposal a single penny. When Washington was offered the command of the army there was little to bring out the unorganized resources of the country. At the very time of Donald McLeod's petition, the provincial congress of New York was engaged with the distracted state of its own commonwealth. Order was not brought out of chaos until the strong hand and great energy of Washington had been felt.

CHAPTER XIII.

HIGHLAND REGIMENTS IN THE AMERICAN REVOLUTION.

The great Pitt, in his famous eulogy on the Highland regiments, delivered in 1766, in Parliament, said: "I sought for merit wherever it could be found. It is my boast that I was the first minister who looked for it, and found it, in the mountains of the north. I called it forth, and drew into your service a hardy and intrepid race of men; men who, when left by your jealousy, became a prey to the artifices of your enemies, and had gone nigh to have overturned the State, in the war before the last. These men, in the last war, were brought to combat on your side; they served with fidelity, as they fought with valor, and conquered for you in every quarter of the world."

ROYAL HIGHLAND EMIGRANT REGIMENT.

These same men were destined to be brought from their homes and help swell the ranks of the oppressors of America. The first attempt made was to organize the Highland regiments in America. The MacDonald fiasco in North Carolina and the Highlanders of Sir John Johnson have already been noticed. But there were other Highlanders throughout the inhabited districts of America, who had emigrated, or else had belonged to the 42nd, Fraser's or Montgomery's Highlanders. It was desired to collect these, in so far as it was possible, and organize them into a distinct regiment. The supervision of this work was given to Colonel Allan MacLean of Torloisk, Mull, an experienced officer who had seen hard service in previous wars. The secret instructions given by George III. to William Tryon, governor of New York, is dated April 3, 1775:

"Whereas an humble application hath been made to us by Allen McLean Eqre late Major to our 114th Regiment, and Lieut

Col: in our Army setting forth, that a considerable number of our subjects, who have, at different times, emigrated from the North West parts of North Britain, and have transported themselves, with their families, to New York, have expressed a desire, to take up Lands within our said Province, to be held of us, our heirs and successors, in fee simple; and whereas it may be of public advantage to grant lands in manner aforesaid to such of the said Emigrants now residing within our said province as may be desirous of settling together upon some convenient spot within the same. It is therefore our Will and pleasure, that upon application to you by the said Allen McLean, and upon his producing to you an Association of the said Emigrants to the effect of the form hereunto annexed, subscribed by the heads of the several families of which such Emigrants shall consist, you do cause a proper spot to be located and surveyed in one contiguous Tract within our said Province of New York, sufficient in quantity for the accommodation of such Emigrants, allowing 100 acres to each head of a family, and 500 acres for every other person of which the said family shall consist; and it is our further will and pleasure that when the said Lands shall have been located as aforesaid, you do grant the same by letters patent under the seal of our said Province unto the said Allen Maclean, in trust, and upon the conditions, to make allotments thereof in Fee Simple to the heads of Families, whose names, together with the number of persons in each family, shall have been delivered in by him as aforesaid, accompanied with the said association, and it is Our further will and pleasure that it be expressed in the said letters patent, that the lands so to be granted shall be exempt from the payment of quit-rents for 20 years from the date thereof, with a proviso however that all such parts of the said Tracts as shall not be settled in manner aforesaid within two years from the date of the grant shall revert to us, and be disposed of in such manner as we shall think fit; and it is our further will and pleasure, that neither yourself, nor any other of our Officers, within our said Province, to whose duty it may appertain to carry these our orders into execution do take any Fee or reward for the same, and that the expense of surveying and locating any Tract of Land in the manner and for the purpose above mentioned be defrayed out of our Revenue of Quit rents and charged to the account thereof. And we do hereby, declare it to be our further will and pleasure, that in case the whole or any part of the said Colonists, fit to bear Arms, shall be hereafter embodied and employed in Our service in America, either as Commission or non Commissioned Officers or private Men, they shall respectively receive further grants of

Land from us within our said province, free of all charges, and exempt from the payment of quit rents for 20 years, in the same proportion to their respective Ranks, as is directed and prescribed by our Royal Proclamation of the 7th of October 1763. in regard to such officers and soldiers as were employed in our service during the last War."

This paltry scheme concocted to raise men for the royal cause could have but very little effect. The Highlanders, it proposed to reach, were scattered, and the work proposed must be done secretly and with expedition. To raise the Highlanders required address, a number of agents, and necessary hardships. Armed with the warrant Colonel Maclean and some followers proceded to New York and from there to Boston, where the object of the visit became known through a sergeant by name of McDonald who was trying to enlist "men to join the King's Troops; they seized him, and on his examination found that he had been employed by Major Small for this Purpose; they sent him a Prisoner into Connecticut. This has raised a violent suspicion against the Scots and Highlanders and will make the execution of Coll Maclean's Plan more difficult."*

The principal agents engaged with Colonel Maclean in raising the new regiment were Major John Small and Captain Alexander McDonald. The latter met with much discouragement and several escapes. His "Letter-Book" is a mine of information pertaining to the regiment. As early as November 15, 1775, he draws a gloomy picture of the straits of the Macdonalds on whom so much was relied by the English government. "As for all the McDonalds in America they may Curse the day that was born as being the means of Leading them to ruin from my Zeal and attachment for government poor Glanaldall I am afraid is Lost as there is no account of him since a small Schooner Arrived which brought an account of his having Six & thirty men then and if he should Not be Lost he is unavoidably ruined in his Means all those up the Mohawk river will be tore to pieces and those in North Carolina the same so that if Government will Not Consider them when Matters are Settled I think they are ill treated"†

The commissions of Colonel Maclean, Major John Small and

---

*Governor Colden to Earl of Dartmouth. New York Docs. Relating to Colonial History, Vol. VIII, p. 588. †Letter Book, p. 221.

REGIMENTS IN THE AMERICAN REVOLUTION.

Captain William Dunbar bear date of June 13, 1775, and all the other captains one day later. The regiment raised was known as the Royal Highland Emigrant Regiment and was composed of two battalions, the first of which was commanded by Lieutenant Colonel Allan Maclean, and was composed of Highland emigrants in Canada, and the discharged men of the 42nd, of Fraser's and Montgomery's Highlanders who had settled in North America after the peace of 1763. Great difficulty was experienced in conveying the troops who had been raised in the back settlements to their respective destinations. This battalion made the following return of its officers:

Isle Aux Noix, 15th April, 1778.

Rank	Names	Former Rank in the Army
Lieut.-Col.	Allan McLean	Lieutenant-Colonel
Major	Donald McDonald	
Captain	William Dunbar	Capt. late 78th Regt.
"	John Nairne	
"	Alexander Fraser	Lieut. late 78th Regt.
"	George McDougall	Lieut. 60th Regt.
"	Malcolm Fraser	Lieut. late 8th Regt.
"	Daniel Robertson	Lieut. 42nd Regt.
"	George Laws	
Lieutenant	Neil McLean, (prisoner)	Lieut. 7th Regt.
"	John McLean	Ensign late 114th Regt.
"	Alexander Firtelier	
"	Lachlan McLean	
"	Fran. Damburgess, (prisoner)	Ensign, 21 Nov. 1775
"	David Cairns	Ensign, 1st June 1775
"	Don. McKinnon	Ensign, 20th Nov. 1775
"	Ronald McDonald	Ensign, 14th June 1775
"	John McDonell	Ensign, 14th June 1775
"	Alexander Stratton, (prisoner)	
"	Hector McLean	
Ensign	Ronald McDonald	
"	Archibald Grant	
"	David Smith	
"	George Darne	
"	Archibald McDonald	
"	William Wood	

Rank	Names	Former Rank in the Army
Ensign......	John Pringle............	....
"	Hector McLean, (prisoner).......	....
Chaplain....	John Bethune....................	....
Adjutant....	Ronald McDonald...............	....
Qr. Master..	Lachlan McLean..............·..	....
Surgeon....	James Davidson................	....
Surg's Mate.	James Walker	....

The second battalion was commanded by Major John Small, formerly of the 42nd, and then of the 21st regiment, which was raised from emigrants arriving in the colonies and discharged Highland soldiers who had settled in Nova Scotia. Each battalion was to consist of seven hundred and fifty men, with officers in proportion. In speaking of the raising of the men Captain Alexander McDonald, in a letter to General Sir William Howe, under date of Halifax, November 30, 1775, says:

"Last October was a year when I found the people of America were determind on Rebellion, I wrote to Major Small desiring he would acquaint General Gage that I was ready to join the Army with a hundred as good men as any in America, the General was pleased to order the Major to write and return his Excellency's thanks to me for my Loyalty and spirited offers of Service, but that he had not power at that time to grant Commissions or raise any troops; however the hint was improved and A proposal was Sent home to Government to raise five Companies and I was in the meantime ordered to ingeage as many men as I possibly Could, Accordingly I Left my own house on Staten Island this same day year and travelled through frost snow & Ice all the way to the Mohawk river, where there was two hundred Men of my own Name, who had fled from the Severity of their Landlords in the Highlands of Scotland, the Leading men of whom most Chearfully agreed to be ready at a Call, but the affair was obliged to be kept a profound Secret till it was Known whether the government approved of the Scheme and otherwise I could have inlisted five hundred men in a months time, from thence I proceeded straight to Boston to know for Certain what was done in the affair when General Gage asur'd me that he had recommended it to the Ministry and did not doubt of its Meeting with approbation. I Left Boston and went home to my own house and was ingeaging as Many men as I Could of those that I thought I could intrust but it was not possible to keep the thing Long a Secret when we had to make proposals to five hundred men; in the Mean time Coll McLean arrived with full power from Government to Collect all the Highlanders who had Emigrated to America Into one place and to give Every man the hundred Acres of Land and if need required to give Arms to as many men as were Capable of bearing them for His Majesty's Service. Coll McLean and I Came from New York to Boston to know how Matters would be Settled by Genl Gage: it was then proposed and Agreed upon to raise twenty Companies or two Battalions Consisting of one Lt Colonl Commandant two Majors and Seventeen Captains, of which I was to be the first or oldest Captain and was confirmed by Coll McLean under his hand Writeing."*

At the time of the beginning of hostilities a large number of Highlanders were on their way from Scotland to settle in the colonies. In some instances the vessels on which were the emigrants, were boarded from a man-of-war before their arrival. In some families there is a tradition that they were captured by a war vessel Those who did arrive were induced partly by threats and partly by persuasion to enlist for the war, which they were assured would be of short duration. These people were not only in poverty, but many were in debt for their passage, and they were now promised that by enlisting their debts should be paid, they should have plenty of food as well as full pay for their services, besides receiving for each head of a family two hundred acres of land and fifty more for each child, while, in the event of refusal, there was presented the alternative of going to jail to pay their debts. The result of the artifices used can be no mystery. Under such conditions most of the able-bodied men enlisted, in some instances father and son serving together. Their wives and children were sent to Halifax, hearing the cannon of Bunker Hill on their passage.

These enlistments formed a part of the Battalion under Major Small,—five companies of which remained in Nova Scotia during the war, and the remaining five joining Sir Henry Clinton and Lord Cornwallis to the southward. That portion of which

---

*Ibid, p. 223.

remained in Nova Scotia, was stationed at Halifax, Windsor, and Cumberland, and were distinguished by their uniform good behavior.

The men belonging to the first battalion were assembled at Quebec. On the approach of the American army by Lake Champlain, Colonel Maclean was ordered to St. Johns with a party of militia, but got only as far as St. Denis, where he was deserted by his men. When Quebec was threatened by the American army under Colonel Arnold, Colonel Maclean with his regiment consisting of three hundred and fifty men, was at Sorel, and being forced to decamp from that place, by great celerity of movement, evaded the army of Colonel Arnold and passed into Quebec with one hundred of his regiment. He arrived just in time, for the citizens were about to surrender the city to the Americans. On Colonel Maclean's arrival, November 13, 1775, the garrison consisted only of fifty men of the Fusiliers and seven hundred militia and seamen. There had also just landed one hundred recruits of Colonel Maclean's corps from Newfoundland, which had been raised by Malcolm Fraser and Captain Campbell. Also, at the same time, there arrived the frigate Lizard, with £20,000 cash, all of which put new spirits into the garrison. The arrival of the veteran Maclean greatly diminished the chances of Colonel Arnold. Colonel Maclean now bent his energies towards saving the town; strengthened every point; enthused the lukewarm, and by emulation kept up a good spirit among them all. When General Carleton, leaving his army behind him, arrived in Quebec he found that Colonel Maclean had not only withstood the assaults of the Americans but had brought order and system out of chaos. In the final assault on the last day of the year, when the brave General Montgomery fell, the Highlanders were in the midst of the fray.

Many of the Americans were captured at this storming of Quebec. One of them narrates that "January 4th, on the next day, we were visited by Colonel Maclean, an old man, attended by other officers, for a peculiar purpose, that is, to ascertain who among us were born in Europe. We had many Irishmen and some Englishmen. The question was put to each; those who admitted a British birth, were told they must serve his majesty in

Colonel Maclean's regiment, a new corps, called the emigrants. Our poor fellows, under the fearful penalty of being carried to Britain, there to be tried for treason, were compelled by necessity, and many of them did enlist."*

Such men could hardly prove to be reliable, and it can be no astonishment to read what Major Henry Caldwell, one of the defenders of Quebec says of it:

"Of the prisoners we took, about 100 of them were Europeans, chiefly from Ireland; the greatest part of them engaged voluntarily in Col. McLean's corps, but about a dozen of them deserting in the course of a month, the rest were again confined, and not released till the arrival of the Isis, when they were again taken into the corps."†

Colonel Arnold despairing of capturing the town by assault, established himself on the Heights of Abraham, with the intention of cutting off supplies and blockading the town. In this situation he reduced the garrison to great straits, all communication with the country being cut off. He erected batteries and made several attempts to get possession of the lower town, but was foiled at every point by the vigilance of Colonel Maclean. On the approach of spring, Colonel Arnold, despairing of success, raised the siege.

The battalion remained in the province of Canada during the war, and was principally employed in small, but harrassing enterprises. In one of these, Captain Daniel Robertson, Lieutenant Hector Maclean, and Ensign Archibald Grant, with the grenadier company, marched twenty days through the woods with no other direction than the compass, and an Indian guide. The object being to surprise a small post in the interior, which was successful and attained without loss. By long practice in the woods the men had become very intelligent and expert in this kind of warfare.

The reason why this regiment was not with the army of General Burgoyne, and thus escaped the humiliation of the surrender at Saratoga, has been stated by that officer in the following language: that he proposed to leave in Canada "Maclean's Corps,

---

*Henry's Campaign Against Quebec, 1775, p. 136. †Invasion of Canada 1775, p. 14.

because I very much apprehend desertions from such parts of it as are composed of Americans, should they come near the enemy. In Canada, whatsoever may be their disposition, it is not so easy to effect it."*

Notwithstanding the conduct of Colonel Allan Maclean at the siege of Quebec and his great zeal in behalf of Britain his corps was not yet recognized, though he had at the outset been promised establishment and rank for it. He therefore returned to England where he arrived on September 1, 1776, to seek justice for himself and men. They were not received until the close of 1778, when the regiment was numbered the 84th, at which time Sir Henry Clinton was appointed its Colonel, and the battalions ordered to be augmented to one thousand men each. The uniform was the full Highland garb, with purses made of raccoons' instead of badger's skins. The officers wore the broad sword and dirk, and the men a half basket sword.

"On a St. Andrew's day a ball was given by the officers of the garrison in which they were quartered to the ladies in the vicinity. When one of the ladies entered the ball-room, and saw officers in the Highland dress, her sensitive delicacy revolted at what she though an indecency, declaring she would quit the room if these were to be her company. This occasioned some little embarrassment. An Indian lady, sister of the Chief Joseph Brant, who was present with her daughters, observing the bustle, inquired what was the matter, and being informed, she cried out, 'This must be a very indelicate lady to think of such a thing; she shows her own arms and elbows to all the men, and she pretends she cannot look at these officers' bear legs, although she will look at my husband's bare thighs for hours together; she must think of other things, or she would see no more shame in a man showing his legs, than she does in showing her neck and breast.' These remarks turned the laugh against the lady's squeamish delicacy, and the ball was permitted to proceed without the officers being obliged to retire."†

With every opportunity offered the first battalion to desert, in consequence of offers of land and other inducements held out by the Americans, not one native Highlander deserted; and only

---

*State of the Expedition, p. VI. †Stewart's Sketches of the Highlanders, Vol. II, p. 186.

one Highlander was brought to the halberts during the time they were embodied.

The history of the formation of the two battalions is dissimilar; that of the second was not attended with so great difficulties. In the formation of the first all manner of devices were entered into, and various disguises were resorted to in order to escape detection. Even this did not always protect them.

"It is beyond the power of Expression to give an Idea of the expence & trouble our Officers have Undergone in these expeditions into the Rebellious provinces. Some of them have been fortunate enough to get off Undiscovered—But Many have been taken abused by Mobs in an Outragious manner & cast into prisons with felons, where they have Suffered all the Evils that revengeful Rage ignorance Bigotry & Inhumanity could inflict— There has been even Skirmishes on such Occasions.*****It was an uncommon Exertion in one of our Offrs. to make his Escape with forty highlanders from the Mohawk river to Montreal havg. had nothing to eat for ten days but their Dogs & herbs & in another to have on his private Credit & indeed ruin, Victualled a Considerable Number of Soldiers he had engaged in hopes of getting off with them to Canada, but being at last taken & kept in hard imprisonmt for near a year by the Rebels to have effected his escape & Collecting his hundred men to have brot them thro' the Woods lately from near Abany to Canada."*

Difficulties in the formation of the regiment and placing it on the establishment grew out of the opposition of Governor Legge, and from him, through General Gage transmitted to the ministry, when all enlistments, for the time being were prohibited. The officers, from the start had been assured that the regiment should be placed on the establishment, and each should be entitled to his rank and in case of reduction should go on half pay. The officers should consist of those on half pay who had served in the last war, and had settled in America. When the regiment had been established and numbered, through the exertions of Colonel Maclean the ranks were rapidly filled, and the previous difficulties overcome.

The winter of 1775-1776, was very severe on the second battalion. Although stationed in Halifax they were without suffi-

---

*Letter-Book, p. 356.

cient clothing or proper food, or pay, and the officer in charge—Captain Alexander McDonald—without authority to draw money, or a regular warrant to receive it. In January "the men were almost stark naked for want of clothing," and even barefooted. The plaids and Kilmarnocks could not be had. As late as March 1st there was "not a shoe nor a bit of leather to be had in Halifax for either love or money," and men were suffering from their frosted feet. "The men made a horrid and scandalous appearance on duty, insulted and despised by the soldiers of the other corps." In April 1778, clothing that was designed for the first battalion, having been consigned to Halifax, was taken by Captain McDonald and distributed to the men of the second. Out of this grew an acrimonious correspondence. Of the food, Captain McDonald writes:

"We are served Served Since prior to September last with Flower that is Rank poison at lest Bread made of Such flower— The Men of our Regiment that are in Command at the East Battery brought me a Sample of the fflower they received for a Months provision, it was exactly like Chalk & as Sower as Vinegarr I asked the Doctors opinion of it who told me it was Sufficient to Destroy all the Regiment to eatt Bread made of Such fflower; it is hard when Mens Lives are So precious and so much wanted for the Service of their King and country, that they Should thus wantonly be Sported with to put money in the pocket of any individuall."*

It appears to have been the policy to break up the second battalion and have it serve on detached duty. Hence a detachment was sent to Newfoundland, another to Annapolis, at Cumberland, Fort Howe, Fort Edward, Fort Sackville and Windsor, but rallying at Halifax as the headquarters—to say nothing of those sent to the Southern States. No wonder Captain McDonald complains, "We have absolutely been worse used than any one Regiment in America and has done more duty and Drudgery of all kinds than any other Bn. in America these thre Years past and it is but reasonable Just and Equitable that we should now be Suffered to Join together at least as early as possible in the Spring and let some Other Regimt relieve the difft. posts we at present Occupy."†

---

*Ibid, p. 303. †Ibid, p. 472.

But it was not all garrison duty. Writing from Halifax, under date of July 13th, 1777, Captain McDonald says:

"Another Attempt has been made from New England to invade this province wch. is also defeated by a detachmt from our Regt & the Marines on board of Captn Hawker. Our Detachmt went on board of him here & he having a Quick passage to the River St John's wch. divides Nova Scotia from New England & where the Rebells were going to take post & Rebuild the old fort that was there the last War. Immediately on Captn Hawker's Arrival there Our men under the Commd. of Ensn. Jno McDonald & the Marines under that of a Lieut were landed & Engaged the Enemy who were abt. a hundred Strong & after a Smart firing & some killed & wounded on both Sides the Rebells ran with the greatest precipitation & Confusion to their boats. Some of our light Armed vessells pursued them & I hope before this time they are either taken or starving in the Woods."*

Whatever may be said of the good behavior of the men of the second battalion, there were three at least whom Captain McDonald describes as "rascales." He also gives the following severe rebuke to one of the officers:

"Halifax 16th Febry 1777
Mr. Jas. McDonald.

I am sorry to inform you that every Accot I receive from Windsor is very unfavorable in regard to you. Your Cursed Carelessness & slovenlyness about your own Body and your dress Nothing going on but drinking Calybogus Schewing Tobacco & playing Cards in place of that decentness & Cleanliness that all Gentlemen who has the least Regard for themselves & Character must & does observe. I am afraid from your Conduct that you will be no Credit or honor to the Memories of those Worthies from whom you are descended & if you have no regard for them or your self I need not expect you'll be at any pains to be of Any Credit to me for anything I can do for you. I am about Giving you Rank agreeable to Col. McLean's plan & on Accot. of your having bro't more men to the Regimt. than either Mr. Fitz Gerd. or Campbell You are to be the Second in Command at that post Lt. Fitz Ger'd. the third & Campbell the fourth. And I hope I shall never have Occasion to write to you in this Manner again.

---

*Ibid, p. 350.

I beg you will begin now to mend your hand to write & learn to keep Accots. that you may be able to do Some thing like an officer if ever you expect to make a figure in the Army You must Change your plan & lay yr. money out to Acquire such Accomplishm'ts. befitting an officer rather than Tobacco, Calybogus and the Devil knows what. I am tired of Scolding of you, so will say no more."*

But little has been recorded of the five companies of the second battalion that joined Sir Henry Clinton and lord Cornwallis. The company called grenadiers was in the battle of Eutaw Springs, South Carolina, fought September 8, 1781. This was one of the most closely contested battles of the Revolution, in which the grenadier company was in the thickest and severest of the fight. The British army, under Colonel Alexander Stuart, of the 3rd regiment was drawn up in a line extending from Eutaw creek to an eighth of a mile southward. The Irish Buffs (third regiment) formed the right; Lieutenant Colonel Cruger's Loyalists the center; and the 63rd and 64th regiments the left. Near the creek was a flank battalion of infantry and the grenadiers, under Major Majoribanks, partially covered and concealed by a thicket on the bank of the stream. The Americans, under General Greene, having routed two advanced detachments, fell with great spirit on the main body. After the battle had been stubbornly contested for some time, Major Majoribank's command was ordered up, and terribly galled the American flanks. In attempting to dislodge them, the Americans received a terrible volley from behind the thicket. Soon the entire British line fell back, Major Majoribanks covering the movement. They abandoned their camp, destroyed their stores and many fled precipitately towards Charleston, while Major Majoribanks halted behind the palisades of a brick house. The American soldiers, in spite of the orders of General Greene and the efforts of their officers began to pillage the camp, instead of attempting to dislodge Major Majoribanks. A heavy fire was poured upon the Americans who were in the British camp, from the force that had taken refuge in the brick house, while Major Majoribanks moved from his covert on the

---

Ibid, p. 330.

right. The light horse or legion of Colonel Henry Lee, remaining under the control of that officer, followed so closely upon those who had fled to the house that the fugitives in closing the doors shut out two or three of their own officers. Those of the legion who had followed to the door seized each a prisoner, and interposing him as a shield retreated beyond the fire from the windows. Among those captured was Captain Barre, a brother of the celebrated Colonel Barre of the British parliament, having been seized by Captain Manning. In the terror of the moment Barre began to recite solemnly his titles: "I am Sir Henry Barre deputy adjutant general of the British army, captain of the 52d regiment, secretary of the commandant at Charleston—" "Are you indeed?" interrupted Captain Manning; "you are my prisoner now, and the very man I was looking for; come along with me." He then placed his titled prisoner between him and the fire of the enemy, and retreated.

The arrest of the Americans by Major Majoribanks and the party that had fled into the brick house, gave Colonel Stuart an opportunity to rally his forces, and while advancing, Major Majoribanks poured a murderous fire into the legion of Colonel Lee, which threw them into confusion. Perceiving this, he sallied out seized the two field pieces and ran them under the windows of the house. Owing to the crippled condition of his army, and the shattering of his cavalry by the force of Major Majoribanks, General Greene ordered a retreat, after a conflict of four hours. The British repossessed the camp, but on the following day decamped, abandoning seventy-two of their wounded. Considering the numbers engaged, both parties lost heavily. The Americans had one hundred and thirty rank and file killed, three hundred and eighty-five wounded, and forty missing. The loss of the British, according to their own report, was sixhundred and ninety-three men, of whom eighty-five were killed.

At the conclusion of the war the transports bearing the companies were ordered to Halifax, where the men were discharged; but, owing to the violence of the weather, and a consequent loss of reckoning, they made the island of Nevis and St. Kitt's instead of Halifax. This delayed the final reduction till 1784. In the distant quarters of the first battalion, they were forgotten. By their agreement they should have been discharged in April 1783, but orders were not sent until July 1784.

It is possible that a roll of the officers of the second battalion may be in existence. The following names of the officers are preserved in McDonald's "Letter-Book":

Major John Small, commandant; Captains Alexander McDonald, Duncan Campbell, Ronald McKinnon, Murdoch McLean, Alexander Campbell, John McDonald and Allan McDonald; Lieutenants Gerald Fitzgerald, Robert Campbell, James McDonald and Lachlan McLean; Ensign John Day; chaplain, Doctor Boynton.

The uniform of the Royal Highland Emigrant regiment was the full Highland garb, with purses made of raccoon's instead of badger's skins. The officers wore the broad sword and dirk, and the men a half basket sword, as previously stated.

At the conclusion of the war grants of land were given to the officers and men, in the proportion of five thousand acres to a field officer, three thousand to a captain, five hundred to a subaltern, two hundred to a serjeant and one hundred to each soldier. All those who had settled in America previous to the war, remained, and took possession of their lands, but many of the others returned to Scotland. The men of Major Small's battalion went to Nova Scotia, where they settled a township, and gave it the name of Douglas, in Hants County; but a number settled on East River.

The first to come to East River, of the 84th, was big James Fraser, in company with Donald McKay and fifteen of his comrades, and took up a tract of three thousand four hundred acres extending along both sides of the river. Their discharges are dated April 10, 1784, but the grant November 3, 1785. About the same time of the occupation of the East River, in Pictou County, the West Branch was occupied by men of the same regiment; the first of whom were David McLean and John Fraser.

The settlers of East Branch, or River, of the 84th, on the East side were Donald Cameron, a native of Urquhart, Scotland; served eight years; possessed one hundred and fifty acres; his son

Duncan served two years as a drummer boy in the regiment. Alexander Cameron, one hundred acres. Robert Clark, one hundred acres. Finlay Cameron, four hundred. Samuel Cameron, one hundred acres. James Fraser, a native of Strathglass, three hundred and fifty acres. Peter Grant, James McDonald, Hugh McDonald, one hundred acres.

On the west side of same river: James Fraser, one hundred acres. Duncan McDonald, one hundred acres. John McDonald, two hundred and fifty acres. Samuel Cameron, three hundred acres. John Chisholm, sen., three hundred acres. John Chisholm, jun., two hundred acres. John McDonald, two hundred and fifty acres.

Those who settled at West Branch and other places on East River were, William Fraser, from Inverness, three hundred and fifty acres. John McKay, three hundred acres. John Robertson, four hundred and fifty. William Robertson, two hundred acres. John Fraser, from Inverness, three hundred acres. Thomas Fraser, from Inverness, two hundred acres. Thomas McKinzie, one hundred acres. David McLean, a sergeant in the army, five hundred acres. Alexander Cameron, three hundred acres. Hector McLean, four hundred acres. John Forbes, from Inverness, four hundred acres. Alexander McLean, five hundred acres. Thomas Fraser, Jun., one hundred acres. James McLellan, from Inverness, five hundred acres. Donald Chisholm, from Strathglass, three hundred and fifty acres. Robert Dundas (four hundred and fifty acres), Alexander Dunbar (two hundred acres), and William Dunbar, (three hundred acres), all three brothers, from Inverness, and of the 84th regiment. James Cameron, 84th regiment, three hundred acres. John McDougall, two hundred and fifty acres. John Chisholm, three hundred acres. Donald Chisholm, Jun., from Inverness, four hundred acres. Robert Clark, 84th, one hundred acres. Donald Shaw, from Inverness, three hundred acres. Alexander McIntosh, from Inverness, five hundred acres, and John McLellan, from Inverness, one hundred acres. Of the grantees of the West Branch, those designated from Inverness, were from the parish of Urquhart and served in the 84th, as did also those so specified. It is more than probable that all the others were not in the Royal Highland Emigrant regiment, or even served in the war.

The members of the first, or Colonel MacLean's battalion settled in Canada, many of whom at Montreal, where they rallied around their chaplain, John Bethune. This gentleman acted as chaplain of the Highlanders in North Carolina, and was taken prisoner at the battle of Moore's Creek Bridge. After remaining a prisoner for about a year, he was released, and made his way to Nova Scotia and for some time resided at Halifax. He received the appointment of chaplain in the Royal Highland Emigrant regiment. He received a grant of three thousand acres, located in Glengarry, and having a growing family to provide for, each of whom was entitled to two hundred acres, he removed to Williamstown, then the principal settlement in Glengarry. Besides his allotment of land, he retired from the army on half pay. In his new home he ever maintained an honorable life.

FORTY-SECOND OR ROYAL HIGHLAND REGIMENT.

The 42nd, or Black Watch, or Royal Highlanders, left America in 1767, and sailed direct for Cork, Ireland. In 1775 the regiment embarked at Donaghadee, and landed at Port Patrick, after an absence of thirty-two years from Scotland. From Port Patrick it marched to Glasgow. Shortly after its arrival in Glasgow two companies were added, and all the companies were augmented to one hundred rank and file, and when completed numbered one thousand and seventy-five men, including serjeants and drummers.

Hitherto the officers had been entirely Highlanders and Scotch. Contrary to the remonstrances of lord John Murray, the lord lieutenant of Ireland succeeded in admitting three English officers into the regiment, Lieutenants Crammond, Littleton, and Franklin, thus cancelling the commissions of Lieutenants Grant and Mackenzie. Of the soldiers nine hundred and thirty-one were Highlanders, seventy-four Lowland Scotch, five English, one Welsh and two Irish.

On account of the breaking out of hostilities the regiment

was ordered to embark for America. The recruits were instructed in the use of the firelock, and, from the shortness of the time allowed, were even drilled by candle-light. New arms and accoutrements were supplied to the men, and the Colonel, at his own expense, furnished them with broad swords and pistols.

April 14, 1776, the Royal Highlanders, in conjunction with Fraser's Highlanders, embarked at Greenock to join an expedition under General Howe against the Americans. After some delay, both regiments sailed on May 1st under the convoy of the Flora, of thirty-two guns, and a fleet of thirty-two ships, the Royal Highlanders being commanded by Colonel Thomas Stirling of Ardoch. Four days after they had sailed, the transports separated in a gale of wind. Some of the scattered transports of both regiments fell in with General Howe's army on their voyage from Halifax; and others, having received information of this movement, followed the main body and joined the army at Staten Island.

When Washington took possession of Dorchester heights, on the night of March 4, 1776, the situation of General Howe, in Boston, became critical, and he was forced to evacuate the city with precipitation. He left no cruisers in Boston bay to warn expected ships from England that the city was no longer in his possession. This was very fortunate for the Americans, for a few days later several store-ships sailed into the harbor and were captured. The Scotch fleet also headed that way, and some of the transports, not having received warning, were also taken in the harbor, but principally of Fraser's Highlanders. By the last of June, about seven hundred and fifty Highlanders belonging to the Scotch fleet, were prisoners in the hands of the Americans.

The Royal Highlanders lost but one of their transports, the Oxford, and at the same time another transport in company with her, having on board recruits for Fraser's Highlanders, in all two hundred and twenty men. They were made prizes of by the Congress privateer, and all the officers, arms and ammunition were taken from the Oxford, and all the soldiers were placed on board that vessel with a prize crew of ten men to carry her into port. In a gale of wind the vessels became separated, and then the carpenter of the Oxford formed a party and retook her, and sailed for the Chesapeake. On June 20th, they sighted Commodore James Barron's vessel, and dispatched a boat with a sergeant, one private and one of the men who were put on board by the Congress to make inquiry. The latter finding a convenient opportunity, informed Commodore Barron of their situation, upon which he boarded and took possession of the Oxford, and brought her to Jamestown. The men were marched to Williamsburgh, Virginia, where every inducement was held out to them to join the American cause. When the promise of miltary promotion failed to have an effect, they were then informed that they would have grants of fertile land, upon which they could live in happiness and freedom. They declared they would take no land save what they deserved by supporting the king. They were then separated into small parties and sent into the back settlements; and were not exchanged until 1778, when they rejoined their regiments.

Before General Sir William Howe's army arrived, or even any vessels of his fleet, the transport Crawford touched at Long Island. Under date of June 24, 1776, General Greene notified Washington that "the Scotch prisoners, with their baggage, have arrived at my Quarters." The list of prisoners are thus given:

"Forty second or Royal Highland Regiment: Captain John Smith and Lieutenant Robert Franklin. Seventy-first Regiment: Captain Norman McLeod and lady and maid; Lieutenant Roderick McLeod; Ensign Colin Campbell and lady; Surgeon's Mate, Robert Boyce; John McAlister, Master of the Crawford transport; Norman McCullock, a passenger; two boys, servants; McDonald, servant to Robert Boyce; Shaw, servant to Captain McLeod. Three boys, servants, came over in the evening."*

General Howe, on board the frigate Greyhound, arrived in the Narrows, from Halifax, on June 25th, accompanied by two other ships-of-war. He came in advance of the fleet that bore his army, in order to consult with Governor Tryon and ascertain the position of affairs at New York. For three or four days after his arrival armed vessels kept coming, and on the twenty-ninth the main body of the fleet arrived, and the troops were immediately

---

*Am. Archives, Fourth Series, Vol. VI, p. 1055.

landed on Staten Island. General Howe was soon after reinforced by English regulars and German mercenaries, and at about the same time Sir Henry Clinton and Admiral Parker, with their broken forces came from the south and joined them. Before the middle of August all the British reinforcements had arrived at Staten Island and General Howe's army was raised to a force of thirty thousand men. On August 22nd, a large body of troops, under cover of the guns of the Rainbow, landed upon Long Island. Soon after five thousand British and Hessian troops poured over the sides of the English ships and transports and in small boats and galleys were rowed to the Long Island shore, covered by the guns of the Phœnix, Rose and Greyhound. The invading force on Long Island numbered fifteen thousand, well armed and equipped, and having forty heavy cannon.

The three Highland battalions were first landed on Staten Island, and immediately a grenadier battalion was formed by Major Charles Stuart. The staff appointments were taken from the Royal Highlanders. The three light companies also formed a battalion in the brigade under Lieutenant-Colonel Abercromby. The grenadiers were remarkable for strength and height, and considered equal to any company in the army. The eight battalion companies were formed into two temporary battalions, the command of one was given to Major William Murray, and that of the other to Major William Grant. These small battalions were brigaded under Sir William Erskine, and placed in the reserve, with the grenadiers and light infantry of the army, under command of lord Cornwallis.

Lieutenant-Colonel Stirling, from the moment of landing, was active in drilling the 42d in the methods of fighting practiced in the French and Indian war, in which he was well versed. The Highlanders made rapid progress in this discipline, being, in general, excellent marksmen.

It was about this time that the broadswords and pistols received at Glasgow were laid aside. The pistols were considered unnecessary, except in the field. The broadswords retarded the men when marching by getting entangled in the brushwood.

The reserve of Howe's army was landed first at Gravesend

Bay, and being moved immediately forward to Flat Bush, the Highlanders and a corps of Hessians were detached to a little distance, where they encamped. The whole army encamped in front of the villages of Gravesend and Utrecht. A woody range of hills, which intersected the country from east to west, divided the opposing armies.

General Howe resolved to bring on a general action and make the attack in three divisions. The right wing under General Clinton seized, on the night of August 26th, a pass on the heights, about three miles from Bedford. The main body pushed into the level country which lay between the hills and the lines of General Israel Putnam. Whilst these movements were in process, Major-General Grant of Ballindalloch, with his brigade, supported by the Royal Highlanders from the reserve, was directed to march from the left along the coast to the Narrows, and make an attack in that quarter. At nine o'clock, on the morning of the 22nd, the right wing having reached Bedford, attacked the left of the American army, which, after a short resistance, quitted the woody grounds, and in confusion retired to their lines, pursued by the British troops, Colonel Stuart leading with his battalion of Highland grenadiers. When the firing at Bedford was heard at Flat Bush, the Hessians advanced, and, attacking the center of the American army, drove them through the woods, capturing three cannon. Previously, General Grant, with the left of the army, commenced the attack with a cannonade against the Americans under lord Stirling. The object of lord Stirling was to defend the pass and keep General Grant in check. He was in the British parliament when Grant made his speech against the Americans, and addressing his soldiers said, in allusion to the boasting Grant that he would "undertake to march from one end of the continent to the other, with five thousand men." "He may have his five thousand men with him now—we are not so many—but I think we are enough to prevent his advancing further on his march over the continent, than that mill-pond," pointing to the head of Gowanus bay. This little speech had a powerful effect, and in the action showed how keenly they felt the insult. General Grant had been instructed not to press an attack until informed by signal-guns from the right wing. These signals were not given until eleven o'clock, at which time lord Stirling was hemmed in. When the truth flashed upon him he hurled a few of his men against lord Cornwallis, in order to keep him at bay while a part of his army might escape. Lord Cornwallis yielded, and when on the point or retreating received large reinforcements which turned the fortunes of the day against the Americans. General Grant drove the remains of lord Stirling's army before him, which escaped across Gowanus creek, by wading and swimming.

The victorious troops, made hot and sanguinary by the fatigues and triumphs of the morning, rushed upon the American lines, eager to carry them by storm. But the day was not wholly lost. Behind the entrenchments were three thousand determined men who met the advancing British army by a severe cannonade and volleys of musketry. Preferring to win the remainder of the conquest with less bloodshed, General Howe called back his troops to a secure place in front of the American lines, beyond musket shot, and encamped for the night.

During the action Washington hastened over from New York to Brooklyn and galloped up to the works. He arrived there in time to witness the catastrophe. All night he was engaged in strengthening his position; and troops were ordered from New York. When the morning dawned heavy masses of vapor rolled in from the sea. At ten o'clock the British opened a cannonade on the American works, with frequent skirmishes throughout the day. Rain fell copiously all the afternoon and the main body of the British kept their tents, but when the storm abated towards evening, they commenced regular approaches within five hundred yards of the American works. That night Washington drew off his army of nine thousand men, with their munitions of war, transported them over a broad ferry to New York, using such consummate skill that the British were not aware of his intention until next morning, when the last boats of the rear guard were seen out of danger.

The American loss in the battle of Long Island did not exceed sixteen hundred and fifty, of whom eleven hundred were prisoners. General Howe stated his own loss to have been, in killed, wounded, and prisoners, three hundred and sixty-seven. The loss of the Highlanders was, Lieutenant Crammond and nine rank and file wounded, of the 42d; and three rank and filed killed, and two sergeants and nine rank and file wounded, of the 71st regiment.

In a letter to lord George Germaine, under date of September 4, 1776, lord Dunmore says:

"I was with the Highlanders and Hessians the whole day, and it is with the utmost pleasure I can assure your lordship that the ardour of both these corps on that day must have exceeded his Majesty's most sanguine wish."*

Active operations were not resumed until September 15th, when the British reserve, which the Royal Highlanders had rejoined after the action at Brooklyn, crossed the river in flat boats from Newtown creek, and landed at Kip's bay covered by a severe cannonade from the ships-of-war, whose guns played briskly upon the American batteries. Washington, hearing the firing, rode with speed towards the scene of action. To him a most alarming spectacle was presented. The militia had fled, and the Connecticut troops had caught the panic, and ran without firing a gun, when only fifty of the British had landed. Meeting the fugitives he used every endeavor to stop their flight. In vain their generals tried to rally them; but they continued to flee in the greatest confusion, leaving Washington alone within eighty yards of the foe. So incensed was he at their conduct that he cast his chapeau to the ground, snapped his pistols at several of the fugitives, and threatened others with his sword. So utterly unconscious was he of danger, that he probably would have fallen had not his attendants seized the bridle of his horse and hurried him away to a place of safety. Immediately he took measures to protect his imperilled army. He retreated to Harlem heights, and sent an order to General Putnam to evacuate the city instantly. This was fortunately accomplished, through the connivance of Mrs. Robert Murray. General Sir William Howe, instead of pushing forward and capturing the four thousand troops under

---

*Ibid, Series V. Vol. II, p. 159.

General Putnam, immediately took up his quarters with his general officers at the mansion of Robert Murray, and sat down for refreshments and rest. Mrs. Murray knowing the value of time to the veteran Putnam, now in jeopardy, used all her art to detain her uninvited guests. With smiles and pleasant conversation, and a profusion of cakes and wine, she regaled them for almost two hours. General Putnam meanwhile receiving his orders, immediately obeyed, and a greater portion of his troops, concealed by the woods, escaped along the Bloomingdale road, and before being discovered had passed the encampment upon the Ineleberg. The rear-guard was attacked by the Highlanders and Hessians, just as a heavy rain began to fall; and the drenched army, after losing fifteen men killed, and three hundred made prisoners, reached Harlem heights.

"This night Major Murray was nearly carried off by the enemy, but saved himself by his strength of arm and presence of mind. As he was crossing to his regiment from the battalion which he commanded, he was attacked by an American officer and two soldiers, against whom he defended himself for some time with his fusil, keeping them at a respectful distance. At last, however, they closed upon him, when unluckily his dirk slipped behind, and he could not, owing to his corpulence, reach it. Observing that the rebel (American) officer had a sword in his hand, he snatched it from him, and made so good use of it, that he compelled them to fly, before some men of the regiment, who had heard the noise, could come up to his assistance. He wore the sword as a trophy during the campaign."*

On the 16th the light infantry was sent out to dislodge a party of Americans who had taken possession of a wood facing the left of the British. Adjutant-General Reed brought information to Washington that the British General Leslie was pushing forward and had attacked Colonel Knowlton and his rangers. Colonel Knowlton retreated, and the British appeared in full view and sounded their bugles. Washington ordered three companies of Colonel Weedon's Virginia regiment, under Major Leitch, to join Knowlton's rangers, and gain the British rear, while a feigned attack should be made in front. The vigilant General

---

*Stewart's Sketches, Vol. I, p. 360.

Leslie perceived this, and made a rapid movement to gain an advantageous position upon Harlem plains, where he was attacked upon the flank by Knowlton and Leitch. A part of Leslie's force, consisting of Highlanders, that had been concealed upon the wooded hills, now came down, and the entire British body changing front, fell upon the Americans with vigor. A short but severe conflict ensued. Major Leitch, pierced by three balls, was borne from the field, and soon after Colonel Knowlton was brought to the ground by a musket ball. Their men fought on bravely, contesting every foot of the ground, as they fell back towards the American camp. Being reinforced by a part of the Maryland regiments of Griffiths and Richardson, the tide of battle changed. The British were driven back across the plain, hotly pursued by the Americans, till Washington, fearing an ambush, ordered a retreat.

In the battle of Harlem the British loss was fourteen killed, and fifty officers and seventy men wounded. The 42nd, or Royal Highlanders lost one sergeant and three privates killed, and Captains Duncan Macpherson and John Mackintosh, Ensign Alexander Mackenzie (who died of his wounds), and three sergeants, one piper, two drummers, and forty-seven privates wounded.

This engagement caused a temporary pause in the movements of the British, which gave Washington an opportunity to strengthen both his camp and army. The respite was not of long duration for on October 12th, General Howe embarked his army in flat-bottomed boats, and on the evening of the same day landed at Frogsneck, near Westchester; but on the next day he re-embarked his troops and landed at Pell's Point, at the mouth of the Hudson. On the 14th he reached the White Plains in front of Washington's position. General Howe's next determination was to capture Fort Washington, which cut off the communication between New York and the continent, to the eastward and northward of Hudson river, and prevented supplies being sent him by way of Kingsbridge. The garrison consisted of over two thousand men under Colonel Magaw. A deserter informed General Howe of the real condition of the garrison and the works on Harlem Heights. General Howe was agreeably surprised by the information, and immediately summoned Colonel Magaw to surrender within an hour, intimating that a refusal might subject the garrison to massacre. Promptly refusing compliance, he further added: "I rather think it a mistake than a settled resolution in General Howe, to act a part so unworthy of himself and the British nation." On November 16th the Hessians, under General Knyphausen, supported by the whole of the reserve under earl Percy, with the exception of the 42nd, who were to make a feint on the east side of the fort, were to make the principal attack. Before daylight the Royal Highlanders embarked in boats, and landed in a small creek at the foot of the rock, in the face of a severe fire. Although the Highlanders had discharged the duties which had been assigned them, still determined to have a full share in the honors of the day, resolved upon an assault, and assisted by each other, and by the brushwood and shrubs which grew out of the crevices of the rocks, scrambled up the precipice. On gaining the summit, they rushed forward, and drove back the Americans with such rapidity, that upwards of two hundred, who had no time to escape, threw down their arms. Pursuing their advantage, the Highlanders penetrated across the table of the hill, and met lord Percy as he was coming up on the other side. By turning their feint into an assault, the Highlanders facilitated the success of the day. The result was that the Americans surrendered at discretion. They lost in killed and wounded one hundred and about twenty-seven hundred prisoners. The loss of the British was twenty killed and one hundred and one wounded; that of the Royal Highlanders being one sergeant and ten privates killed, and Lieutenants Patrick Graeme, Norman Macleod, and Alexander Grant, and for sergeants and sixty-six rank and file, wounded.

The hill, up which the Highlanders charged, was so steep, that the ball which wounded Lieutenant Macleod, entering the posterior part of his neck, ran down on the outside of his ribs, and lodged in the lower part of his back. One of the pipers, who began to play when he reached the point of a rock on the summit of the hill, was immediately shot, and tumbled from one piece of rock to another till he reached the bottom. Major Murray, being a large and corpulent man, could not attempt the steep assent without assistance. The soldiers eager to get to the point of duty, scrambled up, forgetting the position of Major Murray, when he, in a supplicating tone cried, "Oh soldiers, will you leave me!" A party leaped down instantly and brought him up, supporting him from one ledge of rocks to another till they got him to the top.

The next object of General Howe was to possess Fort Lee. Lord Cornwallis, with the grenadiers, light infantry, 33rd regiment and Royal Highlanders, was ordered to attack this post. But on their approach the fort was hastily abandoned. Lord Cornwallis, reenforced by the two battalions of Fraser's Highlanders, pursued the retreating Americans, into the Jerseys, through Elizabethtown, Neward and Brunswick. In the latter town he was ordered to halt, where he remained for eight days, when General Howe, with the army, moved forward, and reached Princeton in the afternoon of November 17th.

The army now went into winter quarters. The Royal Highlanders were stationed at Brunswick, and Fraser's Highlanders quartered at Amboy. Afterwards the Royal Highlanders were ordered to the advanced posts, being the only British regiment in the front, and forming the line of defence at Mt. Holly. After the disaster to the Hessians at Trenton, the Royal Highlanders were ordered to fall back on the light infantry at Princeton.

Lord Cornwallis, who was in New York at the time of the defeat of the Hessians, returned to the army and moved forward with a force consisting of the grenadiers, two brigades of the line, and the two Highland regiments. After much skirmishing in advance he found Washington posted on some high ground beyond Trenton. Lord Cornwallis declaring "the fox cannot escape me," planned to assault Washington on the following morning. But while he slept the American commander, marched to his rear and fell upon that part of the army left at Princeton. Owing to the suddenness of Washington's attacks upon Trenton and Princeton and the vigilance he manifested the British outposts were withdrawn and concentrated at Brunswick where lord Cornwallis established his headquarters.

The Royal Highlanders, on January 6, 1777 were sent to the village of Pisquatua on the line of communication between New

York and Brunswick by Amboy. This was a post of great importance, for it kept open the route by which provisions were sent for the forces at Brunswick. The duty was severe and the winter rigorous. As the homes could not accommodate half the men, officers and soldiers sought shelter in barns and sheds, always sleeping in their body-clothes, for the Americans gave them but little quietude. The Americans, however, did not make any regular attack on the post till May 10th, when, at four in the morning, the divisions of Generals Maxwell and Stephens, attempted to surprise the Highlanders. Advancing with great caution they were not preceived until they rushed upon the pickets. Although the Highlanders were surprised, they held their position until the reserve pickets came to their assistance, when they retired disputing every foot, to afford the regiment time to form, and come to their relief. Then the Americans were driven back with precipitation, leaving upwards of two hundred men, in killed and wounded. The Highlanders, pursuing with eagerness, were recalled with great difficulty. On this occasion the Royal Highlanders had three sergeants and nine privates killed; and Captain Duncan Macpherson, Lieutenant William Stewart, three sergeants, and thirty-five privates wounded.

"On this occasion, Sergeant Macgregor, whose company was immediately in the rear of the picquet, rushed forward to their support, with a few men who happened to have their arms in their hands, when the enemy commenced the attack. Being severely wounded, he was left insensible on the ground. When the picquet was overpowered, and the few survivors forced to retire, Macgregor, who had that day put on a new jacket with silver lace, having besides, large silver buckles in his shoes, and a watch, attracted the notice of an American soldier, who deemed him a good prize. The retreat of his friends not allowing him time to strip the sergeant on the spot, he thought the shortest way was to take him on his back to a more convenient distance. By this time Macgregor began to recover; and, perceiving whither the man was carrying him, drew his dirk, and, grasping him by the throat, swore that he would run him through the breast, if he did not turn back and carry him to the camp. The American, finding this argument irresistible, complied with the request, and, meeting Lord Cornwallis (who had come up to the support of the regiment when he heard the firing) and Colonel Stirling, was thanked for his care of the sergeant; but he honestly told him, that he only conveyed him thither to save his own life. Lord Cornwallis gave him liberty to go whithersoever he chose."*

Summer being well advanced, Sir William Howe made preparations for taking the field. The Royal Highlanders, along with the 13th, 17th, and 44th regiments were put under the command of General Charles Gray. Failing to draw Washington from his secure position at Middlebrook, General Howe resolved to change the seat of war, and accordingly embarked thirty-six battalions of British and Hessians, and sailed for the Chesapeake. Before the embarkation, the Royal Highlanders received one hundred and seventy recruits from Scotland, who, as they were all of the best description, more than supplied the loss that had been sustained.

After a tedious voyage the army, on August 24th, landed at Elk Ferry. It did not begin the march until September 3rd, for Philadelphia. In the meantime Washington marched across the country and took up a position at Red Clay Creek, but having his headquarters at Wilmington. His effective force was about eleven thousand men while that of General Howe was eighteen thousand strong.

The two armies met on September 11th, and fought the battle of Brandywine. During the battle, lord Cornwallis, with four battalions of British grenadiers and light infantry, the Hessian grenadiers, a party of the 71st Highlanders, and the third and fourth brigades, made a circuit of some miles, crossed Jefferis' Ford without opposition, and turned short down the river to attack the American right. Washington, being apprised of this movement, detached General Sullivan, with all the force he could spare, to thwart the design. General Sullivan, having advantageously posted his men, lord Cornwallis was obliged to consume some time in forming a line of battle. An action then took place, when the Americans were driven through the woods towards the main army. Meanwhile General Knyphausen, with his division, made demonstrations for crossing at Chad's Ford, and as soon as

---

Ibid, p. 367.

he knew from the firing of cannon that lord Cornwallis had succeeded, he crossed the river and carried the works of the Americans. The approach of night ended the conflict. The Americans rendezvoused at Chester, and the next day retreated towards Philadelphia, and encamped near Germantown.

The British had fifty officers killed and wounded and four hundred and thirty-eight rank and file. The battalion companies of the 42nd being in the reserve, sustained no loss, as they were not brought into action; but of the light company, which formed part of the light brigade, six privates were killed, and one sergeant and fifteen privates wounded.

On the night of September 20th, General Gray was detached with the 2nd light infantry and the 42nd and 44th regiments to cut off and destroy the corps of General Wayne. They marched with great secrecy and came upon the camp at midnight, when all were asleep save the pickets and guards, who were overpowered without causing an alarm. The troops then rushed forward, bayoneted three hundred and took one hundred Americans prisoners. The British loss was three killed and several wounded.

On the 26th the British army took peaceable possession of Philadelphia. In the battle of Germantown, fought on the morning of October 4, 1777, the Highlanders did not participate.

The next enterprise in which the 42nd was engaged was under General Gray, who embarked with that regiment, the grenadiers and the light infantry brigade, for the purpose of destroying a number of privateers, with their prizes at New Plymouth. On September 5, 1778, the troops landed on the banks of the Acushnet river, and having destroyed seventy vessels, with all the cargoes, stores, wharfs, and buildings, along the whole extent of the river, the whole were re-embarked the following day and returned to New York.

The British army during the Revolutionary struggle took the winter season for a period of rest, although engaging more or less in marauding expeditions. On February 25, 1779, Colonel Stirling, with a detachment consisting of the light infantry of the Guards and the 42nd, was ordered to attack a post at Elizabethtown, in New Jersey, which was taken without opposition.

In April following the Highland regiment was employed on an expedition to the Chesapeake, to destroy the stores and merchandise at Portsmouth, in Virginia. They were again employed with the Guards and a corps of Hessians in another expedition under General Mathews, which sailed on the 30th, under the convoy of Sir George Collier, in the Reasonable, and several ships of war, and reached their destination on May 10th, when the troops landed on the glebe on the western bank of Elizabeth. After fulfilling the object of the expedition they returned to New York in good time for the opening of the campaign, which commenced by the capture, on the part of the British, of Verplanks and Stony Point. A garrison of six hundred men, among whom were two companies of Fraser's Highlanders, took possession of Stony Point. Washington planned its capture which was executed by General Wayne. Soon after General Wayne moved against Verplanks, which held out till the approach of the light infantry and the 42nd, then withdrew his forces and evacuated Stony Point. Shortly after, Colonel Stirling was appointed aide-de-camp to the king, when the command of the 42nd devolved on Major Charles Graham, to whom was entrusted the command of the posts of Stony Point and Verplanks, together with his own regiment, and a detachment of Fraser's Highlanders, under Major Ferguson. This duty was the more important, as the Americans surrounded the posts in great numbers, and desertion had become so frequent among a corps of provincials, sent as a reinforcement, that they could not be trusted on any military duty, particularly on those duties which were most harassing. In the month of October these posts were withdrawn and the regiment sent to Greenwich, near New York.

The winter of 1779 was the coldest that had been known for forty years; and the troops, although in quarters, suffered more from that circumstance than in the preceding winter when in huts. But the Highlanders met with a misfortune that greatly grieved them, and which tended to deteriorate, for several years, the heretofore irreproachable character of the Royal Highland Regiment. In the autumn of this year a draft of one hundred and fifty men, recruits raised principally from the refuse of the streets of London and Dublin, was embarked for the regiment by orders from the inspector-general at Chatham. These men were of the most depraved character, and of such dissolute habits, that one-half of them were unfit for service; fifteen died in the passage, and seventy-five were sent to the hospital from the transport as soon as they disembarked. The infusion of such immoral ingredients must necessarily have a deleterious effect. General Stirling made a strong remonstrance to the commander-in-chief, in consequence of which these men were removed to the 26th regiment, in exchange for the same number of Scotchmen. The introduction of these men into the regiment dissolved the charm which, for nearly forty years, had preserved the Highlanders from contamination. During that long period there were but few courts-martial, and, for many years, no instance of corporal punishment occurred.

With the intention of pushing the war with vigor, the new commander-in-chief, Sir Henry Clinton, who had succeeded Sir William Howe, in May, 1778, resolved to attack Charleston, the capital of South Carolina. Having left General Knyphausen in command at New York, General Clinton with his army set sail December 26, 1779. Such was the severity of the weather, however, that, although the voyage might have been accomplished in ten days, it was February 11, 1780, before the troops disembarked on John's Island, thirty miles from Charleston. So great were the impediments to be overcome, and so cautious was the advance of the general, that it was March 29th before they crossed the Ashley river. The following day they encamped opposite the American lines. Ground was broken in front of Charleston on April 1st. General Lincoln, who commanded the American forces, had strengthened the place in all its defences, both by land and water, in such a manner as to threaten a siege that would be both tedious and difficult. When General Clinton, anticipating the nature of the works he desired to capture, sent for the Royal Highlanders and Queen's Rangers to join him, which they did on April 18th, having sailed from New York on March 31st. The siege proceeded in the usual way until May 12th, when the garrison surrendered prisoners of war. The loss of the British forces on this occasion consisted of seventy-six killed and one hundred and eighty-nine wounded; and that of the 42nd, Lientenant Macleod and nine privates killed, and Lieutenant Alexander Grant and fourteen privates wounded.

After Sir Henry Clinton had taken possession of Charleston, the 42nd and light infantry were ordered to Monck's Corner as a foraging party, and, returning on the 2nd, they embarked June 4th for New York, along with the Grenadiers and Hessians. After being stationed for a time on Staten Island, Valentine's Hill, and other stations in New York, went into winter quarters in the ctiy. About this time one hundred recruits were received from Scotland, all young men, in the full vigor of health, and ready for immediate service. From this period, as the regiment was not engaged in any active service during the war, the changes in encampments are too trifling to require notice.

On April 28, 1782, Major Graham succeeded to the lieutenant-colonelcy of the Royal Highland Regiment, and Captain Walter Home of the fusileers became major.

While the regiment was stationed at Paulus Hook several of the men deserted to the Americans. This unprecedented and unlooked for event occasioned much surpise and various causes were ascribed for it; but the prevalent opinion was that the men had received from the 26th regiment, and who had been made prisoners at Saratoga, had been promised lands and other indulgences while prisoners to the Americans. One of these deserters, a man named Anderson, was soon afterwards taken, tried by court-martial, and shot. This was the first instance of an execution in the regiment since the mutiny of 1743. The regiment remained at Paulus Hook till the conclusion of the war, when the establishment was reduced to eight companies of fifty men each. The officers of the ninth and tenth companies were not put on half-pay, but kept as supernumeraries to fill up vacancies as they occurred in the regiment. A number of the men were discharged at their own request, and their places supplied by those who wished to remain in the country, instead of going home with their regiments. These were taken from Fraser's and Macdonald's Highlanders, and from the Edinburgh and duke of Hamilton's regiments.

The 42nd left New York for Halifax, Nova Scotia, on October 22, 1783, where they remained till the year 1786, when the battalion embarked and sailed for Cape Breton, two companies being detached to the island of St. John. In the month of August, 1789, the regiment embarked for England, and landed in Portsmouth in October. In May, 1790, they arrived in Glasgow.

During the American Revolutionary War the loss of the Royal Highlanders was as follows:

	Killed			Wounded		
	Officers	Serjeants	Drummers and Rank and File	Officers	Serjeants	Drummers and Rank and File
1776, August 22nd and 27th, Long Island, including the battle of Brooklyn..................	...	...	5	1	1	19
September 16th, York Island Supporting Light Infantry........................	1	1	3	3	3	47
November 16th, Attack on Fort Washington	...	1	10	3	4	66
December 22nd, At Black Horse, on the Delaware.............................	...	...	1	...	1	6
1777, February 13th, At Amboy, Grenadier Company......,....................	...	...	3	...	3	17
May 10th, Piscataqua, Jerseys...............	...	3	9	2	3	30
September 11th, Battle of Brandywine......	...	...	6	...	1	15
October 5th, Battle of Germantown, the light company...........................	...	1	...	...	...	4
1778, March 22nd, Foraging parties, Jerseys......	...	...	...	...	...	4
June 28th, Battle of Monmouth, Jerseys.....	...	2	20	1	1	17
1779, February 26th, Elizabethtown, Jerseys......	...	...	...	...	...	9
1780, April and May to 12th, Siege of Charleston.	1	...	12	1	...	14
March 16th, Detachment sent to forage from New York to the Jerseys.................	...	...	...	...	1	3
1781, September and October. Yorktown, in Virginia, light company.................	...	1	5	...	...	6
Total........................	2	9	74	12	17	257

FRASER'S HIGHLANDERS.

The breaking out of hostilities in America in 1775 determined the English government to revive Fraser's Highlanders.

HIGHLANDERS IN AMERICA.

Although disinherited of his estates Colonel Fraser, through the influence of clan feeling, was enabled to raise twelve hundred and fifty men in 1757, it was believed, since his estates had been restored in 1772, he could readily raise a strong regiment. So, in 1775, Colonel Fraser received letters for raising a Highland regiment of two battalions. With ease he raised two thousand three hundred and forty Highlanders, who were marched up to Stirling, and thence to Glasgow in April, 1776. This corps had in it six chiefs of clans besides himself. The regiment consisted of the following nominal list of officers:

FIRST BATTALION.

Colonel: Simon Fraser of Lovat; Lieutenant-Colonel: Sir William Erskine of Torry; Majors: John Macdonell of Lochgarry and Duncan Macpherson of Cluny; Captains: Simon Fraser, Duncan Chisholm of Chisholm, Colin Mackenzie, Francis Skelly, Hamilton Maxwell, John Campbell, Norman Macleod of Macleod, Sir James Baird of Saughtonhall and Charles Cameron of Lochiel; Lieutenants: Charles Campbell, John Macdougall, Colin Mackenzie, John Nairne, William Nairne, Charles Gordon, David Kinloch, Thomas Tause, William Sinclair, Hugh Fraser, Alexander Fraser, Thomas Fraser, Dougald Campbell, Robert Macdonald, Alexander Fraser, Roderick Macleod, John Ross, Patrick Cumming, and Thomas Hamilton; Ensigns: Archibald Campbell, Henry Macpherson, John Grant, Robert Campbell, Allan Malcolm, John Murchison, Angus Macdonell, Peter Fraser; Chaplain: Hugh Blair, D.D.; Adjutant: Donald Cameron; Quarter-Master: David Campbell; Surgeon: William Fraser.

SECOND BATTALION.

Colonel: Simon Fraser of Lovat; Lieutenant-Colonel: Archibald Campbell; Majors: Norman Lamont and Robert Menzies; Captains: Angus Mackintosh of Kellachy, Patrick Campbell, Andrew Lawrie, Æneas Mackintosh of Mackintosh, Charles Cameron, George Munro, Boyd Porterfield and Law Robert Campbell; Lieutenants: Robert Hutchison, Alexander

Sutherland, Archibald Campbell, Hugh Lamont, Robert Duncanson, George Stewart, Charles Barrington Mackenzie, James Christie, James Fraser, Thomas Fraser, Archibald Balnevis, Dougald Campbell, Lodovick Colquhoun, John Mackenzie, Hugh Campbell, John Campbell, Arthur Forbes, Patrick Campbell, Archibald Maclean, David Ross, Robert Grant and Thomas Fraser; Ensigns: William Gordon, Charles Main, Archibald Campbell, Donald Cameron, Smollet Campbell, Gilbert Waugh, William Bain, and John Grant; Chaplain: Malcolm Nicholson; Adjutant: Archibald Campbell; Quarter-Master: J. Ogilvie; Surgeon: Colin Chisholm.

At the time Fraser's Regiment, or the 71st, was mustered in Glasgow, there were nearly six thousand Highlanders in that city, of whom three thousand, belonging to the 42nd, and 71st, were raised and brought from the North in ten weeks. More men had come up than were required. When the corps marched for Greenock, these were left behind. So eager were they to engage against the Americans that many were stowed away, who had not enlisted. On none of the soldiers was there the appearance of displeasure at going.

Sometime after the sailing of the fleet it was scattered by a violent gale, and several of the single ships fell in with, and were scattered by, American privateers. A transport having Captain, afterward Sir Æneas Mackintosh, and his company on board, with two six pounders, made a resolute defence against a privateer with eight guns, till all the ammunition was expended, when they bore down with the intention of boarding; but, the privateer not waiting to receive the shock, set sail, the transport being unable to follow.

As has been previously noticed, General Howe, on evacuating Boston, did not leave a vessel off the harbor to warn incoming British ships. Owing to this neglect, the transport with Colonel Archibald Campbell and Major Menzies on board sailed into Boston Harbor. The account of the capture of this transport and others is here subjoined by the participants. Captain Seth Harding, commander of the Defence, in his report to Governor Trumbull, under date of June 19, 1776, said:

"I sailed on Sunday last from Plymouth. Soon after we came to sail, I heard a considerable firing to the northward. In the evening fell in with four armed schooners near the entrance of Boston harbor, who informed me they had been engaged with a ship and brig, and were obliged to quit them. Soon after I came up into Nantasket Roads, where I found the ship and brig at anchor. I immediately fell in between the two, and came to anchor about eleven o'clock at night. I hailed the ship, who answered, from Great Britain. I ordered her to strike her colors to America. They answered me by asking, What brig is that? I told them the Defence. I then hailed him again, and told him I did not want to kill their men; but have the ship I would at all events, and again desired them to strike; upon which the Major (since dead) said, Yes, I'll strike, and fired a broadside upon me, which I immediately returned, upon which an engagement begun, which continued three glasses, when the ship and brig both struck. In this engagement I had nine wounded, but none killed. The enemy had eighteen killed, and a number wounded. My officers and men behaved with great bravery; no man could have outdone them. We took out of the above vessels two hundred and ten prisoners, among whom is Colonel Campbell, of General Frazer's Regiment of Highlanders. The Major was killed.

Yesterday a ship was seen in the bay, which came towards the entrance of the harbor, upon which I came to sail, with four schooners in company. We came up with her, and took her without any engagement. There were on board about one hundred and twelve Highlanders. As there are a number more of the same fleet expected every day, and the General here urges my stay, I shall tarry a few days, and then proceed for New London. My brig is much damaged in her sails and rigging."

Colonel Campbell made the following report to Sir William Howe, dated at Boston, June 19, 1776:

"Sir: I am sorry to inform you that it has been my unfortunate lot to have fallen into the hands of the Americans in the middle of Boston harbor; but when the circumstances which have occasioned this disaster are understood, I flatter myself no reflection will arise to myself or my officers on account of it. On the 16th of June the George and Annabella transports, with two companies of the Seventy-First Regiment of Highlanders, made the land off Cape Ann, after a passage of seven weeks from Scotland, during the course of which we had not the opportunity of speaking to a single vessel that could give us the smallest information of the British troops having evacuated Boston. On the 17th, at daylight, we found ourselves opposite to the harbor's mouth at Boston; but, from contrary winds, it was necessary to make several tacks to reach it. Four schooners (which we took to be pilots, or armed vessels in the service of his Majesty, but which were afterwards found to be four American privateers, of eight carriage-guns, twelve swivels, and forty men each) were bearing down upon us at four o'clock in the morning. At half an hour thereafter two of them engaged us, and about eleven o'clock the other two were close alongside. The George transport (on board of which were Major Menzies and myself, with one hundred and eight of the Second Battalion, the Adjutant, the Quartermaster, two Lieutenants, and five volunteers, were passengers) had only six pieces of cannon to oppose them; and the Annabella (on board of which was Captain McKenzie, together with two subalterns, two volunteers, and eighty-two private men of the First Battalion) had only two swivels for her defence. Under such circumstances, I thought it expedient for the Annabella to keep ahead of the George, that our artillery might be used with more effect and less obstruction. Two of the privateers having stationed themselves upon our larboard quarter and two upon our starboard quarter, a tolerable cannonade ensued, which, with very few intermissions, lasted till four o'clock in the evening, when the enemy bore away, and anchored in Plymouth harbor. Our loss upon this occasion was only three men mortally wounded on board the George, one killed and one man slightly wounded on board the Annabella. As my orders were for the port of Boston, I thought it my duty, at this happy crisis, to push forward into the harbor, not doubting I should receive protection either from a fort or some ship of force stationed there for the security of our fleet.

Towards the close of the evening we perceived the four schooners that were engaged with us in the morning, joined by the brig Defence, of sixteen carriage-guns, twenty swivels, and one hundred and seventeen men, and a schooner of eight carriage-guns, twelve swivels, and forty men, got under way and made towards us. As we stood up for Nantasket Road, an American battery opened upon us, which was the first serious proof we had that there could scarcely be many friends of ours at Boston; and we were too far embayed to retreat, especially as the wind had died away, and the tide of flood not half expended. After each of the vessels had twice run aground, we anchored at George's Island, and prepared for action; but the Annabella by some misfortune, got aground so far astern of the George we could expect but a feeble support from her musketry. About eleven o'clock four of the schooners anchored right upon our bow, and one right astern of us. The armed brig took her station on our starboard side, at the distance of two hundred yards, and hailed us to strike the British flag. Although the mate of our ship and every sailor on board (the Captain only excepted) refused positively to fight any longer, I have the pleasure to inform you that there was not an officer, non-commissioned officer, or private man of the Seventy-First but what stood to their quarters with a ready and cheerful obedience. On our refusing to strike the British flag, the action was renewed with a good deal of warmth on both sides, and it was our misfortune, after the sharp combat of an hour and a half, to have expended every shot that we had for our artillery. Under such circumstances, hemmed in as we were with six privateers, in the middle of an enemy's harbor, beset with a dead calm, without the power of escaping, or even the most distant hope of relief, I thought it became my duty not to sacrifice the lives of gallant men wantonly in the arduous attempt of an evident impossibility. In this unfortunate affair Major Menzies and seven private soldiers were killed, the Quartermaster and twelve private soldiers wounded. The Major was buried with the honors of war at Boston.

Since our captivity, I have the honor to acquaint you that we have experienced the utmost civility and good treatment from the people of power at Boston, insomuch, sir, that I should do injustice to the feelings of generosity did I not make this particular information with pleasure and satisfaction. I have now to request of you that, so soon as the distracted state of this unfortunate controversy will admit, you will be pleased to take an early opportunity of settling a cartel for myself and officers.

I have the honor to be, with great respect, sir, your most obedient and most humble servant,

Archibald Campbell,
Lieut. Col. 2d Bat. 71st Regiment.

P. S. On my arrival at Boston I found that Captain Maxwell, with the Light-Infantry of the first battalion of the Seventy-First Regiment, had the misfortune to fall into the hands of some other privateers, and were carried into Marblehead the 10th instant. Captain Campbell, with the Grenadiers of the second battalion, who was ignorant, as we were, of the evacuation of Boston, stood into the mouth of this harbor, and was surrounded and taken by eight privateers this forenoon.

In case of a cartel is established, the following return is, as near as I can effect, the number of officers, non-commissioned officers, and private men of the Seventy-First Regiment who are prisoners-of-war at and in the neighborhood of Boston:

The George transport: Lieutenant-Colonel Archibald Campbell; Lieutenant and Adjutant Archibald Campbell; Lieutenant Archibald Balneaves; Lieutenant Hugh Campbell; Quartermaster William Ogilvie; Surgeon's Mate, David Burns; Patrick McDougal, private, and acting Sergeant-Major; James Flint, volunteer; Dugald Campbell, ditto; Donald McBane, John Wilson, three Sergeants, four corporals, two Drummers, ninety private men.

The Annabella transport: Captain George McKinzie; Lieutenant Colin McKinzie; Ensign Peter Fraser; Mr. McKinzie and Alexander McTavish, volunteers; four Sergeants, four Corporals, two Drummers, eighty-one private men.

Lord Howe transport: Captain Lawrence Campbell; Lieutenant Robert Duncanson; Lieutenant Archibald McLean; Lieutenant Lewis Colhoun; Duncan Campbell, volunteer; four Sergeants, four Corporals, two Drummers, ninety-six private men.

Ann transport: Captain Hamilton Maxwell; Lieutenant Charles Campbell; Lieutenant Fraser; Lieutenant ———; four Sergeants, four Corporals, two Drummers, ninety-six private men.

Archibald Campbell,
Lieut. Col. 2d Bat. 71st Regiment."*

On account of the treatment received by General Charles Lee, a prisoner in the hands of Sir William Howe, and the covert threat of condign punishment on the accusation of treason, Congress resolved, January 6, 1777, that "should the proffered exchange of General Lee, for six Hessian field-officers, not be accepted, and the treatment of him as aforementioned be continued, then the principles of retaliation shall occasion first of the said Hessian field-officers, together with Lieutenant-Colonel Archibald Campbell, or any other officers that are or may be in our possession, equivalent in number or quality, to be detained, in order that the same treatment, which general Lee shall receive, may be exactly inflicted upon their persons."

In consequence of this act Colonel Campbell was thrown into Concord gaol. On February 4th he addressed a letter to Washington giving a highly colored account of his severe treatment, making it equal to that inflicted upon the most atrocious criminals; and for the reasons he was so treated declaring that "the

---

*Am. Archives, Series 4, Vol. VI, p. 982.

first of this month, I was carried and lodged in the common gaol of Concord, by an order of Congress, through the Council of Boston, intimating for a reason, that a refusal of General Howe to give up General Lee for six field-officers, of whom I was one, and the placing of that gentleman under the charge of the Provost at New York, were the motives of their particular ill treatment of me."

Washington, on February 28, 1777, wrote to the Council of Massachusetts remonstrating with them and directing Colonel Campbell's enlargement, as his treatment was not according to the resolve of Congress. The following day he wrote Colonel Campbell stating that he imagined there would be a mitigation of what he now suffered. At the same time Washington wrote to the Congress on the impolicy of so treating Colonel Campbell, declaring that he feared that the resolutions, if adhered to, might "produce consequences of an extensive and melancholy nature." On March 6th he wrote to the president of Congress reaffirming his position on the impolicy of their attitude towards Colonel Campbell. To the same he wrote May 28th stating that "notwithstanding my recommendation, agreeably to what I conceived to be the sense of Congress, Lieutenant-Colonel Campbell's treatment continues to be such as cannot be justified either on the principles of generosity or strict retaliation; as I have authentic information, and I doubt not you will have the same, that General Lee's situation is far from being rigorous or uncomfortable." To Sir William Howe, he wrote June 10th, that "Lieutenant-Colonel Campbell and the Hessian field-officers, will be detained till you recognise General Lee as a prisoner of war, and put him on the footing of claim. * * * The situation of Lieutenant-Colonel Campbell, as represented by you, is such as I neither wished nor approve. Upon the first intimation of his complaints, I wrote upon the subject, and hoped there would have been no further cause of uneasiness. That, gentleman, I am persuaded, will do me the justice to say, he has received no ill treatment at my instance. Unnecessary severity and every species of insult I despise, and, I trust, none will ever have just reason to censure me in this respect." At this time Colonel Campbell was not in the gaol but in the jailer's house. On June 2d Congress ordered that Colonel Campbell and the five Hessian officers should be treated "with kindness, generosity, and tenderness, consistent with the safe custody of their persons."

Congress finally decided that General Prescott, who had been recently captured, should be held as a hostage for the good treatment of General Lee, and Washington was authorized to negotiate an exchange of prisoners.

March 10, 1778, in a letter addressed to Washington by Sir William Howe, he concludes as follows:

"When the agreement was concluded upon to appoint commissioners to settle a general exchange, I expected there would have been as much expedition used in returning Lieutenant-Colonel Campbell, and the Hessian field-officers, as in returning Major-General Prescott, and that the cartel might have been finished by the time of the arrival of General Lee. If, however, there should be any objection to General Prescott's remaining at New York, until the aforementioned officers are sent in, he shall, to avoid altercation, be returned upon requisition."

To this Washington replied:

"Valley Forge, 12 March, 1778.

Sir:—Your letter of the 10th came to hand last night. The meeting of our commissioners cannot take place till the time appointed in my last.

I am not able to conceive on what principle it should be imagined, that any distinction, injurious to Lieutenant-Colonel Campbell and the Hessian field officers, still exists. That they have not yet been returned on parole is to be ascribed solely to the remoteness of their situation. Mr. Boudinot informs me, that he momentarily expects their arrival, in prosecution of our engagement. You are well aware, that the distinction originally made, with respect to them, was in consequence of your discrimination to the prejudice of General Lee. On your receding from that discrimination, and agreeing to a mutual releasement of officers on parole, the difficulty ceased, and General Prescott was sent into New York, in full expectation, that General Lee would come out in return. So far from adhering to any former exception. I had particularly directed my commissary of prisoners, to release Lieutenant-Colonel Campbell, in lieu of Lieutenant Colonel Ethan Allen."

It was not, however, until May 5, 1778 that Washington succeeded in exchanging Colonel Campbell for Colonel Ethan Allen.[*] His imprisonment did not have any effect on his treatment of those who afterwards fell into his hands.

---

[*]For Correspondence see Spark's Washington's Writings, Vols. IV, V.

The death of Major Menzies was an irreparable loss to the corps, for he was a man of judgment and experience, and many of the officers and all the sergeants and soldiers totally inexperienced. Colonel Campbell was experienced as an engineer, but was a stranger to the minor and interior discipline of the line. But when it is considered that the force opposed to Fraser's regiment was also undisciplined, the duty and responsibility became less arduous.

The greater part of the 71st safely landed towards the end of July, 1776 on Staten Island and were immediately brought to the front. The grenadiers were placed in the battalion under Lieutenant-Colonel Charles Stuart, and the light infantry in Lieutenant-Colonel Robert Abercromby's brigade; the other companies were formed into three small battalions in brigades, under Sir William Erskine, then appointed Brigadier-General. In this manner, and, as has been noticed, without training, these men were brought into action at Brooklin. Nine hundred men of the 42nd, engaged on this occasion, were as inexperienced as those of the 71st, but they had the advantage of the example of three hundred old soldiers, on which to form their habits, together with officers of long experience.

The first proof of their capacity, energy and steadfastness was at the battle of Brooklin, where they fully met the expectations of their commander. They displayed great eagerness to push the Americans to extremities, and to compel them to abandon their strong position. General Howe, desiring to spare their lives, called them back. The loss sustained by this regiment, in the engagement was three rank and file killed, and two sergeants and nine rank and file wounded.

The regiment passed the winter at Amboy, and in the skirmishing warfare of the next campaign was in constant employment, particularly so in the expeditions against Willsborough and Westfield, with which the operations for 1777 commenced. Immediately afterwards the army embarked for the Chesapeake. In the battle of Brandywine, a part of the 71st was actively engaged, and the regiment remained in Pennsylvania until November, when they embarked for New York. Here they were joined by two hundred recruits who had arrived from Scotland in September. These men along with one hundred more recovered from the hospital, formed a small corps under Captain Colin Mackenzie and acted as light infantry in an expedition up the North river to create a diversion in favor of General Burgoyne's movements. This corps led a successful assault on Fort Montgomery on October 6th, in which they displayed great courage. Captain Mackenzie's troops led the assault, and although so many were recruits, it was said that they exhibited conduct worthy of veterans.

In the year 1778, the 71st regiment accompanied lord Cornwallis on an expedition into the Jerseys, distinguished by a series of movements and countermovements. Stewart says that on the excursion into the Jerseys "a corps of cavalry, commanded by the Polish count Pulaski, were surprised and nearly cut to pieces by the light infantry under Sir James Baird."* This must refer to the expedition against Little Egg Harbor, on the eastern coast of New Jersey, which was a noted place of rendezvous for American privateers. The expedition was commanded by Captain Patrick Ferguson, many of whose troops were American royalists. They failed in their design, but made extensive depredations on both public and private property. A deserter from count Pulaski's command informed Captain Ferguson that a force had been sent to check these ravages and was now encamped twelve miles up the river. Captain Ferguson proceeded to surprise the force, and succeeded. He surrounded the houses at night in which the unsuspecting infantry were sleeping, and in his report of the affair said:

"It being a night-attack, little quarter, of course, could be given; so there were only five prisoners!"

He had butchered fifty of the infantry on the spot, when the approach of count Pulaski's horse caused him to make a rapid retreat to his boats, and a flight down the river.† Such expeditions only tended to arouse the Americans and express the most determined hatred towards their oppressors. They uttered vows of vengeance which they sought in every way to execute.

---
*Sketches, Vol. II, p. 97. †Lossing's Washington and American Republic, Vol. II, p. 643.

An expedition consisting of the Highlanders, two regiments of Hessians, a corps of provincials, and a detachment of artillery, commanded by Lieutenant-Colonel Archibald Campbell, sailed from Sandy Hook, November 29, 1778, and after a stormy passage reached the Savannah river by the end of December. The 1st battalion of the 71st, and the light infantry, under the immediate command of Lieutenant-Colonel Maitland, landed, without opposition a short distance below the town of Savannah. Captain Cameron, without delay, advanced to attack the American advanced posts, when he and three of his men were killed by a volley. The rest instantly charged and drove the Americans back on the main body, drawn up in a line on an open plain in the rear of the town. The disembarkation, with the necessary arrangements for an attack was soon completed. At that time Savannah was an open town, without any natural strength, save that of the woods which covered both sides. Colonel Campbell formed his troops in line, and detached Sir James Baird with the light infantry through a narrow path, to get round the right flank of the Americans, while the corps, which had been Captain Cameron's, was sent round the left. The main army in front made demonstrations to attack. The Americans were so occupied with the main body that they did not perceive the flanking movements, and were thus easily surrounded. When they realized the situation they fled in great confusion. The light infantry closing in upon both flanks of the retreating Americans, they greatly suffered, losing upwards of one hundred killed and five hundred wounded and prisoners, with a British loss of but four soldiers killed and five wounded. The town then surrendered and the British took possession of all the shipping, stores, and forty-five cannon.

Flushed with success Colonel Campbell made immediate preparations to advance against Augusta, situated in the interior about one hundred and fifty miles distant. No opposition was manifested, and the whole province of Georgia, apparently submitted. Colonel Campbell established himself in Augusta, and detached Lieutenant-Colonel Hamilton, with two hundred men to the frontiers of Georgia. Meanwhile General Prevost, having arrived at Savannah from Florida, assumed command. Judging the ground occupied to be too extensive, he ordered Augusta evacuated and the lines narrowed. This retrograde movement emboldened the Americans and they began to collect in great numbers, and hung on the rear of the British, cutting off stragglers, and frequently skirmishing with the rear guard. Although uniformly maintaining themselves, this retreat dispirited the royalists (commonly called tories), and left them unprotected and unwilling to render assistance.

It appears that the policy of General Prevost was not to encourage the establishing of a provincial militia, so that the royalists were left behind without arms or employment, and the patriots formed bands and traversed the country without control. To keep these in check, inroads were made into the interior, and in this manner the winter months passed. Colonel Campbell, who had acted on a different system, obtained leave of absence and embarked for England, leaving Lieutenant-Colonel Maitland in command of the 71st regiment.

The regiment remained inactive till the month of February 1779, when it was employed in an enterprise against Brier Creek, forty miles below Augusta, a strong position defended by upwards of two thousand men, besides one thousand occupied in detached stations. In front was a deep swamp, rendered passable only by a narrow causeway, and on each flank thick woods nearly impenetrable, but the position was open to the rear. In order to dislodge the Americans from this position Lieutenant-Colonel Duncan Macpherson, with the first battalion of the Highlanders, was directed to march upon the front of the position; whilst Colonel Prevost and Lieutenant Colonels Maitland and Macdonald, with the 2d battalion of the Highlanders, the light infantry, and a detachment of provincials, were ordered to attempt the rear by a circuitous route of forty-nine miles. Notwithstanding the length of the march through a difficult country, the movements were so well regulated, that in ten minutes after Colonel Macpherson appeared at the head of the causeway in front, Colonel Maitland's fire was heard in the rear, and Sir James Baird, with the light infantry rushed through the openings in the swamp on the left flank. The attack was made on March 3rd. The Americans under General Ashe were completely surprised. The entire army was lost by death, captivity and dispersion. On this occasion one fourth of General Lincoln's army was destroyed. The loss of the Highlanders being five soldiers killed, and one officer and twelve rank and file wounded.

General Prevost was active and next determined to invade South Carolina. Towards the close of April he crossed the Savannah river, with the troops engaged at Brier's Creek, and a large body of royalists and Creek Indians, and made slow marches towards Charleston. In the meantime General Lincoln had been active and recruited vigorously, and now mustered five thousand men under his command. Whilst General Prevost marched against General Lincoln's front, the former ordered the 71st to make a circuitous march of several miles and attack the rear. Guided by a party of Creek Indians the Highlanders entered a woody swamp at eleven o'clock at night, in traversing which they were frequently up to the shoulders in the swamp. They emerged from the woods the next morning at eight o'clock with their ammunition destroyed. They were now within a half mile of General Lincoln's rear guard which they attacked and drove from their position without sustaining loss. Reaching Charleston on May 11th General Prevost demanded instantly its surrender, but a dispatch from General Lincoln notified the people that he was coming to their relief. General Prevost, fearing that General Lincoln would cut off his communication with Savannah, commenced his retreat towards that city, at midnight, along the coast. This route exposed his troops to much suffering, having to march through unfrequented woods, salt water marshes and swamps. Lieutenant-Colonel Prevost, the Quartermaster-General, and a man of the name of Macgirt, and a person under his orders, had gone on a foraging expedition, and were not returned from their operations; and in order to protect them Colonel Maitland, with a battalion of Highlanders and some Hessians, was placed in a hastily constructed redoubt at Stono Ferry, ten miles below Charleston. On June 20th these men were attacked by a part of General Lincoln's force. When their advance was reported, Captain Colin Campbell, with four officers and fifty-six men, was sent out to reconnoitre. A thick wood covered the approach of the Americans till they reached a clear field on which Captain Campbell's party stood. Immediately he attacked the Americans and a desperate resistance ensued; all the officers and non-commissioned officers of the Highlanders fell, seven soldiers alone remaining on their feet. It was not intended that the resistance should be of such a nature, but most of the men had been captured in Boston Harbor, and had only been recently exchanged, and this being their first appearance before an enemy, and thought it was disgraceful to retreat when under fire. When Captain Campbell fell he directed his men to make the best of their way to the redoubt; but they refused to obey, and leave their officers on the field. The Americans, at this juncture ceased firing, and the seven soldiers carried their officers along with them, followed by such as were able to walk. The Americans advanced on the redoubts with partial success. The Hessians having got into confusion in the redoubt, which they occupied, the Americans forced an entrance, but the 71st having driven back those who attacked their redoubt, Colonel Maitland was enabled to detach two companies of Highlanders to the support of the Hessians. The Americans were instantly driven out of the redoubt at the point of the bayonet, and while preparing for another attempt, the 2d battalion of Highlanders came up, when despairing of success they retreated at all points, leaving many killed and wounded.

The resistance offered by Captain Campbell afforded their friends in the redoubts time to prepare, and likewise to the 2d battalion in the island to march by the difficult and circuitous route left open for them. The delay in the 2d battalion was also caused by a want of boats. Two temporary ferry-boats had been established, but the men in charge ran away as soon as the firing began. The Americans opened a galling fire on the men as they stood on the banks of the river. Lieutenant Robert Campbell plunged into the water and swam across, followed by a few soldiers, returned with the boats, and thus enabled the battalion to cross over to the support of their friends. Five hundred and twenty Highlanders and two hundred Hessians successfully resisted all the efforts of the Americans twelve hundred strong, and this with a trifling loss in comparison to the service rendered. When the Americans fell back, the whole garrison sallied out, but the light troops covered the retreat so successfully, that all the wounded were brought off. In killed and wounded the Americans lost one hundred and forty-six and one hundred and fifty missing. The British loss was three officers and thirty-two soldiers killed and wounded. Three days afterwards, the foraging party having returned, the British evacuated Stono Ferry, and retreated from island to island, until they reached Beaufort, on Port Royal, where Colonel Maitland was left with seven hundred men, while General Prevost, with the main body of the army, continued his difficult and harrassing march to Savannah.

In the month of September 1779, the count D'Estaing arrived on the coast of Georgia with a fleet of twenty sail of the line, two fifty gun ships, seven frigates, and transports, with a body of troops on board for the avowed purpose of retaking Savannah. The garrison consisted of two companies of the 16th regiment, two of the 60th, one battalion of Highlanders, and one weak battalion of Hessians; in all about eleven hundred effective men. The combined force of French and Americans was four thousand nine hundred and fifty men. While General Lincoln and his force were approaching the French effected a landing at Beuley and Thunderbolt, without opposition. General McIntosh urged count D'Estaing to make an immediate assault upon the British works. This advice was rejected, and count D'Estaing advanced within three miles of Savannah and demanded an unconditional surrender to the king of France. General Prevost asked for a truce until next day which was granted, and in the meanwhile twelve hundred white men and negroes were employed in strengthening the fortifications and mounting additional ordnance. This truce General Lincoln at once perceived was fatal to the success of the beseigers, for he had ascertained that Colonel Maitland, with his troops, was on his way from Beaufort, to reinforce General Prevost, and that his arrival within twenty-four hours, was the object which was designed by the truce. Colonel Maitland, conducted by a negro fisherman, passed through a creek with his boats, at high water, and concealed by a fog, eluded the French, and entered the town on the afternoon of September 17th. His arrival gave General Prevost courage, and towards evening he sent a note to count D'Estaing, bearing a positive refusal to capitulate. All energies were now bent towards taking the town by regular approaches. Ground was broken on the morning of September 23rd, and night and day the besiegers plied the spade, and so vigorously was the work prosecuted, that in the course of twelve days fifty-three cannon and fourteen mortars were mounted. During these days two sorties were made. The morning of September 24th, Major Colin Graham, with the light company of the 16th regiment, and the two Highland battalions, dashed out, attacked the besiegers, drove them from their works, and then retired with the loss of Lieutenant Henry Macpherson of the 71st, and three privates killed, and fifteen wounded. On September 27th, Major Macarthur, with the pickets of the Highlanders advanced with such caution and address, that, after firing a few rounds, the French and Americans, mistaking their object, commenced a fire on each other, by which they lost fifty men; and, in the meantime Major Macarthur retired. These sorties had no effect on the general operations.

On the morning of October 4th, the batteries having been all completed and manned, a terrible bombardment was opened upon the British works and the town. The French frigate Truite also opened a cannonade. Houses were shattered, men, women and children were killed or maimed, and terror reigned. Day and night the cannonade was continued until the 9th. Victory was within the grasp of the besiegers, when count D'Estaing became impatient and determined on an assault. Just before dawn on the morning of the 9th four thousand five hundred men of the combined armies moved to the assault, in the midst of a dense fog and under cover of a heavy fire from the batteries. They advanced in three columns, the principal one commanded by count D'Estaing in person, assisted by General Lincoln; another column by count Dillon. The left column taking a great circuit got entangled in a swamp, and, being exposed to the guns of the garrison, was unable to advance. The others made the advance in the best manner, but owing to the fire of the batteries suffered severely. Many entered the ditch, and even ascended and planted the colors on the parapet, where several were killed. Captain Tawse, of the 71st, who commanded the redoubt, plunged his sword into the first man who mounted, and was himself shot dead by the man who followed. Captain Archibald Campbell then assumed the command, and maintained his post till supported by the grenadiers of the 60th, when the assaulting column being attacked on both sides, was completely broken, and driven back with such expedition, that a detachment of the 71st, ordered by Colonel Maitland to hasten and assist those who were so hard pressed by superior numbers, could not overtake them. The other columns, seeing the discomfiture of the principal attack, retired without any further attempt.

It is the uniform testimony of those who have studied this siege that if count D'Estaing had immediately on landing made the attack, the garrison must have succumbed. General Lincoln, although his force was greatly diminished by the action just closed, wished to continue the siege; but count D'Estaing resolved on immediate departure. General Lincoln was indignant, but concealed his wrath; and being too weak to carry on the siege alone, he at last consented to abandon it.

The French loss, in killed and wounded, was six hundred and thirty-seven men, and the American four hundred and fifty-seven. The British lost one captain, two subalterns, four sergeants, and thirty-two soldiers, killed; and two captains, two sergeants, two drummers, and fifty-six soldiers, wounded. Colonel Maitland was attacked with a bilious disease during the siege and soon after died. The British troops had been sickly before Savannah was attacked; but the soldiers were reanimated, and sickness, in a manner, was suspended, during active operations. But when the Americans withdrew, and all excitement had ceased, sickness returned with aggravated violence, and fully one fourth the men were sent to the hospital.

While these operations were going on in Georgia and South Carolina a disaster overtook the grenadiers of the 71st who were posted at Stony Point and Verplanks, in the state of New York. Washington planned the attack on Stony Point and deputed General Wayne to execute it. So secretly was the whole movement conducted, that the British garrison was unsuspicious of danger. At eight o'clock, on the evening of July 15, 1779, General Wayne took post in a hollow, within two miles of the fort on Stony Point, and there remained unperceived until midnight, when he formed his men into two columns, Lieutenant-Colonel Fleury leading one division and Major Stewart the other. At the head of each was a forlorn hope of twenty men. Both parties were close upon the works before they were discovered. A skirmish with the pickets at once ensued, the Americans using the bayonet only. In a few moments the entire works were manned, and the Americans were compelled to press forward in the face of a terrible storm of grape shot and musket balls. Over the ramparts and into the fort both columns pushed their way. At two o'clock the morning of the 16th, General Wayne wrote to Washington:

"The fort and garrison, with Colonel Johnson, are ours. The officers and men behaved like men who were determined to be free."

The British lost nineteen soldiers killed, and one captain, two subalterns, and seventy two soldiers, wounded; and, in all, including prisoners, six hundred. The principal part of this loss fell upon the picket, commanded by Lieutenant Cumming of the 71st, which resisted one of the columns till almost all of the men of the picket, were either killed or wounded, Lieutenant Cumming being among the latter. The Americans lost fifteen killed and eighty-three wounded.

The force which had so ably defended Savannah remained there in quarters during the winter of 1779 and 1780. In the month of March 1780, Sir Henry Clinton arrived before Charleston with a force from New York, which he immediately invested and rigorously pushed the siege. The chief engineer, Captain Moncrieff was indefatigable, and being fearless of danger, was careless of the lives of others. Having served two years with the 71st, and believing it would gratify the Highlanders to select them for dangerous service, he generally applied for a party of that corps for all exposed duties.

After the surrender of Charleston, on May 12, 1780, to the

army under Sir Henry Clinton, the British forces in the southern states were placed under the command of lord Cornwallis. The 71st composed a part of this army, and with it advanced into the interior. In the beginning of June, the army amounting to twenty-five hundred, reached Camden, a central place fixed upon for headquarters. The American general, Horatio Gates, having, in July, assembled a force marched towards Camden. The people generally were in arms and the British officers perplexed. Major Macarthur who was at Cheraw to encourage the royalists, was ordered to fall back towards Camden. Lord Cornwallis, seeing the gathering storm hastily left Charleston and joined lord Rawdon at Camden, arriving there on August 13th. Both generals of the opposing forces on the night of August 15th moved towards each other with the design of making an attack. The British troops consisted of the 23d and 33d regiments, under Lieutenant-Colonel Webster; Tarleton's legion; Irish volunteers; a part of Lieutenant-Colonel Hamilton's North Carolina Regiment; Bryan's corps of royalists, under lord Rawdon, with two six and two three pounders commanded by Lieutenant McLeod; and the 71st regiment. Camden was left in the care of Major Macarthur, with the sick and convalescents.

Both armies were surprised, and each fired at the same moment, which occurred at three o'clock on the morning of August 16th. Both generals, ignorant of each other's force, declined general action, and lay on their arms till morning. When the British army formed in line of battle, the light infantry of the Highlanders, and the Welsh fusileers were on the right; the 33d regiment and the Irish volunteers occupied the center; the provincials were on the left, with the marshy ground in their front. While the army was thus forming, Captain Charles Campbell, who commanded the Highland light companies on the right, placed himself on the stump of an old tree to reconnoitre, and observing the Americans moving as with the intention of turning his flank, leaped down, and giving vent to an oath, called to his men, "Remember you are light infantry; remember you are Highlanders: Charge!" The attack was rapid and irresistible, and being made before the Americans had completed their movement by which they were to surround the British right, they were broken and driven from the field, prior to the beginning of the battle in other parts of the line. When the battle did commence the American center gained ground. Lord Cornwallis opened his center to the right and left, till a considerable space intervened, and then directed the Highlanders to move forward and occupy the vacant space. When this was done, he cried out, "My brave Highlanders, now is your time." They instantly rushed forward accompanied by the Irish volunteers and the 33d, and penetrated and completely overthrew the American column. However the American right continued to advance and gained the ground on which the Highlanders had been placed originally as a reserve. They gave three cheers for victory; but the smoke clearing up they saw their mistake. A party of Highlanders turning upon them, the greater part threw down their arms, while the remainder fled in all directions. The victory was complete. The loss of the British was one captain, one subaltern, two sergeants, and sixty-four soldiers killed; and two field officers, three captains, twelve subalterns, thirteen sergeants, and two hundred and thirteen soldiers wounded. The Highlanders lost Lieutenant Archibald Campbell and eight soldiers killed; and Captain Hugh Campbell, Lieutenant John Grant, two sergeants, and thirty privates wounded. The loss of the Americans was never ascertained, but estimated at seven hundred and thirty two.

General Sumter, with a strong corps, occupied positions on the Catawba river, which commanded the road to Charleston, and from which lord Cornwallis found it necessary to dislodge him. For this purpose Colonel Tarleton was sent with the cavalry and a corps of light infantry, under Captain Charles Campbell of the 71st regiment. The heat was excessive; many of the horses failed on the march, and not more than forty of the infantry were together in front, when, on the morning of the 18th, they came in sight of Fishing Creek, and on their right saw the smoke at a short distance. The sergeant of the advanced guard halted his party and then proceeded to ascertain the cause of the smoke. He saw the encampment, with arms piled, but a few sentinels and no pickets. He returned and reported the same to Captain Campbell who commanded in front. With his usual promptness Captain Campbell formed as many of the cavalry as had come up, and with the party of Highland infantry, rushed forward, and directing their route to the piled arms, quickly secured them and surprised the camp. The success was complete; a few were killed; nearly five hundred taken prisoners, and the rest dispersed. But the victory was dampened by the loss of the gallant Captain Campbell, who was killed by a random shot.

These partial successes were soon counterbalanced by defeats of greater importance. From what had been of great discouragement, the Americans soon rallied, and threatened the frontiers of South Carolina, and on October 7th overthrew Major Ferguson at King's Mountain, who sustained a total loss of eleven hundred and five men, out of eleven hundred and twenty-five. At the plantation of Blackstocks, November 20th, Colonel Tarleton, with four hundred of his command, engaged General Sumter, when the former was driven off with a loss of ninety killed, and about one hundred wounded. The culminating point of these reverses was the battle of the Cowpens.

A new commander for the southern department took charge of the American forces, in the person of Major-General Nathaniel Greene, who stood, in miltary genius, second only to Washington, and who was thoroughly imbued with the principles practiced by that great man. Lord Cornwallis, the ablest of the British tacticians engaged in the American Revolution, found more than his equal in General Greene. He had been appointed to the command of the Southern Department, by Washington, on October 30, 1780, and immediately proceeded to the field of labor, and on December 3rd, took formal command of the army, and was exceedingly active in the arrangement of the army, and in wisely directing its movements. His first arrangement was to divide his army into two detachments, the larger of which, under himself was to be stationed opposite Cheraw Hill, on the east side of the Pedee river, about seventy miles to the right of the British army, then at Winnsborough. The other, composed of about one thousand troops, under General Daniel Morgan, was placed some fifty miles to the left, near the junction of Broad and Parcolet rivers.

Colonel Tarleton was detached to disperse the little army of General Morgan, having with him, the 7th or Fusileers, the 1st battalion of Fraser's Highlanders, or 71st, two hundred in number, a detachment of the British Legion, and three hundred cavalry. Intelligence was received, on the morning of January 17, 1781, that General Morgan was drawn up in front on rising ground. The British were hastily formed, with the Fusileers, the Legion, and the light infantry in front, and the Highlanders and cavalry forming the reserve. As soon as formed the line was ordered to advance rapidly. Exhausted by running, it received the American fire at the distance of thirty or forty paces. The effect was so great as to produce something of a recoil. The fire was returned; and the light infantry made two attempts to charge, but were repulsed with loss. The Highlanders next were ordered up, and rapidly advancing in charge, the American front line gave way and retreated through an open space in the second line. This manœuvre was made without interfering with the ranks of those who were now to oppose the Highlanders, who ran in to take advantage of what appeared to them to be a confusion of the Americans. The second line threw in a fire upon the 71st, when within forty yards which was so destructive that nearly one half their number fell; and those who remained were so scattered, having run a space of five hundred yards at full speed, that they could not be united to form a charge with the bayonet. They did not immediately fall back, but engaged in some irregular firing, when the American line pushed forward to the right flank of the Highlanders, who now realized that there was no prospect of support, and while their number was diminishing that of their foe was increasing. They first wavered, then began to retire, and finally to run. This is said to have been the first instance of a Highland regiment running from an enemy.* This repulse struck a panic into those whom they left in the rear, and who fled in the greatest confusion. Order and command were lost, and the rout became general. Few of the infantry escaped, and the cavalry saved itself by putting their horses to full speed. The Highlanders re-

*Stewart's Sketches, Vol. II, p. 116.

formed in the rear, and might have made a soldier-like retreat if they had been supported.

The battle of the Cowpens was disastrous in its consequences to the British interests, as it inspired the Americans with confidence. Colonel Tarleton had been connected with frequent victories, and his name was associated with that of terror. He was able on a quick dash, but by no means competent to cope with the solid judgment and long experience of General Morgan. The disposition of the men under General Morgan was judicious; and the conduct of Colonels Washington and Howard, in wheeling and manœuvering their corps, and throwing in such destructive volleys on the Highlanders, would have done credit to any commander. To the Highlanders the defeat was particularly unfortunate. Their officers were perfectly satisfied with the conduct of their men, and imputing the disaster altogether to the bad dispositions of Colonel Tarleton, made representations to lord Cornwallis, not to be employed again under the same officer, a request with which compliance was made. This may be the reason that Colonel Tarleton gives them no credit in his "History of the Campaigns," published in 1787. He admits his loss to have been three hundred killed and wounded and near four hundred prisoners.*

After the battle of the Cowpens lord Cornwallis with increased exertions followed the main body of the Americans under General Greene, who retreated northward. The army was stripped of all superfluous baggage. The two battalions of the 71st now greatly reduced, were consolidated into one, and formed in a brigade with the 33d and Welsh Fusileers. Much skirmishing took place on the march, when, on March 16th, General Greene believing his army sufficiently strong to withstand the shock of battle drew up his force at Guilford Court House, in three lines.

The British line was formed of the German regiment of De Bos, the Highlanders, and guards, under General Leslie, on the right; and the Welsh Fusileers, 33d regiment, and second battalion of guards, under General Charles O'Hara, on the left; the

---

*History of Campaigns, p. 218.

cavalry was in the rear supported by the light infantry of the guards and the German Yagers. At one o'clock the battle opened. The Americans, covered by a fence in their front, maintained their position with confidence, and withheld their fire till the British line was within forty paces, when a destructive fire was poured into Colonel Webster's brigade, killing and wounding nearly one-third. The brigade returned the fire, and rushed forward, when the Americans retreated on the second line. The regiment of De Bos and the 33d met with a more determined resistance, having retreated and advanced repeatedly before they succeeded in driving the Americans from the field. In the meantime, a party of the guards pressed on with eagerness, but were charged on their right flank by a body of cavalry which broke their line. The retreating Americans seeing the effect of this charge, turned and recommenced firing. The Highlanders, who had now pushed round the flank, appeared on a rising ground in rear of the left of the enemy, and, rushing forward with shouts, made such an impression on the Americans, that they immediately fled, abandoning their guns and ammunition.

This battle, although nominally a victory for the British commander, was highly beneficial to the patriots. Both armies displayed consummate skill. Lord Cornwallis on the 19th decamped, leaving behind him between seventy and eighty of his wounded soldiers, and all the American prisoners who were wounded, and left the country to the mercy of his enemy. The total loss of the British was ninety-three killed, and four hundred and eleven wounded. The Highlanders lost Ensign Grant, and eleven soldiers killed, and four sergeants and forty-six soldiers wounded. It was long a tradition, in the neighborhood, that many of the Highlanders, who were in the van, fell near the fence, from behind which the North Carolinians rose and fired.

The British army retreated in the direction of Cross Creek, the Americans following closely in the rear. At Cross Creek, the heart of the Highland settlement in North Carolina, lord Cornwallis had hoped to rest his wearied army, a third of whom was sick and wounded and was obliged to carry them in wagons, or on horseback. The remainder were without shoes and worn down with fatigue. Owing to the surrounding conditions, the army took up its weary march to Wilmington, where it was expected there would be supples, of which they were in great need. Here the army halted from April 17th to the 26th, when it proceeded on the route to Petersburg, in Virginia, and to form a junction with General Phillips, who had recently arrived there with three thousand men. The march was a difficult one. Before them was several hundred miles of country, which did not afford an active friend. No intelligence could be obtained, and no communication could be established. On May 25th the army reached Petersburg, where the united force amounted to six thousand men. The army then proceeded to Portsmouth, and when preparing to cross the river at St. James' Island, the Marquis de Lafayette, ignorant of their number, with two thousand men, made a gallant attack. After a sharp resistance he was repulsed, and the night approaching favored his retreat. After this skirmish the British army marched to Portsmouth, and thence to Yorktown, where a position was taken on the York river on August 22nd.

From the tables given by lord Cornwallis, in his "Answer to the Narrative of Sir Henry Clinton"* the following condition of the 71st at different periods on the northward march, is extracted:

January 15, 1781,	1st Battalion 249	2nd Battalion 237	Light Company 69
February 1, 1781,	" —	" 234	
March 1, 1781,	" —	" 212	
April 1, 1781,	" —	" 161	
May 1, 1781,	Two Battalions 175		
June 1, 1781,	Second Battalion 164		
July 1, 1781,	" " 161		
August 1, 1781,	" " 167		
Sept. 1, 1781,	" " 162		
Oct. 1, 1781,	" " 160		

The encampment at Yorktown was formed on an elevated platform, nearly level, on the bank of the river, and of a sandy soil. On the right of the position, extended from the river, a ravine of about forty feet in depth, and more than one hundred yards in breadth; the center was formed by a horn-work of entrenchments; and an extensive redoubt beyond the ravine on the right, and two smaller redoubts on the left, also advanced be-

*Pages 53, 77, 137.

yond the entrenchments, constituted the principal defences of the camp.

On the morning of September 28, 1781, the combined French and American armies, twelve thousand strong, left Williamsburg by different roads, and marched towards Yorktown, and on the 30th the allied armies had completely invested the British works. Batteries were erected, and approaches made in the usual manner. During the first four days the fire was directed against the redoubt on the right, which was reduced to a heap of sand. On the left the redoubts were taken by storm and the guns turned on the other parts of the entrenchments. One of these redoubts had been manned by some soldiers of the 71st. Although the defence of this redoubt was as good and well contested as that of the others, the regiment thought its honor so much implicated, that a petition was drawn up by the men, and carried by the commanding officer to lord Cornwallis, to be permitted to retake it. The proposition was not acceded to, for the siege had reached such a stage that it was not deemed necessary.

Among the incidents related of the Highlanders during the siege, is that of a soliloquy, overheard by two captains, of an old Highland gentleman, a lieutenant, who, drawing his sword, said to himself, "Come, on, Maister Washington, I'm unco glad to see you; I've been offered money for my commission, but I could na think of gangin' hame without a sight of you. Come on."*

The situation of the besieged daily grew more critical, the whole encampment was open to assault, and exposed to a constant and enfilading fire. In this dilemma lord Cornwallis resolved to decamp with the elite of his army, by crossing the river and leaving a small force to capitulate. The first division embarked and some had reached the opposite shore at Gloucester Point, when a violent storm of wind rendered the passage dangerous, and the attempt was consequently abandoned. The British army then surrendered to Washington, and the troops marched out of their works on October 20th.

The loss of the garrison was six officers, thirteen sergeants,

---

*Memoir of General Graham, p. 59.

four drummers and one hundred and thirty-three rank and file killed; six officers, twenty-four sergeants, eleven drummers, and two hundred and eighty-four wounded. Of these the 71st lost Lieutenant Thomas Fraser and nine soldiers killed; three drummers and nineteen soldiers wounded. The whole number surrendered by capitulation was a little more than seven thousand making a total loss of about seven thousand eight hundred. Of the arms and stores there were seventy-five brass, and one hundred and sixty iron cannon; seven thousand seven hundred and ninety-four muskets; twenty-eight regimental standards; a large quantity of cannon and musket-balls, bombs, carriages, &c, &c. The military chest contained nearly eleven thousand dollars in specie.

Thus ended the military service of an army, proud and haughty, that had, within a year marched and counter-marched nearly two thousand miles, had forded streams, some of them in the face of an enemy, had fought two pitched battles and engaged in numerous skirmishes. With all their labors and achievements, they accomplished nothing of real value to the cause they represented.

Fraser's Highlanders remained prisoners until the conclusion of hostilities. During their service their character was equal to their courage. Among them disgraceful punishments were unknown. When prisoners and solicited by the Americans to join their standard and settle among them, not one of them broke the oath he had taken, a virtue not generally observed on that occasion, for many soldiers joined the Americans. On the conclusion of hostilities the 71st was released, ordered to Scotland, and discharged at Perth in 1783.

SEVENTY-FOURTH OR ARGYLE HIGHLANDERS.

The particulars of the 74th or Argyle Highlanders, and the 76th, or Macdonald's Highlanders, are but slightly touched upon by Colonel David Stewart of Garth, in his "Sketches of the Highlanders," by Dr. James Browne, in his "History of the Highlands," and by John S. Keltie, in his "History of the Scottish

Highlands." Even Lieutenant-General Samuel Graham, who was a captain in the 76th, in his "Memoirs," gives but a slight account of his regiment. So a very imperfect view can only be expected in this narration.

The 74th or Argyle Highlanders was raised by Colonel John Campbell of Barbreck, who had served as captain and major of Fraser's Highlanders in the Seven Years' War. In the month of December 1777 letters of service were granted to him, and the regiment was completed in May 1778. In this regiment were more Lowlanders, than in any other of the same description raised during that period. All the officers, except four, were Highlanders, while of the soldiers only five hundred and ninety were of the same country, the others being from Glasgow, and the western districts of Scotland. The name of Campbell mustered strong; the three field-officers, six captains, and fourteen subalterns, being of that name. Among the officers was the chief of the Macquarries, being sixty-two years of age when he entered the army in 1778.

The regiment mustering nine hundred and sixty, rank and file, embarked at Greenock in August, and landed at Halifax in Nova Scotia, where it remained garrisoned with the 80th and the 82d regiments; the whole being under the command of Brigadier-General Francis Maclean. In the spring of 1779, the grenadier company, commanded by Captain Ludovick Colquhoun of Luss, and the light compnay by Captain Campbell of Bulnabie, were sent to New York, and joined the army immediately before the siege of Charleston.

In June of the same year, the battalion companies, with a detachment of the 82d regiment, under the command of Brigadier-General Maclean, embarked from Halifax, and took possession of Penobscot, with the intention of establishing a post there. Before the defences were completed, a hostile fleet from Boston, with two thousand troops on board, under Brigadier-General Solomon Lovell, appeared in the bay, and on July 28th effected a landing on a peninsula, where the British were erecting a fort, and immediately began to construct batteries for a regular siege. These operations were frequently interrupted by sallies of parties from the fort. General Maclean exerted himself to the utmost to strengthen his position, and not only kept the Americans in check, but preserved communication with the shipping, which they endeavored to cut off. Both parties kept skirmishing till August 13th, when Sir George Collier appeared in the bay, with a fleet intended for relief of the post. This accession of strength disconcerted the Americans, and completely destroyed their hopes, so that they quickly decamped and retired to their boats. Being unable to re-embark all the troops, those who remained, along with the sailors of several vessels which had run aground in the hurry of escaping, formed themselves into a body, and endeavored to penetrate through the woods. In the course of this attempt they ran short of provisions, quarrelled among themselves, and, coming to blows, fired on each other till their ammunition was expended. Upwards of sixty men were killed and wounded; the rest dispersed through the woods, numbers perishing before they could reach an inhabited country.

The conduct of General Maclean and his troops met with approbation. In his dispatch, giving an account of the attack and defeat of his foes, he particularly noticed the exertions and zeal of Lieutenant-Colonel Alexander Campbell of the 74th. The loss of this regiment was two sergeants, and fourteen privates killed, and seventeen rank and file wounded.

General Maclean returned to Halifax with the detachment of the 82d, leaving Lieutenant-Colonel Alexander Campbell of Monzie with the 74th at Penobscot, where they remained till the termination of hostilities, when they embarked for England. They landed at Portsmouth whence they marched for Stirling, and, after being joined by the flank companies, were reduced in the autumn of 1783.

SEVENTY-SIXTH OR MACDONALD'S HIGHLANDERS.

In the month of December 1777, letters of service were granted to lord Macdonald to raise a regiment in the Highlands and Isles. On his recommendation Major John Macdonell of Lochgarry was appointed lieutenant-colonel commandant of the regiment. The regiment was numbered the 76th, but called Macdonald's Highlanders. Lord Macdonald exerted himself in the formation of the regiment, and selected the officers from the families of the Macdonalds of Glencoe, Morar, Boisdale, and others of his own clan, and likewise from those of others, as Mackinnon, Fraser of Culduthel, Cameron of Callart, &c. A body of seven hundred and fifty Highlanders was raised. The company of Captain Bruce was principally raised in Ireland; and Captains Cunningham of Craigend, and Montgomery Cunnngham, as well as Lieutenant Samuel Graham, raised their men in the low country. These amounted to nearly two hundred men, and were kept together in two companies; while Bruce's company formed a third. In this manner each race was kept distinct. The whole number, including non-commissioned officers and men, amounted to one thousand and eighty-six. The recruits assembled at Inverness, and in March 1778 the regiment was reported complete. The men on their arrival were attested by a justice of the peace, and received the king's bounty of five guineas. As Major John Macdonell, who had been serving in America in the 71st or Fraser's Highlanders, was taken prisoner, on his passage home from that country, the command devolved on Captain Donaldson, of the 42d or Royal Highland Regiment. Under this officer the regiment was formed, and a code of regulations established for the conduct of both officers and men.

Soon after its formation the 76th was sent to Fort George where it remained a year. It so happened that few of the non-commissioned officers who understood the drill were acquainted with the Gaelic language, and as all words of command were given in English, the commander directed that neither officers nor non-commissioned officers ignorant of the former language should endeavor to learn it. The consequence was that the Highlanders were behind-hand in being drilled, as they had, besides other duties, to acquire a new language. But the Highlanders took uncommon pains to learn their duties, and so exact were they in the discharge of them that upon one occasion, Colonel Campbell, the lieutenant-governor, was seized and made prisoner by the sentry posted at his own door, because the man conceived a trespass had been committed on his post, nor would the sentinel release the colonel until the arrival of the corporal of the guard.

In March 1779 the regiment was removed to Perth, and from there marched to Burnt Island, where they embarked on the 17th. Major Donaldson's health not permitting him to go abroad, the command devolved on lord Berridale, second major, who accompanied them to New York, where they landed in August. The fleet sailed from the Firth of Forth for Portsmouth, and in a short time anchored at Spithead. While waiting there for the assembling of a fleet with reinforcements of men and stores for the army in America, an order was received to set sail for the island of Jersey, as the French had made an attempt there. But the French having been repulsed before the 76th reached Jersey, the regiment returned to Portsmouth, and proceeded on the voyage to America, and arrived in New York on August 27th.

On the arrival of the regiment in New York the flank companies were attached to the battalion of that description. The battalion companies remained between New York and Staten Island till February 1781, when they embarked with a detachment of the army, commanded by General Phillips, for Virginia. The light company, being in the 2d battalion of light infantry, also formed a part of the expedition. The grenadiers remained at New York.

This year, lord Berridale, on the death of his father, became earl of Caithness, and being severely wounded at the siege of Charleston, soon after returned to Scotland. The command of the 76th regiment devolved on Major Needham, who had purchased Major Donaldson's commission.

General Phillips landed at Portsmouth, in Virginia, in March. A number of boats had been constructed under the superintendence of General Benedict Arnold, for the navigation of the rivers, most of them calculated to hold one hundred men. Each boat was manned by a few sailors, and was fitted with a sail as well as oars. Some of them carried a piece of ordnance in their bows. In these boats the light infantry, and detachments of the 76th and 80th regiments, with the Queen's Rangers, embarked, leaving the remainder of the 76th, with other troops, to garrison Portsmouth. The detachment of the 76th which embarked consisted of one major, three captains, twelve subalterns, and three hundred men, under Major Needham. The troops proceeded up the James river destroying warlike stores, shipping, barracks, foundaries and private property. After making many excursions the troops marched to Bermuda Hundreds, opposite City Point, where they embarked, on May 2d; but receiving orders from lord Cornwallis, returned and entered Petersburg on May 10th.

When the 76th regiment found themselves with an army which had been engaged in the most incessant and fatiguing marches through difficult and hostile countries, they considered themselves as inferiors and as having done nothing which could enable them to return to their own country. They were often heard murmuring among themselves, lamenting their lot, and expressing the strongest desire to signalize themselves. This was greatly heightened when visited by men of Fraser's Highlanders. The opportunity presented itself, and their behavior proved they were good soldiers. On the evening of July 6th, the Marquis de Lafayette pushed forward a strong corps, forced the pickets, and drew up in front of the British lines. The pickets in front of the army that morning consisted of twenty men of the 76th and ten of the 80th. When the attack on the pickets commenced, they were reinforced by fifteen Highlanders. The pickets defended the post till every man was either killed or wounded.

A severe engagement took place between the contending armies, the weight of which was sustained on the part of the British by the left of Colonel Dundas's brigade, consisting of the 76th and 80th, and it so happened that while the right of the line was covered with woods they were drawn up in an open field, and exposed to the attack of the Americans with a chosen body of troops. The 76th being on the left, and lord Cornwallis, coming up in rear of the regiment, gave the word to charge, which was immediately repeated by the Highlanders, who rushed forward with impetuosity, and instantly decided the contest. The Americans retired, leaving their cannon and three hundred men killed and wounded behind them.

Soon after this affair lord Cornwallis ordered a detachment of four hundred chosen men of the 76th to be mounted on such horses as could be procured and act with the cavalry. Although four-fifths of the men had never before been on horseback, they were mounted and marched with Tarleton's Legion. After several forced marches, far more fatiguing to the men than they had ever performed on foot, they returned heartily tired of their new mode of travelling. No other service was performed by the 76th until the siege and surrender of Yorktown. During the siege, while the officers of this regiment were sitting at dinner, the Americans opened a new battery, the first shot from which entered the mess-room, killed Lieutenant Robertson on the spot, and wounded Lieutenant Shaw and Quartermaster Barclay. It also struck Assistant Commissary General Perkins, who happened to dine there that day.

The day following the surrender of lord Cornwallis, at Yorktown (October 20th), the British prisoners moved out in two divisions, escorted by regiments of militia; one to the direction of Maryland, the other, to which the 76th belonged, moved to the westward in Virginia for Winchester. On arriving at their cantonment, the officers were lodged in the town on parole, and the soldiers were marched several miles off to a cleared spot in the woods, on which stood a few log huts, some of them occupied by prisoners taken at the Cowpens. From Winchester the regiment was removed to Lancaster in Pennsylvania. After peace was declared they embarked for New York, sailed thence for Scotland, and were disbanded in March 1784 at Stirling Castle.

This regiment maintained a very high standard for their behavior. Thefts and other crimes, implying moral turpitude, were totally unknown. There were only four instances of corporal punishment inflicted on the Highlanders of the regiment, and these were for military offences. Moral suasion and such coercion as a father might use towards his children were deemed sufficient to keep them in discipline or self-restraint.

In the year 1775, George III. resolved to humble the thirteen colonies. In the effort put forth he created a debt of £121,267,993, with an annual charge of £5,088,336, besides sacrificing thousands of human lives, and causing untold misery; and, at last, weary of the war, on July 25, 1782, he issued a warrant to Richard Oswald, commissioning him to negotiate a peace. The definite articles of peace were signed at Paris, September 3, 1783. Then the United States of America took her position among the nations of the earth. George III. and his ministers had exerted themselves to the utmost to subjugate America. Besides the troops raised in the British Isles there were of the German mercenaries twenty-nine thousand eight hundred and sixty-seven. The mercenaries and British troops were well armed, clothed and fed. But the task undertaken was a gigantic one. It would have required a greater force than that sent to America to hold and garrison the cities alone. The fault was not with the army, the navy, or the commanding officers. The impartial student of that war will admit that the army fought well, likewise the navy, and the generals and admirals were skilled and able in the art of war. The British foreign office was weak. Nor was this all. The Americans had counted the cost. They were singularly fortunate in their leader. Thirty-nine years after his death, lord Brougham wrote of Washington that he was "the greatest man of our own or of any age. * * * This eminent person is presented to our observation clothed in attributes as modest, as unpretending, as little calculated to strike or to astonish, as if he had passed unknown through some secluded region of private life. But he had a judgment sure and sound; a steadiness of mind which never suffered any passion or even any feeling to ruffle its calm; a strength of understanding which worked rather than forced its way through all obstacles,—removing or avoiding rather than over-leaping them. His courage, whether in battle or in council, was as perfect as might be expected from this pure and steady temper of soul. A perfectly just man, with a thoroughly firm resolution never to be misled by others any more than by others overawed; never to be seduced or betrayed, or hurried away by his own weaknesses or self-delusions, and more than by other men's arts, nor ever to be disheartened by the most complicated difficulties any more than to be spoilt on the giddy heights of fortune—such was this great man,—whether we regard him sustaining alone the whole weight of campaigns, all but desperate, or gloriously terminating a just warfare by his resources and his courage."*

The British generals proved themselves unable to cope with

---

*Edinburg Review, October, 1838; Collected Contributions, Vol. I, p. 344.

this great and good man. More than six thousand five hundred Highlanders left their homes amidst the beautiful scenery of their native land, crossed a barrier of water three thousand miles in width, that they might fight against such a man and the cause he represented. Their toils, sacrifices and sufferings were in vain. Towards them Washington bore good will. Forgetting the wrongs they had done, he could write of them:

"Your idea of bringing over Highlanders appears to be a good one. They are a hardy, industrious people, well calculated to form new settlements, and will, in time, become valuable citizens."*

War is necessarily cruel and barbarous; and yet there were innumerable instances of wanton cruelty during the American Revolution. No instances of this kind have been recorded against the soldiers belonging to the Highland regiments. There were cruelties perpetrated by those born in the Highlands of Scotland, but they were among those settled by Sir William Johnson on the Mohawk and afterwards joined either Butler's Rangers or else Sir John Johnson's regiment. Even this class was few in numbers.

---

*Letter to Robert Sinclair, May 6, 1792. Spark's Writings of Washington, Vol. XII, p. 304.

CHAPTER XIV.

DISTINGUISHED HIGHLANDERS WHO SERVED IN AMERICA IN THE INTERESTS OF GREAT BRITAIN.

If the list of distinguished Highlanders who served in America in the interests of Great Britain was confined to those who rose to eminence while engaged in said service, it certainly would be a short one. If amplified to those who performed feats of valor or rendered valuable service, then the list would be long. The measure of distinction is too largely given to those who have held prominent positions, or else advanced in military rank. In all probability the names of some have been overlooked, although care has been taken in finding out even those who became distinguished after the American Revolution. The following biographical sketches are limited to those who were born in the Highlands of Scotland:

GENERAL SIR ALAN CAMERON, K. C. B.

Sir Alan Cameron of the Camerons of Fassifern, known in the Highlands as Ailean an Earrachd, almost a veritable giant, was born in Glen Loy, Lochaber, about the year 1745. In early manhood, having fought a duel with a fellow clansman, he fled to the residence of his mother's brother, Maclean of Drimnim, who, in order to elude his pursuers, turned him over to Maclean of Pennycross. Having oscillated between Morvern and Mull for a period of two years, he learned that another relative of his mother's, Colonel Allan Maclean of Torloisk, was about to raise a regiment for the American war. He embarked for America, and was kindly received by his relative who made him an officer in the 84th or Highland Emigrant regiment. During the siege of Quebec, he was taken prisoner and sent to Philadelphia, where he was kept for two years, but finally effected his escape, and returned to his regiment. Being unfit for service, in 1780, he returned to England on sick leave. In London he courted the only heir of Nathaniel Philips, and eloping with her they were married at Gretna Green. Soon after he received an appointment on the militia staff of one of the English counties. In 1782 he was elected a member of the Highland Society of London. In August 1793 Alan was appointed major-commandant, and proceded to Lochaber to raise a regiment, which afterwards was embodied as the 79th, or Cameron Highlanders. Not unmindful of his brother-officers of the Royal Highland Emigrant Regiment, he named two of his own, and five officers of the Clan Maclean. The regiment in January 1794 numbered one thousand, which advanced Alan to the lieutenant-colonelcy. The regiment was then embarked for Flanders to reinforce the British and Austrians against the French. It was in the disastrous retreat to Westphalia, and lost two hundred men. From thence it was sent to the Isle of Wight, and Colonel Cameron was ordered to recruit his regiment to the extent of its losses in Flanders. The regiment was sent to the island of Martinique, and in less than two years, from the unhealthy location, it was reduced to less than three hundred men. But few of the men ever returned to Scotland. Colonel Cameron having been ordered to recruit for eight hundred men, fixed his headquarters at Inverness. Within less than nine months after his return from Martinique he produced a fresh body of seven hundred and eighty men. In 1798 he was ordered with his regiment to occupy the Channel Islands. He was severely wounded at Alkmaar. Colonel Cameron was sent to help drive the French out of Egypt. From Egypt he was transferred to Minorca and from there to England. He took part in the capture of the Danish fleet—a neutral power—and entered Copenhagen. Soon after the battle of Vimiera, Alan was made a brigadier and commandant of Lisbon. He was in command of a brigade at Oporto when that city was besieged. He was twice wounded at the battle of Talavera. After a military career covering a period of thirty-six years, on account of ill-health, he resigned his position in the army, and for several years was not able to meet his friends. He died at Fulham, April 9, 1828.

GENERAL SIR ARCHIBALD CAMPBELL, K. B.

Sir Archibald Campbell second son of James Campbell of Inverneil was born at Inverneil on August 21, 1739. By special rec-

GENERAL SIR ARCHIBALD CAMPBELL.

ommendation of Mr. Pitt he received, in 1757, a captain's commission in Fraser's Highlanders, and served throughout the campaign in North America, and was wounded at the taking of Quebec in 1758. On the conclusion of the war he was transferred to the 29th regiment, and afterwards major and lieutenant-colonel in the 42nd or Royal Highlanders, with which he served in India until 1773, when he returned to Scotland, and was elected to Parliament for the Stirling burgs in 1774. In 1775 he was selected as lieutenant-colonel of the 2nd battalion of Fraser's Highlanders. He was captured on board the George transport, in Boston Harbor June 17, 1776, and remained a prisoner until May 5, 1778, when he was exchanged for Colonel Ethan Allen. He was then placed in command of an expedition against the State of Georgia, which was successful. He was superseded the following year by General Augustine Prevost. Disagreeing with the policy adopted by that officer in regard to the royalist militia, Colonel Campbell returned to England, on leave. In 1779 he married Amelia, daughter of Allan Ramsay, the artist. November 20, 1782, he was promoted major-general, and the following month commissioned governor of Jamaica. His vigilance warded off attacks from the French, besides doing all in his power in sending information, supplies and reinforcements to the British forces in America. For his services, on his return to England, he was invested a knight of the Bath, on September 30, 1785. The same year he was appointed governor and commander-in-chief at Madras. On October 12, 1787, he was appointed colonel of the 74th Highlanders, which had been raised especially for service in India. In 1789 General Campbell returned to England, and at once was re-elected to Parliament for the Stirling burghs. He died March 31, 1791, and was buried in Westminster Abbey.

JOHN CAMPBELL OF STRACHUR.

John Campbell was appointed lieutenant in Loudon's Highlanders in June 1745; served throughout the Rising of 1745-6; made the campaign in Flanders in 1747, in which year he became a captain ;and at the peace of 1748 went on half pay. In 1756 he was called into active service and joined the 42nd. He was wounded at Ticonderoga, and on his recovery was appointed major of the 17th foot. February 1762, he became a lieutenant-colonel in the army, and commanded his regiment in the expedition against Martinico and Havanna. He became lieutenant-col-

HIGHLANDERS WHO SERVED IN AMERICA. 381

onel of the 57th foot, May 1, 1773, and returned to America on the breaking out of the Revolution. On February 19, 1779 he was appointed major-general; colonel of his regiment November 2, 1780, and commanded the British forces in West Florida, where he surrendered Pensacola to the Spaniards, May 10, 1781; became lieutenant-general in 1787, and general January 26, 1797. General Campbell died August 28, 1806.

LORD WILLIAM CAMPBELL.

Lord William Campbell was the youngest son of the 4th duke of Argyle. He entered the navy, and became a captain August 20, 1762, when he was put in command of the Nightingale, of twenty guns. In May 1763, he married Sarah, daughter of Ralph Izard, of Charleston, South Carolina, and in 1764, was elected to represent Argyleshire in parliament. On November 27, 1766 he became governor of Nova Scotia, whose affairs he administered until 1773, when he was transferred to the government of South Carolina, in which province he arrived in June 1775, during the sitting of the first Provincial Congress, which presented him a congratulatory address, but he refused to acknowledge that body. For three months after his arrival he was undisturbed, though indefatigable in fomenting opposition to the popular measures; but in September, distrustful of his personal safety, and leaving his family behind, he retired on board the Tamar sloop-of-war, where he remained, although invited to return to Charleston. Lady Campbell was treated with great respect, but finally went on board the vessel, and was landed at Jamaica. In the attack on the city of Charleston, in June 1776, under Sir Henry Clinton, lord Campbell served as a volunteer on board the Bristol, on which occasion he received a wound that ultimately proved mortal. Presumably he returned with the fleet and died September 5, 1778.

GENERAL SIMON FRASER.

Brigadier Simon Fraser was the tenth son of Alexander Fraser, second of Balnain. The lands of Balnain had been acquired from Hugh, tenth lord of Lovat, by Big Hugh, grandfather of

Simon. Alexander was in possession of the lands as early as 1730, and for his first wife had Jane, daughter of William Fraser, eighth of Foyers, by whom he had issue six sons and one daughter. In 1716 he married Jean, daughter of Angus, tenth Mackintosh of Kyllachy, by whom he had issue five sons and three daughters, Simon being the fourth son, and born May 26th, 1729.

In all probability it would be a difficult task to determine the

date of General Fraser's first commission in the British army owing to the fact that no less than eight Simon Frasers appear in the Army List of 1757, six of whom belonged to Fraser's Highlanders. The subsequent commissions may positively be traced as follows: In the 78th Foot, lieutenant January 5, 1757, captain-lieutenant September 27, 1758, captain April 22, 1759; major in the army March 15, 1761; in the 24th Foot, major February 8, 1762, and lieutenant-colonel July 14, 1768. January 10, 1776,

General Carleton appointed him to act as a brigadier till the king's pleasure could be known, which in due time was confirmed. His last commission was that of colonel in the army, being gazetted July 22, 1777. He served in the Scots Regiment in the Dutch service and was wounded at Bergen ap-Zoon in 1747. He was with his regiment in the expedition against Louisburg in 1758 and accompanied General Wolfe to Quebec in 1759, and was the officer who answered the hail of the enemy's sentry in French and made him believe that the troops who surprised the Heights of Abraham were the Regiment de la Rhine.

After the fall of Quebec, for a few years he did garrison duty at Gibraltar. Through the interest of the marquis of Townshend, who appointed him his aid-de-camp in Ireland, he was selected as quartermaster-general to the troops then stationed in that country. While in Ireland he was selected by General Burgoyne as one of his commanders for his expediction against the Americans. On April 5, 1776, he embarked with the 24th Foot, and arrived in Quebec on the 28th of the following May. He commanded the light brigade on General Burgoyne's campaign, and was thus ever in advance, rendering throughout the most efficient services, and had the singular good fortune to increase his reputation. He assisted in driving the Americans out of Canada, and defeated them in the battle of Three Rivers, followed by that of Hubbardton, July 7, 1777. Had his views prevailed, the blunder of sending heavy German dismounted dragoons to Bennington, and the consequent disaster would never have been committed.

The career of this dauntless hero now rapidly drew near to its close. Up to the battle of Bennington almost unexampled success had attended the expedition of Burgoyne. The turning point had come. The battle of Bennington infused the Americans with a new and indomitable spirit; the murder, by savages, of the beautiful Miss Jane MacRae aroused the passions of war; the failure of Sir Henry Clinton to co-operate with General Burgoyne; the rush of the militia to the aid of General Gates, and the detachment of Colonel Morgan's riflemen by Washington from his own army to the assistance of the imperiled north, all conspired to turn the tide of success, and invite the victorious army to a disaster, rendered famous in the annals of history.

On September 13, the British army crossed the Hudson, by a bridge of rafts with the design of forming a junction with Sir Henry Clinton at Albany. The army was in excellent order and in the highest spirits, and the perils of the expedition seemed practically over. The army marched a short distance along the western bank of the Hudson, and on the 14th encamped on the heights of Saratoga, distant about sixteen miles from Albany. On the 19th a battle was fought between the British right wing and a strong body of Americans. In this action the right column was led by General Fraser, who, on the first onset, wheeled his troops and forced Colonel Morgan to give way. Colonel Morgan was speedily re-enforced, when the action became general. When the battle appeared to be in the grasp of the British, and just as General Fraser and Colonel Breymann were preparing to follow up the advantage, they were recalled by General Burgoyne and reluctantly forced to retreat. Both Generals Fraser and Riedesel (commander of the Brunswick contingent) bitterly criticised the order, and in plain terms informed General Burgoyne that he did not know how to avail himself of his advantage. The next day General Burgoyne devoted himself to the laying out of a fortified camp. The right wing was placed under the command of General Fraser. The situation now began to grow critical. Provisions became scarce. October 5th a council of war was held, and the advice of both Generals Fraser and Riedesel was to fall back immediately to their old position beyond the Batten Kil. General Burgoyne finally determined on a reconnaissance in force. So, on the morning of October 7th, with fifteen hundred men, accompanied by Generals Fraser, Riedesel and Phillips, the division advanced in three columns towards the left wing of the American position. In advance of the right wing, General Fraser had command of five hundred picked men. The Americans fell upon the British advance with fury, and soon a general battle was engaged in. Colonel Morgan poured down like a torrent from the ridge that skirted the flanking party of General Fraser, and forced the latter back; and then by a rapid movement to the left fell upon the flank of the British right with such impetuosity that it wavered. General Fraser noticing the critical situation of the center hurried to its succor the 24th Regiment. Dressed in full uniform, General Fraser was conspicuously mounted on an iron grey horse. He was all activity and vigilance, riding from one part of the division to another, and animated the troops by his example. At a critical point, Colonel Morgan, who, with his riflemen was immediately opposite to General Fraser's corps, perceiving that the fate of the day rested upon that officer, called a few of his sharpshooters aside, among whom was the famous marksman, Timothy Murphy, men on whose precision of aim he could rely, and said to them, "That gallant officer yonder is General Fraser; I admire and respect him, but it is necessary for our good that he should die. Take you station in that cluster of bushes and do your duty." A few moments later, a rifle ball cut the crouper of General Fraser's horse, and another passed through the horse's mane. General Fraser's aid, calling attention to this, said: "It is evident that you are marked out for particular aim; would it not be prudent for you to retire from this place?" General Fraser replied, "My duty forbids me to fly from danger." The next moment he fell wounded by a ball from the rifle of Timothy Murphy, and was carried off the field by two grenadiers. After he was wounded General Fraser told his friends "that he saw the man who shot him, and that he was a rifleman posted in a tree." From this it would appear that after Colonel Morgan had given his orders Timothy Murphy climbed into the forks of a neighboring tree.

General Burgoyne's surgeons were reported to have said had not General Fraser's stomach been distended by a hearty breakfast he had eaten just before going into action he would doubtless have recovered from his wound.

Upon the fall of General Fraser, dismay seized the British. A retreat took place exactly fifty-two minutes after the first shot was fired. General Burgoyne left the cannon on the field, except two howitzers, besides sustaining a loss of more than four hundred men, and among them the flower of his officers. Contemporary military writers affirmed that had General Fraser lived the British would have made good their retreat into Canada. It is claimed that he would have given such advice as would have caused General Burgoyne to have avoided the blunders which finally resulted in his surrender.

The closing scene of General Fraser's life has been graphically described by Madame Riedesel, wife of the German general. It has been oft quoted, and need not be here repeated. General Burgoyne has described the burial scene with his usual felicity of expression and eloquence.

Burgoyne was not unmindful of the wounded general. He was directing the progress of the battle, and it was not until late in the evening that he came to visit the dying man. A tender scene took place between him and General Fraser. The latter was the idol of the army and upon him General Burgoyne placed most reliance. The spot where General Fraser lies buried is on an elevated piece of ground commanding an extensive view of the Hudson, and a great length of the interval on either side. The grave is marked by a tablet placed there by an American lady.

The American reader has a very pleasant regard for the character of General Fraser. His kindly disposition attracted men towards him. As an illustration of the humane disposition the following incident, taken from a rare work, may be cited: "Two American officers taken at Hubbardstown, relate the following anecdote of him. He saw that they were in distress, as their continental paper would not pass with the English; and offered to loan them as much as they wished for their present convenience. They took three guineas each. He remarked to them—'Gentlemen take what you wish—give me your due bills and when we reach Albany, I trust to your honor to take them up; for we shall doubtless over-run the country, and I shall, probably, have an opportunity of seeing you again.'" As General Fraser fell in battle, "the notes were consequently never paid; but the signers of them could not refrain from shedding tears at the fate of this gallant and generous enemy."*

---

*Memoir General Stark, 1831, p. 252.

GENERAL SIMON FRASER OF LOVAT.

General Simon Fraser, thirteenth of Lovat, born October 19, 1726, was the son of the notorious Simon, twelfth lord Lovat, who was executed in 1747. With six hundred of his father's vassals he joined prince Charles before the battle of Falkirk, January 17, 1746, and was one of the forty-three persons included in the act of attainder of June 4, 1746. Having surrendered to the government he was confined in Edinburgh Castle from November, 1746, to August 15, 1747, when he was allowed to reside in Glasgow during the king's pleasure. He received a full pardon in 1750, and two years later entered as an advocate. At the commencement of the seven years' war, by his influence with his clan, without the aid of land or money he raised eight hundren recruits in a few weeks, in which as many more were shortly added. His commission as colonel was dated January 5, 1757. Under his command Fraser's Highlanders went to America, where he was at the seige of Louisburg in 1758, and in the expedition under General Wolfe against Quebec, where he was wounded at Montmorenci. He was again wounded at Sillery, April 28, 1760. In 1762 he was a brigadier-general in the British force sent to Portugal; in the Portuguese army he held the temporary rank of major-general, and in 1768 a lieutenant-general. In 1771 he was a major-general in the British army. By an act of parliament, on the payment of £20,983, all his forfeited lands, lordships, &c., were restored to him, on account of the military services he had rendered the country. On the outbreak of the American Revolution General Fraser raised another regiment of two battalions, known as Fraser's Highlanders or 71st, but did not accompany the regiment. When, in Canada, in 1761, he was returned to par-

GENERAL SIMON FRASER OF LOVAT.

liament, and thrice re-elected, representing the constituency of the county of Inverness until his death, which occurred in Downing Street, London, February 8, 1782.

GENERAL SIMON FRASER.

Lieutenant-General Simon Fraser, son of a tacksman, born in 1738, was senior of the Simon Frasers serving as subalterns in Fraser's Highlanders in the campaign in Canada in 1759-1761. He was wounded at the battle of Sillery, April 28, 1760, and three years later was placed on half-pay as a lieutenant. In 1775 he raised a company for the 71st or Fraser's Highlanders; became senior captain and afterwards major of the regiment, with which he served in America in the campaigns of 1778-1781. In 1793 he raised a Highland regiment which was numbered 133rd foot or Fraser's Highlanders, which after a brief existence, was broken up and drafted into other corps. He became a major-general in 1795, commanded a British force in Portugal in 1797-1800. In 1802 he became lieutenant-general, and for several years second in command in Scotland, in which country he died March 21, 1813.

GENERAL JAMES GRANT OF BALLINDALLOCH.

General James Grant was born in 1720, and after studying law obtained a commission in the army in 1741, and became captain in the Royal Scots, October 24, 1744. General Grant served with his regiment in Flanders and in Ireland, and became major in Montgomery's Highlanders, with which he went to America in 1757. In the following year he was surprised before Fort Duquesne, and lost a third of his command in killed, wounded and missing, besides being captured himself with nineteen of his officers. He became lieutenant-colonel of the 40th foot in 1760, and governor of East Florida. In May, 1761, he led an expedition against the Cherokee Indians, and defeated them in the battle of Etchoe. On the death of his nephew he succeeded to the family estate; became brevet-colonel in 1772; in 1773 was returned to parliament for Wick burghs, and the year after for Sutherlandshire; and in 1775 was appointed colonel of the 55th foot. As a brigadier, in 1776, he went to America with the reinforcement under Sir William Howe; commanded two brigades at the battle of Long Island, Brandywine and Germantown. In May, 1778, was unsuccessful in his attempt to cut off the marquis de Lafayette on the Schuylkill. In December, 1778, he captured St. Lucia, in the West Indies. In 1777, he became major-general, in 1782 lieutenant-general, and in 1796 general; and, in succession, became governor of Dumbarton and Stirling Castles. In 1787, 1790, 1796, and 1801, he was again returned to parliament for Sutherlandshire. He was noted for his love of good living, and in his latter years was immensely corpulent. He died at Ballindalloch April 13, 1806.

GENERAL ALLAN MACLEAN OF TORLOISK.

General Allan Maclean, son of Torloisk, Island of Mull, was born there in 1725, and began his military career in the service of Holland, in the Scots brigade. At the siege of Bergen-op-Zoom, in 1747, a portion of the brigade cut its way with great loss through the French. Lieutenants Allan and Francis Maclean, having been taken prisoners, were carried before General Lowendahl, who thus addressed them: "Gentlemen, consider yourselves on parole. If all had conducted themselves as your brave corps have done, I should not now be master of Bergen-op-Zoom." January 8, 1756, Allan became lieutenant in the 62nd regiment, and on July 8, 1758, was severely wounded at Ticonderoga. He became captain of an independent company, January 16, 1759, and was present at the surrender of Niagara, where he was again dangerously wounded. Returning to Great Britain, he raised the 114th foot or Royal Highland Volunteers, of which he was appointed major commandant October 18, 1761. The regiment being reduced in 1763, Major Maclean went on half-pay. He became lieutenant-colonel May 25, 1772, and early in 1775 devised a colonization scheme which brought him to America, landing in New York of that year. At the outbreak of the Revolution he identified himself with the British king; was arrested in New

York; was released by denying he was taking a part in the dispute; thence went to the Mohawk, and on to Canada, where he began to set about organizing a corps, which became the nucleus of the Royal Highland Emigrants. Of this regiment Major Allan was appointed lieutenant-colonel of the first battalion which he had raised. On the evidence of American prisoners taken at Quebec, Colonel Maclean resorted to questionable means to recruit his regiment. All those of British birth who had been captured were given permission to join the regiment or else be carried to England and tried for treason. But these enforced enlistments proved of no value. Quebec unquestionably would have fallen into the hands of General Arnold had not Colonel Maclean suddenly precipitated himself with a part of his corps into the beleaguered city. Had Quebec fallen, Canada would have become a part of the United States. To Colonel Allan Maclean Great Britain owes the possession of Canada. During the prolonged seige Colonel Maclean suffered an injury to his leg, whereby he partially lost the use of it during the remainder of his life. On May 11, 1776, Colonel Maclean was appointed adjutant-general of the army, which he held until June 6, 1777, when he became brigadier-general, and placed in command at Montreal. As dangers thickened around General Burgoyne, General Maclean was ordered, October 20th, with the 31st and his battalion of the Royal Highland Emigrants, to Chimney Point, but the following month was ordered to Quebec. He left Quebec July 27, 1776, for England, in order to obtain rank and establishment for his regiment which had been promised. He returned to Canada, arriving in Quebec May 28, 1777. In 1778 he again went to England and made a personal appeal to the king in behalf of his regiment, which proved successful. May 1, 1779, he sailed from Spithead and arrived at Quebec on August 16th. He became colonel in the army November 17, 1780, and in the winter of 1782 had command from the ports at Oswegatchie to Michilimackinac. Soon after the peace of 1783, General Maclean retired from the service. He married Janet, daughter of Donald Maclean of Brolass, and died without issue, in London, in March, 1797. From the contents of many letters directed to John Maclean of

Lochbuie, it is to be inferred that he died in comparative poverty. His correspondence during his command of the Highland Emigrants is among the Haldimand MSS. in the British Museum.

General Allan Maclean of Torloisk has been confused by some writers—notably by General Stewart in his "Sketches of the

SIR ALLAN MACLEAN, BART.

Highlands" and Dr. James Brown in his "History of the Highlands and Highland Clans"—with Sir Allan Maclean, twenty-second chief of his clan. Sir Allan served in different parts of the globe. The first notice of his military career is as a captain under the earl of Drumlanrig in the service of Holland. July 16, 1757, he became a captain in Montgomery's Highlanders, and

June 25, 1762, major in the 119th foot or the Prince's Own. He obtained the rank of lieutenant-colonel May 25, 1772, and died on Inch Kenneth, December 10, 1783. He married Anna, daughter of Hector Maclean of Coll. Dr. Samuel Johnson visited him during his tour of the Hebrides, and was so delighted with the baronet and his amiable daughters that he broke out into a Latin sonnet.

GENERAL FRANCIS MACLEAN.

General Francis Maclean, of the family of Blaich, as soon as he was able to bear arms, obtained a commission in the same regiment with his father; was at the defence of Bergen-op Zoom in 1747, and was detained prisoner in France for some time; was appointed captain in the 2nd battalion of the 42nd Highlanders on its being raised in October, 1758. At the capture of the island of Guadaloupe, he was severely wounded, but owing to his gallant conduct was promoted to the rank of major, and appointed governor of the island of Marie Galante. In January, 1761, he exchanged into the 97th regiment, and April 13, 1762, was appointed lieutenant-colonel in the army. In the war in Canada, he commanded a body of troops under General Wolfe, and participated in the capture of Montreal. He was sent, in 1762, to aid the Portuguese against the combined attack of France and Spain, and was made commander of Almeida, a fortified town on the Spanish frontier, which he held for several years; and on being promoted to the rank of major-general, was nominated to the government of Estremadura and the city of Lisbon. On leaving Portugal in 1778, the king presented him with a handsomely mounted sword, and the queen gave him a valuable diamond ring. On his return to England—having been gazetted colonel of the 82nd foot, December 16, 1777—he was immediately dispatched with a corps of the army for America, and appointed to the government of Halifax in Nova Scotia, where he held the rank of brigadier-general. During the month of June, 1779, with a part of his army, General Maclean repaired to the Penobscot, and there proceeded to erect defenses. The American army under General Lovell, from Boston, appeared in the bay on July 28th, and began to erect batteries for a siege. Commodore Sir George Collier, August 13th, entered the bay with a fleet and raised the siege. General Maclean returned to Halifax, where he died, May 4, 1781, in the sixty-fourth year of his age, and unmarried.

GENERAL JOHN SMALL.

General John Small was born in Strathardale in Athole, in the year 1726, and entered the army early in life, his first commission being in the Scotch Brigade. He obtained an ensigncy in 1747, and was on half-pay in 1756, when appointed lieutenant in the 42nd Highlanders on the eve of its departure for America. He accompanied the regiment in 1759 in the expedition to northern New York, and in 1760 went down from Oswego to Montreal. In 1762 he served in the expedition to the West Indies, and on August 6th of the same year was promoted to a company. On the reduction of the regiment in 1763, Captain Small went on half-pay until April, 1765, when he was appointed to a company in the 21st or Royal North British Fusileers, which soon after was sent to America. With this regiment he contiued until 1775, when he received a commission to raise a corps of Highlanders in Nova Scotia. Having raised the 2nd battalion of the Royal Highland Emigrants, he was appointed major commandant, with a portion of which he joined the army with Sir Henry Clinton at New York in 1779, and in 1780, became lieutenant-colonel of the regiment. In 1782 he was quartered on Long Island. November 18, 1790, he was appointed colonel in the army, and in 1794, lieutenant-governor of the island of Guernsey; he was promoted to the rank of major-general October 3, 1794, and died at Guernsey on March 17, 1796, in the seventieth year of his age.

FLORA MACDONALD.

No name in the Scottish Highlands bears such a charm as that of Flora Macdonald. Her praise is frequently sung, sketches of her life published, and her portrait adorns thousands of homes. While her distinction mainly rests on her efforts in behalf of the luckless prince Charles, after the disastrous battle of Culloden;

yet, in reality, her character was strong, and she was a noble type of womanhood in her native isle.

Flora Macdonald—or "Flory," as she always wrote her name, even in her marriage contract—born in 1722, was a daughter of Ranald Macdonald, tacksman of Milton, in South Uist, an island of the Hebrides. Her father died when she was about two

FLORA MACDONALD.

years old, and when six years old she was deprived of the care of her mother, who was abducted and married by Hugh Macdonald of Armadale in Skye. Flora remained in Milton with her brother Angus till her thirteenth year, when she was taken into the mansion of the Clanranalds, where she became an accomplished player on the spinet. In 1739 she went to Edinburgh to complete her studies where, until 1745, she resided in the family

of Sir Alexander Macdonald of the Isles. While on a visit to the
Clanranalds in Benbecula, prince Charles Edward arrived there
after the battle of Culloden in 1746. She enabled the prince to
escape to Skye. For this she was arrested and thrown into the
Tower of London. On receiving her liberty, in 1747, she stayed
for a time in the house of Lady Primrose, where she was visited
by many persons of distinction. Before leaving London she was
presented with £1500. On her return to Scotland she was entertained at Monkstadt in Skye, at a banquet, to which the principal
families were invited. November 6, 1750, she married Allan
Macdonald, younger of Kingsburgh. At first they resided at
Flodigarry; but on the death of her father-in-law they went in
1772 to Kingsburgh. Here she was visited, in 1773, by the celebrated Samuel Johnson. Her husband, oppressed by debts, was
caught in that great wave of emigration from the Highlands to
America. In the month of August, 1774, leaving her two youngest children with friends at home, Flora, her husband and older
children, sailed in the ship Baliol, from Campbelton, Kintyre, for
North Carolina. Flora's fame had preceded her to that distant
country, and her departure from Scotland having become known
to her countrymen in Carolina, she was anxiously expected and
joyfully received on her arrival. Demonstrations on a large scale
were made to welcome her to America. Soon after her landing,
a largely attended ball was given in her honor at Wilmington.
On her arrival at Cross Creek she received a truly Highland welcome from her old neighbors and kinsfolk, who had crossed the
Atlantic years before her. The strains of the Piobaireachd, and
the martial airs of her native land, greeted her on her approach
to the capital of the Scottish settlement. Many families of distinction pressed upon her to make their dwellings her home, but
she respectfully declined, preferring a settled place of her own.
As the laird of Kingsburgh intended to become a planter, he left
his family in Cross Creek until he could decide upon a location.
The house in which they lived during this period was built immediately on the brink of the creek, and for many years afterwards
was known as "Flora Macdonald's house." Northwest of Cross
Creek, a distance of twenty miles, is a hill about six hundred feet

in height, now called Cameron's hill, but then named Mount Pleasant. Around and about this hill, in 1775, many members of the Clan Macdonald had settled, all of whom were of near kin to the laird and lady of Kingsburgh. Hard by are the sources of Barbeque Creek, and not many miles down that stream stood the old kirk, where the clansmen worshipped, and where Flora inscribed her name on the membership roll.

Mount Pleasant stands in the very midst of the pinery region, and from it in every direction stretches the great pine forest. Near this center Allan Macdonald of Kingsburgh purchased of Caleb Touchstone a plantation embracing five hundred and fifty acres on which were a dwelling house and outhouses which were more pretentious than was then customary among Highland settlers. The sum paid, as set forth in the deed, was four hundred and sixty pounds. Here Flora established herself, that with her family she might spend the rest of her days in peace and quiet. But the times were not propitious. There was commotion which soon ended in a long and bitter war. Even this need not have materially disturbed the family had not Kingsburgh precipitated himself into the conflict, needlessly and recklessly. With blind fatuity he took the wrong side in the controversy; and even then by the exercise of patience might have overcome the effects of his folly. Before Flora and her family were settled in America the storm gave its ominous rumble. When Governor Martin, who had deserted his post and fled to an armed cruiser in the mouth of the Cape Fear river, issued his proclamation, Allan Macdonald was among the first to respond. The war spirit of Flora was stirred within her, and she partook of the enthusiasm of her husband. According to tradition, when the Highlanders gathered around the standard Flora made them an address in their own Gaelic tongue that excited them to the highest pitch of warlike enthusiasm. With the due devotion of an affectionate wife, Flora followed her husband for several days, and encamped one night with him in a dangerous place, on the brow of Haymount, near the American forces. For a time she refused to listen to her husband's entreaties to return home, for he thought his life was enough to be in jeopardy. Finally when the army took up its march with banners flying and martial music, she deemed it time to retrace her steps, and affectionately embraced her husband, her eyes dimmed with tears as she breathed an earnest prayer to heaven for his safe and speedy return to his family and home. But alas! she never saw him again in America.

The rebellion of the Highlanders in North Carolina, which ended in a fiasco, has already been narrated. Flora was soon aroused to the fact that the battle was against them, and her husband and one son were confined in Halifax jail. It appears that even she was brought before the Committee of Safety, where she exhibited a "spirited behavior."* Sorrows, indeed, had accumulated rapidly upon her: a severe typhus fever attacked the younger members of the family and two of her children died, a boy and a girl aged respectively eleven and thirteen, and her daughter, Fanny, was still in precarious health, from the dregs of a recent fever. By the advice of her imprisoned husband she resolved to return to her native country. Fortunately for her she secured the favor and good offices of Captain Ingram, an American officer, who promised to assist her. He furnished her with a passport to Wilmington, and from thence she found her way to Charleston, from which port she sailed to her native land, in 1779. In this step she was partly governed by the state of health of her daughter Fanny. Crossing the Atlantic with none of her family but Fanny—her five sons and son-in-law actively engaged in the war—the Scottish heroine met with the last of her adventures. The vessel in which she sailed engaged a French privateer, and during the conflict her left arm was broken. So, in after years, she truthfully said that she had served both the House of Stuart and the House of Hanover, but had been worsted in the cause of each. For some time she resided at Milton, where her brother built her a cottage; but on the return of her husband they again settled at Kingsburgh, where she died March 5, 1790.

---

*Captain Alexander McDonald's Letter-Book, p. 387.

CHAPTER XV.

DISTINGUISHED HIGHLANDERS IN AMERICAN INTERESTS.

The attitude of the Highlanders during the Revolutionary War was not of such a nature as to bring them prominently into view in the cause of freedom. Nor was it the policy of the American statesmen to cater to race distinctions and prejudices. They did not regard their cause to be a race war. They fought for freedom without regard to their origin, believing that a just Providence would smile upon their efforts. Many nationalities were represented in the American army. Men left their homes in the Old World, purposely to engage in the cause of Independence, some of whom gained immortal renown, and will be remembered with honor by generations yet unborn. As has been already noted, there were natives of the Highlands of Scotland, who had made America their home and imbibed the principles of political liberty, and early identified themselves with the cause of their adopted country. The lives of some of these patriots are herewith imperfectly sketched.

GENERAL ALEXANDER M'DOUGALL.

GEN. ALEXANDER MCDOUGALL.

There are few names in the annals of the American Revolution upon which one can linger with more satisfaction than that of the gallant and true-hearted Alexander McDougall. As early as August 20, 1775, Washington wrote to General Schuyler concerning him: his "zeal is unquestionable."* Writing to General McDougall, May 23, 1777, Washington says: "I wish every officer in the army could appeal to his own heart and find the same principles of conduct, that I am persuaded actuate

---
*Spark's Washington's Writings, Vol. III, p. 62.

you."* The same writing to Thomas Jefferson, August 1, 1786, lamented the brave "soldier and disinterested patriot," and exclaimed, "Thus some of the pillars of the revolution fall."†

Alexander McDougall was born in the island of Islay in Scotland, in 1731, being the son of Ranald McDougall, who emigrated to the province of New York in 1735. The father purchased a small farm near the city of New York, and there peddled milk, in which avocation he was assisted by his son, who never was ashamed of the employment of his youth. Alexander was a keen observer of passing events and took great interest in the game of politics. With vigilance he watched the aggressive steps of the royal government; and when the Assembly, in the winter of 1769, faltered in its opposition to the usurpations of the crown and insulted the people by rejecting a proposition authorizing the vote by ballot, and by entering on the favorable consideration of a bill of supplies for troops quartered in the city to overawe the inhabitants, he issued an address, under the title of "A Son of Liberty to the Betrayed Inhabitants of the Colony," in which he contrasted the Assembly with the legislative bodies in other parts of the country, and held up their conduct to unmitigated and just indignation. The bold and deserved rebuke was laid before the house by its speaker, and, with the exception of Philip Schuyler, every member voted that it was "an infamous and seditious libel." A proclamation for the discovery of the author was issued by the governor, and it being traced to Alexander McDougall, he was arrested in February, 1770, and refusing to give bail was committed to prison by order of chief justice Horsmanden. As he was being carried to prison, clearly reading in the signs about him the future of the country, he exclaimed, "I rejoice that I am the first sufferer for liberty since the commencement of our glorious struggle." During the two months of his confinement he was overrun with visitors. He poured forth continued appeals to the people, and boldly avowed his revolutionary opinions. In every circle his case was the subject of impassioned conversation, and in an especial manner he became the idol of the masses. A packed jury found

---

*Ibid, Vol. IV, p. 430. †Ibid, Vol. IX, p. 188.

an indictment against him, and on December 20th he was arraigned at the bar of the Assembly on the same charge, on which occasion he was defended by George Clinton, afterwards the first governor of the State of New York. In the course of the following month a writ of habeas corpus was sued out, but without result, and he was not liberated until March 4, 1771, when the assembly was prorogued. When the Assembly attempted to extort from him a humiliating recantation, he undauntedly answered their threat, that "rather than resign my rights and privileges as a British subject, I would suffer my right hand to be cut off at the bar of the house." When set at liberty he entered into correspondence with the master-spirits in all parts of the country; and when the celebrated meetings in the fields were held, on July 6, 1774, preparatory to the election of the New York delegates to the First General Congress, he was called to preside, and resolutions prepared by him were adopted, pointing out the mode of choosing deputies, inveighing against the Boston Port Bill, and urging upon the proposed congress the prohibition of all commercial intercourse with Great Britain. In March 1775, he was a member of the Provincial Convention, and was nominated as one of the candidates for the Continental Congress at Philadelphia, but was not elected. In the same year he received a commission as colonel of the 1st New York regiment, and on August 9, 1776, was created brigadier-general. On the evening of the 29th of the same month he was selected by Washington to superintend the embarkation of the troops from Brooklyn; was actively engaged on Chatterton's Hill and in various places in New Jersey; and when General William Heath, in the spring of 1777, left Peekskill to assume the command of the eastern department, he succeeded that officer, but was compelled, by a superior force under Sir William Howe, to retreat from the town, after destroying a considerable supply of stores, on March 23rd. After the battle of Germantown, in which he participated, Washington, writing to the president of Congress, under date of October 7, 1777, says:

"I cannot however omit this opportunity of recommending General McDougall to their notice. This gentleman, from the time of his appointment as brigadier, from his abilities, military knowledge, and approved bravery, has every claim to promotion."*

On the 20th of the same month he was commissioned major-general. On March 16, 1778, he was directed to assume the command of the different posts on the Hudson, and, with activity, pursued the construction of the fortifications in the Highlands, and, after the flight of General Arnold, was put in command of West Point, October 5, 1780. Near the close of that year he was called upon by New York to repair to Congress as one of their representatives. It was a critical moment, and Washington urged his acceptance of the post; accordingly he took his seat in the Congress the next January. Congress having organized an executive department, in 1781, General McDougall was appointed Minister of Marine. He did not remain long in Philadelphia, for his habits, friendships, associations and convictions of duty recalled him to the camp. The confidence felt in his integrity and good judgment by all classes in the service, was such, that when the army went into winter quarters at Newburgh, in 1783, he was chosen at the head of the delegation to Congress to represent their grievances. The same year, after the close of the war, he was elected to represent the Southern District in the senate of New York and continued a member of that body until his death, which occurred in the city of New York June 8, 1786. At the time of his decease, General McDougall was president of the Bank of New York. In politics he adhered to the Hamilton party.

GENERAL LACHLAN M'INTOSH.

The history of the emigration of John Mohr McIntosh to Georgia, and the settlement upon the Alatamaha, where now stands the city of Darien, has already been recorded. The second son of John Mohr was Lachlan, born near Raits in Badenoch, Scotland, March 17, 1725, and consequently was eleven years old at the time he emigrated to America. As has been already noted John Mohr McIntosh was captured by the Spaniards at Fort Moosa, carried to Spain, and after several years, returned in broken health.

---

*Ibid, Vol. V, p. 85.

Both Lachlan and his elder brother William were placed as cadets in the regiment by General Oglethorpe. When General Oglethorpe made his final preparations for his return to England, the two young brothers were found hid away in the hold of another vessel, for they had heard of the attempts then being made by prince Charles to regain the throne of his ancestors, and they hoped to regain something that the family of Borlam had lost, of which they were members. General Oglethorpe had the two boys brought to his cabin; he spoke to them of the friendship he had entertained for their father, of the kindness he had shown to themselves, of the hopelessness of every attempt of the house of Stuart, of their own folly in engaging in this wild and desperate struggle, of his own duty as an officer of the house of Brunswick; but if they would go ashore, their secret should be his. He received their pledge and they never saw him again.

GENERAL LACHLAN MCINTOSH.

At that time the means of education in Georgia were limited, yet under his mother's care Lachlan McIntosh was well instructed in English, mathematics and other branches necessary for future military use. Lachlan sought the promising field of enterprise in Charleston, South Carolina, where the fame of his father's gallantry and misfortunes secured to him a kind reception from Henry Laurens, afterwards president of Congress, and the first minister of the United States to Holland. In the house of that patriot he remained several years, and contracted friendships that lasted while he lived, with some of the leading citizens of the southern colonies. Having adopted the profession of surveyor, and married, he returned to Georgia, where he acquired a wide and honorable reputation. On account of his views concerning certain lands between the Alatamaha and St. Mary's rivers which did not coincide with those of Governor Wright of Georgia, it afforded the latter a pretence, for a long and deliberate opposition to the interests of Lachlan McIntosh, which gradually schooled him for the approaching conflict between England and her American colonies. When that event began to dawn upon the people every eye in Georgia was turned to General McIntosh as the leader of whatever force that province might bring into the struggle. When, therefore, the revolutionary government was organized and an order was made for raising a regiment was adopted, Lachlan McIntosh was made colonel commandant; and when the order was issued for raising three other regiments, in September, 1776, he was immediately appointed brigadier-general commandant. About this time Button Gwinnett was elected governor, who had been an unsuccessful competitor for the command of the troops. He was a man unrestrained by any honorable principles, and used his official authority in petty persecutions of General McIntosh and his family. The general bore all this patiently until his opponent ceased to be governor, when he communicated to him the opinion he entertained of his conduct. He received a challenge, and in a duel wounded him mortally. General McIntosh now applied, through his friend Colonel Henry Laurens, for a place in the Continental army, which was granted, and with his staff was invited to join the commander-in-chief. He soon won the confidence of Washington, and for a long time was placed in his front, while watching the superior forces of Sir William Howe in Philadelphia.

While the army was in winter quarters at Valley Forge, the attention of the government was called to the exposed condition of the western frontier, upon which the British was constantly exciting the Indians to the most terrible atrocities. It was determined that General McIntosh should command an expedition against the Indians on the Ohio. In a letter to the President of Congress, dated May 12, 1778, Washington says:

"After much consideration upon the subject, I have appointed General McIntosh to command at Fort Pitt, and in the western country, for which he will set out as soon as he can accommodate his affairs. I part with this gentleman with much reluctance, as I esteem him an officer of great worth and merit, and as I know his services here are and will be materially wanted. His firm disposition and equal justice, his assiduity and good understanding, added to his being a stranger to all parties in that quarter, pointed him out as a proper person."*

With a reinforcement of five hundred men General McIntosh marched to Fort Pitt, of which he assumed the command, and in a short time he gave repose to all western Pennsylvania and Virginia. In the spring of 1779, he completed arrangements for an expedition against Detroit, but in April was recalled by Washington to take part in the operations proposed for the south, where his knowledge of the country, added to his stirling qualities, promised him a useful field. He joined General Lincoln in Charleston, and every preparation in their power was made for the invasion of Georgia, then in possession of the British, as soon as the French fleet under count D'Estaing should arrive on the coast. General McIntosh marched to Augusta, took command of the advance of the troops, and proceeding down to Savannah, drove in all the British outposts. Expecting to be joined by the French, he marched to Beauly, where count D'Estaing effected a landing on September 12th, 13th, and 14th, and on the 15th was joined by General Lincoln. General McIntosh pressed for an immediate attack, but the French admiral refused. In the very midst of the siege the French fleet put to sea, leaving Generals Lincoln and McIntosh to retreat to Charleston, where they were besieged by an overwhelming force under Sir Henry Clinton, to whom the city was surrendered on May 12, 1780. With this event the military life of General McIntosh closed. He was long detained a prisoner of war, and when finally released, retired with his family to Virginia, where he remained until the British troops were driven from Savannah. Upon his return to Georgia, he found his personal property wasted and his real estate much diminished in value. From that time to the close of his life, in a great measure,

Ibid, Vol. V, p. 361.

he lived in retirement and comparative poverty until his death, which took place at Savannah, February 20, 1806.

GENERAL ARTHUR ST. CLAIR.

GENERAL ARTHUR ST. CLAIR.

The life of Major General Arthur St. Clair was a stormy one, full of disappointments, shattered hopes, and yet honored and revered for the distinguished and disinterested services he performed. He was a near relative of the then earl of Roslin, and was born in 1734, in the town of Thurso, Caithness in Scotland. He inherited the fine personal appearance and manly traits of the St. Clairs. After graduating at the University of Edinburgh, he entered upon the study of medicine under the celebrated Doctor William Hunter of London; but receiving a large sum of money from his mother's estate in 1757, he changed his purpose and sought adventures in a military life, and the same year entered the service of the king of Great Britain, as ensign in the 60th or Royal American Regiment of Foot. In May of the succeeding year he was with General Amherst before Louisburg. Gathered there were men soon to become famous among whom were Wolfe, Montcalm, Murray and Lawrence. For gallant conduct Arthur St. Clair received a lieutenant's commission, April 17, 1759, and was with General Wolfe in that brilliant struggle before Quebec, in September of the same year, and soon after was made a captain. In 1760 he married at Boston, Miss Phœbe Bayard, with a fortune of £40,000, which added to his own made him a man of wealth. On April 16, 1762, he resigned his commission in the army, and soon after led a colony of Scotch settlers to the Ligonier Valley, in

Pennsylvania, where he purchased for himself one thousand acres of land. Improvements everywhere sprang up under his guiding genius. He held various offices, among which was member of the Proprietory Council of Pennsylvania, and colonel of militia. The mutterings which preceded the American Revolution were early heard in the beautiful valley of the Ligonier. Colonel St. Clair was not slow to take action, and espoused the cause of the patriots with all the intensity of his character, and never, even for a moment, swerved in the cause. He was destined to receive the enduring friendship of Washington, La Fayette, Hamilton, Schuyler, Wilson, Reed, and others of the most distinguished patriots of the Revolution. Early in the year 1776, he resigned his civil offices, and led the 2nd Pennsylvania Regiment in the invasion of Canada, and on account of the remarkable skill there displayed in saving from capture the army of General Sullivan, he received the rank of brigadier-general, August 6, 1776. He claimed to have pointed out the Quaker road to Washington on the night before the battle of Princeton. On account of his meritorious services in that battle, he was made a major-general, February 19, 1777. On the advance of General Burgoyne, who now threatened the great avenue from the north, General St. Clair was placed in command of Ticonderoga. Discovering that he could not hold the position, with great reluctance he ordered the fort evacuated. A great clamor was raised against him, especially in the New England States, and on account of this he was suspended, and a court-martial ordered. Retaining the confidence of Washington he was a volunteer aid to that commander at the battle of Brandywine. In September 1778, the court-martial acquited him of all the charges. He was on the court-martial that condemned Major John Andre, adjutant-general of the British army, as a spy, who had been actively implicated in the treason of Benedict Arnold, and soon after was placed in command of West Point. He assisted in quelling the mutiny of the Pennsylvania line, and shared in the crowning glory of the Revolution, the capture of the British army under lord Cornwallis at Yorktown. Soon afterwards General St. Clair retired to private life, but his fellow-citizens soon determined otherwise. In 1783 he was on the board of censors for Pennsylvania, and afterwards chosen vendue-master of Philadelphia; in 1786 was elected a member of Congress, and in 1787 was president of that body, which at that time, was the highest office in America. In 1788 he was elected governor of the North West Territory, which imposed upon him the duty of governing, organizing, and bringing order out of chaos, over that region of country. In 1791, Washington made him commander-in-chief of the army, and in the autumn, with an ill-appointed force, set out, under the direct orders from Henry Knox, then Secretary of War, on an expedition against the Indians, but met with an overwhelming defeat on November 4th. The disaster was investigated by Congress, and the general was justly exonerated from all blame. He resigned his commission as general in 1792, but continued in office as governor until 1802, when he was summarily dismissed by Thomas Jefferson, then president. In poverty he retired to a log-house which overlooked the valley he had once owned. In vain he pressed his claims against the government for the expenditures he had made during the Revolution, in aid of the cause. In 1812 he published his "Narrative." In 1813 the legislature of Pennsylvania granted him an annuity of $400, and finally the general government gave him a pension of $60 per month. He died at Laural Hill, Pennsylvania, August 31, 1818, from injuries received by being thrown from a wagon.

Years afterwards Judge Burnet wrote, declaring him to have been "unquestionably a man of superior talents, of extensive information, and of great uprightness of purpose, as well as suavity of manners. * * * He had been accustomed from infancy to mingle in the circles of taste and refinement, and had acquired a polish of manners, and a habitual respect for the feelings of others, which might be cited as a specimen of genuine politeness."*

In 1870 the State of Ohio purchased the papers of General St. Clair, and in 1882 these were published in two volumes, containing twelve hundred and seventy pages.

---

*Notes on the North-Western Territory, p. 378.

SERGEANT DONALD M'DONALD.

The lives of men who have won a great name on the field of battle throw a glamor over themselves which is both interesting and fascinating; and those treading the same path but cut off in their career are forgotten. However, the American Revolution affords many acts of heroism performed by those who did not command armies, some of whom performed many acts worthy of record. Perhaps, among the minor officers none had such a successful run of brilliant exploits as Sergeant Macdonald, many of which are sufficiently well authenticated. Unfortunately the essential particulars relating to him have not been preserved. The warlike deeds which he exhibited are recorded in the "Life of General Francis Marion" by General Horry, of Marion's brigade, and Weems. Just how far Weems romanced may never be known, but in all probability what is related concerning Sergeant Macdonald is practically true, save the shaping up of the story.

Sergeant Macdonald is represented to have been a son of General Donald Macdonald, who headed the Highlanders in North Carolina, and met with an overwhelming defeat at Moore's Creek Bridge. The son was a remarkably stout, red-haired young Scotsman, cool under the most trying difficulties, and brave without a fault. Soon after the defeat and capture of his father he joined the American troops and served under General Horry. One day General Horry asked him why he had entered the service of the patriots. In substance he made the following reply:

"Immediately on the misfortune of my father and his friends at the Great Bridge, I fell to thinking what could be the cause; and then it struck me that it must have been owing to their own monstrous ingratitude. 'Here now,' said I to myself, 'is a parcel of people, meaning my poor father and his friends, who fled from the murderous swords of the English after the massacre at Culloden. Well, they came to America, with hardly anything but their poverty and mournful looks. But among this friendly people that was enough. Every eye that saw us, had pity; and every hand was reached out to assist. They received us in their houses as though we had been their own unfortunate brothers. They kindled high their hospitable fires for us, and spread their feasts, and bid us eat and drink and banish our sorrows, for that we were in a land of friends. And so indeed, we found it; for whenever we told of the woeful battle of Culloden, and how the English gave no quarter to our unfortunate countrymen, but butchered all they could overtake, these generous people often gave us their tears, and said, 'O! that we had been there to aid with our rifles, then should many of these monsters have bit the ground.' They received us into the bosoms of their peaceful forests, and gave us their lands and their beauteous daughters in marriage, and we became rich. And yet, after all, soon as the English came to America, to murder this innocent people, merely for refusing to be their slaves, then my father and friends, forgetting all that the Americans had done for them, went and joined the British, to assist them to cut the throats of their best friends! Now,' said I to myself, 'if ever there was a time for God to stand up to punish ingratitude, this was the time.' And God did stand up; for he enabled the Americans to defeat my father and his friends most completely. But, instead of murdering the prisoners as the English had done at Culloden, they treated us with their usual generosity. And now these are the people I love and will fight for as long as I live."

The first notice given of the sergeant was the trick which he played on a royalist. As soon as he heard that Colonel Tarleton was encamped at Monk's Corner, he went the next morning to a wealthy old royalist of that neighborhood, and passing himself for a sergeant in the British corps, presented Colonel Tarleton's compliments with the request that he would send him one of his best horses for a charger, and that he should not lose by the gift.

"Send him one of my finest horses!" cried the old traitor with eyes sparkling with joy. "Yes, Mr. Sergeant, that I will, by gad! and would send him one of my finest daughters too, had he but said the word. A good friend of the king, did he call me, Mr. Sergeant? yes, God save his sacred majesty, a good friend I am indeed, and a true. And, faith, I am glad too, Mr. Sergeant, that colonel knows it. Send him a charger to drive the rebels, hey? Yes, egad will I send him one, and as proper a one too as ever a soldier straddled. Dick! Dick! I say you Dick!"

"Here, massa, here! here Dick!"

"Oh, you plaguey dog! so I must always split my throat with bawling, before I can get you to answer hey?"

"High, massa, sure Dick always answer when he hear massa hallo!"

"You do, you villian, do you? Well then run! jump, fly, you

rascal, fly to the stable, and bring me out Selim, my young Selim! do you hear? you villiam, do you hear?"

"Yes, massa, be sure!"

Then turning to the sergeant he went on:

"Well, Mr. Sergeant, you have made me confounded glad this morning, you may depend. And now suppose you take a glass of peach; of good old peach, Mr. Sergeant? do you think it would do you any harm?"

"Why, they say it is good of a rainy morning, sir," replied the sergeant.

"O yes, famous of a rainy morning, Mr. Sergeant! a mighty antifogmatic. It prevents you the ague, Mr. Sergeant; and clears a man's throat of the cobwebs, sir."

"God bless your honor!" said the sergeant as he turned off a bumper.

Scarcely had this conversation passed when Dick paraded Selim; a proud, full-blooded, stately steed, that stepped as though he were too lofty to walk upon the earth. Here the old man brightening up, broke out again:

"Aye! there, Mr. Sergeant, there is a horse for you! isn't he, my boy?"

"Faith, a noble animal, sir," replied the sergeant.

"Yes, egad! a noble animal indeed; a charger for a king, Mr. Sergeant! Well, my compliments to Colonel Tarleton; tell him I've sent him a horse, my young Selim, my grand Turk, do you hear, my son of thunder? And say to the colonel that I don't grudge him either, for egad! he's too noble for me, Mr. Sergeant. I've no work that's fit for him, sir; no sir, if there's any work in all this country that's good enough for him but just that which he is now going on; the driving the rebels out of the land."

He had Selim caparisoned with his elegant new saddle and holsters, with his silver-mounted pistols. Then giving Sergeant Macdonald a warm breakfast, and loaning him his great coat, he sent him off, with the promise that he would, the next morning, come and see how Colonel Tarleton was pleased with Selim. Accordingly he waited on the English colonel, told him his name with a smiling countenance; but, to his mortification received no special notice. After partially recovering from his embarrassment he asked Colonel Tarleton how he liked his charger.

"Charger, sir?" said the colonel.

"Yes, sir, the elegant horse I sent you yesterday."

"The elegant horse you sent me, sir?"
"Yes, sir, and by your sergeant, sir, as he called himself."
"An elegant horse! and by my sergeant? Why really, sir, I-I-I don't understand all this."
"Why, my dear, good sir, did you not send a sergeant yesterday with your compliments to me, and a request that I would send you my very best horse for a charger, which I did?"
"No, sir, never!" replied the colonel; "I never sent a sergeant on any such errand. Nor till this moment did I ever know that there existed on earth such a being as you."

The old man turned black in the face; he shook throughout; and as soon as he could recover breath and power of speech, he broke out into a torrent of curses, enough to make one shudder at his blasphemy. Nor was Colonel Tarleton much behind him when he learned what a valuable animal had slipped through his hands.

When Sergeant Macdonald was asked how he could reconcile the taking of the horse he replied:

"Why, sir, as to that matter, people will think differently; but for my part I hold that all is fair in war; and besides, sir, if I had not taken him ColonelTarleton, no doubt, would have got him. And then, with such a swift strong charger as this he might do us as much harm as I hope to do them."

Harm he did with a vengeance; for he had no sense of fear; and for strength he could easily drive his sword through cap and skull of an enemy with irresistible force. He was fond of Selim, and kept him to the top of his metal; Selim was not much his debtor; for, at the first glimpse of a red-coat, he would paw, and champ his iron bit with rage; and the moment of command, he was off among them like a thunderbolt. The gallant Highlander never stopped to count the number, but would dash into the thickest of the fight, and fall to hewing and cutting down like an uncontrollable giant.

General Horry, when lamenting the death of his favorite sergeant said that the first time he saw him fight was when the British held Georgetown; and with the sergeant the two set out alone to reconnoitre. The two concealed themselves in a clump of pines near the road, with the enemy's lines in full view. About sunrise five dragoons left the town and dashed up the road towards the place where the heroes were concealed. The face of Sergeant Macdonald kindled up with the joy of battle. "Zounds, Macdonald," said General Horry, "here's an odds against us, five to two." "By my soul now captain," he replied, "and let 'em come on. Three are welcome to the sword of Macdonald." When the dragoons were fairly opposite, the two, with drawn sabres broke in upon them like a tornado. The panic was complete; two were immediately overthrown, and the remaining three wheeled about and dashed for the town, applying the whip and spur to their steeds. The sergeant mounted upon the swift-footed Selim out-distanced his companion, and single-handed cut down two of the foe. The remaining one would have met a like fate had not the guns of the fort protected him. Although quickly pursued by the relief, the sergeant had the address to bring off an elegant horse of one of the dragoons whom he had killed.

A day or two after the victory of General Marion over Colonel Tynes, near the Black river, General Horry took Captain Baxter, Lieutenant Postell and Sergeant Macdonald, with thirty privates, to see if some advantage could not be gained over the enemy near the lines of Georgetown. While partaking of a meal at the house of a planter, a British troop attempted to surprise them. The party leaped to their saddles and were soon in hot pursuit of the foe. While all were excellently mounted, yet no horse could keep pace with Selim. He was the hindmost when the race began, but with widespread nostrils, long extended neck, and glaring eyeballs, he seemed to fly over the course. Coming up with the enemy Sergeant Macdonald drew his claymore, and rising on his stirrups, with high-uplifted arm, he waved it three times in circles over his head, and then with terrific force brought it down upon the fleeing dragoon. One of the British officers snapped his pistol at him, but before he could try another the sergeant cut him down. Immediately after, at a blow apiece, three more dragoons were brought to the earth by the resistless claymore. Of the twenty-five, not a man escaped, save one officer, who struck off at right angles, for a swamp, which he gained, and so cleared himself. So frightened was Captain Meriot, the British officer, that his hair, from a bright auburn, before night, had turned gray.

On the following day General Horry encountered one third of Colonel Gainey's men, and in the encounter the latter lost one half his men who were in the action. In the conflict, as usual the sergeant performed prodigies of valor. Later in the day Colonel Gainey's regiment again commenced the attack, when Sergeant

SERGEANT MACDONALD AND COLONEL GAINEY.

Macdonald made a dash for the leader, in full confidence of getting a gallant charger. Colonel Gainey proved to have been well mounted; but the sergeant, regarding but the one enemy passed all others. He afterwards said he could have slain several in the charge, but wished for no meaner object than their leader. Only one, who threw himself in the way, became his victim, whom he shot down as they went at full speed along the Black river road. When they reached the corner of Richmond fence, the sergeant had gained so far upon his enemy, as to be able to plunge his bayone into his back. The steel parted from the gun, and, with no time to extricate it, Colonel Gainey rushed into Georgetown, with the weapon still conspicuously showing how close and eager had been the charge, and how narrow the escape. The wound was not fatal.

On another occasion General Marion ordered Captain Withers to take Sergeant Macdonald, with four volunteers, and search out the intentions of the enemy in Georgetown. On the way they stopped at a wayside house and drank too much brandy. Sergeant Macdonald, feeling the effects of the potion, with a red face, reined up Selim, and drawing his claymore, began to pitch and prance about, cutting and slashing the empty air, and cried out, "Huzza, boys! let's charge!" Then clapping spurs to their steeds these six men, huzzaing and flourishing their swords, charged at full tilt into a town garrisoned by three hundred British. The enemy supposing this was the advance guard of General Marion, fled to their redoubts; but all were not fortunate enough to reach that haven, for several were overtaken and cut down in the streets, among whom was a sergeant-major, who fell from a back-handed stroke of a claymore dealt by Sergeant Macdonald. Out of the town the young men galloped without receiving any injury.

Not long after the above incident, the sergeant, as usual employing himself in watching the movements of the British, climbed up into a bushy tree, and thence, with a musket loaded with pistol bullets, fired at the guard as they passed by; of whom he killed one man and badly wounded Lieutenant Torquano; then sliding down the tree, mounted Selim, and was soon out of harm's was. Repassing the Black river he left his clothes behind him, which were seized by the enemy. He sent word to Colonel Watson if he did not immediately send back his clothes, he would kill eight of his men to compensate for them. He felt it was a point of honor that he should recover his clothes. Colonel Watson greatly irritated by a late defeat, was furious at the audacious message. He contemptuously ordered the messenger to return; but some of his officers, aware of the character of the sergeant, urged that the clothes might be returned to the partisan, as he would positively keep his word. Colonel Watson yielded, and when the messenger returned to the sergeant, he said, "You may now tell Colonel Watson that I will kill but four of his men."

The last relation of Sergeant Macdonald, as given by General Peter Horry, is in reference to Captains Snipes and McCauley, with the sergeant and forty men, having surprised and cut to pieces a large party of the enemy near Charleston.

Sergeant Macdonald did not live to reap the fruit of his labors, or even to see his country free. He was killed at the siege of Fort Motte, May 12, 1781. In this fort was stationed a British garrison of one hundred and fifty men under Captain McPherson, which had been reinforced by a small force of dragoons sent from Charleston with dispatches for lord Rawdon. General Marion, with the assistance of Colonel Henry Lee, laid siege to the fortress, which was compelled to surrender, owing to the burning of the mansion in the center of the works. Mrs. Rebecca Motte, the lady that owned the mansion, furnished the bow and arrows used to carry the fire to the roof of the building. Nathan Savage, a private in the ranks of General Marion's men, winged the arrow with the lighted torch. The British did not lose a man, and General Marion lost two of his bravest,—Lieutenant Cruger and Sergeant Macdonald. His resting place is unknown. No monument has been erected to his memory; but his name will endure so long as men shall pay respect to heroism and devotion to country.

APPENDIX.

APPENDIX.

NOTE A.

FIRST EMIGRANTS TO AMERICA.

Parties bearing Highland names were in America and the West Indies during the seventeenth century, none of whom may have been born north of the Grampians. The records fail to give us the details. It has been noted that on May 15, 1635, Henri Donaldson left London for Virginia on the Plaine Joan, the master of which was Richard Buckam. On May 28, 1635, Melaskus McKay was transported from the same port and to the same place, on board the Speedwell, Jo. Chappell, master. Dowgall Campbell and his wife Mary were living in Barbadoes, September 1678, as was also Patric Campel, in August 1679. Malcum Fraser was physician on board the Betty, that carried seventy-five "convicted rebells," one of whom was a woman, in 1685, sailed from Port Weymouth for the Barbadoes, and there sold into slavery. Many persons by name of Morgan also left various English ports during that century, but as they occur in conjunction with that of Welsh names it is probable they were from the same country.

NOTE B.

LETTER OF DONALD MACPHERSON.

Communication between the two countries was difficult and uncertain, which would inevitably, in a short time, stop friendly correspondence. More or less effort was made to keep up old friendships. The friends in the New World did not leave behind them their love for the Highlands, for home, for father and mother. The following curious letter has been preserved from Donald MacPherson, a young Highland lad, who had been sent to Virginia with Captain Toline, and was born near the house of Culloden where his father lived, and addressed to him. It was written about 1727:

"Portobago in Marilante, 2 June, 17—.

Teer Lofen Kynt Fater:

Dis is te lat ye ken, dat I am in quid healt, plessed be Got for dat, houpin te here de lyk frae yu, as I am yer nane sin, I wad a bine ill leart gin I had na latten yu ken tis, be kaptin Rogirs skep dat geangs te Innernes, per cunnan I dinna ket sika anither apertunti dis towmen agen. De skep dat I kam in was a lang tym o de see cumin oure heir, but plissis pi Got for a' ting wi a kepit our heels unco weel, pat Shonie Magwillivray dat hat ay sair heet. Dere was saxty o's a' kame inte te quintry hel a lit an lim an nane o's a' dyit pat Shonie Magwillivray an an otter Ross lad dat kam oure wi's an mai pi dem twa wad a dyit gintey hed bitten at hame. Pi mi fait I kanna kamplin for kumin te dis quintry, for mestir Nicols, Lort pliss hem, pat mi till a pra mestir, dey ca him Shon Bayne, an hi lifes in Marylant in te rifer Potomak, he nifer gart mi wark ony ting pat fat I lykit mi sel: de meast o a' mi wark is waterin a pra stennt hors, and pringin wyn an pread ut o de seller te mi mestir's tebil. Sin efer I kam til him I nefer wantit a pottle o petter ele nor isi m a' Shon Glass hous, for I ay set toun wi de pairns te dennir. Mi mestir seys til mi, fan I kon speek lyk de fouk hier dat I sanna pe pidden di nating pat gar his plackimors wurk, for de fyt fouk dinna ise te wurk pat te first yeer aftir dey kum in te de quintry. Tey speek a' lyk de sogers in Inerness. Lofen fater, fan de sarvants hier he deen wi der mestirs, dey grou unco rich, an its ne wonter for day mak a hantil o tombako; and des sivites anahels and de sheries an de pires grou in de wuds wantin tyks apout dem, De Swynes te ducks and durkies geangs en de wuds wantin mestirs. De tombako grous shust lyk de dockins en de bak o de lairts yart an de skeps dey kum fra ilka place an bys dem an gies a hantel o silder an gier for dem. Mi nane mestir kam til de quintry a sarfant an weil I wot hi's nou wort mony a susan punt. Fait ye mey pelive mi de pirest plantir hire lifes amost as weil as de lairt o Collottin. Mai pi fan mi tim is ut I wel kom hem an sie yu pat not for de fust nor de neest yeir til I gater somtig o mi nane, for I fan I ha dun wi mi mestir, hi maun gi mi a plantashon te set mi up, its de quistium hier in dis quintry; an syn I houp te gar yu trink wyn insteat o tippeni in Innerness. I wis I hat kum our hier twa or tri yiers seener nor I dit, syn I wad ha kum de seener hame, pat Got bi tanket dat I kam sa seen as I dit. Gin yu koud sen mi owr be ony o yur Innesness skeps, ony ting te mi, an it war as muckle clays as mak a quelt it wad, mey pi, gar mi meistir tink te mere o mi. It's tru I ket clays eneu fe him bat oni ting fe yu wad luck weel an pony, an ant plese Got gin I life, I sal pey yu pack agen. Lofen fater, de man dat

wryts dis letir for mi is van Shames Macheyne, hi lifes shust a myl fe mi, hi hes pin unko kyn te mi sin efer I kam te de quintrie. Hi wes porn en Petic an kom our a sarfant fe Klesgou an hes peen hes nane man twa yeirs, an has sax plockimors wurkin til hem alrety makin tombako ilka tay. Heil win hem, shortly an a' te geir dat he hes wun hier an py a lerts kip at hem. Luck dat yu duina forket te vryt til mi ay, fan yu ket ony occashion. Got Almichte plis yu Fater an a de leve o de hous, for I hana forkoten nane o yu, nor dinna yu forket mi, for plise Got I sal kum hem wi gier eneuch te di yu a' an mi nane sel guid. I weit yu will be veri vokie, fan yu sii yur nane sins fesh agen, for I heive leirt a hautle hevens sin I sau yu an I am unco buick leirt.
  A tis fe yur lofen an Opetient Sin,
Tonal Mackaferson.
Directed—For Shames Mackaferson neir te Lairt o Collottin's hous, neir Innerness en de Nort o Skotlan."*

NOTE C.

Emigration During the Eighteenth Century.

The emigration from the Highlands to America was so pronounced that the Scottish papers, notably the "'Edinburgh Evening Courant," the "Caledonian Mercury," and the "Scots Magazine," made frequent reference and bemoan its prevalence. It was even felt in London, for the "Gentleman's Magazine" was also forced to record it. While all these details may not be of great interest, yet to obtain a fair idea of this movement, some record will be of service.

The "Scots Magazine," for September 1769, records that the ship Molly sailed from Islay on August 21st of that year full of passengers to settle in North Carolina; which was the third emigration from Argyle "since the close of the late war." A subsequent issue of the same paper states that fifty-four vessels full of emigrants from the Western Islands and other parts of the Highlands sailed for North Carolina, between April and July 1770, conveying twelve hundred emigrants. Early in 1771, according to the "Scots Magazine," there were five hundred emigrants from Islay, and the adjacent Islands, preparing to sail in the following summer for America "under the conduct of a gentleman of wealth and merit whose predecessors resided in Islay for many centuries past." The paper farther notes that "there is a large

---

*Burt's Letters from the North of Scotland, Vol. I, p. 198.

colony of the most wealthy and substantial people in Skye making ready to follow the example of the Argathelians in going to the fertile and cheap lands on the other side of the Atlantic ocean. It is to be dreaded that these migrations will prove hurtful to the mother country; and therefore its friends ought to use every proper method to prevent them. These Skye men to the number of three hundred and seventy, in due time left for America. The September issue states that "several of them are people of property who intend making purchases of land in America. The late great rise of the rents in the Western Islands of Scotland is said to be the reason of this emigration.

The "Scots Magazine" states that the ship Adventure sailed from Loch Erribol, Sunday August 17, 1772, with upwards of two hundred emigrants from Sutherlandshire for North Carolina. There were several emigrations from Sutherlandshire that year. In June eight families arrived in Greenock, and two other contingents—one of one hundred and the other of ninety souls—were making their way to the same place en route to America. "The cause of this emigration they assign to be want of the means of livelihood at home, through the opulent graziers engrossing the frams, and turning them into pasture. Several contributions have been made for these poor people in towns through which they passed.

During the year 1773, emigrants from all parts of the Highlands sailed for America. The "Courant" of April 3, 1773, reports that "the unlucky spirit of emigration" had not diminished, and that several of the inhabitants of Skye, Lewis, and other places were preparing to emigrate to America during the coming summer "and seek for the sustenance abroad which they allege they cannot find at home." In its issue for July 3, 1773, the same paper states that eight hundred people from Skye were then preparing to go to North Carolina and that they had engaged a vessel at Greenock to carry them across the Atlantic. In the issue of the same paper for September 15th, same year, appears the gloomy statement that the people of Badenoch and Lochaber were in "a most pitiful situation for want of meal. They were reduced to live on blood which they draw from their cattle by repeated bleedings. Need we wonder to hear of emigrations from such a country." On September 1, 1773, according to the "Courant," a ship sailed from Fort William for America with four hundred and twenty-five men, women, and children, all from Knoydart, Lochaber, Appin, Mamore, and Fort William. "They were the finest set of fellows in the Highlands. It is allowed they carried at least £6000 sterling in ready cash with them; so that by this emigration the country is not only deprived of its men, but likewise of its wealth. The extravagant rents started by the landlords is the sole cause given for this spirit of emigration which seems to be only in its infancy." On September 29, 1773, the "Courant," after stating that there were from eight to ten vessels chartered to convey Highland emigrants during that season across the Atlantic, adds: "Eight hundred and forty people sailed from Lewis in July. Alarmed with this Lord Fortrose, their master, came down from London about five weeks ago to treat with the remainder of his tenants. What are the terms they asked of him, think you? 'The land at the old rents; the augmentation paid for three years backward to be refunded; and his factor to be immediately dismissed.'" The "Courant" added that unless these terms were conceded the island of Lewis would soon be an uninhabited waste. Notwithstanding the visit of lord Fortrose, emigration went on. The ship Neptune with one hundred and fifty emigrants from Lewis arrived in New York on August 23, 1773; and, according to the "Scots Magazine," between seven hundred and eight hundred emigrants sailed from Stornoway for America on June 23rd, of the same year.

The "Courant" for September 25, 1773, in a communication from Dornoch, states that on the 16th of that month there sailed from Dornoch Firth, the ship Nancy, with two hundred and fifty emigrants from Sutherlandshire for New York. The freight exceeded 650 guineas. In the previous year a ship from Sutherlandshire paid a freight of 650 guineas.

In October 1773, three vessels with seven hundred and seventy-five emigrants from Moray, Ross, Sutherland, and Caithness, sailed from Stromness for America.

The "Courant" for November 10, 1773, records that fifteen hundred people had left the county of Sutherland for America within the two preceding years. The passage money cost £3 10s each, and it was computed that on an average every emigrant brought £4 with him. "This amounts to £7500, which exceeds a year's rent of the whole county."

The "Gentleman's Magazine" for June 30, 1775, states that "four vessels, containing about seven hundred emigrants, have sailed for America from Port Glasgow and Greenock, in the course of the present month, most of them from the north Highlands:" The same journal for September 23rd, same year, says, "The ship Jupiter from Dunstaffnage Bay, with two hundred emigrants on board, chiefly from Argyleshire, set sail for North Carolina. They declare the oppressions of their landlords are such that they can no longer submit to them."

The perils of the sea did not deter them. Tales of suffering must have been heard in the glens. Some idea of these sufferings and what the emigrants were sometimes called upon to endure may be inferred from the following:

"In December (1773), a brig from Dornock, in Scotland, arrived at New York, with about 200 passengers, and lost about 100 on the passage."*

NOTE D.

APPEAL TO THE HIGHLANDERS LATELY ARRIVED FROM SCOTLAND.

Williamsburgh, November 23, 1775.

FRIENDS AND COUNTRYMEN:—A native of the same island, and on the same side of the Tweed with yourselves, begs, for a few moments, your serious attention. A regard for your happiness, and the security of your posterity, are the only motives that could have induced me to occupy your time by an epistolary exhortation. How far I may fall short of the object I have thus in view, becomes me not to surmise. The same claim, however, has he to praise (though, perhaps, never equally rewarded) who endeavors to do good, as he who has the happiness to effect his purpose. I hope, therefore, no views of acquiring popular fame, no partial or circumstantial motives, will be attributed to me for this attempt. If this, however, should be the case, I have the consolation to know that I am not the first, of many thousands, who have been censured unjustly.

I have been lately told that our Provincial Congress have appointed a Committee to confer with you, respecting the differences which at present subsist between Great Britain and her American Colonies; that they wish to make you their friends, and treat with you for that purpose; to convince you, by facts and argumentation, that it is necessary that every inhabitant of this Colony should concur in such measures as may, through the aid of a superintending Providence, remove those evils under which this Continent is at present depressed.

The substance of the present contest, as far as my abilities serve me to comprehend it, is, simply, whether the Parliament of Great Britain shall have the liberty to take away your property without your consent. It seems clear and obvious to me that it is wrong and dangerous they should have such a power; and that if they are able to carry this into execution, no man in this Country

---

*Holmes' Annals of America, Vol. II, p. 183.

has any property which he may safely call his own. Adding to the absurdity of a people's being taxed by a body of men at least three thousand miles distant, we need only observe that their views and sentiments are opposite to ours, their manners of living so different that nothing but confusion, injustice, and oppression could possibly attend it. If ever we are justly and righteously taxed, it must be by a set of men who, living amongst us, have an interest in the soil, and who are amenable to us for all their transactions.

It was not to become slaves you forsook your native shores. Nothing could have buoyed you up against the prepossessions of nature and of custom, but a desire to fly from tyranny and oppression. Here you found a Country with open arms ready to receive you; no persecuting landlord to torment you; none of your property exacted from you to support court favorites and dependants. Under these circumstances, your virtue and your interest were equally securities for the uprightness of your conduct; yet, independent of these motives, inducements are not wanting to attach you to the cause of liberty. No people are better qualified than you, to ascertain the value of freedom. They only can know its intrinsick worth who have had the misery of being deprived of it.

From the clemency of the English Nation you have little to expect; from the King and his Ministers still less. You and your forefathers have fatally experienced the malignant barbarity of a despotick court. You cannot have forgot the wanton acts of unparalleled cruelty committed during the reign of Charles II. Mercy and justice were then strangers to your land, and your countrymen found but in the dust a sanctuary from their distresses. The cries of age, and the concessions of youth, were uttered but to be disregarded; and equally with and without the formalities of law, were thousands of the innocent and deserving ushered to an untimely grave. The cruel and unmerited usage given to the Duke of Argyle, in that reign, cannot be justified or excused. No language can paint the horrors of this transaction; description falters on her way, and, lost in the labyrinth of sympathy and woe, is unable to perform the duties of her function. This unhappy nobleman had always professed himself an advocate for the Government under which he lived, and a friend to the reigning monarch. Whenever he deviated from these principles, it must have been owing to the strong impulses of honor, and the regard he bore to the rights of his fellow-creatures. 'It were endless, as well as shocking, (says an elegant writer,) to enumerate all the instances of persecution, or, in other words, of absurd tyranny, which at this time prevailed in Scotland. Even women were thought proper objects on whom they might exercise their ferocious and wanton dispositions; and three of that sex, for refusing to sign some test drawn up by tools of Administration, were devoted, without the solemnity of a trial, to a lingering and painful death.'

I wish, for the sake of humanity in general and the royal family in particular, that I could throw a veil over the conduct of the Duke of Cumberland after the last rebellion. The indiscriminate punishments which he held out equally to the innocent and the guilty, are facts of notoriety much to be lamented. The intention may possibly, in some measure, excuse, though nothing can justify the barbarity of the measure.

Let us, then, my countrymen, place our chief dependence on our virtue, and, by opposing the standard of despotism on its first appearance, secure ourselves against those acts in which a contrary conduct will undoubtedly plunge us. I will venture to say, that there is no American so unreasonable as even to wish you to take the field against your friends from the other side of the Atlantick. All they expect or desire from you is, to remain neutral, and to contribute your proportion of the expenses of the war. This will be sufficient testimony of your attachment to the cause they espouse. As you participate of the blessings of the soil, it is but reasonable that you should bear a proportionate part of the disadvantages attending it.

To the virtuous and deserving among the Americans, nothing can be more disagreeable than national reflections; they are, and must be, in the eyes of every judicious man, odious and contemptible, and bespeak a narrowness of soul which the virtuous are strangers to. Let not, then, any disrespectful epithets which the vulgar and illiterate may throw out, prejudice you against them; and endeavor to observe this general rule, dictated at least by humanity, 'that he is a good man who is engaged in a good cause.'

Your enemies have said you are friends to absolute monarchy and despotism, and that you have offered yourselves as tools in the hands of Administration, to rivet the chains forging for your brethren in America. I hope and think my knowledge of you authorizes the assertion that you are friends to liberty, and the natural and avowed enemies of tyranny and usurpation. All of you, I doubt not, came into the Country with a determined resolution of finishing here your days; nor dare I doubt but that, fired with the best and noblest species of human emulation, you would wish to transmit to the rising generation that best of all patrimonies, the legacy of freedom.

Private views, and offers of immediate reward, can only operate on base and unmanly minds. That soul in which the love of liberty ever dwelt must reject, with honest indignation, every idea of preferment, founded on the ruins of a virtuous and deserving people. I would have you look up to the Constitution of Britain as the best and surest safeguard to your liberties. Whenever an attempt is made to violate its fundamental principles, every effort becomes laudable which may tend to preserve its natural purity and perfection.

The warmest advocates for Administration have candor sufficient to admit that the people of Great Britain have no right to tax America. If they have not, for what are they contending? It will, perhaps, be answered, for the dignity of Government. Happy would it be for those who advance this doctrine to consider, that there is more real greatness and genuine magnanimity in acknowledging an error, than in persisting in it. Miserable must that state be, whose rulers, rather than give up a little punctilio, would endanger the lives of thousands of its subjects in a quarrel, the injustice and impropriety of which is universally acknowledged. If the Americans wish for anything more than is set forth in the address of the last Congress to the King and people of Great Britain —if independence is their aim—by removing their real grievances, their artificial ones (if any they should avow) will soon appear, and with them will their cause be deserted by every friend to limited monarchy, and by every well-wisher to the interests of America. I have endeavored, in this uncultivated homespun essay, to avoid prolixity as much as possibly I could. I have aimed at no flowers of speech, no touches of rhetorick, which are too often made use of to amuse, and not to instruct or persuade the understanding. I have no views but your good, and the credit of the Country from whence you came.

In case Government should prevail, and be able to tax America without the least show of representation, it would be to me a painful reflection to think, that the children of the land to which I owe my existence, should have been the cause of plunging millions into perpetual bondage.

If we cannot be of service to the cause, let us not be an injury to it. Let us view this Continent as a country marked out by the great God of nature as a receptacle for distress, and where the industrious and virtuous may range in the fields of freedom, happy under their own fig trees, freed from a swarm of petty tyrants, who disgrace countries the most polished and civilized, and who more particularly infest that region from whence you came.

Scotius Americanus."*

---

*American Archives, Fourth Series, Vol. III, p. 1649.

NOTE E.

Ingratitude of the Highlanders.

"Brigadier-General Donald McDonald was in rebellion in the year 1745, against his lawful sovereign, and headed many of the same clan and name, who are now his followers. These emigrants, from the charity and benevolence of the Assembly of North-Carolina, received large pecuniary contributions, and, to encourage them in making their settlements, were exempted from the payment of taxes for several years. It is a fact, that numbers of that ungrateful people, who have been lately in arms, when they arrived in Carolina, were without the necessaries of life—their passage even paid by the charitable contributions of the inhabitants. They have since, under every encouragement that the Province of North-Carolina could afford them, acquired fortunes very rapidly, and thus they requite their benefactor.—Virginia Gazette."*

NOTE F.

Were the Highlanders Faithful to their Oath Taken by the Americans?

General David Stewart, the faithful and admiring historian of the Highlanders, makes the following strange statements that need correction, especially in the view that the Highlander had a very high regard for his oath: After the battle of Guilford Court House "the British retired southward in the direction of Cross Creek, the Americans following close in the rear; but nothing of consequence occurred. Cross Creek, a settlement of emigrant Highlanders, had been remarkable for its loyalty from the commencement of the war, and they now offered to bring 1,500 men into the field, to be commanded by officers from the line, to find clothing and subsistence for themselves, and to perform all duties whether in front, flanks, or rear; and they required nothing but arms and ammunition. This very reasonable offer was not received, but a proposition was made to form them into what was called a provincial corps of the line. This was declined by the emigrant Highlanders, and after a negotiation of twelve days, they retired to their settlements, and the army marched for Wil-

---

*Ibid, Vol. IV, p. 983.

mington, where they expected to find supplies, of which they now stood in great need.

There was among these settlers a gentleman of the name of Macneil, who had been an officer in the Seven Years' War. He joined the army with several followers, but soon took his leave, having been rather sharply reprimanded for his treatment of a republican family. He was a man of tall stature, and commanding aspect, and moved, when he walked among his followers, with all the dignity of a chieftain of old. Retaining his loyalty, although offended with the reprimand, he offered to surprise the republican garrison, the governor, and council, assembled at Willisborough. He had three hundred followers, one-half of them old country Highlanders, the other half born in America, and the offspring of Highlanders. The enterprise was conducted with address, and the governor, council, and garrison, were secured without bloodshed, and immediately marched off for Wilmington, Macneil and his party travelling by night, and concealing themselves in swamps and woods by day. However, the country was alarmed, and a hostile force collected. He proceeded in zig-zag directions, for he had a perfect knowledge of the country, but without any provisions except what chance threw in his way. When he had advanced two-thirds of the route, he found the enemy occupying a pass which he must open by the sword, or perish in the swamps for want of food. At this time he had more prisoners to guard than followers. 'He did not secure his prisoners by putting them to death;' but, leaving them under a guard of half his force on whom he could least depend, he charged with the others sword in hand through the pass, and cleared it of the enemy, but was unfortunately killed from too great ardor in the pursuit. The enemy being dispersed, the party continued their march disconsolate for the loss of their leader; but their opponents again assembled in force, and the party were obliged to take refuge in the swamps, still retaining their prisoners. The British commander at Wilmington, hearing of Macneil's enterprise, marched out to his support, and kept firing cannon, in expectation the report would reach them in the swamps. The party heard the reports, and knowing that the Americans had no artillery, they ventured out of the swamps towards the quarter whence they heard the guns, and meeting with Major (afterwards Sir James) Craig, sent out to support them, they delivered over their prisoners half famished with hunger, and lodged them safely in Wilmington. Such partizans as these are invaluable in active warfare."*

---

*Sketches of the Highlanders, Vol. II, p. 119.

Dr. James Browne, who follows Stewart very closely, gives*
the first paragraph of the above quotation, but makes no reference
to the exploit of Macneil. Keltie who copies almost literally from
Dr. Browne, also gives † the first paragraph, but no reference to
the second.

General Stewart gives no clue as to the source of his information. If the number of Highlanders reported to have offered their services under such favorable conditions was true, lord Cornwallis was not in a position to refuse. He had been and still was on a very fatiguing campaign. His army was not only worn down but was greatly decimated by the fatigues of a long and harrassing march, and the results of two pitched battles. In his letter to Sir Henry Clinton, ‡ already quoted, not a word of this splendid relief is intimated. From lord Cornwallis' statement he must have made scarcely a stop at Cross Creek, in his flight from Guilford Court House to Wilmington. He says that at Cross Creek "there was not four days' forage within twenty miles"; that he "determined to move immediately to Wilmington," and that "the Highlanders have not had so much time as the people of the upper country, to prove the sincerity of their friendship."‖ This would amount to positive proof that the Highlanders did not offer their services. The language of lord Cornwallis to lord George Germain, under date of Wilmington, North Carolina, April 18th, 1781, is even stronger: "The principal reasons for undertaking the Winter's Campaign were, the difficulty of a defensive War in South Carolina, & the hopes that our friends in North Carolina, who were said to be very numerous, would make good their promises of assembling & taking an Active part with us, in endeavouring to re-establish His Majesty's Government. Our experience has shown that their numbers are not so great as had been represented and that their friendship was only passive; For we have received little assistance from them since our arrival in the province, and altho' I gave the *strongest* & *most pulick assurances* that after refitting & depositing our Sick and Wounded, I *should return to the upper Country*, not above two hundred have been prevailed upon to follow us either as Provincials or Militia." Colonel Tarleton, the principal officer under lord Cornwallis, observes: "Notwithstanding the cruel persecution the inhabitants of Cross creek had constantly endured for their partiality to the British, they yet retained great zeal for the interest of the royal

---

*History of the Highland Clans, Vol. IV, p. 274.   †History of the Highland Clans, Vol. II, p. 473.   ‡See page 141.   ‖Cornwallis' Letter to Sir Henry Clinton, April 10, 1781.

army. All the flour and spirits in the neighborhood were collected and conveyed to camp, and the wounded officers and soldiers were supplied with many conveniences highly agreeable and refreshing to men in their situation. After some expresses were dispatched to lord Rawdon, to advertise him of the movements of the British and Americans, and some wagons were loaded with provisions, earl Cornwallis resumed his march for Wilmington."* Not a word is said of the proposed reinforcement by the Highlanders. Stedman, who was an officer under lord Cornwallis, and was with him in the expedition, says: † "Upon the arrival of the British commander at Cross Creek, he found himself disappointed in all his expectations: Provisions were scarce: Four days' forage not to be procured within twenty miles; and the communication expected to be opened between Cross Creek and Wilmington, by means of the river, was found to be impracticable, the river itself being narrow, its banks high, and the inhabitants, on both sides, for a considerable distance, inveterately hostile. Nothing therefore now remained to be done but to proceed with the army to Wilmington, in the vicinity of which it arrived on the seventh of April. The settlers upon Cross Creek, although they had undergone a variety of persecutions in consequence of their previous unfortunate insurrections, still retained a warm attachment to their mother-country, and during the short stay of the army amongst them, all the provisions and spirits that could be collected within a convenient distance, were readily brought in, and the sick and wounded plentifully supplied with useful and comfortable refreshments." Again he says (page 348): "Lord Cornwallis was greatly disappointed in his expectations of being joined by the loyalists. Some of them indeed came within the lines, but they only remained a few days." Nothing however occurs concerning Highland enlistments or their desire so to engage with the army. General Samuel Graham, then an officer in Fraser's Highlanders, in his "Memoirs," though speaking of the march to Cross Creek, is silent about Highlanders offering their services. Nor is it at all likely, that, in the sorry plight the British army reached Cross Creek in, the Highlanders would unite, especially when the outlook was gloomy, and the Americans were pressing on the rear.

As to the exploit of Macneil, beyond all doubt, that is a confused statement of the capture of Governor Burke, at Hillsboro, by the notorious Colonel David Fanning. This was in Septem-

---
*Campaigns of 1780-1781, p. 281. †History of the American War, Vol. II, p. 352.

ber 1781. His report states, "We killed 15 of the rebels, and wounded 20; and took upwards of 200 prisoners; amongst them was the Governor, his Council, and part of the Continental Colonels, several captains and subalterns, and 71 continental soldiers out of a church." Colonel Fanning was a native of Wake County, North Carolina, and had no special connection with the Highlanders; but among his followers were some bearing Highland names. The majority of his followers, who were little better than highway robbers, had gathered to his standard as the best representative of the king in North Carolina, after the defeat at Moore's Creek.

There is not and never has been a Willisborough in North Carolina. There is a Williamsboro in Granville county, but has never been the seat of government even for a few days. Hillsboro, practically, was the capital in 1781.

The nearest to an organization of Highlanders, after Moore's Creek, was Hamilton's Loyal North Carolina regiment; but this was made up of refugees from over all the state.

It is a fact, according to both history and tradition, that after the battle of Moore's Creek, the Highlanders as a race were quiet. The blow at Moore's Creek taught them a needed lesson, and as an organization gave no more trouble. Whatever numbers, afterwards entered the British service, must have been small, and of little consequence.

NOTE G.

MARVELLOUS ESCAPE OF CAPTAIN MCARTHUR.

The following narration I find in the "Celtic Magazine," vol. I. 1875-76, pp. 209-213 and 241-245. How much of it is true I am unable to discover. Undoubtedly the writer, in some parts, draws on his imagination. Unfortunately no particulars are given concerning either the previous or subsequent life of Captain McArthur. We are even deprived of the knowledge of his Christian name, and hence cannot identify him with the same individual mentioned in the text.

Upon the defeat of the Highlanders at Moore's Creek, "Captain McArthur of the Highland Regiment of Volunteers, was apprehended and committed to the county jail in the town of Cross-Creek. But the gallant officer determined to make a death grasp for effecting his escape; and happily for him the walls of his confinement were not of stone and mortar. In his lonely prison, awaiting his fate, and with horrid visions of death haunting him, he summons up his muscular strength and courage, and with incredible exertion he broke through the jail by night, and once more enjoyed the sweets of liberty. Having thus made his escape he soon found his way to the fair partner of his joys and sorrows. It needs hardly be said that her astonishment was only equalled by her raptures of joy. She, in fact, became so overpowered with the unexpected sight that she was for the moment quite overcome, and unable to comply with the proposal of taking an immediate flight from the enemy's country. She soon, however, regains her sober senses, and is able to grasp the reality of the situation, and fully prepared with mental nerve and courage to face the scenes of hardship and fatigue which lay before them. The thought of flight was, indeed, a hazardous one. The journey to the sea board was far and dangerous; roads were miserably constructed, and these, for the most part, had to be avoided; unbroken forests, immense swamps, and muddy creeks were almost impassable barriers; human habitations were few and far between, and these few could scarcely be looked to as hospitable asylums; enemies would be on the lookout for the capture of the 'Old Tory,' for whose head a tempting reward had been offered; and withal, the care of a tender infant lay heavy upon the parental hearts, and tended to impede their flight. Having this sea of troubles looming before them, the imminent dangers besetting their path, you can estimate the heroism of a woman who was prepared to brave them all. But when you further bear in mind that she had been bred in the ease and delicate refinements of a lairdly circle at home, you can at once conceive the hardships to be encountered vastly augmented, and the moral heroism necessary for such an undertaking to be almost incredible, finding its parallel only in the life of her famous countrywoman, the immortal 'Flora.' Still, life is dear, and a desperate attempt must be made to preserve it—she is ready for any proposal. So off they start at the dead hour of midnight, taking nothing but the scantiest supply of provisions, of which our heroine must be the bearer, while the hardy sire took his infant charge in his folded plaid over one shoulder, with the indispensable musket slung over the other. Thus equipped for the march, they trudge over the heavy sand, leaving the scattered town of Cross-Creek behind in the distance, and soon find themselves lost to all human vision in the midst of the dense forest. There is not a moment to lose; and onward they speed under cover of night for miles and miles, and for a time keeping the main road to the coast. Daylight at length lightened their path, and bright sunrays are pouring through the forest. But that which had lightened the path of the weary fugitives had, at the same time, made wonderful disclosures behind. The morning light had revealed to the astonished gaze of the keeper of the prison the flight of his captive. The consternation among the officials is easily imagined. A detachment of cavalry was speedily dispatched in pursuit; a handsome reward was offered for the absconded rebel, and a most barbarous punishment was in reserve for him in the event of his being captured. With a knowledge of these facts, it will not be matter of surprise that the straits and perplexities of a released captive had already commenced. Who can fancy their terror when the noise of cavalry in the distance admonished them that the enemy was already in hot pursuit, and had taken the right scent. What could they do! Whither could they fly? They dart off the road in an instant and began a race. But alas, of what use, for the tall pines of the forest could afford no shelter or concealment before the pursuers could reach the spot. In their extremity they change their course, running almost in the face of the foe. They rush into the under brush covert of a gum pond which crossed the road close by, and there, in terrible suspense, awaited their fate, up to the knees in water. In a few moments the equestrians, in full gallop, are within a gunshot of them. But on reaching the pond they slacken their speed, and all at once came to a dead halt! Had they already discovered their prey? In an instant their fears were relieved on this score. From their marshy lair they were able, imperfectly, to espy the foe, and they saw that the cause of halting was simply to water their panting steeds. They could also make out to hear the enemy's voice, and so far as they could gather, the subject was enough to inspire them with terror, for the escaped prisoner was evidently the exciting topic. Who could mistake the meaning of such detached prases and epithets as these—'Daring fellow,' 'Scotch dog,' 'British slup,' and 'Steel fix him.' And who can realize the internal emotion of him whom they immediately and unmistakably concerned? But the fates being propitious, the posse of cavalry resumed their course, first in a slow pace, and afterwards in a lively canter, until they were out of sight and out of hearing.

This hair-breadth escape admonished our hero that he must shift his course and avoid the usual route of communication with the coast. The thought struck him, that he would direct his course towards the Cape Fear river, which lay some ten miles to the right; feeling confident, at the same time, that his knowledge of the water in early days could now be made available, if he could only find something in the shape of a boat. And, besides, he saw to his dismay that his fair partner in travel, however ardent in spirit, could not possibly hold out under the hardships incident to

APPENDIX. 433

the long journey at first meditated. For the Cape Fear river then they set off; and after a wearisome march, through swamp and marsh, brush and brier, to the great detriment of their scanty wardrobe and danger of life and limb, they reached the banks of that sluggish stream before the sun had set, foot sore and dispirited, exhausted and downcast. But what is their chance of a boat now? Alas, not even the tiniest craft could be seen. There is nothing for it but to camp in the open air all night and try to refresh their weary limbs and await to see what luck the following morn had in store. Fortunately for them the climate was warm, too much so indeed, as they had found, to their great discomfort, during the day that was now past. In their present homeless situation, however, it was rather opportune; and there was nothing to fear, unless from the effects of heavy dew, or the expected invasion of snakes and mosquitoes. But for these there was a counteracting remedy. The thick foliage of a stately tree afforded ample protection from dew, while a blazing fire, struck from the musket flint, defied the approach of any infesting vermin or crawling reptiles, and also answered the needed purpose of setting to rights their hosiery department which had suffered so much during the day. Here they are snug and cozy, under the arching canopy, which nature had provided, and prepared to do fair justice to the scanty viands and refreshments in their possession, before betaking themselves to their nocturnal slumbers which nature so much craved. But can we take leave of our pilgrims for the night without taking a glance at the innocent babe as it lay upon the folded plaid in blissful ignorance of the cares and anxieties which racked the parental breast. The very thought of its sweet face and throbbing little heart as it breathed in unconscious repose under the open canopy of heaven, was enough to entwine a thousand new chords of affection around the heart of its keepers, like the clasping ivy around the tree which gave them shelter, and to nerve them anew, for its sake, for the rough and perilous journey upon which they had entered. The fond mother imprints a kiss upon its cheek, and moistens it with tears of mingled joy and grief, and clasping it to her bosom is instantly absorbed in the sweet embrace of Morpheus. The hardy sire, it was agreed, would keep the first watch and take his rest in turn, the latter part of the night. He is now virtually alone, in deep and pensive meditation. He surveys with tender solicitude his precious charge, which was dearer to him than his own life, and for whose sake he would risk ten lives. He paces the sward during the night watches. He meditates his plans for the following day. He deliberates and schemes how he can take advantage of the flow-ing sheet of water before him, for the more easy conveyance of his precious belongings. The mode of travel hitherto adopted, he saw, to be simply impossible. The delay involved might be ruinous to his hopes. With these cogitations he sat down, without bringing any plan to maturity. He gazed at the burning embers as if in a reverie, and as he gazed he thought he had seen, either by actual vision or by the 'second sight,' in which he was a firm believer, the form of a canoe with a single sable steersman coming to his rescue. He felt tempted to communicate the vision to his sleeping partner; but, thinking it unkind to disturb her slumbers, he desists from his resolution, reclines on the ground, and without intending it, he falls fast asleep. But imagine his astonishment and alarm when he came to consciousness, to find that he had slept for three full hours without interruption. He could hardly realize it, the interval seemed like an instant. However, all was well; his wife and babe were still enjoying unbroken rest, and no foe had discovered their retreat; and withal, the gladsome light of day is now breaking in around them and eclipsing the glare of the smouldering embers. Up starts our hero much refreshed and invigorated, and exulting in surprising buoyancy of spirit for running the race of the new day now ushering in. He withdraws a gunshot from the camp; and what does he descry in the grey dawn but, apparently, a small skiff with a single rower crossing the river towards them, but a short distance down the stream. The advancing light of day soon confirmed his hopes. He at once started in the direction of the skiff, having armed himself with his loaded musket, and resolved to get possession of it by fair means or by foul. A few minutes brought him to the spot, and to his great astonishment he found himself in the undisputed possession of the object of his wishes, a tiny little canoe drawn up on the beach. In connection with the night's vision he would have positively declared that there was something supernatural in the affair, but having marked the bare footprints of its late occupant on the muddy soil, and heard the rustling of leaves in the distance, calling attention to the woolly head of its owner getting out of sight through the bush, and making his way for a neighboring plantation. He could explain the event upon strict natural principles. The happy coincidence, however, filled him with emotions of joy, in so readily securing the means of an earlier and more expeditious transit. He retraces his steps and joins his little circle, and in joyous ecstacy relates to his sympathetic spouse, just aroused from her long slumbers, the tenor of his lucky adventure. There is now no time to lose. The crimson rays of the rising sun peering through a dense morning atmosphere and a dense forest, are reflected upon the surface of the stream to which they are about to commit their fortune, and admonish them to be off. They break their fast upon the remnants of the dry morsels with which they last appeased their hunger. This dispatched, they hasten to the beach, and speedily embark, seating themselves with the utmost caution in the narrow hull, which good luck and Sambo had placed at their disposal, and with less apprehension of danger from winds and waves than from the angry billows of human passion. A push from the shore and the voyage is fairly and auspiciously begun, the good lady seated in the prow in charge of the tender object of her unremitting care, and giving it the shelter of her parasol from the advancing rays of the sun, and the skilful Palinurus himself squatted in the stern, with a small paddle in his hand, giving alternate strokes, first to the right and then to the left, and thus, with the aid of the slow current propelling his diminutive barque at the rate of about six knots an hour, and enjoying the simultaneous pleasure of 'paddling his own canoe.' Onward they glide, smoothly and pleasantly, over the unruffled water, the steersman taking occasional rests from his monotonous strokes, while having the satisfaction of noting some progress by the flow of the current. Thus, hours passed away without the occurrence of anything worth noting, except the happy reflection that their memorable encampment was left several leagues in the distance. But lo! here is the first interruption to their navigation! About the hour of noon a mastless hull is seen in the distance. Their first impulse was fear, but this was soon dispelled on discovering it to be a flat or 'pole boat,' without sail or rigging, used for the conveyance of merchandise to the head of navigation, and propelled by long poles which the hardy craftsmen handled with great dexterity. It was, in fact, the steamer of the day, creating upon its arrival the same stir and bustle that is now caused by its more agreeable and efficient substitute, the 'Flora Macdonald.' The sight of this advancing craft, however, suggested the necessity of extreme caution, and of getting out of its way for a time. The Highland royalist felt greatly tempted to wait and hail the crew, whom he felt pretty sure to be his own friendly countrymen, and who, like their sires, in the case of prince Charlie, thirty years before, would scorn to betray their brother Celt, even for the gold of Carolina. Still, like the royal outlaw in his wanderings, he also deemed it more prudent to conceal his whereabouts even from his most confidential friends. He at once quits the river, and thus for a good while suspends his navigation. He takes special precaution to secure his little transport by drawing it a considerable distance from the water, a feat which required no great effort. The party stroll out of the way, and up the rising beach, watching for a time the tardy movement of the 'flat.' Tired of this they continue their slow ramble further into the interior, in hopes, at the same time, of making some accidental discovery by which to replenish their commissariat, which was quite empty, and made their steps faint and feeble, for it was now considerably past noon. As 'fortune favors the brave' they did succeed in making a discovery. They saw 'the opening' of a small plantation in the forest, an event which, in Carolina, is hailed with immense satisfaction by those who chance to lose their way in the woods, as suggestive of kindness and hospitality. Nothing short of such a treatment woud be expected by our adventurers as a matter of course, if they could only afford to throw themselves upon the hospitality of settlers. In their situation, however, they must take their bearings with anxious circumspection, and weigh the consequences of the possibility of their falling into the hands of foes. But here, all of a sudden, their path is intercepted by the actual presence of a formidable foe. One of the pursuers? No, but one equally defiant. It is a huge serpent of the 'Whip snake' species, which never gives way, but always takes a bold and defiant stand. It took its stand about fifty yards ahead, ready for battle, its head, and about a yard of its length, in semi-erect posture, and displaying every sign of its proverbial enmity to Adam's race. It has no poison, but its mode of attack is still more horrible, by throwing itself with electric speed in coils around its antagonist, tight as the strongest cord, and lashing with a yard of its tail, till it puts its combatant to death. Knowing its nature, the assailed levels his piece, and in an instant leaves the assailant turning a thousand somersaults until its strength is spent, and, is at last, wriggling on the ground.

The discharge of the musket was the signal to those within hearing that somebody was about. It awakened to his senses an old negro, the honest 'Uncle Ned,' and brought him to the edge of the 'clearing,' in order to satisfy his curiosity, and to see if it was 'old Massa' making an unceremonious visit to the farm of which Ned was virtually overseer. Our disconsolate party could not avoid an interview even if they would. They summoned their courage and affected to feel at ease. And truly they might, for Ned, like the class to which he belonged, would never dream of asking impertinent questions of any respectable white man, his known duty being to answer, not to ask, questions. Our weary party invited themselves to 'Uncle Ned's' cabin, which stood in the edge of the clearing close by, and turned out to be a tidy log cottage. The presiding divinity, of its single apartment was our

APPENDIX. 437

kind hostess, 'Aunt Lucy,' Ned's better half, who felt so highly charmed and flattered by the visit of such distinguished guests that she scarcely knew what she was saying or doing. She dropt her lighted pipe on the floor, hustled and scraped and curt-sied to the gentle lady over and over, and caressed the beautiful little 'Missie' with emotions which bordered on questionable kindness. This ovation over, our hungry guests began to think of the chief object of their visit—getting something in the shape of warm luncheon—and with this in view they eyed with covetous interest the large flock of fine plump pullets about the door. There was fine material for a feast to begin with. The hint was given to 'Aunt Lucy,' and when that aged dame became conscious of the great honor thus to be conferred upon her, she at once set to work in the culinary department with a dexterity and skill of art which is incredible to those who are ignorant of the great speciality of negresses. There was sudden havoc among the poultry, and fruit and vegetables found their way from the corn field in abundant variety to the large chimney place. Meanwhile the captain shouldered his piece and brought, from an adjacent thicket, two large fox squirrels to add to the variety of the feast, extorting from the faithful Ned the flattering compliment 'b' gollies, Boss, you is the best shot I ever see'd.' Preparation is rapidly advancing, and so is the appetite of the longing expectants. But such preparation was not the work of a moment, especially, from the scantiness of Lucy's cooking utensils. So the guests thought they would withdraw for a time in order to relieve the busy cook of all ceremony, and at the same time relieve themselves of the uncomfortable reflection of three blazing fires in the chimney place. After partaking of a few slices of a delicious water-melon, they retired to the shade of a tree in the yard, and there enjoyed a most refreshing nap. In due course the sumptuous meal is ready; the small table is loaded with a most substantial repast, the over plus finding a receptacle upon the board floor of the apartment, which was covered with white sand. It is needless to say that the guests discharged their duty with great gusto, notwithstanding the absence of any condiments, save pepper and salt, in their case hunger being the best sauce. Who but an epicure could grumble at the repast before them? What better than stewed fowls and squirrels, boiled rice, Indian hoe cake and yams smoking hot from the ashes, squashes, pumpkin pies and apple dumpling, and all this followed by a course of fruit, peaches and apples, musk and water-melons, all of a flavor and size inconceivable by any but the inhabitants of the sunny climes which brought them to maturity. Her ladyship could not help making the contrast with a service of fruit upon an extra occasion in her home circle, which cost several golden guineas, and yet was not to be compared with that furnished for the merest trifle by these sable purveyors—so much for the sun rays of the latitude. There was, however, the absence of any beverage stronger than water, not even tea, a name which the humble hostess scarcely comprehended. But a good substitute was readily presented, in the form of strong coffee, without cream or sugar. It was now drawing late in the afternoon, and our party refreshed and delighted with their adventure, must begin to retrace their steps towards the canoe. The reckoning was soon settled. A few shillings, the idex of the late regime of George in the colony, more than satisfied all demands, and surpassed all expectations. But the fair visitor was not content, without leaving an additional, and more pleasant memento. She took a beautiful gold ring, bearing the initials B. J. C., and placed it upon the swarthy finger of 'Aunt Lucy,' with many thanks and blessings for her kindness, on that eventful occasion. This kindly expression was heartily reciprocated by the negress, and responded by a flood of tears from her eyes, and a volley of blessings from her lips. The party bade a final adieu to their entertainers, and they had to veto their pressing offer of escorting them to the river. Off they went, leaving the aged couple gazing after them, and lost in amazement as to who they could be, or whither they were going, and all the more astonished that the mysterious visitors had supplied themselves with such a load of the leavings of the repast.

The navigation was at length resumed, and onward they glide as before, without the sight of anything to obstruct their course. Their prosperous voyaging continued till about midnight, for they resolved to continue their course during the whole night, unless necessity compelled them to do otherwise. Long before this hour, the mother and child resigned themselves to sleep, which was only interrupted by occasional starts, while the indefatigable steersman watched his charge, and plied his vocation with improving expertness. At this hour again, in the dim light of the crescent moon, a second 'pole boat' was discovered making towards them, but which they easily avoided by rowing to the opposite side of the river, thus continuing their course, and escaping observation. In passing the 'flat' an animated conversation was overheard among the hands, from which it was easily gathered that the escape of the rebel was the engrossing topic in the town of Wilmington, the place of their departure, and towards which the rebel himself was now finding his way as fast as the tide and padle could carry him. At present, however, he felt no cause of alarm. One of the hands speaking in vulgar English accent was heard to depone, 'By George if I could only get that prize I'd be a happy man, and would go back to old h-England.' To this base insinuation a threatening proof was administered by other parties, who replied in genuine Gaelic idiom and said, 'It's yourself that would need to have the face and the conscience, the day you would do that;' and they further signified their readiness to render any assistance to their brave countryman should opportunity offer. Those parties were readily recognized from their accent to be no other than Captain McArthur's intimate acquaintances, Sandie McDougall and Angus Ray, and who were so well qualified from their known strength and courage to render most valuable assistance in any cause in which their bravery might be enlisted. If he only gave them the signal of his presence they would instantly fly into his service and share his fate. However, it was deemed the wisest course to pass on, and not put their prowess to the test. Hours had now passed in successful progress without notice or interruption; and they are at long last approaching Wilmington, their seaport, but a considerable distance from the mouth of the river. The question is how are they to pass it, whether by land or water, for it is now approaching towards day. What is to be done must be done without a moment's delay. It is at length resolved to hazard the chance of passing it by canoe rather than encountering the untried perils of a dismal swamp. The daring leader puts his utmost strength to the test, striking the water right and left with excited vigor. His feeling is 'now or never'; for he knew this to be the most critical position of his whole route; unless he could get past it before break of day his case was hopeless. The dreaded town is at length in view, engendering fear and terror, but not despair. Several large crafts are seen lying at the wharf, and lights are reflected from adjacent shipping offices. Two small boats are observed crossing the river, and in rather uncomfortable proximity. With these exceptions the inhabitants are evidently in the enjoyment of undisturbed repose, and quite unconscious of the phenomenon of such a notorious personage passing their doors with triumphant success. Scarcely a word was heard, it was like a city of the dead. Who can imagine the internal raptures of our lucky hero, on leaving behind him, in the distance, that spot upon which his fate was suspended, and in having the consciousness that he is now not far from the goal of safety. Even now there are signals which cheer his heart. He begins already to inhale the ocean breeze, and from that he derives an exhilirating sensation such as he had not experienced for many years. He gets the benefit of the ocean tide, fortunately, in his favor, and carrying his

little hull upon its bosom at such a rate as to supersede the use of
the paddle except in guiding the course. The ocean wave, however, is scarcely so favorable. It rocks and rolls their frail abode
in such a way as to threaten to put a sad finish to the successful
labors of the past. There is no help for it but to abandon the
canoe a few miles sooner than intended. There is, however, little
cause for complaint, for they can now see their way clear to their
final terminus, if no untoward circumstance arises. They leave
the canoe on the beach, parting with it forever, but not without a
sigh of emotion, as if bidding farewell to a good friend. But the
paddle they cling to as a memento of its achievements, the operator remarking—'It did me better service than any sword ever put
into my hand.' A few miles walk from the landing, which is on
the southern shore of the estuary, and they are in sight of a small
hamlet, which lies upon the shore. And what is more inspiring of
hope and courage, they are in sight of a vessel of considerable
tonnage, lying at anchor off the shore, and displaying the British
flag, floating in the morning breeze, evidently preparing to hoist
sail. Now is their chance. This must be their ark of safety if
they are ever to escape such billows of adversity as they have been
struggling with for some days past. To get on board is that upon
which their hearts are set, and all that is required in order to defy
all enemies and pursuers. Not thinking that there is anything in
the wind in this pretty hamlet, they make straight for the vessel,
but they go but a few paces in that direction before another crisis
turns up. Enemies are still in pursuit. A small body of men, apparently under commission, are observed a short distance beyond
the hamlet as if anticipating the possibility of the escaped prisoner
making his way to the British ship. Nor is the surmise groundless, as the signal proves. In their perplexity the objects of pursuit have to lie in ambush and await the course of events. Their
military pursuers are now wending their way in the opposite direction until they are almost lost to view. Now is the time for a
last desperate effort. They rush for the shore, and there accost a
sallow lank-looking boatman followed by a negro, on the lookout
for custom, in their marine calling. A request is made for their
boat and services, for conveyance to the ship. At first the man
looks suspicious and sceptical, but on expostulation that there was
the utmost necessity for an interview with the captain before sailing, and important dispatches to be sent home, and a hint given
that a fee for services in such a case was of no object, he at once
consents; the ferry boat is launched, and in a few minutes the
party are off from the shore. But the military party observing
these movements begin to retrace their steps in order to ascertain

what all this means, and who the party are. They put to their heels and race towards the shore as fast as their feet can carry them. They feel tantalised to find that they have been sleeping at their post, and that the very object of their search is now halfway to the goal of safety. They signal and halloo with all their might, but getting no answer they fire a volley of shot in the direction of the boat. This has no effect, except for an instant, to put a stop to the rowing. The boatman gets alarmed as he now more than guesses who the noted passenger is, and he signifies his determination to put back and avoid the consequences that may be fatal to himself. The hero puts a sudden stop to further parley. He flings a gold sovereign to the swarthy rower, commands him simply to fulfil his promise, but to refund the balance of change upon their return from the ship—'he must see the captain before sailing.' To enforce his command the sturdy Highlander, who was more than a match for the two, took up his loaded musket and intimated what the consequences would be if they refused to obey orders. This had the desired effect. The rowers pulled with might and main, and in a few minutes the passengers were left safe and sound on board the gallant ship, and surrounded by a sympathising and hospitable crew. The fugitives were at last safe, despite rewards and sanguine pursuers. But their situation they could scarcely realize, their past life seemed more like a dream than a reality. Our brave heroine was again quite overcome. The reaction was too much for her nerves. In being led to the cabin she would have fallen prostrate on the deck had she not been supported. And who can wonder, in view of her fatigues and privations, her hair-breadth escapes and mental anxieties. But she survived it all. Sails are now hoisted to the favoring breeze, anchor weighed, and our now rejoicing pilgrims bade a lasting farewell to the ever memorable shores of Carolina. In care of the courteous commander they, in due time, reached their island home in the Scottish Highlands, and there lived to a good old age in peace and contentment. They had the pleasure of seeing the tender object of their solicitude grow up to womanhood, and afterwards enjoying the blessings of married life. And the veteran officer himself found no greater pleasure in whiling away the hours of his repose than in rehearsing to an entranced auditory, among the stirring scenes of the American Revolution, the marvellous story of his own fate; the principal events of which are here hurriedly and imperfectly sketched from a current tradition among his admiring countrymen in the two hemispheres."—*John Darroch.*

NOTE H.

HIGHLANDERS IN SOUTH CAROLINA.

There was no distinctively Highland settlement in South Carolina, although there was quite an influx of emigrants of this class into the province. Efforts were made to divert the Highlanders into the new settlements. As early as 1716 Governor Daniel informed the Assembly that he had bought thirty of the Highland Scots rebels at £30 per head, for whom the London agent had petitioned, and requested power to purchase more. This purchase was sanctioned by the Assembly, but wished no more "till we see how these behave themselves." On August 4th another issue of £15000 in bills was authorized to be stamped to pay for these Scots, who were to be employed as soldiers in defending the province.

Inducements were held out to the Highlanders, who had left their homes after the battle of Culloden, to settle in South Carolina. The "High Hills of Santee," which lie between Lynche's creek and the Wateree, in what is now Sumter County, were designed for them. The exiles, however, baffled by contrary winds, were driven into the Cape Fear, and from thence a part of them crossed and settled higher up, in what is now Darlington County, the rest having taken up their abode in North Carolina.

The war fever engendered by the Revolution was exhibited by these people, some of whom, at least, took up arms against their adopted country. October 31, 1776, at Charleston, South Carolina, the following, who had been taken prisoners by the navy, signed their parole, which also stipulated that they should go to Salisbury, North Carolina:

Dun McNicol, Cap. R. H. E., Hugh Fraser, Lieut. R. H. E., Dun MacDougall, Walter Cunningham, Angus Cameron, Laughlin McDonald, Hector McQuary, Alexr. Chisholm.

"We also undertake for Neal McNicol, James Fraser, Alexr. McDonald & David Donaldson, that they shall be on the same footing with ourselves."*

"Jany 28. 177.

These are to certify that Duncan Nicol, Hugh Fraser, Alex. Chisholm, Angs. Cameron, Lach. MacDonald, Hector McQuarrie, Walter Cunningham, Duncan MacDougall, Alen. McDonald, David Donaldson, Jas. Fraser, Niel McNicol—prisoners of war

---

*North Carolina Colonial Records, Vol. X, p. 830.

from the neighboring state of South Carolina have been on Parole in this town and within ten miles Y. of for upwards of ten weeks —during which time they have behaved themselves agreeable to their Parole and that they are now removed to Halifax by order of the commanding officer of the District, in order to be forwarded to the northward agreeable to order of Congress.

(Signed) Duncan McNicol, Capt., Hugh Fraser, Lieut. R. H. E., Alex. McDonald, James Fraser, David Donaldson, Niel McNicol, Alex Chisholm, Angus Cameron, Lach McDonald, Hector Mc Quarrie, Walter Cunningham, Privates, Dun, McDougall, Ensign.

N. B. The Parole of the prisoners of war above mentd was sent to the Congress at Halifax, at their last sitting. They are now sent under the direction of Capt. Martin Fifer—Certified by orders of Committee at Salisbury this 28 Jan'y, 1777.
(Signed) May Chambers, Chr. Com."*

NOTE I.

ALEXANDER MCNAUGHTON.

Miss Jennie M. Patten of Brush, Colorado, a descendant of Alexander McNaughton, in a letter dated Feb. 26th, 1900, gives some very interesting facts, among which may be related that at the close of the Revolution all of the Highland settlers of Washington county would have been sent to Canada, had it not been for Hon. Edward Savage, son-in-law of Alexander McNaughton, who had been an officer in the Revolutionary army, and had sufficient influence to prevent his wife's relatives and friends being sent out of the country on account of their tory proclivities. They considered that they had sworn allegiance to the king, and considered themselves perjured persons if they violated their oath. This idea appeared to be due from the fact that the land given to them was in "the name of the king." From this the colonists thought the land was given to them by the king.

The colonists did not all come to Washington county to occupy the land allotted to them, for some remained where they had settled after the collapse of Captain Campbell's scheme, but those who did settle in Argyle were related either by blood, or else by marriage.

Alexander McNaughton came to America in 1738, accom-

*Ibid, Vol. XI, p. 370.

panied by his wife, Mary McDonald, and his children, John, Moses, Eleanor and Jeannette. They first settled at a place called Kaket, where they lived several years, when they removed up the river to Tappan, and there continued until the grant was made in Argyle. Alexander McNaughton died at the home of his son-in-law, Edward Savage, near Salem, and was buried on the land that had been granted him. The first to be interred in the old Argyle cemetery was the daughter Jeannette. The wife, Mary, died on the way home from Burgoyne's camp. The children of the colonists were loyal Americans, although many of the colonists had been carried to the British camp for protection.

NOTE J.

ALLAN McDONALD'S COMPLAINT TO THE PRESIDENT OF CONGRESS.

"Philadelphia, March 25, 1776.

Sir: It is now several weeks since the Scotch inhabitants in and about Johnstown, Tryon County, have been required by General Schuyler to deliver up their arms; and that each and all of them should parade in the above place, that he might take from this small body six prisoners of his own nomination. The request was accordingly complied with, and five other gentlemen with myself were made prisoners of. As we are not conscious of having acted upon any principle that merits such severe proceedings from Congress, we cannot help being a good deal surprised at such treatment; but are willing to attribute this rather to malicious, ill-designing people, than to gentlemen of so much humanity and known character as the Congress consists of. The many difficulties we met with since our landing on this Continent, (which is but very lately,) burdened with women and children, we hope merit a share in their feeling; and that they would obtain the surest conviction, before we were removed from our families; as, by a separation of the kind, they are rendered destitute, and without access to either money or credit. This is the reason why you will observe, in the article of capitulation respecting the Scotch, that they made such a struggle for having their respective families provided for in their absence. The General declared he had no discretionary power to grant such, but that he would represent it, as he hoped with success, to Congress; and in this opinion two other gentlemen present supported him. The request is so just in itself that it is but what you daily grant to the meanest of your prisoners. As we cannot, we do not claim it by any agreement.

Though, by a little attention to that part of the capitulation, you will observe that we were put in the hope and expectation of having them supported in their different situations.

As to ourselves, we are put into a tavern, with the proper allowance of bed and board. This is all that is necessary so far. But what becomes of the external part of the body? This requires its necessaries, and without the decent part of such, a gentleman must be very intolerable to himself and others. I know I need not enter so minutely in representing those difficulties to Congress or you, as your established character and feelings will induce you to treat us as gentlemen and prisoners, removed from all means of relief for ourselves or families, but that of application to Congress. I arrived here last night in order to have the honor of laying those matters personally, or in writing, before you and them. Shall accordingly expect to be honored with an answer.

I am, most respectfully, sir, your most obedient humble servant,

Allan McDonald."*

NOTE K.

THE GLENGARRY SETTLERS.

Major General D. McLeod, of the Patriot Army, Upper Canada, in his "Brief Review of the Settlement of Upper Canada," published in 1841, adds the following interesting statements: "Gen. Howe, the then commander in chief of the British forces in North America, on hearing that the Scots in Virginia had joined the continentals, and were among the most active of the opposers of British domination, despatched Sir John Johnstone to the Scots settlement on the Mohawk—Captain James Craig, afterwards Governor of Lower Canada, and Lieut. Donald Cameron of the Regulars, to other parts, to induce the Highlanders to join the Royal Standard, and to convince them, that their interest and safety depended on their doing so.

They persuaded the uninstructed Highlanders, that the rebels had neither money, means, nor allies; that it was impossible they could for any length of time, withstand the mighty power and means of Great Britain; that their property would be confiscated, and apportioned to the royalists who should volunteer to reduce them to subjection. The Highlanders having duly

---

*American Archives, Fourth Series, Vol. V, p. 495.

weighed these circumstances, came to the conclusion, that the Americans would, like the Scots, in 1746, be ultimately overpowered;—that it was therefore to their interest, as they would not be permitted to remain neutral, to join the British standard.

The greater part of them volunteered under the command of Sir. J. Johnstone, and served faithfully with him until the peace of 1783. On the exchange of the ratification of peace, these unfortunate Highlanders, saw themselves once more bereft of house and home. The reward of their loyalty, and attachment to British supremacy, after fighting the battles of England for seven long and doubtful years, and sacrificing their all, was finally, an ungenerous abandonment by the British government of their interests, in not securing their property and personal safety in the treaty of peace. The object for which their services were required, not being accomplished, they were unceremoniously left to shift for themselves in the lower Province, among a race of people, whose language they did not understand, and whose manners and habits of life were quite dissimilar to their own. Col. McDonald, a near kinsman of the chief of that name, and who had, also, taken an active part in the royal army, during the revolution, commiserating their unfortunate condition, collected them together, and in a friendly manner, in their own native language, informed them, that if it were agreeable to their wishes, he would forthwith apply to the governor for a tract of land in the upper Province, where they might settle down in a body; and where, as they spoke a language different to that of the natives, they might enjoy their own society, and be better able to assist each other.

This, above all things, was what they wished for, and they therefore received the proposal with gratitude. Without much further delay, the Colonel proceeded to the Upper Province, pitched upon the eastern part of the eastern District; and after choosing a location for himself, directed his course to head quarters—informed the Governor of his plans and intentions, praying him to confirm the request of his countrymen, and prevent their return to the United States. The governor approved of his design, and promised every assistance. Satisfied that all was done, that could be reasonably expected, the Colonel lost no time, in communicating the result of his mission to his expectant countrymen; and they, in a short time afterwards, removed with him to their new location. The Highlanders, not long after, proposed to the Colonel as a mark of their approbation for his services, to call the settlement Glengarry, in honor of the chief of his clan, by which name it is distinguished to this day. It may be proper, to remember, in this place, that many of these were the immediate descendants of the proscribed Highlanders of 1715, and not a few the descendants of the relatives of the treacherously murdered clans of Glencoe (for their faithful and incorruptible adherence to the royal family of Stuart,) by king William the 3d, of Bloody memory, the Dutch defender of the English christian tory faith. But by far the major part, were the patriots of 1745,—the gallant supporters of the deeply lamented prince Charles Edward, and who, as before stated, had sought refuge in the colonies, from the British dungeons and bloody scaffolds.

It was not, therefore, their attachment to the British crown, nor their love of British institutions, that induced them to take up arms against the Americans; but their fears that the insurrection, would prove as disastrous to the sons of Liberty, as the Rebellion and the fatal field of Culloden had been to themselves; and that if any of them were found in the ranks of the discontented, they would be more severely dealt with in consequence of their former rebellion. Their chagrin was great indeed, especially, when they compared their former comfortable circumstances, in the state of New York, with their present miserable condition; and particularly, when they reflected how floolishly they had permitted themselves to be duped, out of their once happy homes by the promises of a government, which they knew from former experience, to be as false and treacherous, as it was cruel and overbearing. They settled down, but with no very friendly feelings towards a government which had allured them to their ruin, and which at last, left them to their own resources, after fighting their battles for eight sanguinary years. Nor are their descendants, at this day, remarkable for either their loyalty, or attachment, to the reigning family. These were the first settlers of Glengarry. It is a singular circumstance, that, nearly all the Highlanders, who fought for liberty and independence, and who remained in the U. S., afterwards became rich and independent, while on the other hand, with a very few exceptions, every 'individual, whether American or European, who took up arms against the revolution, became blighted in his prospects," (pp. 33-36).

Having mentioned in particular Butler's Rangers the following from Lossing's "Pictorial Field-Book of the War of 1812," may be of some interest: "Some of Butler's Rangers, those bitter Tory marauders in Central New York during the Revolution, who in cruelty often shamed Brant and his braves, settled in Toronto, and were mostly men of savage character, who met death by violence. Mr. John Ross knew a Mr. D——, one of these Rangers, who, when intoxicated, once told him that 'the sweetest steak he ever ate was the breast of a woman, which he cut off and broiled,'" (p. 592).

NOTE TO CHAPTER VIII.

The method of warfare carried on by Sir John Johnson and his adherents did not sway the lofty mind of Washington, as may be illustrated in the following narration furnished the author by Rev. Dr. R. Cameron, grandson of Alexander Cameron, who was a direct descendant of Donald Dubh of Lochiel. This Alexander Cameron came to America in 1773, and on the outbreak of the Revolution enlisted as a private under Sir John Johnson. Three times he was taken prisoner and condemned to be executed as a spy. How he escaped the first time is unknown. The second time, the wife of the presiding officer at the court-martial, informed him in Gaelic that he would be condemned, and assisted him in dressing him in her own clothes, and thus escaped to the woods. The third time, his mother, Mary Cameron of Glennevis, rode all the way from Albany to Valley Forge on horseback and personally plead her cause before Washington. Having listened to her patiently, the mighty chief replied: "Mrs. Cameron, I will pardon your son for your sake, but you must promise me that you will take him to Canada at once, or he will be shot." The whole family left for Canada.

NOTE L.

Moravian Indians.

It is now scarcely known that one company of Montgomery's Highlanders took part in the attempted expatriation of the Christian Indians—better known as Moravian Indians—in Pennsylvania. Owing to an attack made by savages, in 1763, against a Scotch-Irish settlement, those of that nationality at Paxton became bitterly inflamed against the Moravian Indians and determined upon their extermination. As these Indians were harmless and never engaged in strife, they appealed to the governor of Pennnsylvania for protection. These people, then living at Nazareth, Nain and Bethlehem, under the decree of the Council and the Assembly, were ordered by Governor Penn to be disarmed and taken to Philadelphia. Although their arms were the insignia of their freedom, yet these they surrendered to Sheriff Jennings, and on the eighth of November the procession moved towards Philadelphia. On their arrival in Philadelphia they were ordered to the "British Barracks," which had been erected soon after Braddock's defeat. At this time several companies of Montgomery's Highlanders were there quartered. On the morning of the eleventh, the first three wagons, filled with women and children, passed in at the gate. This movement aroused the Highlanders, and seizing their muskets, they rushed tumultuously together, stopped the rest of the wagons, and threatened to fire among the cowering women and children in the yard if they did not instantly leave. Meanwhile a dreadful mob gathered around the Indians, deriding, reviling, and charging them with all the outrages committed by the savages, threatening to kill them on the spot. From ten o'clock until three these Indians, with the missionaries, endured every abuse which wild frenzy and ribald vulgarity could clothe in words. In the midst of this persecution some Quakers braved the danger of the mob and taking the Indians by the hand gave them words of encouragement. During all this tumult the Indians remained silent, but considered "what insult and mockery our Savior had suffered on their account."

The soldiers persisting in their refusal to allow the Moravian Indians admission, after five hours, the latter were marched through the city, thousands following them with great clamor, to the outskirts, where the mob dispersed. The Indians were from thence conveyed to Province Island.

The Scotch-Irish of Paxton next turned their attention to a party of peaceable Indians who had long lived quietly among white people in the small village of Canestoga, near Lancaster, and on the fourteenth of December attacked and murdered fourteen of them in their huts. The rest fled to Lancaster and for protection were lodged in the work-house, a strong building and well secured. They were followed by the miscreants who broke into the building, and though the Indians begged their lives on their knees, yet all were cruelly murdered and their mangled remains thrown into the court-yard.

The assassins became emboldened by many hundreds from Paxton and other parts of the county of Lancaster joining their number, and planned to set out for Philadelphia, and not rest until all the Indians were massacred. While these troubles were brewing the Moravian Indians celebrated the Lord's Supper at the commencement of the year 1764, and renewed their covenant to show forth his death in his walk and conversation.

In order to protect them the government determined to send them out of the colony and place them under the care of Sir William Johnson, in New York, as the Indians had expressed their desire to be no longer detained from their families.* On January 4, 1764, the Moravian Indians numbering about one hundred and

---
*Colonial Records of Penna., Vol. IX, p. 111.

forty persons,* were placed under the convoy of Captain James Robertson, of Montgomery's Highlanders, and seventy Highlanders, for New York City. The Highlanders "behaved at first very wild and unfriendly, being particularly troublesome to the young women by their profane conversation, but were persuaded by degrees to conduct themselves with more order and decency." On arriving at Amboy, one of the soldiers exclaimed: "Would to God., all the white people were as good Christians, as these Indians."

The Indians were not allowed to enter New York, but were returned to Philadelphia under a guard of one hundred and seventy men from General Gage's army, commanded by Captain Schloffer, one party leading the van, and the other bringing up the rear. Captain Robertson and his Highlanders passed over to New York.†

NOTE M.

Highlanders Refused Lands in America.

"To the King's Most Excellent Majesty in Council,

The Humble Petition of James Macdonald, Merchant in Porterie in the Isle of Sky and Normand Macdonald of Slate in the said Island for themselves and on behalf of Hugh Macdonald Edmund Macqueen John Betton and Alexander Macqueen of Slate. The Reverend Mr. William Macqueen and Alexander Macdonald of the said Island of Sky and county of Inverness

Most Humbly Sheweth

That your petitioners having had in view to form a settlement to themselves and Families in your Majesty's Province in North Carolina have for some time been making Dispositions for that purpose by engaging Servants and disposing of their effects in this country.

And being now ready to embark and carry their intentions into Execution.

They most humbly pray your Majesty will be graciously pleased to Grant unto your petitioners Forty thousand Acres of Land in the said province of North Carolina upon the Terms and Conditions it has been usual to give such Grants or as to your Majesty shall seem proper,

And your petitioners shall ever pray,
Jas Macdonald,
Normand Macdonald."‡

---

*Ibid. †See Loskiel's Hist. Indian Mission, Book II, Chapter XVI. Schweinitz's Life of Zeisberger, Chap. XV. ‡North Carolina Colonial Records, Vol. VIII, p. 620.

APPENDIX.

"To the Right Honble the Lords of the Committee of his Majesty's most Honble Privy Council for Plantation Affairs.
Whitehall 21st of June 1771.
My Lords,
In obedience to His Majesty's Order in Council, dated June 14th, 1771, we have taken into consideration, the humble Petition of James Macdonald, Merchant in Porterie in the Isle of Sky and Normand Macdonald of Slate in the said Island for themselves and on behalf of Hugh Macdonald, Edmund Macqueen, John Belton and Alexander Macqueen of Slate the Reverend Mr William Macqueen and Alexander Macdonald of the said Isle of Sky and County of Inverness, setting forth that the Petitioners having had in view to form a Settlement to themselves and their Families in His Majesty's province of North Carolina, have for some time been making dispositions for that purpose by engaging servants and disposing of their effects in this Country and being now ready to embark and carry their said intention into execution, the Petitioners humbly pray, that His Majesty will be pleased to grant them forty thousand Acres of Land in the said Province upon the terms and conditions it hath been usual to grant such Lands. Whereupon We beg leave to report to your Lordships,

That the emigration of inhabitants of Great Britain and Ireland to the American Colonies is a circumstance which in our opinion cannot fail to lessen the strength and security and to prejudice the landed Interest and Manufactures of these Kingdoms and the great extent to which this emigration hath of late years prevailed renders it an object well deserving the serious attention of government.

Upon the ground of this opinion We have thought it necessary in Cases where we have recommended Grants of Land in America, to be made to persons of substance and ability in this Kingdom, to propose amongst other conditions, that they should be settled by foreign Protestants; and therefore We can on no account recommend to your Lordships to advise His Majesty to comply with the prayer of a Petition, founded on a resolution taken by a number of considerable persons to abandon their settlements in this Kingdom and to pass over into America, with their Families and Dependants in a large Body and which therefore holds out a Plan that we think, instead of meriting the Encouragement, ought rather to receive the discountenance of government.
We are My Lords &c.
Hillsborough
Ed: Eliot
John Roberts
Wm Fitzherbert."*

---
*ature*Ibid*, p. 621.

"At the Court of St James's
the 19th day of June 1772.
Present
The King's most Excellent Majesty in Council.

Whereas there was this day read at the Board a Report from the Right Honourable the Lords of the Committee of Council for plantation affairs Dated the 17th of this Instant in the words following viz,

Your Majesty having been pleased by your order in council of the 14th June 1771, to refer to the Lords Commissioners for Trade and Plantations the humble petition of James Macdonald Merchant of Portrie in the Isle of Sky and Norman Macdonald of Slate in the said Island for themselves and on behalf of Hugh Macdonald Edmund Macqueen John Betton and Alexander Macqueen of Slate and Reverend Mr Wm Macqueen and Alexander Macdonald of the said Isle of Sky and County of Inverness setting forth that the petitioners have had in view to form a settlement to themselves and their families in your Majesty's Province of North Carolina have for sometime been making Dispositions for that purpose by engaging servants and disposing of their Effects in this Country and being now ready to embark and carry their said intention into execution the petitioners humbly pray that your Majesty will be pleased to grant them Forty thousand acres of Land in the said Province upon the terms and conditions it hath been usual to grant such Lands. The said Lords Commissioners have reported to this Committee "that the emigration of the Inhabitants of Great Britain and Ireland to the American Colonies is a circumstance which in their opinion cannot fail to lessen the strength and security and to prejudice the landed Interest and manufactures of these Kingdoms and the great extent to which this emigration has of late years prevailed renders it an object well deserving the serious attention of Government that upon the Ground of this opinion they have thought it necessary in cases where they have recommended Grants of Land in America to be made to persons of substance and ability in this Kingdom to propose amongst other conditions that they should be settled by foreign protestants and therefore the said Lords Commissioners can on no account recommend to this committee to advise your Majesty to comply with the prayer of a petition founded on a resolution taken by a number of considerable persons to abandon their settlements in this Kingdom and to pass over to America with their Families and Dependants in a large body and which therefore holds out a plan that they think instead of meeting the encouragement ought

APPENDIX. 453

rather to receive the discouragement of Government. The Lords of the Committee this day took the said Representation and petition into consideration and concurring in opinion with the said Lord Commissioners for Trade and Plantations do agree humbly to report as their opinion to your Majesty that the said Petition of the said James and Norman Macdonald ought to be dismissed.

His Majesty taking the said Report into consideration was pleased with the advise of his Privy Council to approve thereof and to order as it is hereby ordered that the said Petition of the said James and Norman Macdonald be and it is hereby dismissed this board."*

NOTE N.

CAPTAIN JAMES STEWART COMMISSIONED TO RAISE A COMPANY OF HIGHLANDERS.

The Records of the New York Convention of July 25, 1775, contain the following:

"The Committee appointed to take into consideration and report the most proper mode for employing in the service of this State Mr. James Stewart, late Lieutenant in Colonel Livingston's Regiment, delivered in their Report, which was read; and the same being read, paragraph by paragraph, and amended, was agreed to, and is in the words following, to wit:

Resolved, That the said James Stewart is desiring a Captain's Commission in the service of this State, and that a Warrant be immediately given to him to raise a Company with all possible despatch.

That the said Company ought to consist of Scotch Highlanders, or as many of them as possible, and that they serve during the war, unless sooner discharged by this Convention, or a future Legislature of this State.

That the said Company shall consist of one Captain, one Lieutenant, one Ensign, four Sergeants, four Corporals, one Drum, one Fife, and not less than sixty-two Privates.

That a Bounty of fifteen dollars be allowed to each Non-Commissioned Officer and Private.

That they be entitled to Continental Pay and Rations, and subject to the Continental Articles of War, till further orders from this Convention or a future Legislature of this State.

That the said James Stewart shall not receive pay as a Cap-

---
*N. C. Colonial Records, Vol. IX, p. 303.

tain until he shall have returned to this Convention, or a future Legislature of this State, a regular muster roll, upon oath, of thirty able-bodied men, duly inlisted.

That the Treasurer of this Convention be ordered to advance to the said James Stewart £144, in order to enable him to advance the bounty to those he may inlist taking his receipt to account for the same to the Treasurer of this State.

That as soon as the said James Stewart shall have returned to this Convention, or a future Legislature of this State, a regular muster-roll of thirty able-bodied men, duly inlisted, certifying that the said men have been mustered, in the presence of a person to be appointed by the Chairman of the Committee of the City and County of Albany, or of a person to be appointed by the Chairman of the Committee of the City and County of New York, that then, and not before, the said James Stewart shall be authorized to draw upon the Chairman of the Committee of the City and County of Albany for the further sum of £100 in order that he may be enabled to proceed in his inlistment, giving his receipt to account for the same to the Treasurer of this State; and that when the said James Stewart shall have been duly inlisted and mustered, in the presence of a person to be appointed by the Chairman of the Committee of the City and County of Albany, the whole of his Company, or as many as he can inlist, and then he shall be entitled to receive of the said Chairman of the County Committee the remaining proportion of bounty due to the non-commissioned officers and privates which he shall have inlisted.

That if the said James Stewart shall not be able to complete the inlistment of this Company, that he shall make a report of the same, with all dispatch, to the President of this Convention, or to a future Legislature, who will either order his Commission to issue, or make such further provision for his trouble in recruiting as the equity of the case shall require.

That the Treasurer of this Convention be ordered to remit into the hands of John Barclay, Esquire, of the City of Albany, the sum of £288, on or before the last day of December next, in order to enable him to make unto the said James Stewart the disbursements aforesaid.

That the said James Stewart shall be authorized to engage to each man the sum of 7s. per week, billeting money, till such time as further provision is made for the subsistence of his recruits.

That the said Company, when raised, shall be either employed as an independent Company, or incorporated into any Bat-

APPENDIX.

tallion as to this Convention, or to a future proper authority of this State, shall appear advisable."*

There is no evidence that this action of the Convention terminated in any thing tangible. There was a James Stewart, captain of the third company, in the Fifth regiment of the New York Line, and while there was a large percentage in that regiment bearing Highland names, yet Captain Stewart's company had but five. It is not to be assumed that the two names represented the same person.

---

*American Archives, Fifth Series, Vol. I, p. 1441.

Since the publication of "Scotch Highlanders in America," I have secured the following complete list of the officers of the 2nd Battalion of the 84th or Royal Highland Emigrant Regiment, from Hon. Aeneas A. Macdonald, Charlottetown, Prince Edward Island. He also has a complete list of the enlisted men. The original document is in private hands in St. John, N. B.

LIST OF OFFICERS OF 2ND BATTALION OF ROYAL HIGHLAND EMIGRANTS.

Muster of January 21st, 1778, at Halifax 2nd Battalion of His Majesty's Young Royal Highland Regiment of Foot whereof the Honble Lieut. Genl. Thomas Gage is Colonel in Chief.

1st Company, Major Commandant, John Small, Commissioned June 13th, 1775, and April 8th, 1777; Captain Lieutenant, John MacLean, Commissioned April 9th, 1776 ; Ensign, Lauchlan McQuarrie, Commissioned April 9th, 1776; Chaplain, Revd Alexr McKenzie, Commissioned July 12th, 1776, Absent by leave, Revd Doctr Brinston officiating; Adjutant, Hector MacLean, Commissioned April 25th, 1776; Quarter Master, Angus Macdonald, Commissioned June 14th, 1775; Surgeon, George Fr. Boyd, Commissioned May 8th, 1776; Surgeon's Mate, Donald Cameron, Commissioned Oct 25th, 1776. 3 Sergeants 3 Corporals 2 Drummers and 46 Privates.

2nd Company, Captain, Alexr Macdonald, Commissioned June 14th, 1775; Lieutenant, Gerald Fitzgerald, Commissioned June 14th, 1775; On recruiting service in Newfoundland; Ensign, Kenneth Macdonald, Commissioned June 14th, 1775. 8 non-commissioned officers and 38 Privates.

3rd Company, Captain, Duncan Campbell, Commissioned June 14th, 1775; Lieutenant, Thomas Lunden, Commissioned June 14th, 1775; Ensign, Christr Seaton, Commissioned April 9th, 1777. 8 non-commissioned officers and 48 Privates.

4th Company, Captain, Ronald McKinnon, Commissioned June 14th, 1775; Lieutenants, Robert Campbell, Commissioned June 14th, 1775, and James McDonald, Commissioned June 14th, 1775. 8 non-commissioned officers and 50 Privates.

5th Company, Captain, Alexr Campbell, Commissioned

June 14th, 1775, Absent on Comr in Chief's leave; Lieutenant, Samuel Bliss, Commissioned June 14th, 1775; Ensign, Joseph Hawkins, Commissioned Decr 25th, 1775. 8 non-commissioned officers and 50 Privates.

6th or Grenadier Company, Captain, Murdoch McLaine, Commissioned June 14th, 1775, Recruiting; Lieutenants, Lauchlin McLaine, Commissioned June 14th, 1775, Charles McDonald, Commissioned May 18th, 1776. 8 non-commissioned officers and 50 Privates.

7th Company, Captain, Neil McLean, Commissioned June 14th, 1775, Serving with the Army in Canada and under orders to join; Lieutenant, Hugh Frazier, Commissioned Feby 27th, 1776, Prisoner with the Rebels; Ensign, John Macdonald, Commissioned Octr 7th, 1776. 8 non-commissioned officers and 32 Privates.

8th Company, Captain, Allen Macdonald, Commissioned June 14th, 1775, Prisoner with Rebels; Lieutenant, Alexr Macdonald, Commissioned June 14th, 1775, Prisoner with Rebels; Ensign, Alexr Maclean, Commissioned Decr 25th, 1776. 8 non-commissioned officers and 34 Privates.

9th Company, Captain, John Macdonald, Commissioned June 14th, 1775; Lieutenant, Alexr McDonell, Commissioned June 14th, 1775, Prisoner with the Rebels; Ensign, James Robertson, Commissioned Oct 30th, 1776. 8 non-commissioned officers and 34 Privates.

10th Company, Captain, Allan Macdonnell, Commissioned June 14th, 1775, Prisoner with the Rebels; Lieutenant, John Macdonnell, Major Genl Massey's leave; Ensign, Hector Maclean, Commissioned June 14th, 1775. 8 non-commissioned officers and 40 Privates.

At this Muster the 3rd or Captain Duncan Campbell's Company and the 5th or Captain Alexr Campbell's Company could not have been present as the Muster Rolls of these Companies, while containing the list of Officers and Men, are not completed and not signed by the officers or by the Deputy Officer taking the Muster. The 5th Company was in Newfoundland at the time and the 3rd probably there also.

At a Muster of the Regiment held at Halifax on 2nd of September 1778 the Regiment appears as His Majesty's Royal Highland Regiment of Emigrants.

INDEX

----, Big Hugh 381 Dick 409-410 Flora 431 George 178 Hughy 192 Jenny 212 Joan 47 Sandy 189
ABERCHALDER, Alexander 213 Chichester 214 Hugh 213 John 214
ABERCROMBIE, 48 259 263
ABERCROMBY, 259 269 Gen 258 James 252-253 257 283 James Jr 283 Lt-Col 327 Robert 350
AGRICOLA, 32
ALAN, 378
ALEXANDER, 77 Brigadier-Gen 139 John Mcnitt 119
ALEXANDER III, King Of? 33
ALLAN, Maj 390 Sir 391
ALLEN, 190 Ethan 190-191 349 380 John 194 Mrs 194
ALLINE, Henry 251
ALMACK, 69
AMHERST, 269 273 295 Gen 268-271 278 283-284 405 Jeffrey 263 Maj-Gen 258 William 288
ANDERSON, 340 Andrew 86 Eben'r 225 John 93-94 236 Joseph 225 Mary 184 186 Sam'l 224-225
ANDRE, John Maj 406
ANGUS, 34 300
ANNE, Duchess Of Hamilton 78
ARCHIBALD, 248 Thomas 239
ARDTORNISH, 255
ARGYLE, 79 368 Duke Of 381 423 Earl Of 80
ARGYLL, Earle Of 83
ARMAGH, Archbishop Of 41
ARNOLD, 193 Benedict 372 406 Col 314-315 Gen 217 390 401
ARNOTT, Hugh 253
ASHE, Col 131 Gen 354 John 117 Mr 110
ATHOL, 79
AUGUST, Capt 381
AUGUSTIN, Walter 154
AUSTIN, Charles 225
BAILIES, 151
BAILLIE, Capt 264-265 David 255 Robert 175 William 253 261
BAIN, James 254 John Mackintosh 166 William 343
BAINE, Mary 186
BAIRD, James 342 351-353
BAKER, Capt 175 Samuel 104

BALFOUR, Capt 265
BALNEAVES, Archibald 347
    Patrick 253 261 279
BALNEVIS, Archibald 343
BANCROFT, 295
BARBA, 169
BARCALDINE, Alexander 265
BARCLAY, Capt 174 David 279
    John 454 Quartermaster
    374
BARRE, 321 Capt 321 Col 321
    Henry 321
BARRON, Cammodore 326
    James 326
BARTRAM, Wm 104
BAXTER, Capt 412
BAYARD, Phoebe 405
BAYLIE, Robert 82
BAYNE, Duncan 254 Shon
    418
BEATTY, James 188
BELLOMONT, 94 Earl Of 94
    101
BELTON, John 451 Mary 185
BEMBO, Adm 94
BENNET, James 251
BERRIDALE, Lord 372
BETHUNE, John 136 141 312
    324
BETTON, John 450 452
BISSET, Majory 41
BLACKWOOD, Robert 85
BLAICH, 392
BLAIKIE, Charles 242
BLAIR, Hugh 342 Simon 279
BLANING, Hugh 104 106
BLISS, Samuel 458
BLOODGOOD, S D W 191
BOISDALE, 232 371
BOONE, Daniel 60
BOQUET, 266 280-281 283
    Col 280 282-283 288

BOQUET (Cont.)
    Henry 279
BORLAM, 402
BORLAND, John 97
BOSCAWEN, Adm 263
BOSWELL, 69
BOUDINOT, Mr 349
BOYCE, Robert 326
BOYD, George Fr 457 William
    46
BOYNTON, Dr 322
BRADDOCK, 53-54 266 448
BRADSTREET, Col 263
BRANT, 200 220 447 Joseph
    198 217 220 223 316
BREYMANN, Col 384
BRIAN, King Of Ireland 40
BRINSTON, Rev Dr 457
BROOKS, Francis 162
BROUGHAM, Lord 375
BROWN, 238 Archibald 187
    James 391 William 279
BROWNE, Dr 428 James 368
    428
BRUCE, 34 371 Capt 371
BRYAN, 360 Col 139
BRYANT, Lt-Col 137
BUCHANAN, 67 69 George 87
    John 87 William 86
BUCKAM, Richard 417
BUEA, Archibald 111 Duncan
    111 Malcolm 111 Mary 111
    Neill 111
BUG, Arch 105
BUIE, Archibald 144 Duncan
    144
BULLOCK, 175
BUNYON, 49
BURGES, Joseph 166
BURGOGNE, 53
BURGOYNE, 48 191-193 195
    383 386 444

BURGOYNE (Cont.)
  Gen 193 215-216 315 351
  383-386 390 406
BURKE, Gov 429 William 291
BURNET, Judge 407
BURNS, David 347
BURRINGTON, Gov 54
BURT, 31 419
BURTON, Col 272
BUSSES, 70
BUTE, Lord 110
BUTLER, 215 217 219-221
  376 447 Capt 221 Col 216
  John 218-220 228 Walter
  N 220-221
BUY, James Macsorley 42
  Sorley 42
BYRNS, 226
C, B J 438
CAIRNS, David 311
CAITHNESS, Earl Of 372
CALDWELL, Elizabeth 186
  Henry 315 Mr 208
CAMEL, Angus 113
CAMERON, 30 34 245 371
  377-378 396 Alan 377 Alex
  242 Alexander 210-211
  244-245 255 274 323 448
  Allan 254-255 Angs 442
  Angus 442-443 Capt 278
  352 Charles 342 Col 378
  Daniel 135 Donald 22 84
  144 241 243 255 322 342-
  343 445 457 Duncan 225
  277 323 Ewen 22 255
  Fassifern 255 Finlay 323
  Hugh 255 James 323 John
  84 Mary 448 Mrs 448 R
  448 Samuel 323 William
  210-211
CAMPBEL, Duncan 104 106
  Jas 106

CAMPBELL, 34-35 43 50 63
  100 119 182-183 319 369
  Agnes 86 Alan 253
  Alexander 85 96 99 185
  191 253-255 261 265 275
  277 322 370 Alexr 457-458
  Allan 278 283 Amelia 380
  Angus 135 Ann 186
  Archibald 87 183-185 188
  253 255 261 275 277 279
  342-343 346-347 352 358
  361 379 Capt 100 112 133
  177-178 181-182 273 314
  346 355 361-362 369 443
  Catharine 184 Charles 342
  347 360 Col 344 347-350
  352-353 371 380 Colen 85
  Colin 80-82 96 253-254
  267 326 354 Colline 81-82
  Daniel 86 114 210 David
  342 Donald 176 182 191
  253-254 281 Dougald 342-
  343 Dougall 84 Dowgall
  417 Dugald 347 Duncan 80
  83 85 104-105 185 187 253
  261 279 281 283 322 347
  457-458 Duncan Jr 185
  Duncan Sr 186 Elizabeth
  184-185 Farquard 119
  Farquhar 108 112
  Farquhard 113 115 117-
  121 134 136 Ferqd 113 141
  Gen 380-381 George 84
  182 185 253 279 Gilbert
  80-82 Glenlyon 277 Hugh
  87 97 343 347 361 James
  80 83 85 143 145 166 182
  185 253 279 379 John 83
  85 97 111 114 119 132 186
  253-255 260-261 276-277
  279 283 342-343 369 380
  John Jr 279 John Sr 253

CAMPBELL (Cont.)
Lachlan 188 Lady 381
Lady Neil 84 Lauchlan 176
191 Lauchlin 177 Law
Robert 342 Lawrence 347
Lord 381 Lt 176 Lt-Col
348-349 Malcolm 185
Marian 185 Mary 184 186
417 Matthew 87 Monzie 86
Mr 119-120 Mungo 84 87
Patrick 81 83 85-86 342-
343 Robert 75 301 322 342
355 457 Robert Jr 186
Ronald 81 84 Sarah 381
Sgt 97 Smollet 343
Thomas 83 218 William 56
125 239 381
CAMPEL, Patric 417
CAMPLEY, Arch 106
CARGILL, Elizabeth 184
James 185 Jane 185 John
185
CARGYLE, Margaret 186
CARLETON, Gen 314 383
CARLTON, Richd 106
CASWELL, 131 Col 121 130-
132 137-139 Gov 121
Richard 136
CHAD, 336
CHAPPELL, Jo 417
CHARLES, 35
CHARLES, Prince 107 229
245 387 393 395 402
CHARLES EDWARD, 395
Prince of ? 395 447
CHARLES I, 34
CHARLES II, 423
CHARLIE, Prince 435
CHATHAM, 295
CHATTERTON, 400
CHESSION, William 210
CHISHOLM, Alex 442-443

CHISHOLM (Cont.)
Alexr 442 Archibald 244
Colin 343 Donald 323
Duncan 342 Hugh 210
John 277 323 William 210
CHISOLM, John 255
CHISSEM, Donald 210
CHISSIM, Donald 211 Wm 211
CHISSIMS, Hugh 211
CHLORUS, Constantius 33
CHOISEUL, 290
CHRISTIE, Alexander 185
James 343
CHRISTY, John 210
CHURCH, Oliver 227
CLANDONALD, 41
CLANRANALD, 231 394-395
CLARK, Daniel 166 185-186
Donald 159 166 George
Rogers 53 Gilbert 144 Jno
105 Mr 48 Neill 111 Robert
323 Robt 106 Thomas 48
William 186
CLARKE, 164 Alexander 166
George 177 180 Gov 177
181
CLARKS, Thos 105
CLAUS, Col 225 Daniel 198
William 225
CLAYTON, Jno 106 John 104
CLEPHANE, James 254
CLERK, George 85
CLINTON, Gen 328 339
George 400 Henry 123 125
141-142 313 316 320 327
339-340 359-360 366 381
383-384 393 404 428
COCHRAN, Jonathan 173
Robert 113 190
COCK, Daniel 251 Mr 251
COCKBURN, Archibald 304
James 253

INDEX

COCKBURNE, William 279
COFFIN, Mr 225 William 225
COLDEN, Gov 310
COLHOUN, Lewis 347
COLLACHIE, 197 203 205
  Alexander 214 Allan 214
  Allan Of 206
COLLIER, George 338 370 393
COLLOTTIN, 418
COLQUHON, Robert 97
COLQUHOUN, Humphrey 80
  Lodovick 343 Ludovick 369
CONNOLLY, John 225
CONSTANS, 33
CONWAY, Gen 295
CORBETT, 131
CORNWALLIS, 54 57-58 428
  Earl 141-142 429 Lord 313
  320 327 329 334-337 351
  360-362 364-367 373-374
  406 428-429
CORNWELL, 46
COSBY, Col 176 Gov 177 180
COTTON, 128 131
COUTTS, Patrick 82
COX, Longfield 139
CRAIG, James 427 445 Maj 427
CRAIGHEAD, Capt 268
CRAMMOND, Lt 324 330
CRAWFORD, 227 326
  Archibald 254 Capt 227
  Wm Redf'd 226
CRERAR, Peter 72
CROCKETT, John 243
CROMWELL, 24 35
CROSSET, 219
CRUGER, Lt 415 Lt-Col 320
CULTON, Anthony 243
CUMBERLAND, Duke Of 424
CUMING, James 85

CUMING (Cont.)
  Mattheu 86 Robert 86
CUMMING, Lt 359 Patrick 342
CUMYNG, Alexander 86
CUNISON, Thomas 279
CUNNINGHAM, Capt 371
  Montgomery 371 Walter 442-443
CUTHBERT, 151 John 166
  255 Lt 264-265
CYRUS, 77
D, Mr 447
D'ESTAING, Count 356-358 404
DALGLEISH, Alexander 97
DALING, Richard 96
DALL, Rory 29
DALRYMPLE, John 75
  Secretary 76
DALY, Patrick 224
DAMBURGESS, Fran 311
DANIEL, Gov 442
DARACH, Jenny 111
DARNE, George 311
DARROCH, John 441
DARTMOUTH, Earl Of 117 120 205 310
DAVIDSON, 44 James 312
  Marion 86
DAY, John 322
DAYTON, Col 207-208 Elias 205
DEBOS, 364-365
DELEVI, 259 261 276 278
DELLIUS, Godfrey 181
DEMERE, Raymond 173-174
DESWYNES, 418
DIES, 227
DIESKAU, 48
DILLON, Count 357
DINWIDDIE, Gov 103
DONALD, 189 Corporal 189

DONALDSON, Alexander 279
283 Capt 371 David 442-
443 Henri 417 Maj 372
DONEGAL, Marquis Of 45
DOTY, John 225
DOUGLAS, John 255 Lt 275
DOUGLASS, Arch 106 Colin
239 243 251 James 279
DRAKE, 22
DRUMLANRIG, Earl Of 391
DRUMMOND, 34 Adam 86
David 81-83 Helen 82
James 81 83-85 James
Lord 86 John 80 82-86
Lodovick 85 Lord 85
Robert 93 279 Thomas 80
86 William 80
DUBH, Donald 448
DUCOUR, Chevalier 263
DUFF, James 254 William 86
DUFFE, Alexander 86
DUMBARTON, 389
DUN, Private 443
DUNBAR, 151 Alexander 323
Capt 151 153 George 149-
151 Lt 162 William 311
323
DUNCAN, Capt 97 Richard 224
Walter 96
DUNCANSON, Robert 343 347
DUNDAS, Col 373 Henry 304
Mrs Hamilton 232 Robert
323
DUNDEE, 35 Bonnie 35
DUNDONALD, Earl Of 264
DUNLAP, 52
DUNMORE, Lord 330
DUNVEGAN, 150
EARL, Rd 105
EARLE, Archibald 83 George
81
EARRACHD, Ailean An 377

EASTCHURCH, Gov 54
EDDINGTON, James 284
EDWARD, 33 EFFINGHAM,
Lord 295-296
EGLINTON, Earl Of 253
ELBERT, Col 175
ELIOT, Col 140
ELIZABETH, 42
ELLICE, James 210
ENSIGN, Private 443
ENTERKIN, Lady 84
ERC, 41
ERSKINE, John 36 William
327 342 350
EVERETT, Peter 225
FALCONER, Alexander 244
FANNING, Col 430 David 429
FARIS, Wm 106
FARQUHARSON, Alexander
279 Charles 254 George
253 261
FARRAND, Jacob 225
FERGURSONE, David 87
FERGUS, 41 James 106 Son
Of Erc 41
FERGUSON, 43 Adam 253
Alex 210 Alexander 211
Capt 351 James 82 Jenette
185 Maj 338 362 Patrick
351
FERQUHAR, 96 Francis 87
FIFER, Martin 443
FINGAL, 229
FINLAYSON, Alexander 84
FINLEY, John 60
FIRTELIER, Alexander 311
FITZGERALD, Gerald 322 457
Lt 234
FITZHERBERT, Wm 451
FLETCHER, Thomas 279 283
FLEURY, Lt-Col 359
FLINT, James 347

FONAB, 100
FONDA, Jellis 211 John 200
   Maj 212 Mrs 212
FORBES, 266 Alexander 83
   Arthur 80 83 343 Charles
   87 David 84 Duncan 80
   Gen 267 John 80-82 84
   265 323 Samuell 81-82
   Thomas 82 Wm 104
FORTROSE, Lord 421
FOX, 49 294
FOYERS, 382
FRANKLIN, Dr 294 Lt 324
   Robert 326
FRASER, 34 131 155 227 245
   254 256 263-264 270 273-
   274 276 288-289 305 308
   311 325 334 338 340-341
   343 350 363 368-369 371
   373 379-380 382 387-388
   429 Alex 243-244 Alex Jr
   243 Alexander 241 245
   255 274-275 277 311 342
   381-382 Alexander Jr 273
   Barbara 83 Capt 241
   Charles 243 Col 273 277
   342 David 241 Elizabeth
   185 Gen 382 384-387
   Hugh 240 242-243 255 342
   442-443 J Alexander 265
   James 255 322-323 343
   442-443 Jane 382 Jas 442
   Jean 382 John 82 255 322-
   323 Kenneth 243-244 Lt
   347 Malcolm 255 273 277
   311 314 Malcum 417 Peter
   342 347 Robert 83-84 86
   Simon 243 254-255 275
   277 279 342 381-382 387-
   388 Simon Jr 277 Simon
   Sr 277 Thomas 166 244
   255 323 342-343 368

FRASER (Cont.)
   William 186 227 244 323
   342 382
FRAZER, Gen 344
FRAZIER, Francis 134 Hugh
   458 Jeremiah 119
FRENCH, Jeremiah 227
FURGUSON, 57 Col 56
GAGE, Gen 118 312 317 450
   Genl 313 Thomas 457
GAINEY, Col 413-414
GALANTE, Marie 392
GALGACUS, 32
GARDENIER, 216 Jacob 216
GASCOIGNE, Capt 156
GATES, Gen 383 Horatio 360
GEORGE, 438
GEORGE, King of ? 132
GEORGE, King Of England
   124
GEORGE, Viscount Of Tarbat
   81
GEORGE I, King Of England
   35
GEORGE III, 54 188 292 294
   297-298 301 308 374-375
GEORGE KING, The Third 198
GER'D, Fitz 319
GERD, Fitz 319
GERMAIN, George 172 215
   428
GERMAINE, George 330
GETMAN, Capt 223
GIBSON, James 96 Walter 109
   117
GILCHRIST, Alexander 185
   188 Duncan 186-187 John
   185 188 Margaret 186
   Peter 191
GILLASPIE, Neil 183-184
GILLES, James 188
GILLIS, Alexander 188

GILLIS (Cont.)
James 185
GILMER, Gov 58
GLANALDALL, 310
GLASS, Shon 418
GLEN, Jacob 225 John 86 225
GLENALADALE, 233-234
GLENALADALL, 234
GLENALADEL, 234
GLODSMITH, H 235
GOLDSMITH, 152
GOOSE, Frederick 210-211
GORDON, Adam 80 82 Charles 342 Cosmo 255 277 Hugh 254 James 82 John 80 85 254 Miss Of Baldornie 233 Robert 80 Thomas 82 William 343
GORDONE, William 85
GORDOUN, Alexander 81
GORDOUNE, Alexander 81
GRAEME, 87 David 82 85 Mungo 80 86 Patrick 333 Thomas 81-82 253 278
GRAHAM, 27 43 87 147 Alexr 114 Angus 185 Charles 279 338 Colin 357 Daniel 113 Donald 244 Duchray 261 Gen 367 Gordon 253 261 278 283 John 81 86 253 261 279-281 283 Maj 340 Malcolm 113 Margaret 86 Mary 186 Michael 113 Murdock 113 Samuel 369 371 429 Thomas 261 283 Walter 97 William 81 119 185
GRAHAME, John 87 166 Patrick 166 Thomas 85
GRANT, 34 97 267 328 Alexander 210-211 254 267 333 340 Allan 211 279

GRANT (Cont.)
Allen 210 Angus 210-211 Archibald 311 315 Charles 279 Donald 211 229-230 244 Ensign 365 Francis 80 253 278 283 Gen 328-329 388 George 279 James 243-245 253-254 261 266 279 283 294 388 John 279 342-343 361 Joseph 254 Lewis 279 Lt 324 Maj 174 266 284 Maj-Gen 328 Peter 261 279 323 Robert 254 283 343 U S 246 William 253 261-262 279 283 327
GRANVILLE, Lord 54
GRAY, Charles 336 Gen 337 James 207 224 253 279 Maj 225 Robert 253 261
GREEN, Gretna 378
GREENE, 57 Gen 320-321 326 362 364 Nathaniel 362
GREER, 43
GREGOR, 43 Alexander 279 John 279
GREGORIE, James 81 84
GREGORSON, Alexander 255 277 Ensign 275
GREGORY, James 81
GRIER, 43
GRIERSON, Christian 83 John 83
GRIFFITHS, 332
GUMMESELL, Thos 226
GWINNETT, Button 403
HABERSHAM, Maj 174
HACO, King Of Norway 33
HAGGART, William 254
HALDANE, David 279 John 83 85-86
HALDIMAND, Col 278 Gen 209

INDEX

HALL, 219
HALLIDAY, Thomas 85
HAMILTON, 406 430 Duke Of 101 340 Lt-Col 352 360 Robert 104 Thomas 342
HAMMEL, Mary 186
HANOVER, 397
HARDENBURGH, Jacobus 217
HARDING, Seth 343
HARDWICKE, Lord 291
HARDY, Robt 106
HARRIS, Dr 239
HARRISON, Charles 106
HASSOCK, Provost 151
HAVILAND, Col 278
HAWKER, Captn 319
HAWKINS, 47 Joseph 458
HAY, 227 Gov 227
HAYS, James 243
HEATH, William 400
HECTOR, Sir 24
HENDERSON, 60 James 255
HENRY, 53 315 John 46 Patrick 53 William 257
HENRY VIII, 42
HEPBURN, David 253 279 James 117 Joseph 119
HERKIMER, 217 Gen 209 216
HERRING, Elbert 279
HEWES, Joseph 116
HILL, John 82 87
HOLLAND, John F 225 Maj 225
HOLMES, 46 422
HOME, Walter 340
HOOK, Paulus 340
HOOPER, William 116 141
HORRY, Gen 408 411-413 Peter 415
HORSMANDEN, Chief Justice 399
HORTON, Mr 159
HOUSTON, Lewis 254
HOWARD, Col 364 John 226
HOWE, 259 327 Gen 137-138 325-329 332-334 336 343 348 350 445 Lord 48 258-259 262 347 William 139 312 326 330 336 339 344 347-349 389 400 403
HUGH, Fifteenth Of Coll 232 Tenth Lord Of Lovat 381
HUNTER, William 185 405
HUTCHINSON, 174
HUTCHISON, 190 Charles 190-191 Robert 342
IGNATIO, Don 155
INDIAN, Attakullakulla 170 Le Loup 193 195
INGRAM, Capt 397
INNES, Alexander 82 James 103
IRVINE, 50
IZARD, Ralph 381 Sarah 381
JAMES, 34-35 42
JAMES, King Of ? 21
JAMES, King Of Britain 42 King Of Great Britain 36
JAMES, Sir 427
JAMES, Thomas 92
JAMES I, King Of England 42
JAMES II, King Of England 35
JAMES IV, 34
JEFFERIS, 336
JEFFERSON, Thomas 399 407
JENNINGS, Sheriff 448
JOHN, Sir 198 201-208 213 220-221
JOHN OF ISLAY, 41
JOHNSON, 69 196-200 204-206 217 227 Col 199 359 Daniel 185 Guy 198-200 215 220 John 188 200-201 203 206-208 210-213 215

JOHNSON (Cont.)
218 221 224-226 228 230
308 376 448 Lady 207-208
Samuel 392 395 William
95 196-197 230 376 449
Wm 224 227
JOHNSTON, Alexander 83
Gabriel 102 George 87
John 119 Lauchlan 279
Samuel 97 119 124
Secretary 89 William 84
JOHNSTONE, J 446 John 445
Thomas 83
JOHNSTOUN, James 86
Rachell 82 Thomas 86
JOHNSTOUNE, Alexander 82
Jesper 83
JONES, David 191 Griffeth 104 Thomas 165 William 173 Wm 106
KALM, 290
KELTIE, 67 71 428 John S 368
KENNEDY, 273
KENNON, William 117
KEPPEL, Adm 295
KEPPOCH, 20
KERR, R 227
KILMORE, George 188 194
KINLOCH, David 342 Lady 86
KIRK, 232
KLOCK, 221
KNOWLES, Adm 298
KNOWLTON, 331-332 Col 331-332
KNOX, 43 Henry 407
KNYPHAUSEN, Gen 333 336 339
L, John Mcintosh 158
LA FAYETTE, 406
LAFAYETTE, Marquis De 366 373 389

LAFOREY, Capt 265
LAIRD, Billie 211
LAMON, Duncan 119
LAMONT, Archibald 253 279 Hugh 343 Norman 342
LANGAN, Patrick 226
LANSINGH, Phil P 227
LAURENS, Henry 402-403
LAWRENCE, 405 Brig-Gen 263 Gen 264
LAWRIE, Andrew 342
LAWS, George 311
LEAKE, Robert 226
LECKY, 39 294 299
LEE, 175 Charles 142 347 Col 321 Gen 347-349 Henry 321 415
LEEK, 197 Allan 213 Archibald 213 Ronald 213
LEEKY, 298
LEGGATE, John 135 Lt-Capt 135
LEGGE, Gov 317
LEITCH, 332 Maj 331-332
LEITH, John 279
LEPSCOMB, 226
LESLIE, 332 Gen 331-332 364 George 279
LEWES, Brigadier 140
LEWIS, Brigadier-Gen 142
LIGETT, John 141
LILLINGTON, Col 131-132
LINCOLN, Col 357 Gen 339 354 356 358 404
LINDSEY, David 184 Duncan 186 188
LITTLETON, Gov 170 Lt 324
LIVINGSTON, Archibald 187 Col 301 453 Isabella 186
LOGAN, James 50
LONDON, Lord 224
LONG, Col 139

LOSKIEL, 450
LOSSING, 351 447
LOUDON, 380 Lord 256-257
LOVAT, Hugh Tenth Lord Of
  381 Lord 21 254 Simon
  Twelfth Lord 387
LOVELL, Gen 392 Solomon
  369
LOVETT, Rich 105
LOWDEN, Capt 249
LOWELL, 47
LOWENDAHL, Gen 389
LUDLOW, 269
LUNDEN, Thomas 457
LUTHER, 222
LYNVILGE, John Mackintosh
  166 John Mcintosh 158
LYON, James 104 Richard 113
M'DONALD, Donald 408
M'DOUGALL, Alexander 398
M'INTOSH, Lachlan 401
MACALLISTER, Archibald 255
MACARTHER, Alexr 113 Neill
  113
MACARTHUR, Maj 357 360
MACBEAN, John 277
MACBRIAR, 268
MACCASKILL, Murdo 141
MACDONALD, 30 34 41 63
  114-115 127 130-131 133
  308 310 340 368 370-371
  396 412 A 140 Aeneas A
  457 Alexander 66 133-134
  140 209 231-232 254-255
  267 395 450-452 Alexr
  457-458 Allan 114-115 124
  137 395-396 Allen 135 140
  458 Angus 394 457
  Clanranald 255 Donald
  124 233 254-255 265 277
  408 Fanny 397 Flora 114
  144 233 393-397 435

MACDONALD (Cont.)
  Flory 394 Gen 125-130
  132-135 137 Hector 255
  277 Hugh 394 450-452
  James 134 141 450-453
  Jas 450 John 134 209 231-
  233 254 265 267 370 458
  Kenneth 457 Kennith 134
  Lach 442 Lord 371 Lt-Col
  353 Marjory 233 Norman
  452-453 Normand 450-451
  Ranald 394 Robert 342
  Roderick 233 Sgt 408 410-
  415 Sorley Buy 41 63
  William 233 254 267
MACDONALDS, 20
MACDONEL, 268
MACDONELL, 197 215 227
  Alexander 209-210 214
  229 Allan 210-211 213-214
  Angus 213 215 342 Arch'd
  214 Archibald 213 Capt
  213 274 288-289 Charles
  255 277 Chichester 214
  Helen 211 Hugh 213
  James 213 John 209-210
  213-214 255 273 342 371
  Miles 213 Of Dunluce 42
  Ronald 213-214 255
  William 255
MACDONNELL, Allan 458
  John 458
MACDOUGALL, Dun 442
  Duncan 442 John 342
MACFARLANE, 34
MACGIRT, 354
MACGREGOR, 34 43 335 Sgt
  335
MACHEMIE, Francis 49
MACHEYNE, Shames 419
MACINTOSH, 163 171
  Alexander 254 Capt 163

MACINTOSH (Cont.)
  John Mohr 155-157 164
  Lachlan 171 Old Borlum
  164 William 164 169 171
MACKAFERSON, Shames 419
  Tonal 419
MACKAY, 34 127 151 154 168
  Alexander 279 Capt 157
  Daniel 80 Ensign 156
  Hugh 35 149 152-155 159
  Lt 162 168
MACKENZIE, 30 34 127
  Alexander 254 267 332
  Capt 288 351 Charles
  Barrington 343 Colin 342
  351 Hugh 254 267 James
  80 255 John 343 Lt 324
  Robert 254 267 William
  254 267
MACKINNON, 43 371 John 66
  Lt 286 Ronald 254
MACKINTOSH, 34 Aeneas
  342-343 Alexander 261
  Angus 342 382 James 280-
  281 Jean 382 John 166
  332 Mr 161
MACLACHLAN, 127 268
MACLACHLANE, John 254
MACLAINE, A 113 Alexander
  135 Archibald 117 119
MACLEAN, 24 34 125 127 131
  314-315 377-378
  Alexander 125 283-284
  Alexr 458 Allan 234 254
  308 311 316 377 389-391
  Allen 309 Anna 392
  Archibald 343 Brigadier-
  Gen 369 Col 310 314-315
  317 324 390 Coll 310
  Donald 390 Francis 369
  389 392 Gen 370 390 392-
  393

MACLEAN (Cont.)
  Hector 232 315 392 457-
  458 James 254 Janet 390
  John 166 255 390 457
  Torloisk 389 William 254
MACLEOD, 29 115 127 150
  Alexander 255 277 Alexr
  141 Donald 125 132 Hugh
  237-238 John 150 158 Lt
  333 340 Maj 132-133
  Malcolm 66 Murdoch 141
  Norman 66 333 342
  Roderick 342
MACMAHON, 41
MACMASTER, Lt 286
MACNAB, John 254
MACNEIL, 427-429 Donald
  255 Roderick 255
MACNISH, 43
MACPHARLANE, John 79
MACPHERSON, 34 286 Allan
  286 Capt 273 Cluny 255
  Col 353 Donald 417
  Duncan 332 335 342 353
  Henry 342 357 Hugh 261
  James 254 John 254-255
  Robert 255
MACQUARRIE, 34
MACQUEEN, Alexander 450-
  452 Edmund 450-452
  William 450-451 Wm 452
MACRAE, 127 Jane 383
MACVICAR, Archibald 254
MAGALANE, 63
MAGAW, Col 332-333
MAGUIRE, 41
MAGWILLIVRAY, Shonie 418
MAHON, Lord 36
MAIN, Andrew 243 Charles
  343
MAITLAND, Col 353-356 358
  Lt-Col 352-353 Maj 174

INDEX 471

MAJORIBANKS, Maj 320-321
MAKEMIE, Francis 45
MALCOLM, Allan 342
MALCOLM THE SECOND, 40
MANN, Isaac 225 John 225
MANNING, Capt 321
MAR, 36 63 Earl Of 36
MARION, 58 408 Francis 408
   Gen 412 414-415
MARQUESS, James 82
MARQUESSE, John 83
MARSDEN, Rufus 106
MARSHALL, Robert 243 250
MARTILEER, Jno 106
MARTIN, 28 117 125 Col 129
   Cosmo 254 Gov 112 115
   119 123-124 136 139 396
   Josiah 117 128
MASSEY, Maj-Gen 458
MATHESON, Charles 244
   William 244
MATHEWS, Gen 338
MAURER, Jacob 226
MAXWELL, Capt 346 Gen 335
   Hamilton 342 347
MC-, Donald 244
MCALISTER, Alexander 113
   117-119 144 Archibald 277
   Coll 104 James 105 John
   326
MCALLISTER, Barbara 186
   Charles 185 Margaret 186
MCALPINE, Dougall 184
   Robert 186
MCANTHONY, Ann 184
MCARDEN, 145
MCARTHUR, 193 Alexander
   186 Capt 134 430 439
   Charles 186 Duncan 185-
   188 193 John 186 Neal
   125 Neil 135 Neill 134 141
   Patrick 185

MCASKELL, Murdoch 134-135
MCBAIN, Archibald 166
MCBANE, Donald 347
MCBRAINE, Murdock 106
MCBRIDE, Malcolm 113
MCCABE, 244 James 242
MCCANNON, 43
MCCARTER, Archibald 185
   Catharine 186 Donald 210-
   211 John 185-186
MCCARTHY, Francis 225
MCCAULEY, Capt 415
MCCLEAN, Hugh 109
MCCLELAND, Andw 114 John
   114
MCCLELLAND, John 173
   Samuel 173
MCCLOUD, 124
MCCOLLISTER, Alexander
   108
MCCONNELL, George 243
MCCORE, Archibald 185 John
   186
MCCOULSKEY, Neil 113
MCCOULSKY, Archd 114
   James 114
MCCOY, Edward 185
MCCRACKEN, 187 Joseph 187
   191
MCCRAINE, Hugh 105
MCCREA, Jane 191 193 195
MCCULLOCH, Henry 54
   James 243 Jno 173
   Nathaniel 279
MCCULLOCK, Norman 326
MCCULLOM, Archibald 185-
   186
MCCULLOUGH, Seth 173
   William 173
MCDANIEL, Daniel 135
MCDONALD, 43 117 217 220
   222-223 230 234 310 322

MCDONALD (Cont.)
326 Alen 442 Alex 186 443
Alexander 119 125 134-
135 219-220 233-234 310
312 318 322 397 Alexr 141
442 Allan 118 125 184 322
444-445 Allan Of Collachie
206 Allen 117 135 218
Angus 134-135 141 218
Archibald 311 Capt 220
233-234 318-319 Charles
171 173 458 Col 446
Daniel 166 Don 128 130
Donald 125-126 135-136
138 221-222 234 239 241
243 276 311 426 Duncan
323 Gen 134 136-139
Hugh 135 323 James 113
134-135 185 242 322-323
457 Jas 319 Jno 319 John
135 141 166 185 210-211
217 322-323 Kenn 126
Kennith 136 Lach 443
Laughlin 442 Lt 217 Maj
118 Mary 444 Mr 139 206
234 Mrs 206 Neil 185
Roderick 210-211 Ronald
158 166 311-312
MCDONALL, Alexander 213
MCDONELL, 205 219 Alex 224
Alexander 205 230 275
Alexr 458 Allan 203 205
225 Allan Jr 205 Allen 202
207 Angus 217-218 224
228 Arch 225 Archibald
205 Capt 225 Donald 228
Helen 212 Hugh 225
James 226 John 205 224-
225 275 311 Miles 225 Mr
203 205 Ron 227 Ronald
205 275
MCDONNEL, 124

MCDOUGAL, Patrick 347
MCDOUGALD, Alexander 111
Angus 111 Donald 111
Dougald 111 John 111
Malcolm 111 Peggy 111
MCDOUGALL, 43 Agnes 185
Alex 186 Alexander 188
398-399 Angus 186
Archibald 185 Donald 184
Duncan 185 Gen 398 400-
401 George 311 Hugh 185
John 185 191 323 Private
443 Ranald 399 Sandie
439
MCDOWELL, 50 57 Charles 57
MCDUFFIE, Ann 184 Donald
185 Duncan 185 John 114
185 Malcolm 185
MCDUGAL, Reynold 113
MCDUGALD, James 105
MCEACHERN, Archibald 134
Neil 186
MCELOROY, Hugh 185
MCELROY, 50
MCEWEN, Archibald 185
Hannah 186 John 185-186
Marian 185
MCFADDEN, Duncan 186 Neil
186
MCFARLAND, 43 Malcolm 113
MCFARLANE, John 81
MCFARTHER, Daniel 113
John 113
MCFERSON, Jno 105
MCGILL, Arch 106
MCGLENNY, John 210-211
MCGOWAN, John 185 John Sr
186
MCGOWNE, Archibald 184
John Jr 185 Mary 184
MCGREGOR, 43 251 James
46-47 251 John 244

INDEX 473

MCGREGOR (Cont.)
  William 103
MCGUILVERY, Farquhar 166
MCGUIRE, Duncan 185 John 186
MCILFENDER, Catharine 186
MCINTIRE, 190 Duncan 210 John 166
MCINTOSH, 43 158 162
  Alexander 253 279 323
  Benjamin 166 Col 174 Gen 356 403-404 George 173
  James 279 John 84 166 173 John Mohr 162 401 Lach 173 Lachlan 173 401-403 Moore 161 Mr 161
  Roderick 173 Thomas 96 William 402
MCINTYRE, 43 Donald 186 Duncan 210 John 186
MCIVER, Collin 135
MCKALLOR, Dougall 185 Edward 185
MCKAY, 249 Alex 243
  Alexander 117-118 134 Alexr 141 Archibald 144 Capt 153 227 Colin 243 Daniel 81 166 Donald 244 249 322 Donald Jr 243 Donald Sr 243 Hugh 81 243 Iver 114 James 243 John 166 227 236 244 323 Melaskus 417 Peter 166 Rod Sr 243 Roderick 239 243-245 249 Samuel 227 Wiliam 243 William 226 Wm 243
MCKEAN, 44
MCKEITHEN, Archibald 113 Donald 113 Duncan 113 Gilbert 113
MCKENNA, 43

MCKENZIE, 43 226 Alex 227
  Alexander 244 Alexr 457 Angus 244 Capt 345 Colin 243-244 Donald 244 Ensign 275 Florence 185 George 185 John 136 185 242 Kenneth 80 William 243-244
MCKERWAN, Duncan 184
MCKEY, Alex 106
MCKINNEN, Rory 134
MCKINNON, Don 311 Laughlin 134 Ronald 322 457
MCKINZIE, Colin 347 George 347 John 134 Kenneth 119 Mr 347 Thomas 323
MCKLARTY, Alexr 113 James 113
MCKOWN, John 113-114 Robert 114 William 114
MCLACHLAN, James 105
MCLACHLEN, James 106 Jas 106
MCLAGAN, George 253
MCLAINE, Lauchlin 458 Murdoch 458
MCLASON, Jno 114
MCLEAN, 43 Alex 243
  Alexander 125 244 323 Alexd 118 Allan 118 311 Allen 308-309 Archibald 347 Catherine 184 Col 315 319 Coll 313 Daniel 135 David 322-323 Donald 111 Duncan 111 Hector 311-312 323 James 84 John 111 311 Lachlan 311-312 322 Murdoch 322 Nancy 111 Neil 279 311 458 Neill 111 Peter 111 William 84
MCLEANE, Alexander 84
MCLELLAN, Donald 243

MCLELLAN (Cont.)
  James 242 323 John 243-
  244 323 Samuel 85
  William 242 244
MCLELLAND, Samuell 80
MCLEOD, Aeneas 81
  Alexander 125 134-135
  244 Alexd 117 Alexr 118
  135 Capt 120 326 D 445
  Donald 125 134 136 306-
  307 Hugh 244 James 243-
  244 John 114 117 134-135
  141 143-145 166 Lt 360
  Mary 186 Mr 167 Murdoch
  134 Murdock 136 Norman
  134 253 326 Owen 166
  Philip 244 Roderick 326
  Wm 243
MCMARTIN, Mal 225
MCMONTS, Hugh 219
MCMULLAN, Evin 114
MCMULLIN, Donald 186
MCNAB, Archibald 279
MCNACHTEN, Alexander 186
MCNATT, Benja 113
MCNAUGHTON, 190
  Alexander 183 187 190
  443-444 Chas 114 Eleanor
  444 Jeannette 444 John
  444 Mary 444 Moses 444
MCNEAL, Daniel 104 Dugald
  104 Neal 104
MCNEICE, 43
MCNEIL, 114 192 Archibald
  184 Dan 104 106 Daniel
  106 Donald 277 Dugold
  104 Elizabeth 186 Hector
  105 108 John 187 278 Lt
  276 Malcolm 105 Matcolm
  136 Morgan 185 Neil 105-
  106 Roger 185 William 114
MCNEILE, John 253

MCNEILL, Bluff Hector 104
  143 Duncan 119 Hector
  104 143 Malcolm 135-136
  Neil 104 Of Barra 275
  Roderick 275
MCNICOL, Dun 442 Duncan
  443 Neal 442 Niel 442-443
MCNIEL, Archibald 188 John
  188
MCNISH, George 46
MCPHARLANE, John 80
MCPHERSON, 43 Capt 276
  415 Hugh 253 James 153
  John 275
MCQUARRIE, Hector 442-443
  Lauchlan 457
MCQUARY, Hector 442
MCRAW, Alexander 135
MCRAY, Alexander 135 Lt-
  Capt 134
MCREI, Wm 114
MCRITCHIE, Kenneth 244
MCTAVISH, Alexander 347
MCVARICK, Florence 185
MCVICAR, Neill 87
MEARNS, 300
MEINZIES, Archibald 85
  James 83 William 83
MENEES, 43
MENS, James 135
MENZIES, 34 Charles 279
  James 86-87 John 81 84
  Maj 343 345-346 350
  Robert 84 255 277 279 342
  William 81
MERCER, 43
MERIOT, Capt 412
MIDDLETON, Peter 183
MILEROSS, Andrew 210
MILLER, Adam 216 Capt 96
  David 261 Gov 54 James
  96

MILLS, David 279
MILROSS, Andrew 211
MITCHELL, 50
MONCK, 340
MONCKTON, 271 Gov 179
MONCRIEFF, Capt 359
MONIES, 43
MONK, 409
MONRO, Alexander 84 166
  Willliam 158
MONROE, 157 Alexander 156 158
MONTAGUE, Gov 58
MONTCALM, 257 259-261 263 270-272 405
MONTGOMERY, 43 252-256 265 269 279 281 284-289 296 305 308 311 388 391 448 450 Alex 185 Alexander 254 Archibald 253-254 Capt 274 Col 284-285 287 294 Gen 314 Hugh 186 254
MONTROSE, 35 79
MOORE, 128 130-131 136 138 142 324 408 430 Brigadier Gen 129 Gen 128-129 131-132 137-139 Henry 189 James 128-130 John Mackintosh 166
MOR, John 41 171
MORAR, 371
MORE, John Mcintosh 158 Mcintosh 158-159 William 158
MORFOFF, George 210
MORGAN, 44 57 417 Col 383-385 Daniel 53 362 Gen 363-364
MORISON, Alexander 141
MORPHEUS, 433
MORRISON, 43 Alexander 134

MORRISON (Cont.)
  Alexr 135 Capt 134 285-286 Donald 128 134 George 243 Hugh 166 John 47 Roderick 29 Wm 226
MORVERN, 377
MOTTE, Rebecca 415
MULL, 377
MUNNIS, 43
MUNRO, 34 Alexander 166 Assistant-Surgeon 286 Col 257 George 254 267 342 Hector 301 Henry 254-255 267 277 Hugh 225 John 224-225 William 166
MUNROE, Donald 244 James 134 John 244
MURCHISON, John 136 141 342
MURDOFF, George 210
MURPHY, Timothy 385
MURRAY, 21 277 405
  Alexander 80-81 Andrew 84 Archibald 83 Brig-Gen 258 274 Brigadier 275 Dr 83 Gen 271 274 276-278 George 81 86 277 283 James 82-84 106 244 255 261 265 279 283 John 80 82-85 253 324 Lord 21 85 278 Maj 331 333-334 Mary 84 Mrs 331 Mrs Robert 330 Patrick 81 85 279 Robert 83-85 331 Thomas 80 Walter 83 85 243-244 William 85 279 283 327
NAIRN, John 255 277
NAIRNE, John 311 342
  William 342
NEEDHAM, Maj 372-373
NELSON, Robert 113

NEVIN, Archibald 186 Rachael 185
NEWMARKET, 69
NEWTE, 69
NICHOLSON, Lt 264 Malcolm 343
NICOL, Duncan 442
NICOLS, 418
NORTH, Lord 293-294 299
NUTT, James 185
O'BRIEN, 268
O'CAHAN, 41
O'DOHERTY, 41
O'DONNEL, 268
O'DONNELL, 41
O'HARA, Charles 364
O'LACHLAN, 268
O'NEILL, 41 50 Shane 41
OFFERY, John 188
OGILVIE, J 343 Patrick 83 William 85 347
OGILVY, 27 Charles 85
OGLETHORPE, 146-151 153-155 157 160-171 252 Gen 164 170 402 James 146 Mr 159
ORR, James 236
OSSIAN, 229
OSWALD, Richard 374
OWEN, Jon 106
PAGAN, 236 John 236
PAIN, Samuel 191
PALINURUS, 435
PALMER, 163 Col 163
PARKER, Adm 327
PATERSON, 76-78 88 92-93 William 76
PATTEN, Jennie M 443
PATTERSON, 248 Edward 187 John 243 248 250 Robert 239-240 242 248 250
PATTISON, Gilbert 105

PEEBLES, John 281
PENN, Gov 448 John 116
PENNANT, 69
PENNICUIK, Capt 94 Robert 93
PERCY, Earl 333 Lord 333
PERKINS, Gen 374
PHILIPS, Nathaniel 378
PHILLIPS, Gen 366 372 384
PHILP, George 161
PICKENS, 58
PINCARTON, Robert 95
PINKERTON, 290
PITCAIRN, Maj 294
PITT, 308 Earl Of Chatham 295 Mr 379 William 267 290
PORTERFIELD, Boyd 342
PORTEVINT, Sam 106
POSTELL, Lt 412
PRENTISS, John 225
PRESCOT, Gen 138
PRESCOTT, Gen 138 349 Maj-Gen 349
PREVOST, Augustine 380 Col 353 Gen 352-354 356-357 Lt-Col 354
PRIDEAUX, John 269
PRIMROSE, Lady 395
PRINGLE, John 312
PULASKI, Count 351
PUTNAM, 331 Gen 330-331 Israel 328
RALEIGH, 22
RAMSAY, Amelia 380 James 85
RAMSEY, Allan 380
RANIER, Gen 169
RATTRAY, George 261
RAWDON, Lord 360 415 429
RAY, Angus 439 Archibald 144 Elizabeth 185

INDEX

READ, John 253
REED, 406 Adjutant-Gen 331 Roger 186
REID, Alexander 279 Arthur 192 Duncan 183 185 188 John 186 278 283 Roger 187
RICE, 174
RICHARDSON, 332
RICHMOND, Duke Of 296
RIEDESEL, Gen 384 Madame 386
RILEY, D L 13
ROBERTS, Daniel 174 John 451
ROBERTSON, 34 43 Andrew 81 Archibald 254 267 Capt 450 Daniel 279 311 315 Donald 283 Hugh 84 James 80 254 279 450 458 Jerome 80 John 80 86 279 323 Leonard 99 Lt 374 Mrs 59 Mrs James 59 Neal 226 Thomas 83-84 William 84 277 323
ROBERTSONE, Alexander 82 Andrew 85 David 80 Donald 83 George 85 John 87 Leonard 81 Robert 87 Umqll James 87 William 80
ROBERTSTONE, George 81
ROBINSOUNE, George 86 John 86
RODERICK, Lt 275
ROGER, 143
ROGERS, 187
ROGIRS, Kaptin 418
ROS, Mr 275
ROSE, Alexander 166 Arthur 255 277 Robert 84
ROSLIN, Earl Of 405

ROSS, 34 236 239 418 Alex 243-244 Alex Jr 243 Capt 274 Charles 87 David 343 Donald 210-211 John 236 244 342 447 Maj 219 221 Thomas 210-211 255 275 William 82
ROWAN, Mathew 104 Robert 115 117
RUTHERFORD, Col 134-135 Thomas 115 118-119 127
RUTLEDGE, 44 John 58
RYCAUT, Paul 89
SAINTCLAIR, 43 405 Arthur 405 Col 406 Duncan 135 Gen 406-407 John Charles 279 Matthew 80
SAINTLEGER, 216-217 Barry 215
SALTZBURGHER, 160
SAMMONS, Jacob 216
SAVAGE, Edward 443-444 Jeanette 444 Nathan 415
SCARSBOROUGH, 219-220
SCHLOFFER, Capt 450
SCHULYER, Gen 204
SCHUYLER, 406 Gen 202-209 211 217 398 444 Philip 399
SCHWEINITZ, 450
SCOT, Adam 92
SCOTAS, John 213 Miles 213
SCOTT, Mr 243 Thomas 83 279
SCOTUS, Marianus 40
SCREVEN, Capt 175
SEATON, Christr 457
SERGEANT, Mr 409-410
SETON, Henry 255
SEVERUS, Emperor 32
SEVIER, 57 John 56
SHAW, 326 Catharine 186

SHAW (Cont.)
  Donald 186 323 Duncan 186 John Sr 185-186 Lt 374 Neal 188 Neil 185
SHELBURNE, 294
SHELBY, 57 Isaac 56
SHELL, 221-223 John Christian 221 Mrs 222
SHIELS, Alexander 97-98
SHUTE, Gov 46
SIM, Robert 244
SIMMONDS, Mr 150
SIMON, Twelfth Lord Lovat 387
SIMS, 219
SINCLAIR, 34 Archibald 84 Charles 83 John 82 254 Patrick 279 Peggy 111 Robert 82-83 376 William 342
SINGLETON, Geo 226
SKELLY, Francis 342
SKENE, 40
SKIBLEY, Henry 106
SLAVE, Aunt Lucy 437-438 Dick 409-410 Lucy 437 Ned 436-437 Uncle Ned 436
SLOCUM, Lt 133
SMALL, Capt 223 393 John 233 253 279 283 310 312 322 393 457 Maj 310 312-313 322
SMALWOOD, Jas 106
SMITH, David 119 251 311 Dr 225 John 136 141 243 246-247 261 279 326 Joseph 136 Malcolm 144 Mr 178 Thomas 225 William 176
SNIPES, Capt 415
SOMERSET, Duke Of 34

SOTHEL, Gov 54
SOUTHERLAND, 168 George 80 Lt 168
SPALDING, James 175
SPARK, 349 376 398
SPARKS, 285 Jared 193
SPEARS, John 236
SPEIR, Jno 106 Wm 106
SPENCER, Hazelt'n 227 Samuel 117
STANDISH, Samuel 193
STARK, 44 48 Alexander 95 Gen 386 John 258
STEDMAN, 429
STEPHENS, Gen 335
STEUART, Helen 83 John 84
STEVENS, Mr 166 Thomas 166 Wm 106
STEWART, 34 43 255 277 287 316 331 351 363 428 Adam 279 Alexander 84 96 Allan 254-255 Allen 125 Anne 83 Capt 455 Charles 97 255 277 David 242 247 368 426 Donald 166 254 Dougal 106 Gen 262 391 428 George 343 Innernaheil 255 James 82 225 261 278-279 453-455 John 60 82-83 243 Maj 359 Patric 106 Patrick 261 Robert 83 William 83 85 335
STILLE, 51
STIRLING, 342 370 374 380 389 Col 335 337-338 Gen 138 339 George 83 Lord 138-139 328-329 Lt-Col 327 Thomas 279 283 325
STONE, 200 217 223
STRANRAER, Lord 80
STRATTON, Alexander 311
STUART, 35-36 107 150 397

STUART (Cont.)
402 447 Adam 279
Alexander 135 320 Allen 173 Capt 169-170 Charles 36 327 350 Col 321 328 Donald 135 John 169-170 227 279 Kenneth 135 Lt-Capt 135 Patrick 253
STULL, Samuel 279
SULLIVAN, 43-44 220 Gen 138 336 406 John 207 220
SUMTER, 58 Gen 361-362
SUNDHOPE, 84
SUTHERLAND, 34 Alexander 342-343 Capt 286 John 243-244 253 261 279 Nichol 254 Walter 226
TARBAT, Viscount Of 80
TARLETON, 360 374 Col 361-364 409-411 428
TARLIN, Peter 173
TAUSE, Thomas 342
TAWSE, Capt 358
TAYLOR, Duncan 186 Thomas 210-211
THAYENDANEGEA, 198
THOMPSON, 147 Dougall 185 Eleanor 184 Timothy 227
THREADCROFT, George 173
THUCYDIDES, 295
TOLINE, Capt 417
TOLME, Kenneth 253
TOLMIE, Kenneth 279
TONDEE, 173
TORQUANO, Lt 414
TORREY, David 186 John 185
TORRY, Mary 186
TOUCHSTONE, Caleb 396
TOWNSEND, Brig-Gen 258
TRUMBULL, Gov 343
TRYON, 56-57 Gov 55 112 116 190 205 326

TRYON (Cont.)
William 109 202 308
TURNBULL, Alexander 253 279 283 Thomas 243
TURNER, 48
TWEEDDALE, Lord High Commissioner 89
TYNES, Col 412
UGIN, Mr 140
URCHAD, Wm 210
URGHAD, William 211
URQUHART, David 243-244 James 96 Wm 210
VALENTINE, James 225 John 225
VERELST, H 157 162
VERGENNES, 290
VERNON, Adm 162
WADE, Thomas 117
WALKER, James 130 312 Mr 47 Robt 106 Thomas 60
WASHINGTON, 53 55 102 123 139 175 220 266-267 285 307 325-326 329-332 334 336 338 347-349 351 358-359 362 376 383 398 400-401 403-404 406-407 448 Col 364 George 103 Maister 367
WATSON, Col 414-415
WAUGH, 247 249 Gilbert 343 Wellwood 246 249
WAYNE, 43 Anthony 51 Gen 337-338 358-359
WEBB, 272 Gen 257
WEBSTER, Col 365 Lt-Col 360
WEDDERBURN, 294 Mr 294
WEEDON, Col 331
WEEMS, 408
WESENT, John 173
WESLEY, Andrew 243
WHER, Christian 227

WHITE, Alexander 200
WHITMORE, Brig-Gen 263
WIDROW, Jane 185
WIER, Thos 136
WILLETT, 219
WILLIAM, 35 76 88 96 99
WILLIAM, King 75-76 King Of ? 21 89 91 94
WILLIAM, Sir 196 198 230
WILLIAM THE 3RD, King Of ? 447
WILLIAMS, Col 48 191
WILSON, 406 John 347
WITHERS, Capt 414
WITHERSPOON, John 173 235 306
WOLFE, 48 264-265 271-272 405 Brig-Gen 258 263 Gen 269-273 383 387 392 405
WOOD, William 311
WOODFORD, Col 122
WRIGHT, Gov 58 403 James 172 175
YATES, Christopher 184
YORK, Seymore 135
YOUNG, Henry 226 John 46
ZEISBERGER, 450

www.ingramcontent.com/pod-product-compliance
Lightning Source LLC
Chambersburg PA
CBHW050424240426
43661CB00055B/2267